*"If the wind and rain could play guitar...*
*they would sound a lot like Doc Watson."*

- Greg Brown[1]

# BLIND BUT NOW I SEE

## The Biography of Music Legend Doc Watson

Photo by John Cohen ©

*"Doc Watson is the kind of musician who learned his music in the purest form and he still plays it the way he learned it."*

- President Jimmy Carter[2]

*"There may not be a serious, committed Baby Boomer alive who didn't at some point in his or her youth try to spend a few minutes at least trying to learn to pick a guitar like Doc Watson."*

- President Bill Clinton[3]

*"I recorded 'Strawberry Jam' with Doc at MerleFest. After we played the set, the camera was on me, and I said, 'Oh my God, that was as good as sex.'"*

- Michelle Shocked[4]

*"Doc spoke to 13,000 people at Newport as he speaks to a single friend while riding in a car; with the same relaxed, informal voice."*

- Ralph Rinzler[5]

*"Doc had more taste in the end of his little finger than most people had in their whole approach."*

- Alan O'Bryant[6]

*"Doc Watson…can play the guitar with such ability…just like water running."*

- Bob Dylan[7]

*"There's a sense of grace, effortlessness, and fluidity to Doc Watson's musicianship and singing that is nothing short of miraculous."*

- Ben Harper[8]

*"I looked at Doc as the J.S. Bach of country music."*

- Ed Pearl[9]

*"Doc Watson represents a fierce honesty and a fierce simplicity that pierces like an arrow straight to a place that is true."*

- Joe Crookston[10]

*"Doc Watson is the platonic form of the flatpicker, and anyone who picks up an instrument should aspire to that level of intention."*

- Jonathan Byrd[11]

*"He's a hell of a singer and guitar player."*

- Chet Atkins[12]

*"Doc seemed to be a hundred years old on his first record and he just gets better."*

- Bela Fleck[13]

*"I consider Doc a real father of music. Every time I'm around him I always try to bless him, love on him, pray over him, and just thank God for him, because he is a true treasure."*

- Ricky Skaggs[14]

*"Doc Watson is such a great guitar player, but I don't think that would be nearly enough if it weren't for his way of talking to people while on stage. It's just exceptional, and unique."*

- Mike Seeger[15]

*"Doc is a force of nature. In fact, without Doc there would have been no anchor for the last 40 years to keep us remembering the simplicity of the old tunes."*

- Peter Rowan[16]

*"Doc's music is authentic, raw, pure and uncontrived. It has the depth of generations."*

- Paul Chasman[17]

*"There isn't a musician anywhere who isn't saying, 'My God, I'll never even get close to that.'"*

- Mike Marshall[18]


*"I remember when I finally got a record player I would listen to Doc over and over trying to figure out those licks he was doing."*

- Pat Donohue[19]


*"Mr. Doc Watson knows no strangers. Meeting him for the first time felt more like a reunion with my long lost grandfather…"*

- Rebecca Lovell[20]


*"One night in the studio I was struggling hard to get a guitar solo right, and I thought I had it, and I walked in there and I finally said, 'Doc, what do you think?' He said, 'Well, son if you're looking for something that's a little bit overplayed and a little out of tune, I think you got it.' And I thought, 'Okay, back to the drawing board.'"*

- Marty Stuart[21]


*"I hear my own music here. Irish music. With edges knocked off by its leaving and corners replaced by its landing. Doc helps me come and go and feast on this music. Like a picnic with a flat pick."*

- Tommy Sands[22]


*"You can feel the joy in his playing and hear it in his voice and the way he talks to the audience. You can just feel the joy."*

- Sam Bush[23]


*"Doc Watson truly believes in the song."*

- Si Kahn[24]

*"We all owe him a lot for breaking down the barriers and being such a musical genius, and giving us a direction to go in."*

- Jerry Douglas[25]

*"Doc Watson is one of the great traditional musicians of the 20th Century.*

- Tom Paxton[26]

*"I think Doc's contribution is very deep. He's always showed us an unwavering authenticity in his playing, his singing and his character."*

- Tommy Emmanuel[27]

*"When you listen to what Doc is doing on the guitar, it hits you right in the soul."*

- Warren Haynes[28]

*"There was a feeling, on the west coast at least, that Doc was sort of like a spectacular natural feature of the landscape; inevitable, fully formed, iconic. He seemed ageless, and his so-called 'disability' and spectacular transcendence of that along with his folksy manner made him a kind of mythic character, sort of a household god."*

- Darol Anger[29]

*"Doc bridges many stylistic gaps: between country blues and balladry, between white and black traditions, and between early and later popular folk forms. He is a one-of-a-kind."*

- David Grisman[30]

*"People all the world round can speak Doc Watson's name and can picture him in their mind, and in their ears can hear his very one-of-a-kind sound."*

- Ketch Secor[31]

## Quote Attributions

1.      *Gustavson, Kent, Email Interview with Greg Brown. April 1, 2009.*
2.      *Doc and Merle Playing at White House, Video, Ralph Rinzler Folklife Archives, SI-FP 1990-VTR-29 #65, 1980.*
3.      *Clinton, Bill, Remarks on presenting the arts and humanities medals. (Pres Bill Clinton's speech during the awards presentation of the 1997 National Medal of Arts and National Medal of Humanities) (Transcript). October 6, 1997: Washington.*
4.      *Gustavson, Kent, Telephone Interview with Michelle Shocked. March 12, 2009.*
5.      *Rinzler, Ralph, Doc Watson: Folksinging is a Way of Life. Sing Out!, February-March 1964. 14(1): p. 8-12.*
6.      *Gustavson, Kent, Telephone Interview with Alan O'Bryant. May 6, 2009.*
7.      *Cohen, John, Conversations with Bob Dylan. Sing Out!, 1968. 18(4): p. 6-23,67.*
8.      *Gustavson, Kent, Telephone Interview with Ben Harper. June 4, 2009.*
9.      *Gustavson, Kent, Telephone Interview with Ed Pearl. May 29, 2009.*
10.     *Gustavson, Kent, Telephone Interview with Joe Crookston. March 25, 2009.*
11.     *Gustavson, Kent, Email Interview with Jonathan Byrd. April 2, 2009.*
12.     *Harrington, Richard, Doc Watson, Strumming Home. The Washington Post, January 25, 1988. Washington D.C.: p. C1,C8.*
13.     *Gustavson, Kent, Email Interview with Bela Fleck. April 24, 2009.*
14.     *Gustavson, Kent, Telephone Interview with Ricky Skaggs. April 29, 2009.*
15.     *Gustavson, Kent, Telephone Interview with Mike Seeger. May 23, 2009.*
16.     *Gustavson, Kent, Telephone Interview with Peter Rowan. June 1, 2009.*
17.     *Gustavson, Kent, Telephone Interview with Paul Chasman. April 13, 2009.*
18.     *Gustavson, Kent, Telephone Interview with Mike Marshall. March 26, 2009.*
19.     *Gustavson, Kent, Telephone Interview with Pat Donohue. March 11, 2009.*
20.     *Gustavson, Kent, Email Interview with Rebecca Lovell. March 28, 2009.*
21.     *Gustavson, Kent, Telephone Interview with Marty Stuart. May 18, 2009.*
22.     *Gustavson, Kent, Email Interview with Tommy Sands. July 7, 2009.*
23.     *Gustavson, Kent, Telephone Interview with Sam Bush. April 9, 2009.*
24.     *Gustavson, Kent, Telephone Interview with Si Kahn. May 26, 2009.*
25.     *Gustavson, Kent, Telephone Interview with Jerry Douglas. April 10, 2009.*
26.     *Gustavson, Kent, Telephone Interview with Tom Paxton. April 14, 2009.*
27.     *Gustavson, Kent, Email Interview with Tommy Emmanuel. April 24, 2009.*
28.     *Gustavson, Kent, Telephone Interview with Warren Haynes. May 20, 2009.*
29.     *Gustavson, Kent, Email Interview with Darol Anger. April 24, 2009.*
30.     *Gustavson, Kent, Email Interview with David Grisman. March 25, 2009.*
31.     *Gustavson, Kent, Telephone Interview with Ketch Secor. March 19, 2009.*

# BLIND BUT NOW I SEE

The Biography of Music Legend Doc Watson

KENT GUSTAVSON, PhD

**2010**
BLOOMING TWIG BOOKS / NEW YORK, NY

BLIND BUT NOW I SEE
Copyright © 2010 Kent Gustavson, PhD
*www.docwatsonbook.com*
*www.kentgustavson.com*

Front cover photo by Rob Garland
*www.robgarland.com*

Additional photographs by:
Tony Cartledge, *www.tonycartledge.com*
John Cohen, *www.johncohenworks.com*
Rob Garland, *www.robgarland.com*
John Hudson, *www.flickr.com/photos/botetourt/*
Mark Reid, *www.markreidphotography.com*
Bill Revill, *www.billrevill.com*
John Rocklin, *www.johnrocklinphotography.com*
Peter Shenkin, *www.bluegrasstime.com*
Nic Siler, *nws3m@virginia.edu*
Bob Voors, *www.voorsphotography.com*
Bill Walsh, *www.clearlyseen.org*

Scans of archival documents courtesy of the Ralph Rinzler Folklife Archives were made by
Stephanie Smith. All scanned documents are reprinted here with the permission of the Ralph
Rinzler Folklife Archives at the Smithsonian Institution in Washington.

Interior and Cover Illustrations by Kristina Tosic, *www.eskalicka.com*

Published by:
Blooming Twig Books LLC
PO Box 4668 #66675
New York, NY 10163-4668
*www.bloomingtwigbooks.com*

Printed in the United States of America.

ISBN 978-1-933918-43-3

First Edition
10 9 8 7 6 5 4 3 2 1

*To my mother and father*, *for gifting me with a love of music.*

*To Micah*, *for introducing me to these songs.*

*To Katharina*, *for giving me a reason to sing.*

*To all of the teachers* *who saw sound radar inside of me.*

# TABLE OF CONTENTS

**Introduction** ............................................................ 003

**Chapter 01**. Lone Pilgrim ............................................. 011

**Chapter 02**. Sound Radar ............................................ 025

**Chapter 03**. Blind School ............................................ 035

**Chapter 04**. Crosscut Saw ........................................... 051

**Chapter 05**. Catskin Banjo .......................................... 059

**Chapter 06**. Fretting a Fence ....................................... 069

**Chapter 07**. Wildcat Girl ............................................. 081

**Chapter 08**. Williams & the Rail-Riders ...................... 095

**Chapter 09**. Ralph Rinzler .......................................... 101

**Chapter 10**. The Watson Family .................................. 121

**Chapter 11**. Friends of Old Time Music ..................... 131

**Chapter 12**. The Clarence Ashley Group .................... 149

**Chapter 13**. One Man Band ........................................ 167

**Chapter 14**. Pete & Doc ............................................. 197

**Chapter 15**. Doc & Merle ........................................... 213

**Chapter 16**. Midnight Rider ........................................ 233

**Chapter 17**. After Merle ............................................. 265

**Chapter 18**. Traditional Plus ...................................... 279

**Chapter 19**. Doc's Guitar ............................................ 289

**Chapter 20**. Amazing Grace ....................................... 309

**Acknowledgments** ................................................... 329

**About the Author** ..................................................... 333

**About the Charities** ................................................. 334

# BLIND BUT NOW I SEE

## The Biography of Music Legend Doc Watson

# INTRODUCTION

*"There is a deep tradition within our collective music. And Doc is central to it. In some West African countries there are people called* griot, *figures whose role in their community is to pass on the songs and stories that belong to that community. They're perpetuators of tradition, they're living historians. And that's how I think of Doc."*

- Si Kahn[1]

On a simple wooden stage in a brand new elementary school auditorium in New York City's Greenwich Village, Doc Watson, a handsome blue-eyed blind man with a sun-browned and craggy brow, wavy hair and worker's hands, sat on a stool in front of a crowd filled with a who's who of Washington Square folkies and musicians, and he sang into the microphone at center stage, "Amazing grace, how sweet the sound..." with a handful of other musicians gathered behind him, humming soft harmony.

Only a few blocks from this 37-year-old bard and his borrowed guitar, the Twin Towers of the World Trade Center had not yet been built in Battery Park. No one in attendance that early spring night in 1961 could have guessed that Doc Watson's version of "Amazing Grace" would travel around the world to land again in New York City in the aftermath of September 11th, 2001; used as salve and as solace for an entire nation.

A simple search of online videos yields countless tributes to fallen 9/11 police and firefighters, nearly all of them set to the moving melody of "Amazing Grace." And memorial ceremonies each year are not complete without a bagpipe corps tolling the long, somber and majestic notes of "Amazing Grace."

Not unlike the bagpipes, Doc's singing was simple, straight and true. He added no frills, displaying nothing but true piety and emotion as shut his eyes tightly and sang the hymn's stanzas. John Cohen of the New Lost City Ramblers recalled Doc's performance of "Amazing Grace" at the March 25th, 1961 concert: "I was in the audience and I remember how moved I was by that moment when a blind man was leading us on those verses: '...was blind, but now I see.' Then the mythology about 'Amazing Grace' grew."[2]

Cohen continued: "I think we all knew 'Amazing Grace' before this. But it never had an impact. It never sank in the same way... With Doc leading it, it was this sweet, accessible tune."[2] Soon the hymn was performed all across the folk music circuit, and within a few years, had crossed the globe. People of every color and creed around the world now sing the verses and melody of the hymn as Doc first heard them as a child.

Written by repentant slave trader John Newton in the 18th century, the lyrics first crossed the Atlantic to the new world and found their way into the shape note hymnals of 19th century America; Doc's family learned their version from the 1866 version of *The Christian Harmony*. Blind from birth, the inspirational words of the hymn spoke to Doc even as a child. In a 1999 interview, while talking about "Amazing Grace," Doc said: "When I leave this world, and these are my honest feelings, I'll be able to see like you can, only maybe a bit more perfect."[3] Doc truly believed in the song's message, and the Greenwich Village audience caught a glimpse of his inner world that night in the elementary school's auditorium.

Like the hymn "Amazing Grace," Doc Watson came from humble beginnings. Even as he sat on the PS 41 stage in Greenwich Village, his family still lived in poverty; Doc, his wife and two children lived off of welfare and garden vegetables. Little did he know that he was starting out on a music career that would span four continents and half a century.

By 1966, Doc had started to earn a good living for his family; he had completed a national solo tour, signed with Vanguard Records, and was now planning to record with country superstars Flatt and Scruggs in Nashville for their upcoming instrumental release *Strictly Instrumental*. But he almost did not make it to the recording session.

Just after arriving in Nashville to start recording, Doc's appendix ruptured. He had been under terrible stress during his first few years on the road, traveling from town to town by airplane and bus, never knowing more than a name of the person who would greet him at the other end. He smoked cigarettes to ease the edge, but of course that did not help his health. He had suffered from ulcers, and now he was in a Music City hospital bed.

A giant was on his knees, and the world scarcely knew it. When Bob Dylan had his 1966 motorcycle crash, newspapers everywhere reported it. But Doc

Watson was not yet a household name, and his illness went largely unknown. The family was left to circle his bed, praying that Doc would recover.

Doc fought hard for his life in that Nashville hospital. He recalled his morphine-induced dreams in a 1988 interview: "I was walking along by a big cornfield, and I was barefooted, just like I did when I was a boy... And there was grass along there, and I came to this guy wire that went up to a utility pole that was setting over on the edge of that cornfield... And I could smell that green corn...just as plain as reality... And I reached up and put my hand on that thing, and bent over to swing around to go under that guy cable. And about that time, some big bruiser monster or another jumped out of that cornfield. And it was trying to tie my arm up to that wire and was gonna kill me. And I was whuppin' him. I was getting the better of him."[4] Doc was fighting for his life.

Doc spoke about striking a deal with God from his hospital bed: "I was lying on a bed where they'd moved me up in the hospital, and it was like almost being out there...sort of half in this world, and sort of not, and over here, there was the almost presence of God and eternity, the whole thing... And over here was Rosa Lee and the kids, and the world as it is. And [I] talked to the Lord that time. I said, 'I'd like to get up from here, Lord, if it's your will, and work for my family, but your will be done. If it's not right, if I shouldn't, whatever I've done wrong, you know about it, and I've lain it aside.'"[4] After delivering that unspoken prayer from his hospital bed, Doc recalled, "It was like they lifted a 10-ton load off of my chest."[4]

Doc's ruptured appendix soon fully healed. He went on to record with Flatt and Scruggs, and went back out on the road with his son Merle to earn a living. If it had not been for Doc Watson's morphine dreams, for the love and support of his family, and then the nudge by Earl Scruggs a few days later, Doc never would have hit the road again.

Though Doc soon recovered from his own physical ailment, he soon spent years of watching his son Merle suffer under the demons of addiction, eventually ending in his death at the young age of 36. Despite Doc's blindness, and despite the hardships he ran into on the road, from a ruptured appendix in 1966 to severe ulcers, by far the greatest pain he suffered was the death of his son. Merle's grave is within sight of Doc and Rosa Lee's kitchen window, and the family still mourns for him a quarter of a century after his passing. To this day, Doc never grants an interview without mentioning his talented, now absent, son.

Jack Lawrence, Merle's close friend and Doc's longtime road partner (since Merle's death in 1985), witnessed Doc's last moment with his son's earthly remains: "We had held up pretty well through this whole thing. And it came to the end of the service and nobody had taken Doc up to the casket to say goodbye. So T. Michael Coleman [Doc and Merle's long-time bass player on the road] takes Doc up, and Doc has his arms and head down on the casket, says goodbye, and he's crying."[5]

Lawrence and the other young musicians present watched as Doc laid his head on his son's casket and wept for his best friend and musical soul mate. None of them had imagined that this king of guitar could appear so small and frail. And when they saw Doc with his head and hands on Merle's casket weeping, they could not help but also break down crying. Jack Lawrence recalled: "At this point Coleman and Merle's friend Cliff Miller and I just lost it. So here the three of us are standing around, we're all just sobbing."[5]

Shortly after Merle's death, Doc recorded a hymn called "Did Christ O'er Sinners Weep" for his all-gospel album *On Praying Ground*, supported by the pristine a capella harmonies of The Nashville Bluegrass Band:

> *Did Christ o'er sinners weep,*
> *Then shall our cheeks be dry,*
> *Let floods of penitential grief,*
> *Spring forth from every eye,*
>
> *The Son of God in tears,*
> *The blessed angels see,*
> *Those tears were shed for everyone,*
> *They were shed for even me.*[6]

In Benjamin Beddome's original version of the text from the 18th century, the second line in the first stanza reads, "*And* shall our cheeks be dry..."[7] not, as Doc sang, "*Then* shall our cheeks be dry..."[6] Although different by only one word, the change implies a world of difference in the meaning of the song. In Beddome's version, he implied to listeners, "Christ wept over sinners and so should we." Doc's version alternatively said, "Christ wept for sinners so that we don't have to," very much falling in line with the Appalachian Baptist tradition he grew up within, where congregants believe that Jesus Christ "died for their sins" and for the "sins of the world." Doc surely had his son in mind when he sang the hymn, possibly believing that Christ wept for Merle just as Doc and Rosa Lee had, despite his boy's sins here on earth.

Don Rigsby, the director of Morehead State University's Kentucky Center for Traditional Music, and award-winning gospel and bluegrass singer, said of "Did Christ O'er Sinners Weep," "It's one of the most amazing pieces of gospel music I've ever heard in any genre. Doc feels it so deeply and completely. That's a masterful recording..."[8] Over the top of the a capella harmonies Doc voiced over verses from John 3:16-17 out of the King James version of the Bible:

*For God so loved the world*
*That he gave his only begotten son*
*That whosoever believeth in him*
*Shall not perish but have everlasting life,*
*For he sent not his son to the world for to condemn the world*
*But that the world through him might be saved.*

Doc certainly knew how difficult it was to give up a son. And if God loved the world enough to send his Son to earth in order for everyone to have everlasting life, Doc believed that God must have truly cared for the earth's inhabitants. This loving image of God certainly helped Doc to understand his own loss, and to believe in Merle's redemption and grace.

After Merle's death, the young musicians around Doc watched him return to the deeply spiritual mindset he had grown up within. Ricky Skaggs spoke of his own deep spiritual connection to Doc: "We've had some good conversations about faith... That's one of the things that I love about Doc. It doesn't have to be music that we talk about when we're together. We talk about the love that we have for God, and how blessed we are, and how it would be impossible to do what we do without the blessing of God, and how blessed we are to be able to play music, and the gift that He's given us in that. And that's just one of the things that Doc and I share that is really, really deep and thick. And it's bountiful. There's always sweet honeycomb that we share when we talk. Even if it's five minutes, or if it's an hour, we're just eating honey. We're feasting on the Lord and His love for us."[9]

Doc had by that point "feasted on honey" for most of his life; he grew up surrounded by the love of his church and his family, and as he nears his 90th year of life, he continues to value religion above all else. He still sings the hymn "Amazing Grace" on stage, asking the audience to join in on the now-familiar chorus.

When Doc was young, his father led his family in a daily devotional each evening with readings from the Bible and hymns from *The Christian Harmony*. Doc remembered: "[Dad] always had the family order at home, and we usually sang some of the old songs and he'd read a chapter or two out of his Bible, and it didn't make any difference whether it was the Old or the New Testament common. He studied both of them for the benefit of his boys and girls as we grew up. And we always had family prayer unless Dad was sick, up until I was...a grown man. And I guess that doesn't hurt a fellow's moral life to grow up like that... I can attribute a lot of my street thinking to the way Dad raised us."[10]

"Street thinking" took a whole new connotation when Doc stepped off of the Greyhound bus into the bustle of Manhattan in the spring of 1961. He had lived nearly four decades in the mountains, and he would never lose that world. But now he was on a new street, one that would lead him around the world. PS 41, the little elementary school in Greenwich Village, was Doc Watson's first step into the public spotlight, a world that he has since occupied for fifty years.

On Saturday, March 25th, 1961, Doc Watson sat in front of a packed elementary school crowd with his fellow musicians from Appalachia and he sang a simple version of a country hymn he had known all of his life.

# CHAPTER NOTES

1.  Gustavson, Kent, *Telephone Interview with Si Kahn*. May 26, 2009.
2.  Gustavson, Kent, *Personal Interviews with John Cohen*. April 8 & August 6, 2009.
3.  Watson, Doc and David Grisman, *Doc Watson and David Grisman - In Concert (1999)*, DVD, Vestapol, 2001.
4.  Earle, Eugene, *Interview with Doc Watson*, Audio Cassette, Southern Folklife Collection: Eugene Earle Collection, 1988.
5.  Gustavson, Kent, *Telephone Interview with Jack Lawrence*. April 13, 2009.
6.  Watson, Doc, *On Praying Ground*, Audio CD, Sugar Hill Records, 1990.
7.  Beddome, Benjamin, *Twenty discourses adapted to village worship or the devotions of the family*. Vol. 1. 1807: J.W. Morris.
8.  Gustavson, Kent, *Telephone Interview with Don Rigsby*. April 1, 2009.
9.  Gustavson, Kent, *Telephone Interview with Ricky Skaggs*. April 29, 2009.
10. Lloyd, Bert, *Interview with Doc Watson*, Audio CD, Ralph Rinzler Folklife Archives, Smithsonian Institution, 1976.

# CHAPTER ONE
## Lone Pilgrim

*"I can remember sitting on your lap, must have been about two years old, hearing them sing at the church, with Marshall, and Everett and all the people, you know... To me as a tiny little boy, I remember thinking it must sound like that in heaven."*

- Doc to his mother Annie[1]

*"I know you was always mighty quiet, you was always listening."*

- Annie's response.[1]

E ven as the birds began to sing before dawn on Sunday mornings, so too did the residents of Wildcat Creek valley begin to sing and pray. Up the winding road towards Deep Gap proper, before summer's heat filled the valley with soup-like warmth, the cool morning air was filled with the sound of chanted prayers and hymns. The nine Watson children and their parents would dress in their Sunday finest, then walk the three miles over the creek and down into the valley, joyfully anticipating songs and fellowship with their neighbors. And all through the valley, other fathers helped their boys slip into hard-soled shoes and home-sewn pant-waists, and other mothers squeezed their girls into Sunday dresses.

Even as a toddler, Doc Watson remembered the trip through snow or rain, sun or shadow, down into the valley where Mount Paran Baptist Church stood. Before he was able to make the entire journey on foot, his parents would carry him.

Doc can surely still smell the sweet scent of homemade soap on the ladies in their calico Sunday dresses and of pomade in the hair of gentlemen in their best trousers, with hands scrubbed as clean as workers' hands can get after a week of hard labor. And of course Doc remembered the sound: "It was so strange, and yet it was so pretty... The singing was very pure then. No vibrato in the voices at all, you know, just good straight harmonies, and some of those mountain people had voices like you wouldn't believe!"[2]

Doc's father was the singing leader at the church, and the weekly trip around the side of the mountain, over the creek and into the valley was a part of life for the Watson family. The little church required only that sinners come forward to be saved: dipped in the deep waters of the Baptist faith. They did not believe in *sprinkling*, the local term for when Protestant pastors sprinkle water on a child's head in baptism. They believed in full immersion. Body and spirit below the water. Spitting and gurgling for air.

The small boy in his mother's arms was baptized by this music, this harmony, embraced by a wash of a capella voices, bouncing around the uncoated planks of the small sanctuary, strong, sure, and free.

Doc recalled the small church choir: "I remember when our little church choir [with] about 16 people in it, won...as best singers. They'd have big singings as you know at the church back then, and I guess they must have been pretty good, because they won a lot of them. There was no [sheet] music in the church at all then [and] they didn't have any piano."[2]

His father, as the leader of the group, would start everyone singing and count out time with his arm. Doc's father's favorite hymn was "The Lone Pilgrim," a hymn that Doc Watson later made famous on his first record on Vanguard, his self-titled *Doc Watson* LP, and which was later recorded by countless other musicians, including Bob Dylan in 1993 on his record *World Gone Wrong*.

Doc later recalled an amusing anecdote about his father's choir: "Whenever [Dad] got a frog in his throat or missed a note to cough, the whole congregation had to stop singing until Dad could start up again. Once, the congregation was singing along, but Dad coughed so everyone stopped except for a lady with a real high-pitched voice. She didn't realize that everyone had stopped singing, so she just stuck up there on a high note. Everybody was giggling, and the service was just about ruined, but Dad just finished coughing and started the congregation up singing again. You could hear a trace of a chuckle in his voice, though."[3]

Doc's daughter Nancy, in recalling the original church building that has long since been torn down and replaced by a brick building across the street, wrote: "There was an old painted wood church...where my brother Merle and I were first introduced to music. Kerosene lanterns were suspended from the ceiling, lighted at night. Moths repeatedly circled the yellow glow as the familiar scent of burning wicks filled the air, mixing with the ever-present one of the pine wood walls. In a similar setting our parents were introduced to music; the same as their parents, and their parents before them... People knew [the church] as a place to rest and forget for a while the hardness of life. They could sing their soul's sorrows and frustrations away."[4]

Doc's childhood was stunningly simple. He knew church, family and little else. His brothers and sisters were his closest friends, and his family lived on the side of the mountain, where they grew vegetables and lived in harmony. The small blind boy thought little about the future, let alone a wife, kids, and a career as a professional musician. He learned to navigate the world around him, and enjoyed the same freedoms as any of his sighted siblings.

From a young age, little blind Doc Watson decided to ignore his disability as best he could. He learned how to walk like his brothers, talk like his brothers, and even fight like his brothers. He sledded down precipices and jumped on corn-cribs, often coming home bloodied and hurt just like all of the others. He learned the hard-knock lessons of life far before most blind children even have the opportunity to walk alone down the street. Doc certainly did not know it at the time, but he was training for his later career, when he would be sleeping on couches in apartments owned by friends of friends, paying for dive motels that cost nearly as much as he netted from weeklong engagements, hopping buses and planes, hoping that the correct contact would greet him at the other end. It is not hard to see why Doc decided to record "The Lone Pilgrim" on his first major album.

Doc had no limit to what he believed he could do, learn, or achieve. John Cohen, who, in partnership with Ralph Rinzler, organized the Friends of Old Time Music concert that featured Doc in New York, remembered being shocked by the depth of Doc's independence, curiosity, and intelligence: "I remember one time it was either me alone, or with several others. We took Doc down to Spring Street and 6th Avenue. There was a library there, a public library that had books for the blind. We'd take him there and Doc would spend his time just reading things, listening to Library of Congress books on record. And during those times we began to realize that there was a different person inside this country guy: a different personality, a deeper personality who was interested in all kinds of things, and articulate. He could describe things... It was not like a country boy at all. And I was very impressed by that."[5] Doc had a natural ability to interact and meld with New York City culture, as he was able, throughout his career, to comfortably play music in both Nashville and New York.

Doc blended folk music with rock, country, jazz and many other styles of music, just as smoothly as he was personally able to blend into whatever subculture he visited in his career on the road. Doc became an expert houseguest. But entertaining his hosts was hard work, and he was grateful when his son Merle joined him on the road in 1965. Merle then spent more than half of his life on the road with his father before his death at the young age of 36.

Doc was in no way prepared for his son's death in 1985, but he had been always thought about the issues surrounding death and the hereafter. In a conversation with Studs Terkel, Doc remembered: "From the time I can remember, I was vaguely aware of death... [As] I was sitting on my mother's lap – I must have been about two – they were singing 'The Lone Pilgrim'... I can remember thinking about the fellow who went to the old boy's grave and stood there in contemplation of the man's life: 'I came to the place where the lone pilgrim lay / and [pensively] stood by his tomb.' I think that headed me in the right direction to a little later think about death for what it really was, because they took us to funerals from the time I was just a little boy. Death was talked about, and Heaven, and the danger of being lost. They didn't fully understand how to clarify the truths to young children, [so] I had to learn about that later... But death was certainly there, very present from the time I was a little boy."[6]

As Doc grew older, his faith remained as strong as his father's. When asked by Terkel about his father's beliefs, Doc said that many people called his father a "fundamentalist," but in Doc's words, "He wasn't exactly that. He wasn't as strict as a lot of people."[6] In fact, although he cautioned his family about the dangers of parties, he later encouraged his son to play music at the same parties, knowing that Doc might be able to make a living at it. General had a strong moral compass, but he knew when not to be rigid in his beliefs.

Others in Doc's extended family didn't agree with General. One of Doc's cousins who was a Baptist preacher gave Doc a great deal of trouble about his performance at dances around the community. Doc remembered that his cousin came to his and Rosa Lee's house one day in the early 1950s: "One day, right after I moved out with my sweetie on our own, he came up to the house and I knew he was going to get on the subject in about two minutes."[6] Doc knew his cousin, and he knew what was coming, so Doc cut him off before he even started. Doc said, "Brother, you were talking to me the other day about music... I've been thinking about the good old book that you and I both love... In that book, it says the man that provides not for his own house is denied the faith and is worse than an infidel. I figure if I can get out there and earn a little of that money [that those] old boys are blowing on booze and beer and the slot machines at the VFW clubs and help my sweetheart raise these two children, I don't think I'm doing too bad."[6] Doc had thought out his argument beforehand, and he said to his cousin, "Can you help what they do with the lumber you cut at your sawmill? They may build beer joints or houses of prostitution or whatever."[6] Doc's reasoning was waterproof, and his cousin had no way to argue. He said, "I never thought about that,"[6] to which Doc quickly replied, "Well, you better think about it."[6]

Doc's cousin had no idea that Doc would someday bring the gospel songs of Appalachia to the world, and that he would nearly singlehandedly put a new face on Appalachian culture: *hillbilly* no more. Doc never lampooned his own culture, nor misrepresented it in the public. He allowed the world to drink from the rich cup of Appalachian music tradition, and he always then returned home to the mountain to replenish his cup. He was born on the mountain, and he will someday die on the mountain, just like his father and grandfather before him, and like his beloved son Merle.

Arthel Lane Watson was born on March 3rd, 1923, at 9 o'clock on a Tuesday evening.[7] He didn't acquire the nickname *Doc* until he was much older, once he was already doing amateur performances around his local area. His family christened him with a totem of courage and intelligence. Arthel, Doc's given first name, comes from the Gaelic words *àirdeil* for "ingenious" and *gal* for "valor." Doc's middle name is Lane or "roadway," fitting for a man destined to spend the second half of his life on the road.

Doc's father General (a given name, not a military title) was a gentle bear of a man; a farmer and manual laborer who loved his family and God above all else. His mother, Annie, was a homemaker, running around after nine children and tending household chores and the garden. Though Annie was descended from a line of preachers and singers, she was not able to read, and though General could not read much better, she relied on him to do the nightly Bible readings with their children by lamplight. But Annie was versed in oral tradition, knowing many ballads passed down by generations of Scotch-Irish Appalachian women, and most of the hymns out of *The Christian Harmony* that they would sing on Sundays and during nightly devotionals. She would hum or sing while churning butter, hanging the laundry, sewing, or tucking the children in at night.

Annie was happy in the small cabin that General had built for them on a small parcel of the 3000 acres that had once belonged to their ancestor David Watson (five generations before Doc was born). The home was built of trees pulled from the steep hillsides all around; the chinks between the logs were filled with mud, and the roof was made of tin. The cabin was about a mile from Wildcat Creek, down a winding path across the side of the mountain. There was a cellar cut into the hillside full of preserves in the winter; there was a garden in back, and a hill on the side. Doc's father cut the lumber off the hillsides to burn in winter, and to sell to the local lumber company for cash.

The town nearest to Doc's family home was Deep Gap, only a few miles up the road. Though Deep Gap is well known as the hometown of Doc Watson, it is little more than a ghost town now. The new Highway 421 recently blasted its way through the mountain towards Boone, and old Highway 421, which runs directly through Deep Gap, sits abandoned and empty. One of the only signs in town is painted on the side of a barn, and reads, "Jesus Saves," with an arrow pointed up towards the sky.

Doc's ancestor David Watson likely trained as an apprentice before marrying and traveling to the colonies, but no records show for certain. David Watson might have been the son of shoemaker John Watson in Edinburgh, Scotland, trained as a saddler's apprentice for six years in the 1770s.[8] Or he might have trained in another trade, working hard to save for his long voyage to the new world with his young bride. Whatever the true David Watson's training in Scotland, he came to the American colonies just before the Revolutionary War, and signed up to fight the British in exchange for the promise of land, should the Americans prevail in their struggle.

David Watson fought valiantly as a cavalryman, and on one retreat, he narrowly escaped capture by the Redcoat army. According to John Preston Arthur's history of Watauga County, Watson's horse jumped a ditch that his pursuer's horse could not cross. Watson returned safely to his family as a hero, and in the 1790s was given his promised piece of land, soon bringing his wife and children to the wild Watauga region of North Carolina along with their seven slaves. He also brought along his father John Watson for the journey, who eventually lived to be 100 years old, his life spanning two continents and two centuries. David and his wife Mary Beda had 12 children.[9]

Life in the wilderness was hard for David's family: clearing land and guarding against wild animals and neighboring Cherokee tribes. But his risk soon paid off, and as the Watauga River valley became a hotbed of settlement in the coming generations, the family land became more and more valuable. David owned miles of the countryside near present-day Boone, North Carolina, now settled and owned in little parcels by hundreds and thousands of his progeny.[9]

David Watson's son Thomas is buried in a cemetery atop the hill in Deep Gap that had once overlooked over old Highway 421 into Boone. The settlement of Deep Gap was one of the main stops along Daniel Boone's original Wilderness Road westward across the Appalachians towards Kentucky at the end of the 18th century, but it wasn't until the Good Roads Program of North Carolina Governor Cameron Morrison in the early 1920s that the town began to truly develop. Now the cemetery sits just off the shoulder of new Highway 421.

Although only miles from the eastern Tennessee border, Deep Gap belonged, like the rest of North Carolina to the Confederacy. Nearby Tennessee, however, was the last state to join the Confederacy, and was a place of heavy fighting throughout the Civil War. Doc's great-grandfather Thomas Watson, Jr. was a soldier for the Confederacy,[10] and just after returning from the war, he had a child named Smith, Doc's grandfather. Smith's wife Charlotte was the midwife who delivered her grandson Doc at his birth in the late winter days of 1923.[11] Through Charlotte Carlton, Doc is also distantly related to his wife Rosa Lee Carlton; they are second cousins, sharing a great-grandparent.

In 1891, Smith and Charlotte had a son, General. Despite being named according to a military rank, he was born into a world far removed from the times of the Revolutionary War within which David Watson had fought, or the Civil War within which Thomas Watson, Jr. fought. After the Civil War, isolation came to Appalachia, and family clans stuck to their own hollows, keeping to ancestral traditions, and living a subsistence-based lifestyle.

When General was born, education was secondary to survival. He never received a formal education, and though still a 9-year old boy when the 1900 census was taken, his profession was already listed as "farm labor."[12] In that same census, General's name was misspelled as *Jenarl*. Later in life, General learned to read a few passages in the Bible and to sing hymns out of the family shape-note hymnal, but that was the extent of his literacy.

On his birth certificate, 32 years after his father was born, Doc was also falsely christened, marked forever by his humble beginnings: the child of two nearly illiterate parents. Little Arthel was listed as *Örthel* Watson.[11]

Doc's mother was born Annie Greene in a one-room cabin in the nearby town of Meat Camp, North Carolina. Meat Camp had been a Confederate camp in the Civil War where meat and supplies were kept in a cave, hidden under close guard from enemy raids. Annie's father soon built a new home of split and flattened logs, cutting chinks out of pine to fill the gaps between the logs. Annie's mother stuffed newspapers into these gaps, coating them with a paste of flour and water, in order to insulate the cabin against the cutting winter winds. They lived a simple life, lighting the house by pine torches at night.[1]

Annie grew up in the last vestige of 17th century European culture, though she was born in 1896. Among other traditions kept through 200 years of American domesticity, her father still made shoes for his family, affixing their soles with wooden pegs. Her six brothers and four sisters watched as their shoes emerged from the weathered and expert hands of their father.[1]

When little Annie was eight years old, her family moved from Meat Camp to Deep Gap, just a few miles away from the Watson clan. Times at the turn of the century were not easy, and with a rising population in Appalachia, there was simply not enough land to support everyone. The land was not tilled sustainably, and once a pasture or field was "used up," farmers would move on, until only barren hillsides remained. Logging was then lucrative for a time, until all of the good lumber was removed. All of Annie's brothers and sisters except for one soon moved to Ohio, where there was a promise of good farmland and abundant jobs. Annie, however, did not follow her family. She was in love. At age 15, she married Doc's father in 1911 and moved into the Watson family's home.

As most young girls do, Annie Greene had longed for a handsome suitor. One night she had an especially vivid dream: she was shelling corn upstairs with her brother, getting ready to go to the mill. They were hard at work, sitting for hours, silently peeling the leaves away from the precious yellow and white kernels of corn, when suddenly a dog barked. Annie leapt to the window, dumping the corn out of her apron, looking off down the road to see who was approaching. She saw two men coming up the road, still far away.[1]

According to Annie in an interview in the early 1970s, her dream soon came true. One day while silently shucking corn upstairs with her brother, she heard a dog bark. She ran as quickly as she could to the window, dumping her corn in excitement. Indeed, she saw the two men from her dream walking up the road, still off in the distance. She ran downstairs to her mother, and shouted, "There's two men coming!" Her mother said, coolly, "Get the broom and brush up the hearth right quick...and get you on a clean dress!"[1] She did her best to brush her hair, and then donned a simple and clean dress to meet the man she would soon marry.

Soon enough, the two strange men came in the door. One man was Annie's cousin, Wade Greene, and the other was young General Watson, 19 years old, thin and handsome, hands and face brown from hard work, his eyes bright with danger. The two men had walked 16 miles to arrive at the Greenes' house. General had been in trouble with the law in Deep Gap, and was required to go to court near the Greenes' house, so Wade had suggested he stay the night with the Greenes on his long journey.[1]

On part of the long walk through the mountains, Wade said to General, a mischievous grin on his face, "There are pretty girls up there at the Greene's." General, with a sly grin, replied to Wade, "If there are, I'm gonna help them wash the dishes!"[1]

General's strategy worked. His eye was set soon after his arrival upon young Annie, and after dinner, when she was in the kitchen cleaning up, General came into the kitchen with his hands stuffed into his trouser pockets. Annie could barely move. She could hardly look up. This was a strange man, and she was shy; she just stood silent, barely lifting her eyes to look at General. At the same time, General just stood there and watched as she washed the dishes. He didn't help, (as he had said he would) but after the women finished, he offered to Annie, "When I get back home, I might write you a letter. Will you answer it?"[1]

Though hardly the fare of a Blockbuster love story, this was romance of the highest degree for young Annie. She, in shy modesty, said that she might answer his letter. In a week, she got a letter as promised. Every two weeks after that, General would walk 16 miles to the Greene's home to come courting.

General and Annie were married in the gentle, thawing days of May 1911, in Meat Camp Township at her father's home. The ceremony was simple. The newlyweds soon after moved to Tennessee, and General found a well-paying job there. But they were homesick for the hills they had left behind. Annie remembered that General was so lonely he would pull his banjo out in the middle of the night and play a tune or two. She remembered in her interview with Bert Lloyd: "Oh, he wouldn't sleep... He'd get up and he'd get that banjo and he'd get me up and I'd have to...try to dance with him for hours and hours... He'd sit and pick that old banjo and want me to dance and dance. You know, I tried to do anything to pacify him."[1]

Though General played a few tunes for his young wife, they never attended any dances or public events together where there might be music or other such merriment. The early 1900s in Appalachia were filled with many community events: molasses-making, quilt-making, log-rolling, ground-clearing, bean-stringing, house-raising and many other happenings. But at such gatherings, jugs of moonshine often were passed from hand to hand, and General was a devout Baptist, and did not believe they should participate in such debauchery.

When homesickness overtook them both, General and Annie moved back to Deep Gap where General soon built the home within which Doc began his early forays into the world of music.

Though of humble birth, Doc's lineage traces back to European royalty through his great-grandmother on his father's side, Betsey Triplett, who was the great-grandchild of a man named "Yankee" John Church. Although he was not given as much land by the young American government as David Watson had been, Church also moved to Wilkes County in North Carolina after the Revolutionary War in 1773.[13]

"Yankee" John had a long history in the United States: his great-great-grandfather William Goodrich had traveled to the colonies in 1648. The adventure of crossing the seas had been quite dangerous in the 17th century, and sometimes as much as half of each ship's "human cargo," boarding below decks with the rats, did not survive the grueling voyage. Even upon arrival in the colonies, a rough existence awaited each traveler. Because of the rough conditions, travel to the New World did not become commonplace until decades later. But 19-year old William survived the treacherous journey with his 16-year old newlywed wife in tow.[13]

William's lineage is well documented back to 1390 in Lincolnshire, England, some 17 generations before Doc was born. In his heritage are knights, lords, barons, and 33 generations back, kings of England. And 44 generations before Doc first breathed the North Carolina air, his distant relative Charlemagne was appointed by the Pope to rule the Holy Roman Empire.

Charlemagne and Doc trace their common ancestry to kings of Italy, Austrasia, France, the Ostragoths, Franks, Al Manie, and even, 80 generations before Doc was born, Germanicus Julius Caesar of Rome.

Charlemagne had an all-encompassing passion for learning that has moved historians to write biographies of him ever since. He was responsible for reforms in all worlds of academia, from art to script. He probably did not know how to write (most of the kings were not able to write or read), but he is said to have kept a tablet under his bed so that he could practice writing in secret.

Doc Watson, too, grew up with parents who knew little about reading and writing, but who nevertheless valued the education of their children. Doc grew up with Bible lessons each day, and was later sent to study at one of the best schools for the blind in the country. After he dropped out of school, Doc continued to study hundreds of so-called "talking books" made available by the Library of Congress on any subject imaginable.

Though later known as the father of the *guitar* instead of the father of *Europe*, Doc, like Charlemagne, kept his metaphoric tablet under his bed, always valuing education and innovation in his own life.

The Depression came early to Appalachia, and in the mid-1920s, Doc's parents took solace in the simple plank walls of Mount Paran Baptist Church on Sunday mornings and summer nights. Annie carried her little blind son in her arms, and the rest of the children gathered around her as General led the church choir and congregation in song: "I came to a place where the lone pilgrim lay…"

Young Doc drifted away on the human harp of voices filling up the small, sweaty sanctuary. Far from the wealth of the European kings in his lineage, a young king was christened in the wash of harmony in that summer church; women and men around him singing and shouting out the songs of glory in their piercing tenor and soprano voices, the turn of their tongues inherited from mouths long forgotten. He certainly would not have traded the throne of his mother's arms in that summer church for the plush velvet chairs of Roman kings.

# CHAPTER NOTES

1.  Lloyd, Bert, *Interview with Annie & Doc Watson*, Audio CD, Ralph Rinzler Folklife Archives, Smithsonian Institution, 1976.
2.  Lloyd, Bert, *Interview with Doc Watson*, Audio CD, Ralph Rinzler Folklife Archives, Smithsonian Institution, 1976.
3.  Watson, Doc and Ralph Rinzler, *The Songs of Doc Watson*. 1971, New York City: Oak Publications.
4.  Watson, Nancy, *Liner Notes to The Doc Watson Family: Songs from the Southern Mountains*, Sugar Hill Records, 1994.
5.  Gustavson, Kent, *Personal Interviews with John Cohen*. April 8 & August 6, 2009.
6.  Terkel, Studs, *Will the Circle Be Unbroken: Reflections on Death, Rebirth, and Hunger for a Faith*. 2002: Ballantine Books.
7.  Holt, David and Doc Watson, *Doc Watson and David Holt: Legacy*, Audio CD, High Windy Audio, 2002.
8.  *Register of Edinburgh Apprentices 1756-1800, Addenda et Corrigenda*. 1800.
9.  Arthur, John Preston, *A History of Watauga County, North Carolina*. 1915.
10. *Civil War Compiled Military Service Records*. 2005, Civil War Service Records at the US National Archives: Ancestry.com.
11. *Birth Certificate for Örthel (sic) Lane Watson*. 1923.
12. *1900 U.S. Federal Census*. 1900.
13. Revis, Linda Johnson, *Genealogical Data on Yankee John Church*, W.R.P. Barrett, Editor. 2005.

Photo by John Cohen ©
*Doc Watson onstage at the Chicago Folk Festival, 1962.*

# CHAPTER TWO
## Sound Radar

*"I could walk a country road and not get in the ditch, I mean I could do it without a stick, and not go up and bump into the bank – I could walk right straight down the middle of the road. It's not like that now. Oh, I'd give a million dollars if I could."*

- Doc Watson[1]

*"He told us how he had a little white cane. He said he occasionally used it to kind of feel whether there was something in front of him. He told me he'd go down the road and go visit a cousin or brother or whatever. We said, 'How do you do it?' He said he did it by tapping; it was like radar."*

- Maria Muldaur[2]

Though he was born without eyesight, young Doc knew freedom like few other blind children of the 1920s. As a young boy, he roamed unencumbered, running with his brothers down deer and Indian paths along Wildcat Creek, exploring the fields and woods around his home without worry or fear. Doc was able to play nearly all of the games the other children played. He told Cara Ellen Modisett in 2004: "I went and did as I pleased. And I never got hurt, either. Not really."[1]

Early in his life, Doc discovered that he had very sensitive hearing, which he called *sound radar*, and from the wild sounds of his country life, to the hymns in his little valley church, to the songs his granny sang on the porch while shelling peas, Doc learned to listen. Doc said of his sound radar: "If I was walking through the grass at 20 years old; the rustle of the grass as I walked by a fence – oh, maybe five, six feet away from it – if the wind wasn't blowing and covering up the high end sound, I could count the stakes by the sound, the high-end sound, bouncing off the stakes as I rustled the grass and walked through it. That was my radar. Sound radar."[1] Doc talked in another interview about his bat-like ability:

"Well, you know, a bat uses a radar system – they can hear much higher than any human can; I began to do that when I was a little boy."[3]

Doc Watson was born with, and quickly developed his sound radar. *Sound* in both senses of the word: *sound* like the mountains that have been his foundation for the greater part of a century, the Appalachians that, 450 million years ago, were the tallest mountains in the world, and *sound* as in the twisting partials and harmonics racing to the inner ears of the lucky, somewhere above 20,000 Hz; the cast-off melodies beyond ordinary human perception.

Donna Hill, a blind singer-songwriter who interviewed Doc a number of times, recalled that her own childhood was, like Doc's, uncommonly free for a blind child: "My mother would just say, 'Get out of the house, leave.' And if I fell out of a tree or if I stumbled or did whatever, well that happens. I don't know Doc's parents so I don't know if they had any philosophy with regard to raising him as a blind child, or if they simply said, 'Look, he is one of nine kids. These are the rules, and everybody gets treated the same way; everybody's expected to pull their own weight, and if he's going to go out there and wants to be out there with the kids, then he goes out there with other kids. If he has a problem he has a problem.' I mean, he has to learn to adapt, and that's what you need to do with your kids because otherwise, if you don't let them test the limits of their own abilities and get in with the other children, they're not going to be properly socialized. They're not going to know what their limits are, they are not going to be able to find acceptable alternatives to do anything when they are young and their minds are more open to things. They're going to be stuck with a limited life. But I'm sure it wasn't easy for my mom to know that I was going out unaided being legally blind and doing some of the things that I did. Maybe that's why I don't have kids."[4]

Doc believed that he could do nearly anything. Not only did Doc have aspirations of being a mechanic, engineer or the like, he, rather remarkably, *was* able to fix nearly anything. Just about everyone who knew Doc in the early part of his career remembers a story about him fixing something. Folk singer Jean Ritchie recalled being on the road with Doc in the 1960s: "I went on an automobile trip with Doc somewhere one day. I was in the car, and Doc said, 'There's a funny knocking in the engine.' And he listened to it for a while and he said, 'Let's get out and look at it.' So he got out and he looked at it, and just by listening to it he told them exactly what was wrong with the car. And they were able to get it fixed."[5] B. Townes, former Executive Director of MerleFest, recalled similar situations in the late 1980s: "Riding down the road late at night, just me and Doc in the car, he would often say things like, 'You know, B., I believe that right front tire's a little low on air,' or, 'I believe you better check the oil, I hear the fifth cylinder clicking a little bit.'"[6]

Doc's greatest skill was to use his talents of charm and even of car repair in order to make friends along the road. He inspired young musicians, and entertained his hosts along the way, sleeping on couches and making lifelong friends. Doc never had temper tantrums, never threw furniture out of windows. He made friends, and one by one, he won over fans that came out to support him time after time, through both good and lean times.

George McCeney, who made fast friends with Doc during the 1960s, told a story about Doc's uncanny navigation ability: "I guess this is true of all blind people, but he had the most amazing sense of where he was. He was sort of like a GPS or something. We had some letters to mail, so he had given them to me, and we were walking down the street in Boone. And all of a sudden he pulled on my arm and said, 'I think we have to mail those letters.' I looked across the street, and as God is my judge, at exactly 90 degrees to us was the door to the post office. I looked at my friend Gary, and he looked at me. I said, 'Yeah, okay Doc,' and went across the street."[7]

Doc's amazing ability to judge where he was according to sound quickly became a game for him as a child, especially with his older cousin Willard, who would come up the road wanting to surprise him. Willard would stand in front of him, and Doc would know exactly who it was. Doc remembered: "Well, they've tried that many times, and if they forgot and were trying to hide, they would breathe a little harder than they normally would – and their breath comes through their voice box, and I'd hear it good enough. I'd say, 'Well, hello Herb,' or 'How are you, Willard,' and they could not believe it."[8] Doc continued to play these sound games throughout his career, much to the delight of his musical friends. Everyone who knew Doc at some point in his career tested him at one time or another.

Blues and popular music vocalist Maria Muldaur spoke about surprising her old friend Doc near her home: "It was many years since I had seen Doc, and he came and played at the Sweetwater in Mill Valley, which is a nightclub near here. He had no idea where I lived or anything, but you bet I was going to come there, and I walked into the dressing room and said, 'Doc, do you know who this is?' He knew it was me, and nobody announced me."[2]

Roland White, another of Doc's early friends in the music business, surprised Doc in a similar way in Nashville: "I came to Nashville in 1967, and I saw Doc a couple times in early '70s playing the Exit Inn, which is kind of a leftover coffee-house-type scene in Nashville. And he played another club, and another listening room. I probably saw him five or six times through the years. I would come up to him after a gig, and I wouldn't tell him I was there in advance. I'd say, 'Hello, Doc, how are you doing?' And he would say, 'Is that you, Roland?' and reach out his hand. That's what really fooled me! I saw him several times through the years, and then I saw him once a year, every year, at MerleFest once I joined the Nashville Bluegrass Band in 1989."[9]

Doc did not just amuse his colleagues and friends in the music business. He amazed them with his virtuosity, his kindness, and his ability to transcend his disability. George McCeney even took it one level further while speaking about Doc's incredible sensitivity to sound: "Being blind, of course, means you have to listen more acutely than you might otherwise. And people who listen carefully understand more. And I just wonder whether Doc, not uniquely because of his blindness, but in part because of his blindness, listened in ways in which you and I would not. And I think that probably contributed to his greatness, that kind of sensitivity to what a song is really all about."[7] Indeed, Doc's sound radar did more than lead him safely down the road to Boone. It brought him to millions of listeners across the world.

Despite countless interviews about his life and also at times about his blindness, Doc has never spoken at length publicly about what caused his disability. At times, he suggested that the silver nitrate drops that were put in his eyes at birth might have caused his blindness: "When I was born, some kind of infection got in my eyes and destroyed the corneas. It was thought that contaminated silver nitrate drops did it – I don't know…"[3]

In 1881, German researcher Karl Credé discovered that a drop of two-percent silver nitrate solution placed into each eye at birth could prevent infection, a discovery that dramatically decreased the incidence of blindness.[10] By 1923, researchers had found that a one-percent solution was just as effective, and the state of North Carolina prescribed the smaller amount to be administered into each newborn's eyes. On Doc Watson's birth certificate, the midwife or clerk who filed his paperwork wrote "yes" after question number 21 on the certificate, which read, "Did you use drops in baby's eyes at birth to prevent blindness?"[11] The state legislature of North Carolina also required that midwives wash the eyes of newborn children with a solution of 15 percent "antiseptic solution," which was often boric acid, and 85 percent water. It was a painful process, but one that could potentially ward off other infections causing blindness.[12]

Though Doc was blind from birth, he never showed acute outward effects of infection, which could cause the eyelids of afflicted children to curl up uncomfortably. Despite a cataract in one eye, Doc's eyes are deep blue like robin's eggs, often intensely focused on some unseen target.

He told Terry Grosz on the NPR program Fresh Air how people tried to get him to wear sunglasses, and how he always refused: "Boy, they used to try to get me to wear them. I reckon they didn't like the way my eyes looked. Lot of people would say, 'You ought to wear sunglasses,' but I hated them; I wouldn't do it... I just never have worn them. I don't know if the blind that wear them, their eyes look really abnormal or what, I don't know. I never did care to wear them, just didn't do it. No particular reason except what I told you."[13]

Though most journalists throughout Doc's career have cited a childhood infection as the reason for his blindness, a small number speculated the cause to be congenital, perhaps even the result of inbreeding. Doc's blindness might indeed be congenital, especially because his sister Ethel was also blind, but was certainly not the result of inbreeding, a word that had already maliciously cast its pall over the perception of Appalachians in American culture by the late 1950s. Of course, inbreeding was a problem in certain remote hollows of the Appalachian Mountains, but not within respected churchgoing families who were careful to trace their family lines back, and not within Doc's family.

Doc's wife Rosa Lee is his second cousin. While that might seem like evidence of familial overlap, the practice of cousin marriage is widespread in the United States and beyond. Second cousin marriage is legal around the world to this day, and is practiced with few congenital problems. Even first cousin marriage is legal in most of the world. However, Doc's parents were not related, making the argument that Doc's blindness was a result of inbreeding impossible. There is no evidence of any inbreeding, at least as far back as his ancestors' emigration from Europe.

In 1964, Lee Winfrey, falsely speculating that inbreeding was the cause of Doc's blindness, wrote in the *Detroit Free Press* (for Knight Newspapers, Inc.): "Isolated in their coves and glens, the mountain people married their friends and neighbors. Often, there was no one around to marry except relatives – a cousin or a niece. The inbreeding produced congenital defects which run today through many mountain bloodlines. Blindness, for example, runs through the Watson family. Doc's sister is blind, too... Doc Watson is beating the game, but he is a decided exception. Not one man in a million can play a guitar like he can. For most of his neighbors, Deep Gap is a valley getting deeper all the time."[14] Such a gross misunderstanding of Doc's condition and of his careful and loving upbringing is shockingly familiar to those who study Appalachian history. Similar articles about the Appalachians helped to form the stereotypes today that still so comfortably lampoon *rednecks* and *hillbillies*. Whatever caused Doc's blindness, it could probably have happened to the wealthiest and most socially connected children, and had little or nothing to do with his parents being, as Winfrey wrote, either isolated or inbred.

Although Doc Watson never really complained publicly about his blindness, he had a brief flash of hope in 1962, when doctors developed certain techniques to transplant corneas and possibly restore sight. Unfortunately, Doc had been blind too long, and was not even a remote candidate for the procedure.[15] The possibility to see had given Doc and his family great hope, and he was crushed when it turned out that the operation could not work: "I felt like a little boy who had lost his best friend. I had a world-renowned doctor, so naturally I had big hopes. I thought, finally I was going to be able to see. You know how it is when you have that sinking feeling in your stomach...like the whole world has just dropped out from under you? Whew! That's how it was when Dr. Jaffe told me that even if I had the operation, I still wouldn't be able to see. Not ever. Not in this life, anyway. But...I soon decided to take heart about it. He's not God, I thought. I had always had the handicap to deal with, and there was no reason to grieve over it. It wouldn't be any worse now. I'd just go on like I always had."[16]

Despite the despair Doc felt that he would never be able to see within his lifetime, gospel hymns like "Amazing Grace" gave him hope that he would see like everyone else in the afterlife he believed awaited good Christians. At the same time, Doc also began to try to explain his blindness within his belief system. He began to feel that his blindness had been gifted to him by his loving God as a hindrance to his natural ego: "I think that [blindness] was allowed to be mine as a deterrent – I think I might have been maybe a bit stuck up, or haughty, if it hadn't have been for that. And I think maybe the good Lord thought I needed it. I really have come to that conclusion over the past few years."[17]

Despite his blindness, Doc believed that *trying* something was the best way to learn it. His father taught him that early in his life, and Doc courageously went out into the dark, even though his footsteps often stumbled. Doc learned to *live* in courage, every day of his life, whether on the road by himself, or at home, chopping wood behind his home.

Marty Stuart, the well-known country and gospel star, who had many opportunities to share a stage with Doc and Merle in his early years, recalled once visiting Doc at his home before going out on the road with him on a tour: "One time we were up in Boone up on the mountain. Doc had just built a new home, and right across the pasture was the old place where Doc's daughter Nancy lived. And I was going to take him down there to say goodbye to Nancy before we went on the road, and it was pitch black, and I was trying to lead him across the way to Nancy's house and almost got us killed. This is the truth. He said, 'Son, you get behind me,' and he led me to Nancy's house in the middle of the night."[18]

In life and in the music industry, not only has Doc been able to not only navigate for himself, but he has walked into the darkness with Virgil's lantern on his back, lighting the way for young musicians from around the world, like Marty Stuart that night in the dark. Young musicians have gathered around Doc his entire career, and he has been like a father to all of them. Like Merle, they could go off and party on the mountain, but when they returned, there was Doc, honest and authentic, ready to embrace them like the *papa* of so many prodigal sons, teaching them to be humble on stage and within their lives. He led them all and shone his lantern brightly, though he himself was wrapped in darkness.

Doc recalled singing with Bill Monroe for President Jimmy Carter on the front lawn of the White House on August 7, 1980: "When I got up there, I said, 'Well, when I was a little boy playing with a little homemade wooden wagon in the yard, I never thought I'd be setting here on the stage on the White House lawn, playing music for the president, but since I'm here, I'm gonna try to do my best...' Jimmy Carter had bragged on me some, and I said, Jimmy, you make me nervous, buddy."[19]

Doc's courageous adventure out into the world had begun early in his life. Already, Doc possessed an uncommon fearlessness. Doc and his brother David described one incident in which Doc's intrepid behavior could have gotten him severly injured. The boys, Linney, Arnold, Doc and David, were playing on a cliff together, near a tall tree, swinging out on a grapevine over the side. Doc pleaded for a while to have a turn on the vine, at which point the boys passed it to him. Doc remembered, "I had to try it, and about 20 feet off the ground the grapevine just slipped out of my hand and I went crashing down the hillside. I sure was sore but I wasn't injured."[8]

The brothers were terrified. David remembered: "We thought he was really hurt bad. His nose was bleeding and everything. It turned out he was awfully sore, but he was all right. I don't know why he turned loose – I think he thought he could fly."[20]

And Doc Watson never stopped thinking he could fly, metaphorically speaking, although in the 1970s, he stopped taking airplanes, blaming them for the ulcers that had plagued him the first decade of his career. Doc's success throughout his life came, for the most part, because he had the ability, using his sound radar, to swing freely on every grapevine: gauging the highest point of the arc, 20 feet above the cliff, only then letting go, believing he could fly.

# CHAPTER NOTES

1.     Modisett, Cara Ellen, *The Roanoker Talks to... Doc Watson*. The Roanoker, November 2, 2004.
2.     Gustavson, Kent, *Telephone Interview with Maria Muldaur*. April 1, 2009.
3.     Holt, David and Doc Watson, *Doc Watson and David Holt: Legacy*, Audio CD, High Windy Audio, 2002.
4.     Gustavson, Kent, *Telephone Interview with Donna Hill*. May 6, 2009.
5.     Gustavson, Kent, *Telephone Interview with Jean Ritchie*. May 6, 2009.
6.     Gustavson, Kent, *Telephone Interview with B. Townes*. July 10, 2009.
7.     Gustavson, Kent, *Telephone Interview with George McCeney*. May 22, 2009.
8.     Holt, David, *Liner Notes to Doc Watson and David Holt: Legacy*, High Windy Audio, 2002.
9.     Gustavson, Kent, *Telephone Interview with Roland White*. June 12, 2009.
10.     Credé, Karl *Die Verhütung der Augenentzündung der Neugeborenen*. Archiv für Gynäkologie, 1881. 17: p. 50-53.
11.     *Birth Certificate for Örthel (sic) Lane Watson*. 1923.
12.     Rogers, Sam L., Director of Department of Commerce, Bureau of the Census, *The Blind of the United States 1910*. 1917: Washington.
13.     Grosz, Terry, *Interview with Doc Watson*, from *Fresh Air*. 1988, National Public Radio.
14.     Winfrey, Lee, *Inbreeding and Ignorance Plague the Hill Folk*. Detroit Free Press, May 19, 1964. Detroit, MI.
15.     *Doc Watson Family Timeline*, Doc Watson Museum: Cove Creek, NC.
16.     Watson, Nancy, *Doc Watson: A Closer Look*. Bluegrass Unlimited, August 1984. 19(2): p. 8-11.
17.     Humphrey, Mark, *Liner Notes to Doc Watson Rare Performances 1982-1993*, Stefan Grossman's Guitar Workshop, Vestapol/Rounder Records, 1995.
18.     Gustavson, Kent, *Telephone Interview with Marty Stuart*. May 18, 2009.
19.     Murphy, Joe, *Doc and Merle -The Lives and Music of Doc & Merle Watson (1985)*, VHS, Vestapol, 1996.
20.     Brinson, Linda, *Doc Watson: He Takes His Gift and Shares It With the World*. Winston-Salem Journal, March 29, 1987. Winston-Salem, NC: p. A13,A16.

# CHAPTER THREE
## Blind School

*"[One time, Doc] was telling the time by feeling the face of his [braille] pocket watch. My son asked me and Doc shyly what [he] was doing, and [Doc] told him he was telling time. Doc then asked, 'How old are you son?' and Mark held up three fingers. [I] told Mark that Doc couldn't see his fingers and that he would have to tell Doc his age, at which time he voiced, 'Three.' Mark then asked me and, in turn, Doc, why he couldn't see and Doc turned to him in the most grandfatherly voice [and said,] 'Well, son, my light bulbs are burned out.'"*

- Steve Kaufman[1]

Doc and his siblings were familiar with the walk uphill around the lush mountainside, up the steep switchbacks in the road where Wildcat creek cut its narrow trough. They had often walked into Deep Gap for supplies that they could not grow or kill. Doc remembers even having walked the dozen or so miles into nearby Boone with only the guidance of his cane. But this time was different. Doc was wearing his best outfit: perhaps his little knee pants and shirt, his hair combed and his shoes freshly cleaned. His family walked with him the few miles into Deep Gap proper, so that ten-year old Doc could catch the Greyhound bus to Raleigh, 200 miles to the east, where he would be enrolling in the Raleigh School for the Blind.

The late summer day would have been a perfect one for Doc to be out with his younger brother David or his other friends, climbing trees and playing in the barn. But there was no time for Doc to play outside today. His long journey was just beginning. David Watson recalled his big brother Doc's departure from home: "Boy, when he went off to school, talk about somebody who was lonesome!... I didn't have anyone to play with."[2] David would not see his brother for months at a time, but when Doc returned home during holidays, David recalled the trip they would make to see Doc: "At the end of the school term, they let him come home and we'd go over to Deep Gap and wait. Sometimes that Greyhound bus would be way in the cotton-picking night getting up there. And we get him off and then walk all the way back around that mountain at least five miles. Boy he was glad to be home though. Always glad to get home."[2] Doc, always overjoyed to return home and see David and the rest of his family, surely picked up quickly where he had left off with his brothers, going out to climb trees, play in the barn, and frail* on his little homemade catskin banjo.

Over the four years that Doc attended the Raleigh School for the Blind, he began to hate his time there more and more: every summer, when he had the chance to return home, he wallowed in the freedom the mountains held for him. The restrictions put on him at school must have seemed like prison to a boy used to swinging on ropes and sledding down mountains with his brothers. Little wonder that rambunctious and free-spirited Doc got himself into a good measure of trouble.

Even before he left home at age ten, Doc already knew a little about getting into trouble. He often recounts, in his recent concert tours, a story of his father's two corncribs in the barn. One stored feed corn, and the other stored corn that would later be ground into cornmeal. His little brother David and he would put planks between the two of them, playing games that little boys play, until one day, they broke through the edges of the cribs, and they had to tell their father what they had done. Their father gave them what Doc calls a *nettling* the next morning. Doc recalled getting another "pretty good spanking, not a real dangerous one," for scratching a record while trying to play with his family's Victrola record player.[3]

Though he felt the sting of his father's hand, he also learned the value of hard work from him, and the beautiful sound of hymn singing. And though he and his brothers had run-ins with the hickory switch a number of times, his brothers were always there to both mock and comfort him; something he would not have traded for the world.

His family's modest home certainly was not a luxury hotel, but during long and cold winter months, they kept each other warm. Doc shared a bed with two of his brothers as a child during the Depression. He recalled that mornings in his childhood home were often bitterly cold: "You'd wake up in the morning with frost on your pillow."[4]

The nine children took care of each other, at home, and out in the world. That was especially true for Doc and his younger brother David. They were inseparable as boys. David Watson spoke of his close friendship with his brother: "Any kind of meanness I got into, Doc was right there with me, whatever it was.

---

* *"Frailing," also called "clawhammer," is a technique used on the banjo that was popularized in the 1920s. It involves the performer striking the banjo strings with the cupped fingers of their right hand and alternately plucking the drone string with their thumb.*

We had a couple of cousins that lived out there, Howard and Sylvester Green, and we'd get out there with them boys and fight. I hold one of them 'til Doc could get a hold of him, then I'd take care of the other. Boy, you talk about beat on him. If Doc could just get a hold of him, he was fine! Doc is strong as an ox!"[2] Doc had learned how to survive in the school of hard knocks, and was already roaming the hills as an independent, free-willed boy.

A 10-year old country boy stepped onto a Greyhound bus clutching his few belongings tightly. As he felt his way down the aisle to find an empty seat, perhaps he wondered how he would fare in his adventures. As the bus drove stop-by-stop east towards Raleigh and his new life, maybe he listened to the conversations around him, imagining where the other passengers were from, and where they were going. The bus bumped and rolled through every little town, out of the Blue Ridge, into the foothills, and down into the flatlands. Surely the driver helped the young boy exit the bus at his final destination, his unseeing silvery blue eyes staring out towards the bustling new scenery of Raleigh's city streets. The bus then pulled away from Doc, and his escape route disappeared. Here he was, on the edge of his new destiny. Little did he know that more than half of his life would be this coming and going, traveling on buses and planes and in automobiles, from little town to big city, all across the country.

It was mandatory, under North Carolina state law, that young Arthel Watson attend the Raleigh School for the Blind by the age of seven. Beginning in 1908 in the state of North Carolina, there was a compulsory education law in place for blind children between the ages of 7 and 17, which was soon further extended to the age of 21. They were required to attend nine months of school per year. If the child's parents could not afford the expense of sending their child to the school, the government asked for two "respectable citizens" to verify that the parents were "unable to provide for the child's clothing and expenses to and from the institution," whereupon "the governor must order the amount to be paid by the state."[5] The state government then charged the child's county government for the costs. Doc qualified for assistance, and Wilkes County picked up the bill for him.

The state of North Carolina was very progressive in offering quality education for blind children. Doc never thought of it that way, but he was a lucky child, because his education was far better than even that of his siblings or friends attending public schools in the Deep Gap area. In 1921, twelve years before Doc attended, the Raleigh School for the Blind had been placed on a list of accredited high schools, and was then held to the same standards as regular academic public high schools in Raleigh.

The first school for the blind in the United States was the New England Asylum for the Blind in Massachusetts. Opened to the public in 1832, it accepted students from every state. In 1842, North Carolina governor John Motley Morehead first recommended to his legislature that they follow suit. He met with resistance, but continued to push for the school. In 1844, he wrote of the blind and deaf students he wanted to educate, "Many of them, if educated and instructed in useful employment, would be able to maintain themselves and enjoy life as rational creatures. Without these advantages, we often find them huddled together within the confines of a loathsome poor house, doomed to while away a miserable existence in wretchedness to themselves, and at an increased expense to those whose duty it is to make for them more ample provision."[6] Finally, Governor Morehead succeeded in his quest, and nearly 30 years after the first attempts, a School for the Blind and Deaf was established in North Carolina. While Doc was in attendance there, it was named the Raleigh School for the Blind, but the school is now named in honor of its chief advocate: The Governor Morehead School for the Blind.

The Raleigh School for the Blind took pride in its strict educational and academic policies. This was a school that, in its bylaws, stood for "moral, intellectual and physical training."[6] This was not simply a school for the disabled; students came to this school to learn to be teachers, academics, handworkers, musicians, and more. And students did not simply come to study at the Raleigh School; they were also taught to work, from planting grass and shade trees to learning trades alongside their academic training. They were taught to be self-sufficient in every way possible.

At the Raleigh School, educators focused on two goals of study for their students. One was to train them to be teachers in similar institutions to the one they were attending, and the other was to train them to be musicians, with professions as church organists or teachers of music. The authorities of the school believed that music would be one of the most lucrative and practical fields for the students, and therefore, much of their education was focused around music.

The music department at the Raleigh School was extensive. Students were given lessons on many instruments, including piano, organ, guitar and pipe organ. They were trained vocally, and were given instruction in composition, notation, harmony, piano tuning, and the profession of teaching. Students studied many instruments, including: violin, viola, cello, bass, clarinet, flute and trombone... They used the same instruments that sighted people use, and their sheet music was sometimes printed in raised type, but they usually learned by ear. Other high schools in the area and across the country offered music as an extra-curricular activity in the 1930s, but certainly a public institution with extensive training such as the Raleigh School provided to Doc was highly uncommon. Essentially, Doc was trained at one of the finest institutions for musical study of the time, whether for sighted or unsighted children.

Though he often discounts the four years he spent there as having been horrible years, they were certainly beneficial to his future career as a professional musician and eventual music legend. Doc was trained in the rudiments of classical music, and, combined with the exposure he had to radio, records and live performances there, Doc was in a virtual breeding ground for musical talent. He has often claimed that he had little or no formal musical training, or that he never studied classical music. But he correctly contradicts himself in other interviews, and admits some of the musical background the Raleigh School afforded him. In a 1994 interview, Doc recalled studying piano at school: "I took about three months of piano, when I was going to school in Raleigh, and they wouldn't let me mess around with anything but classical music."[7]

Though Doc did not like his piano lessons and soon quit them, he found piano tuning fascinating. Little did he know that piano tuning would pay many of his family's bills a decade later during hard times. In 1888, one of the teachers and administrators at the Raleigh School, exploring the need for another vocation among the boys of the school, had learned the art of piano tuning, and began teaching the boys.[5] Pianos at the time were still remarkably rare across the country, but within the next 20 years, piano makers began producing them by the thousands, and pianos reached all corners of the countryside. The program in piano tuning expanded and by the time Doc attended the school nearly half a century later, piano tuning had already become a lucrative career for generations of graduates from the Raleigh School.

Doc absorbed the classical records they listened to so often in their residence hall, the live performances he heard on the radio from WPTF, the powerful local Raleigh radio station of hillbilly singers and more. The Monroe Brothers, Wade Mainer and the Mountaineers, and The Tobacco Tags were all live groups that came through the studio when Doc listened, rapt at the other end of the radio set.

Doc was also exposed to jazz music for the first time. His teachers played him records of jazz guitarists Nick Lucas and Django Reinhardt, and the records of all the era's big jazz bands. When later asked about Django, the great gypsy guitarist who had also grown up playing banjo, Doc replied, "[I] couldn't figure out what the devil he was doing he went so fast on most of it, but I loved it."[8] At home, Doc's family had head heard many records on his family's Victrola before going to school, and he had certainly listened to the radio in stores, and at friends' homes, but never had he heard such a wonderful variety of music. Anything he could imagine was on the radio, and instead of the raw sounds he was accustomed to in the mountains, on the porches and in the church, now he was hearing the produced, sweet sounds of professional country, classical and jazz music.

The music department at the Raleigh School was in the basement. There were 12 practice rooms, an orchestra room, five studios for the instructors, and a big choral room. The practice rooms were all grouped closely together, and did not have sound-proofing, which created quite a melee of sound on busy days, but there was plenty of space to accommodate all of the students comfortably.

Doc quit the official course on piano tuning, perhaps more interested in the technical science and technology courses at the school, but he was still interested enough to sit in the window of one of those basement rooms, listening in on the instructor talking about the hammers and guts of the piano, and about the tuning forks that were used to tune the giant instruments. Little did Doc know that someday he would use all of those skills, not only for piano tuning, but for tuning up his guitar in front of thousands of audiences around the country. Doc recalled how he would sit in the window and listen: "[The teacher] Mr. Cox could see a little bit – and he explained to them...how to fit [the tuning hammer] over the pins to tune... Anyway, I don't want to give a lesson in tuning over here, but by listening I learned...even how to string a piano, but I never did do it – I never did have to... I learned a bunch of things..."[3]

Doc lived in a small cottage designed to house 28 boys. There was a piano inside, and a console radio, and most of the bedrooms had record players that the students would use to listen to their Library of Congress "talking books." His cottage was well lit by electric light, though for Doc and most of his fellow blind students, the light would have been largely unnecessary. The small dormitory had also both hot and cold running water, and a full kitchen, with gas ranges, refrigerators and cabinets.

Every morning, Doc and his fellow pupils crawled out of bed early enough to make it to chapel in time for the morning religious services. A passage from the Bible would be read and interpreted, and the entire school body would join together in prayer. A similar prayer service was held late in the afternoon, after all courses and chores were completed.

Besides their school courses, the students took part in various activities every day: walking, football, baseball, other outdoor sports and bowling (in an on-campus bowling alley). The students were only allowed to leave the school premises with special permission, or with a staff member from the institution, and all visitors and correspondence had to happen through the hands of the administration. Male and female students were not allowed to associate unless in the presence of a teacher, and conversation was forbidden between the students at mealtime.

Because he had never been to school before, Doc was required to start at the beginning, and work his way through school, one grade at a time, until he reached the grade level that corresponded to his age. Primary education at the Raleigh School consisted mostly of the alphabet, spelling, reading, and arithmetic. Doc began kindergarten soon after he stepped off of the bus into the humid, warm Raleigh air, and soon sped through several more grade levels before returning home the next summer. He flew through Penmanship, Geography, Rhetoric, Grammar, Arithmetic, History and more, showing that his hunger for book learning was as great as his later hunger for musical skill.

The main portion of every day was filled with study, with 40-minute class periods throughout, and there was a recreation hour between 5 and 6 PM. Students had an hour for lunch, and one of their class periods was devoted to physical education. The chapel service began at 8:10 in the morning, and the 10th period finished at 5 PM. The last four class periods were slightly longer, and students could choose in which activities they wanted to participate, whether orchestra, chorus, shop work, library, or another activity.

Doc spoke about his first teacher at the Raleigh School: "I was 10 years old; turned 11 shortly after I went there…and they had a kindergarten that was truly a kindergarten… I learned to read and write in two weeks… Pretty amazing, but not when you're ten years old, if you have any mind at all, and if you have a *number one-A D-double-A number one* teacher. She was a blind lady, and she was a Godsend to that school: Miss Nora Norris… She lived near Asheville…"[3] Nora Norris had been teaching at the Raleigh School for nearly twenty years, after having started out at the salary of $25 per year as a kindergarten assistant, then taking the job of *kindergartner* when her predecessor retired.[9] Doc was grateful for Nora Norris' mentorship and encouragement since it was his first time away from home, and he was terribly homesick. He would live at the Raleigh School for three months or more at a time without visits home, and when other students went home for interim holidays, Doc stayed on campus and waited for them to return again. The state would only pay transportation costs for him to return home in the summer.

Doc recalled that his first week was especially hard: "The first Sunday I was at the school I was so homesick I was just sitting around crying. The old matron of the school scolded, 'If you can't do any better than that, you can stay here and I will take the rest of the children to Sunday school.' Well, I sat down crying on a great big bench in the hall. A black woman who worked there came in and said, 'Honey, is you homesick?' I said, 'Yes, Bessie, I wish I was home.' She said, 'I'll tell you what, there are a whole bunch of toys that is never used. I'll get them out on the floor and you can play to your heart's content.' She got those toys out, they belonged to the rest of the kids, I didn't have any toys. That cheered me up and helped me get over that spell of homesickness."[2]

The school matron's callousness was the first sign to Doc that he would not have the same freedoms he had enjoyed at home. However, in a time when corporal punishment was the standard in the nation's schools, the Raleigh School had already been outlawing it for more than 70 years by the time Doc arrived (since 1858). If teachers used violence, they were acting against school policy. All cases of disobedience, delinquency, etc. went straight to the principal, who took care of the matter without outward violence. However, blind students are particularly vulnerable to neglectful and abusive treatment, and even today, there are still issues with abuse at blind institutions, including the Raleigh School. In 1991, several claims of abuse were investigated, and, though the school was found not to be abusive in general, there were isolated incidents that were disturbing, including one student being tied to a door, and another falling down a staircase while not being well supervised.[10]

Because Doc was a boy funded by the state, and, among other things that displayed his country character, frailed on the fretless banjo his father and brothers had crafted for him, he was discriminated against by the students and by some of the staff members at the school. But Doc was also a troublemaker by many definitions; he still calls the staff members *overlords*, and says that he rebelled against them. That kind of language or anti-authoritarian behavior would certainly not have been well received by his teachers and matrons. Doc never revealed why precisely his experience at the Raleigh School was so terrible, but he has used strong language to describe his caretakers at the school: "I don't know if 'sadistic' is the word, [but] they should have been in an institution, rather than controlling little children, especially blind people."[11] And in another interview with Donna Hill, a fellow blind musician, he told her that the school was being run by people who considered a school for the blind to be an asylum for freaks.[12]

Though the school was ranked just as highly as Raleigh standard public schools, Doc was still convinced that his general education at the Raleigh School could have been much stronger, and that their methods often hindered the students' progress rather than supporting them: "Most blind people, unless there are other things wrong with them, are pretty well normal or they can be made so with the right environment and reasonable training. The Raleigh School had the facilities down there and the means. It wouldn't have cost the state anything. Boys with scientific interest like I had, with just a little of effort on the school's part, their minds could have been kept totally busy and, even blind, they could have come out of there some kind of engineers. No telling what they could have done."[11]

Doc is still spiteful sometimes that he could not become scientist or an engineer. He feels that the teachers at his school gifted him with an inferiority complex that discouraged him from being all he could be. Doc talked about the fine line that education systems of the blind must walk: "I was talking to Rosa Lee today, I said, 'Honey, there's two things that affect the life of a blind person, and that is if you are in a school or are governed by people that make you feel inferior because of your handicap, and, on the other hand, if your folks shelter you too much at home... Those two things can absolutely destroy a blind person's confidence to the point where they will not – even though they have brilliant minds – they will not be a success. They give it up.' Shucks, I went out and climbed trees and fell out just like the rest of my brothers did."[11] Doc's teachers did not see his free thinking and rebelliousness as a positive, to say the least. Doc took up smoking, and got into fights. He felt restricted, stuck in a situation where every activity and every movement was carefully scrutinized and planned, and he rebelled.

Upon reaching eighth grade at the Raleigh School, students were required to choose between the four specialized courses of study: academic, vocational, commercial or music. Though Doc never reached that point before quitting school, he probably would not have chosen the music route. In all of his interviews, when the subject of school was brought up, Doc has said that if he had been sighted, he would have chosen engineering, carpentry, or another job where he could have worked with his hands.

At the Raleigh School, boys took all standard subjects, including science, math and history. But what Doc loved the most was engineering; he loved pulling things apart, and he loved figuring things out. Many of the other boys at the school accepted what their teachers said as the whole truth. They believed *all* they could be was a musician, or a peddler on the street corner, or at best, a teacher. But Doc heard what his teachers said and he saw the message *beneath* it.

He saw that he could be *anybody* he wanted to be. He could study anything that sighted people could study. He could do anything sighted people could do.

If Doc knew a certain freedom as a child to wander in the woods and valleys of home, he began to know a new kind of freedom at the Raleigh School. He was given the freedom of good education, and he saw that his teachers functioned in the world despite their blindness, that they were just like anyone else; that they could teach, that they could play music; they could tune pianos. Soon, he could read Library of Congress "talking books" and braille books, and for the rest of his life, he could study anything, and be anyone he wanted to be. Years later, he spent hours in the New York Public Library where he listened to book after book during the idle hours between gigs and recording sessions. Whether Doc acknowledges it or not, it was at the Raleigh School that Doc acquired his true passion for learning.

He also first learned how to play the guitar at the Raleigh School. He met another student who played a little left-handed guitar, and taught Doc his first few chords: "Paul Montgomery could see just a tiny bit, [and] he told me where to put my fingers – at first, the C, the G, the D and the A chord. And, man, I loved the guitar so good that every time he'd set down, I'd get him over to show me – oh, about the fourth time, I had 'em."[3] Both Paul and Doc were very protective of their instruments; Paul of his little Kalamazoo guitar, and Doc of his homemade banjo. Paul remembered that Doc held his banjo, "like it was a baby in his lap and wouldn't let it out of his sight."[2] Paul and Doc became good friends, and did a lot of playing on the weekends, when little was scheduled for the boys at the school.

The two boys started talking one day, and decided to try swapping instruments for a few minutes. Paul recalled their conversation: Doc suggested, "I'll let you play my banjo if you let me play your guitar." Paul responded, "That is a step in the right direction!"[2] Paul played left-handed, and used a standard guitar upside down. He taught Doc how to play the chords just like a left-handed player before Doc figured out how to finger them right side up.

Despite the friendships he had formed, and his forays into guitar, Doc simply could not stand school any more at age 13. He quit, hiding from his family before they were supposed to leave for the bus.

Doc often cited an experience he had when he was 12 as having been the last straw. In an interview with Peter Siegel, Doc talked about an experience that, in his words, "almost ruined [him] as a performer." He remembered, "There was an amateur hour on the stage of the auditorium on Friday evenings. I got up there with my little homemade fretless banjo and played 'Cripple Creek,' 'Shortening Bread' and 'I Like Mountain Music' just as happy as I can be, tapping my little old foot and picking that banjo the best I could. I got back to the little boys' dormitory and the matron slapped my face and told me I was conceited. That about fixed it for me forever as an entertainer. They had almighty authority, you know, and to do a thing like that to me at that time in my life...well, it drove deep. There were other factors, I guess, but nothing like that. It took a long long time [to get over that experience]. Even in later years when I had an opportunity to really get out there and play music for people, sometimes I'd go on the stage at a college folk festival and I was so scared my heart beat would be flying."[13]

Paul Montgomery also recalled that fateful day that was almost the end of Doc's career in music: "It was a Christmas program. They couldn't send us all home for the holidays, so we would have programs in the auditorium. Doc and I and another fellow played and sang 'I Like Mountain Music.' Well, the matron of our dormitory was embarrassed by the fact that we had gotten up on stage and publicly played some country music. She was upset by it, and that is what she slapped Doc over. They didn't like jazz, either, only classical."[2]

Doc says he dropped out of school because of the *overlord* attitudes of his teachers, but, in actuality, he had first been suspended by the school for smoking before he decided not to return, and hid from his parents on the day he was supposed to depart. Doc recalled quitting school: "I went to that school 'til the seventh grade. I didn't even go to high school, and I quit. I got suspended one year for smoking, and they wanted me to come back and I told my Daddy, 'I won't go back because if I do I'll go to jail, because I'll have to hurt somebody bad.' I hid... until the bus was gone. They couldn't find me."[11]

The rebellious boy wanted to be free of the restraints the school put on him, free of their specific courses, their detailed schedule, and the discriminatory staff members. One morning, a few days after Doc had refused to return to the Raleigh School on the bus, Doc's father said, "Come here, son, I want to talk with you." Doc went and sat down next to his father on the porch, birdsong thick in the air outside, and the humid late summer air just steaming up. General Watson continued, "Don't you know, son, that you need an education?" Doc replied, "Yeah, Dad. I know it, maybe not the way you do, but I realize that. But I can't go back to that school."[11]

Doc sat on the porch that morning and he told his father the entire story. He recounted a tale of the "overlords" and the helpless blind students and the prejudice against a little boy with a fretless banjo. He told his father about the lonely weekends, when all of the other children went home. He told him the entire truth from his perspective of how his life had been at the Raleigh School for the Blind. Whether the tales he told his father were 100-percent fact or not, they hit home with General. Doc's father took a long breath, and did not say anything in response. He surely thought about it during that long day of work, and Doc overheard him that night, speaking to his mother Annie: "Honey, if that place is half as bad as he says, I won't send him back there. I won't drive him to go. If he don't want to go he don't have to."[11]

According to state law, it would be a misdemeanor for the parents of a blind child to "fail to send the child to some school for the instruction of the blind for at least eight sessions of nine months each."[5] But this law had one exception: "...this law is not enforceable against the parents... until the authorities of some school for the blind serve written notice on them directing that the child be sent to the school of which they have charge."[5] Because Doc had been a troublemaker, it is possible that the Raleigh School had no interest in enforcing the child's attendance. The law stated, "The authorities of the state school for the blind are not compelled to retain in their custody or under instruction any incorrigible person, or person of confirmed immoral habits."[5] Whether or not Doc had been deemed *incorrigible* by the Raleigh School, he only returned once: to pick up his things and say goodbye to his friends and teachers. And then he returned home to Deep Gap.

Like any kid who drops out of school, or any person who stops some project mid-stream, Doc was disappointed in himself. He felt depressed; he did not know what to do. He had enjoyed freedoms in Raleigh that he now missed. At the school, he had been frustrated by the rigid schedules and constant planned activities, but in Deep Gap, there was nothing for him to do other than sit around and sulk.

Surely the valley had gotten smaller while he was away. What was he supposed to do day after day? What was his life goal? What was next?

When Doc went back to pick up everything he had left behind at the Raleigh School, his favorite teacher, Hessie James, took him aside and said, "Your education doesn't have to quit. There are plenty of books. You can read and keep learning."[14] Doc listened to his teacher, and he continued to study for the rest of his life: "I guess I got a little too restless to stay in school...[but] I didn't quit with my education; I tried to read and learn a few other things about the world and about what there is to learn...out of books after I quit going to school."[4]

Doc was, indeed, able to become a teacher, an innovator, and a musical genius who has since influenced generations of musicians and educated the world about Appalachian history and culture. He has been the guest of presidents and earned just about every award in the book, including honorary doctoral degrees. It seems he made the right decision to hide from the bus that day in 1937. And he still stands by it. Doc said in an interview with Bert Lloyd: "No offense meant to the school that I went to, but they didn't understand blind people then, and they made you feel like a misfit, a misfit in society. It was out of ignorance, of course, some of it was, I'll leave it to that right there. But if I had gone on to that school or been left feeling like that by my parents, I wouldn't have been worth the salt on my bread."[4]

Lucky for Doc, and lucky for all of his listeners around the world, Doc had wonderful parents who taught him next the greatest lesson of his life: the value of hard work.

# CHAPTER NOTES

1. Watson, Doc and Steve Kaufman, *The Legacy of Doc Watson*. 1999, Pacific, MO: Mel Bay Publications.
2. Holt, David, *Liner Notes to Doc Watson and David Holt: Legacy*, High Windy Audio, 2002.
3. Holt, David and Doc Watson, *Doc Watson and David Holt: Legacy*, Audio CD, High Windy Audio, 2002.
4. Lloyd, Bert, *Interview with Doc Watson*, Audio CD, Ralph Rinzler Folklife Archives, Smithsonian Institution, 1976.
5. Rogers, Sam L., Director of Department of Commerce, Bureau of the Census, *The Blind of the United States 1910*. 1917: Washington.
6. Strickland, Eugenia Love, *A Century of Educating the Deaf and the Blind in North Carolina*, from *History*. 1950, UNC at Chapel Hill: Chapel Hill, NC.
7. Reamy, Margaret, *The Real Thing: Doc Watson*. The Record Exchange Music Monitor, April 1994: p. 1.
8. Miller, Dan, *Doc Watson: Flatpicking Legend*. Flatpicking Guitar, September/October 1998.
9. Instruction, Dept. of Public, *Biennial report and recommendations of the Superintendent of Public Instruction of North Carolina*. Journal of The Senate of the General Assembly of the State of North Carolina, 1919(Session 1919): p. 760.
10. *No "abuse" at school in Raleigh*. Associated Press, June 16, 1991.
11. Stewart, Jean, *A Conversation with Doc Watson*. Sing Out!, January/February 1981. 29(1).
12. Gustavson, Kent, *Telephone Interview with Donna Hill*. May 6, 2009.
13. Siegel, Peter K., *Liner Notes from Doc Watson at Gerde's Folk City*, Sugar Hill Records, 2001.
14. Brinson, Linda, *Doc Watson: He Takes His Gift and Shares It With the World*. Winston-Salem Journal, March 29, 1987. Winston-Salem, NC: p. A13,A16.

Photo by Nic Siler ©
*Doc Watson onstage.*

# CHAPTER FOUR
## Crosscut Saw

*"Being on the road is tough on a man. And there was a time in 1963 when I came close to quitting. I almost said 'The hell with it.' But music was the only trade I knew. My father instilled in me the fact that if a man can work, he should. That's why Daddy put me on one end of a crosscut saw when I was 14. So the road was lonely, but it was a way to provide for my family."*

- Doc Watson[1]

After deciding not to return to the Raleigh School for the Blind, Doc sunk into a depression. He was happy not to be in the highly-controlled environment of his school, but when he returned home, things were not the way he envisioned either. His brothers all worked all day, as did his father. And Doc did not yet play much music: he only fiddled around now and then with the guitar, and played from time to time on the porch with his brothers, when there was a special day or holiday. While his family worked, Doc did little else but mope around the house; he simply sat in the corner for hours every day.

Before he went off to school, Doc had always been willing to help his parents shuck corn, shell peas, and other small tasks he could easily learn, and in which he did not need to navigate much. Doc recalled the first time his mother had him picking up potatoes, and the first time his father encouraged him to shuck corn like the rest of his brothers: "I remember the first thing they put me doing, one fall they were picking up potatoes and, being a little active boy, I was out there running around. Mama said to me, 'Son, I believe you can pick up some of these potatoes.' She said, 'I'll show you where the piles are,' and that got me started. And I was as proud as I could be you know, thinking I was doing something to help them, in the field. And, all at once, the corn-shucking time came along and they'd hand-stack the corn...in a huge pile and then we'd all gather it up on a good warm day in the late fall and shuck it out... Dad said, '[There] isn't a reason in the world why you can't shuck corn, son. Come on...let's see if you can beat me.' [He was] just kidding with me, you know, [of course] I never could beat him, but I tried awful hard."[2]

However, after Doc quit the Raleigh School, General Watson knew he had to do something to snap Doc out of his depression and get him contributing to family life again. One morning, General decided that he would try to teach Doc how to work like any other boy his age; but this would not be as simple as a seasonal potato-picking or corn-shucking. He wanted to teach his boy how to do daily work just as his other sons did. That first morning, General took a sip from his coffee, and said, "Son, do you think you can learn to pull a crosscut saw like the rest of the boys?"[3] Doc recalled, "I had what some people refer to as a 'complex'... If it hadn't been for my dad putting me on the other end of a crosscut saw and teaching me that I was of some benefit other than just to sit around in the corner somewhere, I don't think I would have had much incentive in life to do anything."[4]

In 1937, logging was the largest industry in North Carolina, and local farmers all across the Blue Ridge felled their own trees and sold them to industrial corporations for cash, as well as using the lumber for their own heat and cooking fuel. Doc's father used a felling saw to fell the trees, and then a two-man crosscut saw to cut the felled trees into lumber. The felling saw had a narrow blade in order to cut a wedge, which allowed the logger to predict where the tree would fall. The crosscut saw had a thick blade with saw teeth that would clear the sawdust with each powerful pull across the tree's girth.

General Watson did not want his blind son out in dangerous areas where trees might fall on him, so he instead put him on the other end of a two-man saw, carefully teaching him how to do a hard day's work without putting him in harm's way, and without making him perform a job on his own. This was a way that General could also spend time with his rebellious young son. Doc was nervous; he had never done hard work like this before, but he acquiesced to his father's urging, and decided to pretend he was like his brothers, and could fulfill this task and make his father and family proud: "I had to kind of sound like a man, whether I was or not, you know."[2]

There was nothing Doc loved more than being drawn into the working world of his family and neighbors. However, his initial reaction was a bit hesitant. His mother Annie was also resistant to General's idea that first morning over coffee. She was sure that Doc would be hurt by falling trees or the sharp blades of the large saw. Doc recalled his mother's first reaction to General's idea: "Mama was afraid he'd let me get hurt, but he said, 'Don't you worry... When I get ready to fell a tree, I'll get him out of the way.'"[5] Doc spoke at length about his parents' discussion: "Dad knew I was physically able to work and the handicap wouldn't limit me to everything... Mama was kind of protective and wanted to shield me a little too much but he said to her, 'Now Mama, don't you worry about it, he can do some work the same as the rest of us.' And I'm really proud of my father for that thing, that he didn't shelter me too much."[2] General assured his wife that their boy was very healthy despite his disability, and would quickly learn how to work. And he would be looking out for Doc, making sure nothing happened to him.

Even though Doc felt like this was the hardest work in the world at the time, he recalled that his father took it easy on him, not wanting Doc to tire too quickly: "That day, I was 14. I thought he was tough on me. But when I think back on it, he was really easy on me, because we cut off a cut, then he'd trim the limbs and piled brush and roll that out to the pile of logs where he was piling all of it to burn. And sometimes he'd chop down some smaller stuff and let me rest, and put me back to sawing again, until I got used to it."[1]

Doc had made his father proud, and he was a happy boy at the end of the day. However, he had never worked so hard in his life, and was thoroughly exhausted: "I tell you...that first day after pulling that crosscut saw this boy was ready to go to sleep. It made every muscle in my body sore and if you've ever done that, it requires just about every muscle in your body to do it. And it's like swimming, but once you get the knack of it, it doesn't hurt you anymore."[2] Not only did Doc get used to sawing wood, but he also began to see the fruit of his labor; he was able to help his father cut that winter's firewood: "I was awful proud that I could learn to do it and I was happy that I could help him cut the winter's firewood."[6]

Doc gained confidence in his abilities, and the work strengthened his belief that he could do anything to which he put his mind. At school he learned that he could study and do anything that sighted people could do. Now his father taught him that he could even do manual labor. Doc again drew the connection to his later ability to go out on tour alone, hoping to make a living for his family: "You know, that one thing, him putting me to work, realizing I was worth something, might have been the thing that gave me the nerve to tackle music as a profession and get out there and face the world."[2]

The Depression came early to Appalachia. The lumber industry had all but died after the First World War, and there was not much to replace it. Coal and textiles still ran their machinery in large towns, but there were few industrial jobs near Deep Gap. That left subsistence agriculture as the primary lifestyle. The people in the hollows near Deep Gap knew how to grow their own food, chop their own wood, shoot their own game, though there was little or no work to be found, but times were certainly lean and belts were tightened.

With the election of Franklin Delano Roosevelt to the White House in 1932, the New Deal established relief agencies within Appalachia for the first time, and the nation started to form a picture of the desperate times in the region, seeing images and reading descriptions of the despicable conditions there. As part of the plan to employ thousands of chronically unemployed Appalachians, the national government invested in improving roads, bridges and public buildings. Doc's father was one of the men who benefitted from the New Deal, and he worked with the Works Progress Administration (WPA) to help build the highways around Deep Gap as well as the buildings of Appalachian State University in Boone. The WPA was one of the most successful programs that came out of the Emergency Relief Appropriation Act of April 1935, and it provided about three million jobs to unemployed heads of households across the country.

Doc recalled his father coming home after days of working for the WPA: "[My father] was an old hard-working mountain man, and when he wasn't working on the little dirt farm we had... as it's been referred to sometimes, he did a lot of public works... [He] helped build a lot of the buildings when [Appalachian State University in Boone] was growing here as a college...putting down floor and all kinds of things like that, [and] kept work on the highway during the WPA days, when times were really hard... Sometimes, in the beginning of that, they'd work for 80 cents a day – 10 cents an hour."[3]

Though Doc had enough food and clothing, luxuries were scarce. His family never had indoor plumbing, for example. In winter, when inclement weather came, their home was not very well prepared. In an interview with Bert Lloyd, Doc recalled what snowstorms were like as a child: "When a hard blowing snow came, you had to go up in the attic to sweep up the snow and put it out through the shutter window. If you let it go until you got your big fire hot, it would melt and wet everything."[7]

Doc's mother Annie, present for this part of the interview, continued: "When it come a snowstorm, there was a window up there, a wooden window and you'd pull the shutters together and close it. But still there were cracks, and the snow would blow in up there, upstairs, we just had planks you know, laid on top of the door so it wouldn't [get through]. The snow would blow in and when the snowstorm would be over they'd have to go up there and shovel and throw it out that window, throw it out... We'd have to cover up the table, have to cover up the beds."[7]

Doc continued to describe the lean years of his childhood: "Mum, can you remember how hard the times were during the Depression, you know the hard years, 'round about 1930...when it was so hard to get any clothes for us to wear? We grew most of what we ate... The main thing I can remember about the hard times was wearing patched overalls."[7]

Annie responded: "We raised everything that we went upon. [We hardly ever had] coffee and sugar... [We were hardly able] to buy a sack of flour, I don't think, not very often. Maybe we had biscuits for breakfast, or corn bread."[7]

By mentioning food, all of a sudden Doc's mother hit a chord with her son, and in the middle of the interview, Doc started salivating, thinking of the food his mother had prepared during the Depression years, nearly half a century before this 1970s interview. He said to his mother, "Oh Mam...you bring it all back to mind... Mam, about those homemade molasses biscuits. And the homemade pancakes. I'll never forget the big field of buck wheat."[7]

Annie continued, encouraged by Doc's recollection of her cooking: "We raised our own corn, we raised our own sorghum, you know. Molasses: we nearly always had a big barrel of that. We had two good cows, I churned a lot of butter, and that went good with the molasses, you know."[7]

Likely making the connection to his own life, and his struggle to provide for his family as a blind man, Doc remembered, "You know...Momma, I guess we thought of ourselves as very poor, but we actually lived good compared to a lot of folks in the cities... I've heard boys tell that grew up around then, that they went to bed hungry, but we never did. We always had plenty to eat, such as it was."[7] Annie said, "No, never went to bed hungry."[7] Doc responded: "That's something to be thankful for..."[7]

When Doc was growing up, his family grew what they ate, and they ate what they grew. If General or one of his boys were able to bring home a few dollars, they would purchase coffee, sugar or flour. Otherwise, they just did with what they pulled out of the garden, or in winter, what they could find in the root cellar. Doc's father and brothers would also go out hunting for food. Doc remembered: "[My brothers were] used to foraging for animals...during the Depression... Those years were pretty tough... Luckily there was plenty of game."[2] And of course the Watson men also chopped firewood for the stove and for winter heat.

Donna Hill spoke about Doc's work ethic and a conversation they once had about life during the Depression years: "Doc Watson grew up with the attitude that, if you're alive, you work. You know, that's the way it is; you've got to pull your load. Especially because he grew up in the Depression, when any little contribution that a family member could make was very important, because of how little everybody had during that time. Doc told me there was only one short time during the Depression when his dad was ill that they really had a problem getting food on the table. But he talks about making the sorghum molasses and having buckwheat pancakes, and that sort of thing. But they got by with hard work, and that's where he learned that attitude."[8]

Through the years Doc has astounded friends and musicians alike with remarkable skills outside of music, ranging from electronics to caning chairs. Wayne Henderson, the world-famous guitar luthier from Virginia, for example, will never forget the straight-back chair that Doc caned for him years ago: "I usually try to trade stuff with Doc. I've done repair work on his guitars in exchange for him caning chair bottoms for me. Did you know he was a real good craftsman? Those chairs are my favorite pieces of furniture in my house. I actually just now sat in one of those chairs and had breakfast. He used to come over to the shop and pick quite a bit, and Doc always wants an old straight back chair to sit in. And the bottom of this particular chair was real frazzled out, just about shot. And he was feeling along the edge of that, and he said, 'Wayne, I need to fix this thing for you.' I guess I expressed some doubt in my voice whether that was something a blind guy could do; that's a pretty complicated job to cane a chair, you know, and put that nice pattern in it. You know, I actually wouldn't doubt him to do it, but I was just sort of shocked a little bit that he would say he could do that, and I guess he detected that."[9]

Doc then had his friend Charles Welsh put the chair in the back of his truck, and he left for home. A week later, Doc wanted to come back. Henderson recalled, "And he comes back, and he had that chair, and it was an absolute beautiful job. With that herringbone design and wood cane, you know. It was amazing what a beautiful job he did doing that. And that chair; I still have that thing, and it's one of my prized possessions, and I use it every day. And it still holds up, and that's been several years ago."[9]

Henderson added, "Doc's just amazing, what he can do. I think that comes from his childhood when his dad put him to doing something, you know, on the end of a crosscut saw. I've heard him talk about that. Instead of just letting him sit over in the corner because he was blind and couldn't do anything, like a lot of blind people got, they put him to work. His parents figured out stuff he could do, if it was running the end of a crosscut saw, or doing whatever work around the house there was, and putting him to do it."[9]

Every adult has to learn to carry his or her own load, and for General Watson, Doc was no exception. From the lessons Doc learned that first day on the other side of a crosscut saw, Doc was able to go out and make his way in the world.

# CHAPTER NOTES

1. Stambler, Irwin and Lyndon Stambler, *Folk and Blues: The Premier Encyclopedia of American Roots Music*. 2001: Thomas Dunne Books. 816.
2. Lloyd, Bert, *Interview with Doc Watson*, Audio CD, Ralph Rinzler Folklife Archives, Smithsonian Institution, 1976.
3. Holt, David and Doc Watson, *Doc Watson and David Holt: Legacy*, Audio CD, High Windy Audio, 2002.
4. Humphrey, Mark, *Liner Notes from Doc Watson: Rare Performances 1963-1981*, Vestapol/Rounder, 2002.
5. Hurst, Jack, *Good Pickin's: Guitarist Watson's Name Was Doctored*. The Milwaukee Journal. Milwaukee, WI.
6. Reamy, Margaret, *The Real Thing: Doc Watson*. The Record Exchange Music Monitor, April 1994: p. 1.
7. Lloyd, Bert, *Interview with Annie & Doc Watson*, Audio CD, Ralph Rinzler Folklife Archives, Smithsonian Institution, 1976.
8. Gustavson, Kent, *Telephone Interview with Donna Hill*. May 6, 2009.
9. Gustavson, Kent, *Email Interview with Wayne Henderson*. April 2, 2009.

# CHAPTER FIVE
## Catskin Banjo

*"I feel sometimes that Doc Watson with his blind eyes can better view the colors of music than we, who claim to see, can envisage with ours. His notes are not those plucked from a page or supped easily from a silver spoon. Rather they are picked lovingly from between hard roads and rocks and prickly places."*

- Tommy Sands[1]

David Watson nearly killed his brother Doc, robbing the world of its greatest guitarist before Doc had even learned his first chord. The two boys were playing a game that is every parent's worst nightmare. David was supposed to find flat rocks, then throw them just above Doc's head. The curious boy loved to hear the rocks whiz past, and insisted that his brother engage in this odd game. After throwing countless rocks, David's focus drifted, and one of his stones curved directly towards his blind brother's head. Of course, Doc could not see the stone coming, and it hit him squarely in the forehead. As the blood was running down his face, Doc heard David shout, "Lord, I killed my brother!"[2] Of course their mother was furious, though David recalls Doc calmly telling her, "Why, he didn't intend to hit me. I had him throwing them stones."[2]

When he wasn't dreaming up dangerous games with his brother, Doc found many other ways to entertain himself. One of his favorite pastimes was banging on anything that could produce an interesting sound. Indeed, who could resist the pots, pans, whisks, ladles and spoons in their mother's kitchen? Annie probably did not expect that her son's pounding would someday lead him to play with the giants of country music history, but at least it was less dangerous than the boys' game of rocks.

Doc remembered: "Anything that had a tone to it, I would have to beat on it some. Sometimes Mama would say, 'Honey, get off the porch with that! I've got a headache; you're bustin' my head!' I'd go on the porch and hammer and beat on something that I thought had a good sound... Some of the time... I'd get me...two little tin cans; one of them had different tones. Or I loved the cowbell – especially where they'd have two or three there... To me, anything that had a pleasant tone to it...like the gear of the T-model, if it had a pleasant ring to it – it was musical."[3]

When she was not being driven crazy by Doc's primitive drumming, Annie would often sing around the house. He talked with her about that in their joint interview with Bert Lloyd: "I remember when I was a boy, thinking of music and singing, some of the little poems that I used to hear you saying around the house, sometimes. There was one...that you used to sing, with a tune, something about – 'Peter's at the gate, waiting for the butter cake. Come butter, come.' You remember?"[4] Annie then replied, "Yes, I remember. I don't think I can do it alto-gether."[4] Doc reassured his mother, "Well you needn't try to sing it, honey, I won't ask you to do that right now."[4]

General Watson, too busy in the fields to worry about his young son's creative hammerings, was also a talented musician. He rarely showed it outside of the daily hymn sung with his wife and children from *The Christian Harmony*, and in church on Sunday, but for Doc he made an exception: "[Dad] could play some on the [harmonica] – he was pretty good... He would play a bunch of the old break-downs. Like 'Jimmy Sutton' and 'Molly Hare,' 'Sally Gooden.'"[5]

Doc and his siblings did not have many luxuries growing up, but one thing that Doc would get from Santa Claus every Christmas without fail was a harmon-ica. He learned to play with a few lessons from his father, and he would carry the small instrument with him wherever he went; which also meant that the boy would most often lose the harmonica within a few weeks of receiving it. Fortunately for Santa Claus, that made it possible to bring another new har-monica the next year.

Doc's brief lessons from his father were his first real lessons in music theory, and started Doc yet another step down the road towards his eventual career. His father taught him the major scale using the harmonica, referencing the seven-note scale that Doc already knew from church singing: "Son, now this thing's got notes on it – just like the ones you hear me sing in the songbook – like, Do, Re, Mi, Fa, So, La, Ti, Do."[6] General continued, encouraging his son to practice; "Now Son, when you get used to it, it'll come about natural, like whistling, and then you can begin to know it with your tongue, [and] get some of the special effects that I can't even get."[6] Little did Doc's father know that Doc would still be playing "Molly Hare" and "Jimmy Sutton" more than 80 years later on stages in New York City, Chicago, Seattle, Los Angeles, and all across the world, in front of thousands of fans.

Many of Doc's relatives played musical instruments when he was a boy, but music was not as omnipresent in his world as many of his listeners might imagine. The musicians in his family did not play music every day, and in fact *rarely* made music. In a world where music is now piped into shopping malls, and into the night sky outside of restaurants, and where movies have 90-minute long soundtracks, it is sometimes hard to remember that in Doc's childhood, there were no soundtracks in the country outside of cicadas and birdsong. When Doc was lucky, he could persuade his mother or father to sing, and his relatives and older siblings sometimes gathered together on a porch in midsummer, or during the holidays, and picked and sang a tune or two. But the amount of music Doc heard each day as a child amounted to minutes, not hours.

When Doc was given harmonicas, he was able, for the first time, to begin exploring musically on his own. With his harmonica in one hand, he would thump a long wire attached to his father's barn, and he'd play the tunes to the rhythm of the makeshift bass he had rigged up. It was the first string instrument he ever played, and likely led to his later fascination with the banjo. But his ingenuity was clear. He had made a handmade *barn*-banjo, and had taught himself to frail it at the same time as he played "Home Sweet Home" on the harmonica. Not even his later feats of guitar wizardry could hold a candle to the joy Doc felt at humbly executing these songs for the first time.

Doc explained the details of his musical invention: "After I had learned to play the harmonica a little bit, my dad built a big new woodshed and granary which had a sliding door at the front, where you went to stack wood in, and went up the steps to the place where you cured out the ham shoulders... He had a couple of corn cribs in [the shed] – one for what he called the pig corn, and one for the good old bread corn that we took to the mill and had ground for corn bread... I got me a piece of steel wire (from a car rim), and I strung it from the door (that was a handled wooden door, so you could open and close it; it didn't have any rollers on it); it took [all of] your might to slide the thing. And there was a big old staple in the doorpost so you could put a lock in it, in order to lock it so nobody could get in there, and I [strung the steel wire to that, and then] pushed that door 'til I got that wire to get that old bass note, you know, [in] the same key as my harmonica. I sure had a lot of fun picking on the wire and playing the harmonica along with it, but I guess it had a kind of primitive sound. I could play along with 'Home Sweet Home' and some other little tunes. Boy, I thought I had accomplished something."[6]

Before Doc left for the Raleigh School for the Blind, General already noticed that Doc's love of music and his talent, whether for banging harmoniously on tin cans, or playing a few tunes on the harmonica. And when his son came home the next summer for three months, General decided to build Doc a banjo so that he would be able to pick it all summer and back at school when he was homesick.

Doc remembered: "When I came home [after] that first spring at school, my dad said, 'Son, I might make you a little banjo this summer.'"[7] Doc excitedly replied: "I ain't never seen one of them [being made]."[7] General continued: "Well, I used to pick a little, and I know where to get a-hold of some of them tension hooks, so I believe I can make you one."

Doc spoke about the steps his father took to make the banjo: "He carved the neck out of maple and made little friction tuning pegs like dulcimers have."[7] Then, because he wanted his son to have a quality banjo that would sound like a factory-made banjo, he carved the tension hoop out of maple.[8] Doc continued: "When he got the hoop done, he stretched a groundhog hide over it, but that just didn't work right. It was too stiff and didn't give a very good tone."[7]

Frustrated by the dull tone the groundhog hide produced, Doc's father tried to come up with a solution to make the banjo more resonant. Doc remembered: "We solved the problem...when Granny's 16-year-old cat passed on. That made one of the best banjo heads you ever seen and it stayed on that thing, I guess, as long as I picked it. Dad got it made and tuned it up and the first piece I ever heard him play was 'Rambling Hobo.' He showed me a few tunes to get me started. Then one day he picked it up and put it in my hands and said, 'Here, son. Take this and learn to play it good...' He never would pick no more after he got me started."[7]

Doc's father would not often play secular music. Though he was just about always kind to his children, he did not tolerate what he viewed as more profane aspects of society, and he brought up his children to be respectful and to avoid places such as square dances. General Watson forbade his wife and children from going near them. Doc recalled: "Up until I was grown I never had the pleasure of going to any of those square dances. My dad...thought a fellow might get into trouble if he wasn't old enough to take care of himself."[5]

Doc remembered his father being very serious about his religious beliefs: "He was a pretty serious fellow and devoted most of his evenings to trying to see that we got enough of the word of God, so that we knew the Golden Rule and the way to live morally decent lives, and that we knew some of the songs so that we could sing along when he took us to church."[9]

General Watson did not craft a banjo for his son so that he could play at dances and other such parties. He put the instrument together so that Doc could play it at the Raleigh School when he was homesick, and in the summertime at home when he was bored. He knew that the instrument could get his boy through troubled times as it had helped him in the early days of his marriage to Annie when the young couple had moved away from Deep Gap. General could not have imagined the importance of the homemade banjo and his simple lessons with Doc towards his eventual career in music.

The catskin head of Doc's little homemade banjo was an innovation thought up by Doc's father and his older brother Linney, after General saw an ad in a Sears catalog for a catskin banjo head. Doc's homemade catskin would be quite a lesson in "using all the parts of an animal" for the young brothers.

Doc's granny had given Linney 50 cents to kill her cat, telling him, "I just ain't got the heart."[6] The cat was 16 years old, blind, and had now stopped eating, and she wanted the cat to be humanely put down. Doc remembered: "I was picking up a load of stove wood for Mama where Dad was splitting wood...[when] my brother Linney came up in the yard with a little burlap sack in one hand, one of those little 20 lb. bags or something, and Dad said, 'Son, what you got in that bag?'... [Linney] said, 'I got Granny's old cat in there...it's about to die and she wanted me to put it out of its misery.' [Dad] stopped splitting wood a minute and thought about it and he said, 'Well, if you boys will skin her...I'll make you a banjo head out of [her].' And I thought, 'Lord, what a job!' But to make a long story short, we did. And I like to never got the [blood] washed off my hands, but Linney put the cat out of its misery without it even hollering or anything; he knew how to do it."[3]

In an interview with Charles Wolfe, Doc talked about the incredible strength of the catskin drum on his banjo: "My father tanned [the cat skin] in a very special way, taking the hair off, of course, but not weakening the unbelievable strength of the skin."[10] Through sixteen years of life, the cat's skin had grown tougher and tougher, and when General and Linney tanned its hide, they were able to make it paper-thin. Doc was proud of that instrument for the rest of his life; he always said there was no sound like that banjo.

Some of Doc's first attempts at playing music were, of course, based on the tunes his father had taught him. However, it was not long before Doc started picking out songs he heard on records and on the radio. Even into the first years of his career, records and radio remained vital to his music. He learned much of the repertoire that he performed in the 1960s from records, and if he needed a refresher of this tune or that, he would ask Eugene Earle or other friends in the folk world to find him the original 78-record, and he would learn the music and words.

Doc is often thought of as a traditional artist who *only* learned songs from his family and his tradition. That is simply not true. In fact, he learned *most* of his giant repertoire from the records that he heard on his family's Victrola, and from his subsequent record acquisitions. Doc wrote in 1970: "While I learned a lot of music from my family and the people who lived near us, I also learned a great deal of music from records."[9]

Doc often recounts the story of his Uncle Jerome, the owner of a sawmill, who bought a floor model Victrola and wanted to sell his tabletop model to Doc's father. A deal was struck whereby Doc's brothers and father would work a week at the sawmill to purchase the Victrola that came with fifty different 78-rpm records. Doc recalled that, when they brought that Victrola home with all of those records, he felt like they had the "king's treasure,"[11] and the family listened so much, they wore the records out.

In different interviews, Doc spoke of many varied records that the family received with the tabletop Victrola. In a 1976 interview, Doc recalled: "The first records we had were the original Carter Family, a few recordings by them, and a couple by Clarence Ashley and the Tar Heels, and there was one or two old blues records; I believe there was one by Mississippi John Hurt, 'Spike Driver's Blues,' and I don't remember what the other side of that disc was…We had a few by the

JD Vaughan Gospel Singers, Sacred Smith Singers and JD Vaughan Quartet. And then we had some recordings by Earl Johnson, a fiddler from Texas, 'Johnson's Old Grey Mule' and a bunch of other things that he had done. Then later along we began to add Jimmie Rodgers recordings to the pile; we didn't have any of his [at the beginning]."[3]

Steadily, the pile of recordings next to the record player grew. And in 1939, the family bought its first radio, and they had access to a wide range of performers. Doc remembered listening to the Delmore Brothers, the Carter Family, Sam & Kirk McGee, Dave Macon, Roy Acuff, Merle Travis, and many more.[12] Doc's family also crowded around the radio all together on Saturday nights to hear the Grand ol' Opry, with acts like the Blue Sky Boys, the Monroe Brothers, J.E. Mainer and the Mountaineers, Jack Shook and the Missouri Mountaineers, The Possum Hunters, and new acts every week. Doc remembered that he listened to whatever he could tune in: "We could pick up anything from Del Rio, Texas to Minneapolis, Minnesota. I heard a lot of big band music. I remember getting interested in Dixieland jazz. I thought that was some kind of fine. And later I began to like the Dorseys and Phil Harris. You name it and I began to like the sound. When you begin to understand music and your ear is being educated to the theory, then you can really learn to love it. You can't really love something until you can understand it."[7]

Doc also began frequenting the Greene Inn, a bed and breakfast in downtown Boone, where, in the basement, Richard Greene sold instruments and records, as well as country, big band, and blues records. Doc bought many records there, paid for with the few dollars he could earn by busking on the streets of Boone. Doc recalled many of the records that he purchased through the years: "All kinds of people came up through the years and I listened to all of 'em, Riley Puckett, Frank [Hutchinson], Gene Austin, Vernon Dalhart, Burl Ives, Charlie Poole, the Carolina Tar Heels, everybody from the Skillet Lickers and the original Carter Family to a recording by John Hurt... I listened to music, whoever and whatever they played."[13]

Ben Harper is a well-known singer-songwriter who grew up steeped in folk, blues and rock, and who integrates essences of all these styles into his music. In an interview about Doc's diverse interests in music with regards to records, Harper said: "I'm sure that Doc was as much bit by old, early American and English and Irish folk songs as he was the blues...as much by Stephen Foster Campbell as he was by Robert Johnson, because that's what they had at the time when Doc was coming up. He couldn't just go to iTunes and pull up every blues song ever written."[14]

Doc listened to whatever he could get his hands on. And the same passion he had for listening, he soon had for playing. At first, he played music on the streets alone or with his brother Linney. Then he joined any group who would have him, and sat on the porch for the rest of the day, figuring out melodies and chords from songs he heard on records and on the radio.

The catskin banjo was Doc's first exposure to the joys of playing and singing. The virus took hold. The seed was planted. Forever in debt to his granny's late cat, Doc has carried the sound of that humble homemade banjo with him for the rest of his career.

## CHAPTER NOTES

1.     Gustavson, Kent, *Email Interview with Tommy Sands*. July 7, 2009.
2.     Holt, David, *Liner Notes to Doc Watson and David Holt: Legacy*, High Windy Audio, 2002.
3.     Lloyd, Bert, *Interview with Doc Watson*, Audio CD, Ralph Rinzler Folklife Archives, Smithsonian Institution, 1976.
4.     Lloyd, Bert, *Interview with Annie & Doc Watson*, Audio CD, Ralph Rinzler Folklife Archives, Smithsonian Institution, 1976.
5.     Spitzer, Nick, *Interview with Doc Watson*. 1987, Smithsonian Institution, Ralph Rinzler Folklife Archives: Washington D.C.
6.     Holt, David and Doc Watson, *Doc Watson and David Holt: Legacy*, Audio CD, High Windy Audio, 2002.
7.     Sievert, Jon, *Doc Watson: 'Like Some Kind of Fine'*. Frets, March 1979. 1(1): p. 20-26.
8.     Watson, Doc with Ron Stanford, *Draft of "Introduction" for "Songs of Doc Watson" Book*. 1970, Ralph Rinzler Folklife Archives, Smithsonian Institution: Washington.
9.     Watson, Doc and Ralph Rinzler, *The Songs of Doc Watson*. 1971, New York City: Oak Publications.
10.     Wolfe, Charles K, *Classic Country*. 2001, United Kingdom: Routledge.
11.     Havighurst, Craig, *Living Legacy*. Acoustic Guitar, 2003. 13(12): p. 54-64.
12.     Aldin, Mary Katherine, *Liner Notes to Doc Watson: The Vanguard Years*, Vanguard Records, 1995.
13.     *Doc Watson Quotes*. 2005 [Last accessed Sept. 11, 2005]; Available from: http://www.merlefest.org/DocsQuotes.htm.
14.     Gustavson, Kent, *Telephone Interview with Ben Harper*. June 4, 2009.

Photo by Tony Cartledge ©

# CHAPTER SIX
## Fretting a Fence

*"A good guitar is like a friend. Sometimes when you're lonely, bored, or depressed, you pick that guitar up and play and all at once it's gone. It's like a conversation with a good friend, I imagine. You play an old song, and you remember all kinds of wonderful things. Or you come across a sad song and recall some bad things..."*

- Doc Watson[1]

**M**any guitars have accompanied Doc Watson in his nearly 75 years of playing the instrument. From his first borrowed beater to the Gallagher workhorse that traveled more than a million miles with him on the road, the stories of Doc's guitars tell the story of Doc himself.

The first time Doc ever heard a guitar in person was as a very small boy, before he had even gotten his first harmonica. His teenaged step-cousin Princess, or Prinzie for short, came to visit, and he remembered her strumming the guitar in the style of Maybelle Carter and singing just like Sara Carter from the original *Carter Family* recordings. Not only did Prinzie play and sing beautifully, but she was blind, as he was. Surely, that started General and Annie thinking about Doc's future as a blind man, and they saw how excited their boy was to hear the music coming from his older cousin's fingers.

The first guitar that Doc played extensively was Paul Montgomery's instrument at the Raleigh School, Paul recalled, "I was left-handed and played upside down. I taught Doc his first chords upside down and backwards. He learned them and then turned them around for a right-handed person."[2] The banjo was still Doc's instrument of choice, but he was intrigued by his friend's guitar, and that summer, when 13-year old Doc came home from the Raleigh School, he convinced his brother Linney to borrow a guitar from their neighbor Spencer Miller.

Doc messed around with his cousin's guitar, and was able to do a few things on it, doing his best to make it sound like Jimmie Rodgers, Maybelle Carter or Riley Puckett. General Watson, upon hearing his son play around with the borrowed guitar one morning made a deal with him, and promised Doc he would help the boy purchase his own guitar if he could play an entire song by the time General came home from work that day.

Doc already knew a few chords from playing around with his friend Paul at school, and he was able to play and sing "When the Roses Bloom in Dixieland" by The Carter Family when his father returned from work that evening. General kept his word and added a few dollars to Doc's savings so that he could purchase his own guitar from the furniture store down the road.

Doc recalled the guitar his father helped him buy: "It was a little Stella guitar; you could get them for about $12... [I had it for] about two years."[3] Doc got his Stella a few years before that merger. Many pre-war blues musicians, including Skip James, Barbecue Bob and Charley Patton played Stellas, partially for their low price, but also for their loud volume. At the time, music shops could order a dozen flat-backed Stella guitars with various decals at the reasonable price of $66. Stella guitars, manufactured by the Oscar Schmidt company before the brand was bought by Harmony in 1939, was ladder-braced, not x-braced, which helped the volume significantly. The guitar was made of birchwood with a black satin finish and a white pearlette fingerboard. The binding and sound hole ring were both painted white, and the front of the guitar had a beautiful curve to it, with f-holes on either side of the bridge.[4]

Equipped with his very own guitar, Doc now began to be more serious about music, and tried to make a few dollars with his talent. Doc soon spent a lot of time playing music on the streets, at times with his brother Linney, and other times just by himself. He would catch a ride to town with his father or another relative, carrying his little guitar or a borrowed steel-rim banjo from his brother Arnold in tow. He had learned about busking at the Raleigh School, where teachers taught their blind students to sell pencils on the streets in order to supplement their income from the state. Doc simply took that to the next level, selling pencils at first, but soon becoming a semi-professional street musician, selling only his music instead of knick-knacks.

In a 1999 interview, Doc talked about performing on the street: "The first time I ever played music for money was on the street, buddy, with a cup on the guitar. And I ain't never been ashamed of it. I used to be a little bit. But I've thought back about that since then, and I was selling something, just like I do now, if a person buys a ticket to come in to hear me pick. I'd get somewhere, if there was an ordinance, wouldn't block up the sidewalk, usually at somebody's stand, where it was back out of the way, and pick. Or on a back lot where they had a cab stand."[5] His first amateur appearance was at a Fiddler's Convention at the

Blowing Rock High School nearby. He played and sang Bill Monroe's popular and high-energy "Muleskinner Blues."

Like any self-respecting guitar player, though he loved his Stella, Doc soon had a desire to upgrade. When General Watson complained that all of his chestnut saplings were dying of blight, 17-year old Doc and his 15-year old brother David came up with a plan.

Their father showed them how to saw up dead chestnut saplings, each between 6 and 10 inches thick, into small pieces with the two-man crosscut saw. Then the boys could sell them to the local tannery as extract wood. Their cousin Paul Green came in with his truck and sold the wood to the tannery for them. The boys split the money they got for the wood among themselves, and David purchased a new blue serge suit with his share, and four years after he purchased his Stella guitar, Doc ordered himself a brand new guitar out of the Sears catalog. Doc remembered: "I bought me a guitar with my part of the money; ordered it from Sears Roebuck. And [David ordered] a suit of clothes with his part of the money. I don't remember, I think my guitar cost about $25 or something. It was a pretty nice box, it was an archtop, but it had a good sound. I had that about a year and a half."[3]

Doc's guitar was a 1940 Silvertone, similar in appearance to the Vogue Model G guitars Harmony had made in the 1930s, with a maple body and spruce top. It was much larger than Doc's Stella guitar had been, and was able to put out a great deal of volume. For an extra dollar, Doc ordered a copy of the *Nick Lucas Plectrum Guitar Method*, a flimsy paperback book that was to soon change his life forever. The book, which was subtitled, "A comprehensive course of Modern Instruction for the Plectrum Guitar," had step-by-step instructions and pictures. Since Doc could not read it himself, his brother David read it for him, and then showed Doc how to hold the pick correctly according to the book's diagrams and pictures. A flatpicking guitar legend was born.

Doc has said in certain interviews that he briefly traded his Silvertone for a Gibson Kalamazoo, which would have been his first flattop guitar. Kalamazoo was a small factory owned by Gibson where the guitar maker produced its less-expensive guitars. Doc's Kalamazoo would have been very resonant and responsive to a flat pick, and was made of Brazilian rosewood, Adirondack spruce and mahogany.

Doc began to really hone his skills on the acoustic guitar, and people in the area started to respect his playing. Doc recalled that he had a lot of success playing and singing at taxi stands: "I used to pick some on the street in different places, especially along the back lots where they would have taxi stands. Them ol' boys wanted you to come and pick, 'cause it got them a whole lot of customers – and you could make a couple of bucks."[6] Every weekend in the summertime, Doc would catch a ride down to Boone or Lenoir, the other nearby town, and he'd often earn quite a bit of money on the streets: "I played on the street nearly every Saturday when the weather was warm at a cab stand in Lenoir, NC. Sometimes I'd make as much as fifty dollars..."[7]

He still lived at home, and trusted his father for guidance about a number of matters. Doc recalls General putting his hand on Doc's shoulder, saying, "Son, you are old enough to behave yourself... Go out and play some music for them folks that they enjoy and earn you a few dollars, but behave."[8] Doc truly looked up to his father, and it meant the world to him that his father supported him in his fledgling music career. Doc remembered, "He was always giving me advice even after I was grown, you know, and was a man of my own."[8]

Doc wanted to play in an ensemble that might earn him more income, but there was a problem: despite Doc's unbelievable talent on the guitar, he was not able to do a flashy show as was customary in the 1940s in country music. He could not dance while he was playing, or otherwise ham it up. He was simply an incredible picker, and a solid singer. Doc remembered: "I think blindness kept me out of music as a professional during the later '40s. In those days, most of the time you had to do flashy shows, and I don't think I would've fit in too well on the stage. I think that was the reason, maybe, that people wouldn't hire me as a sideman. That aggravated me but it didn't really make me bitter."[9]

As Doc played on the street, he did get plenty of praise, however, from passers-by, and from other local musicians who came up and talked with him from time to time. Presumably, that is how Doc first ran into Clarence Ashley, who had recorded with the Carolina Tarheels in the 1920s, as well as made his own records. As a young man, Doc began to play backup for Clarence Ashley at land sales. Ashley would work to entertain the large crowds of people that came to the auctions, but he did not play an instrument anymore, since he had injured his hand years before. At times, as many as 100 lots of land would be up for sale, and in a society where land was the wealth of choice, these were popular events in the community. When the auctioneer took a break, Ashley and Doc would take the stage and perform before the auctioneer started up again.

Land sales were big money, high-rolling events, and after one such sale, Doc remembered finding a wallet with a lot of cash: "There must have been 3,000 dollars in there. And I gave it to him. I didn't even think none. I come back and tell Dad about it, and he said, 'Son, you have to be honest about it,' and he said, 'You know, the fellow is a rascal – he could have thanked you at least!' I said, 'Yeah, [but] it didn't belong to me – and he probably would have figured out I've got it, anyway...' Dad laughed, he says, 'Oh, you were afraid you'd get *caught*!'"[10]

By this time, Doc was nearly twenty years old, and had moved up to a Martin guitar. If Doc had even taken one hundred dollar bill from the stack of money, he could have paid off the new D-18 he was paying off month by month.

Doc recalled the conversation he had with the local music store proprietor: "Richard Greene used to have a little music store under his boarding house...in Boone, and I went in there one day...and he said, 'Why don't you let me help you get you a good guitar?' And I said, 'Gosh, it cost too much.' And he said, 'Tell you what I can do. I can get you a good Martin D-18 that will be a price you can afford, and I'll take the payments down to 5 dollars a month. And I couldn't beat that...with a stick. And at that time, I was playing at the little fruit stand and a couple of the little bean markets they had in Boone and making me a few *shekels* on Saturday, having a good time picking and I paid for the guitar that summer. He got me that thing at his cost, and it cost 90 bucks, and I paid for it. Oh, Lord, I was proud of that guitar. But in all truth, compared to my guitar now, it was like fretting a fence."[11]

Years later, Doc spoke with the *Washington Post* about the difficulty he had playing the Martin guitar he had purchased from Mr. Greene's shop: "[It] was very hard to play – the neck was a second off the line and I got it rather cheap. It did have a real beautiful tone, but there was no craftsman in the area that could fix the neck, so I had to put up with it the way it was. It was awfully hard to play it. I think that's one of the reasons I traded it in on the electric guitar."[12] *Fretting a fence* was Doc's playful way of saying that his guitar's strings were far from the fingerboard, forcing him to push them down with a great deal of force. However, such exercise was great training for the eager young fingers of a man who would soon become the king of flatpicking. Legend has it that Doc used heavy gauge strings in the 1960s, and the volume he was able to produce out of any guitar was immense. *Fretting a fence* in his early years certainly had not hurt him any.

Doc began to develop his own sound, and instead of simply imitating Bill Monroe's high tenor on "Muleskinner Blues," or playing Jimmie Rodgers runs or Riley Puckett runs on the guitar, Doc began to find his own voice. And he found it between all of his influences, somewhere between jazz and hillbilly, country and classical. He listened to everything, and took a little bit from each genre.

Ben Harper, also a singer-songwriter with great ability to cross barriers of genre, spoke about his own influences: "You sort of find your strength through challenge. You can't come up into music and not be influenced at this time in history, because there's so much music that's been out there. But you listen to Doc Watson, you listen to Jimi Hendrix, you listen to Robert Johnson, you listen to Muddy Waters, and somehow you reach for that sound. But as much as you think at a young age you want to sound like someone else, you really quickly realize you want to sound like yourself. You want to incorporate elements of the greats into what you do."[13]

Soon Doc Watson would also be great, but it was not yet his time. For now, the Martin guitar helped him discover the limits of what an acoustic guitar could do. And then Doc went electric.

In 1952, while Bob Dylan was still in grade school trying to keep warm during long Minnesota winters, Doc picked up a Les Paul, and started to play rock and roll. Doc had found that his Martin guitar simply could not get loud enough when he was trying to play over the top of crowd noise at dances or on the street. Doc looked for ways to amplify his instrument, but he did not like the sound that pickups produced, so he traded in his beloved Martin D-18 for a 1952 Les Paul Gold Top Standard. The Gold Top Standard was the least expensive of the Gibson line of Les Paul electric guitars. On the current market, they go for astronomical sums of money, and they are coveted, like all 1950s Les Pauls, by rock musicians because of their weight (around nine pounds), and their strong, P-90 single coil pickups.

Though he was excited about his new acquisition, the bridge on the Les Paul was problematic for Doc; he was not to mute the strings Merle Travis-style because the strings went *underneath* the bridge instead of over it. But Doc was able to solve the problem by removing the bridge and putting a standard bridge onto the instrument. He told Bob Edwards in a 2002 interview: "I hated the thing, and I got me a regular bridge, and a regular tailpiece to go on that thing, and fixed it so I could pick it."[14] Doc recalled that the guitar did not look quite as good afterwards, and his father joked with him, kidding him about his "cobbling on it," but his tinkering had allowed him to play in the style of Merle Travis, who was recording hit record after hit record at the time.[5]

Now that Doc was hooked up with a guitar that could take the top off of a dance hall, he went out and played in several groups around the local area. He enjoyed the sounds of spinning feet vibrating the floor of the dance halls, and the cheering and shouting voices. Doc recalled the joy he felt at these local all night long picking parties: "Sometimes we'd get together and pick some after a corn shucking – or we'd just go to somebody's house – especially in late fall after everything was done, or in the winter when it was cold, and you couldn't work outside, *son*,[*] and just play for half a night and just enjoy it, oh Lord…I'd give anything to get into and really enjoy it [like that again] – but when you're learning, you can enjoy ten times more than you do after all of it's kind of down pat in your head, you know. If we get a good audience now, I still feel that joy."[8]

After owning the Les Paul for several years, Doc decided to trade it in on another electric guitar, a solid-body Fender Telecaster. The Telecaster was lighter, and fit the current trends in the mid-fifties much better than his Les Paul did. According to Paul Asbell, guitarist for Kilimanjaro and guitar teacher of Trey Anastasio of Phish fame, the difference between a Telecaster and Les Paul is clear: "A Les Paul guitar is a little jazzier, and more rock and roll-like; the rock and roll of more modern interpretation, not like Elvis Presley or something, but like Guns n' Roses. Les Pauls at this point are the standard issue rock and roll weapon of choice, kind of, and it's the thing that everything else is compared against. It's much easier to get a screaming, distorted lead sound out of it. You overdrive the amp with the pickups on a Les Paul. But that's not the thing that a country guy typically wants to do."[15]

Asbell spoke about Doc's switch to a Fender electric: "In the days before Guns n' Roses, Doc's upgrade to a mid-fifties Telecaster was the modern and hip choice. The Fender was a little bit like an acoustic Martin guitar; a Martin has a

---

[*] *Doc can often be heard to use the word "son" in the same way many say "man;" it is an expression of emphasis from his home region's vernacular.*

signature tone that has become synonymous in this case with bluegrass that may not be perfect for any number of other things, but it's sort of the sound that people have gotten used to hearing and then want to hear when you're playing bluegrass flatpicking or whatever. It just sort of seems to go hand in hand with it. A Fender Telecaster for sort of twangy country music sort of has that. And there's just no way to get that out of a Les Paul."[15]

In the late 1950s, while trying to make ends meet with two small children running around the house, Doc could only afford to have one guitar, so he kept his Telecaster around the house; if anyone wanted him to play acoustic, Doc had to borrow an instrument. And in 1960, when Ralph Rinzler came down from New York with Eugene Earle in tow, and wanted to record Clarence Ashley, 37-year old Doc recorded on a borrowed Martin D-18, similar to the one he had owned in the 1940s.[16]

That was not the last time Doc would borrow an instrument. Once he was traveling solo, he did not like the encumbrance and bother instruments caused him, and he would write ahead to venues where he would be performing, asking for various instruments to be on hand when he arrived. John Cohen recalled that both Doc and Clarence Ashley used his banjo on stage in New York at their first appearance in 1961, and many other musicians have had the honor of having Doc perform using their instruments during one performance or another. In his music workshops in the 1960s, Doc would pick up any instrument within arm's reach, demonstrating to his fascinated students how it could best be played, whether banjos, guitars, lutes, harps, autoharps, mandolins, or just about anything else with strings.

Doc had one guitar that traveled more miles with him and played more notes than any of his other guitars, and it never even truly belonged to him. The guitar is called *Ol' Hoss*, and was loaned to Doc by J.W. Gallagher. Doc first met J.W. Gallagher under a tree at a music festival in 1968. The Gallaghers walked over to Doc and his 19-year old son Merle as they sat beneath the tree with a guitar case. They took it out and offered it to Doc to try, and he enjoyed the sound of the instrument so much, when he went to hand it back, they struck a deal. J.W. Gallagher told him, "Keep it, for as long as you play it."[17]

On the 1972 *Will the Circle Be Unbroken* album with the Nitty Gritty Dirt Band, there is a passage of dialogue between Doc Watson and his idol Merle

Travis, and they talk about the guitar Doc was playing. Their now-legendary conversation went as follows. Merle Travis: "...That guitar, by the way, rings like a bell..."[18] Doc Watson: "It's a pretty good little box, isn't it? Mr. Gallagher made this thing. Lives down in Wartrace, Tennessee..."[18] That was all it took for the Gallagher guitar company to become a household name for guitar enthusiasts.

Doc has favored a number of different guitars through the years, depending on his mood, the newest guitar in his collection, or the people he joins onstage. One of his favorite guitars is now a Bourgeois guitar given to him by Ricky Skaggs, and he also often plays the guitar his friend Wayne Henderson made for him.

Doc's touch on the strings of any luthier's instrument is akin to a blessing. And over his 75 years of playing the guitar, he has christened countless instruments with his calloused hands.

# CHAPTER NOTES

1. Aldin, Mary Katherine, *Liner Notes to Doc Watson: The Vanguard Years*, Vanguard Records, 1995.
2. Holt, David, *Liner Notes to Doc Watson and David Holt: Legacy*, High Windy, 2002.
3. Lloyd, Bert, *Interview with Doc Watson*, Audio CD, Ralph Rinzler Folklife Archives, Smithsonian Institution, 1976.
4. *Stella Decalomania*. Oscar Schmidt Catalog, 1936.
5. Watson, Doc and David Grisman, *Doc Watson and David Grisman - In Concert (1999)*, DVD, Vestapol, 2001.
6. Humphrey, Mark, *Liner Notes from Doc Watson: Rare Performances 1963-1981*, Vestapol/Rounder, 2002.
7. Sievert, Jon, *Doc Watson: 'Like Some Kind of Fine'*. Frets, March 1979. 1(1): p. 20-26.
8. Spitzer, Nick, *Interview with Doc Watson*. 1987, Ralph Rinzler Archives, Smithsonian Institution: Washington D.C.
9. Sievert, Jon, *Interview with Doc Watson*. Frets, March 1987. 9(3): p. 30-36,40-43,67.
10. Murphy, Joe, *Doc and Merle -The Lives and Music of Doc & Merle Watson (1985)*, VHS, Vestapol, 1996.
11. Grosz, Terry, *Interview with Doc Watson*, from *Fresh Air*. 1988, National Public Radio.
12. Harrington, Richard, *Doc Watson, Strumming Home*. The Washington Post, January 25, 1988. Washington D.C.: p. C1,C8.
13. Gustavson, Kent, *Telephone Interview with Ben Harper*. June 4, 2009.
14. Edwards, Bob, *Interview with Doc Watson*, from *Morning Edition*. 2002, National Public Radio.
15. Gustavson, Kent, *Telephone Interview with Paul Asbell*. March 16, 2009.
16. Watson, Doc and Steve Kaufman, *The Legacy of Doc Watson*. 1999, Pacific, MO: Mel Bay Publications.
17. *History of Gallagher Guitars*. 2009 [Last accessed 12/10/2009]; Available from: gallagherguitar.com/history.
18. Nitty Gritty Dirt Band, The, *Will the Circle Be Unbroken*, LP Record, 1972.

Photo by Nic Siler ©
*Doc Watson playing Ol' Hoss with luthier J.W. Gallagher looking on.*

# CHAPTER SEVEN
## Wildcat Girl

*"When a young neighbor girl eight years his junior struck up a conversation one day, 'You might as well have hit me over the head with a bludgeon,' says Doc... 'Every breath of the day was her name,' he says softly. 'That's the way it was.'"*

- Roger Wolmuth[1]

Doc's music has a sense of honesty and authenticity that draws listeners in, time and time again. Doc learned the skill of simplicity to a great extent from his father-in-law Gaither Carlton, through whose sinewy fiddle playing Doc first truly connected with old-time mountain music. Carlton soon became like Doc's second father, both musically and personally; and of course, Doc soon courted his sweet daughter Rosa Lee.

Doc came to know Gaither's kindness shortly after meeting him as a boy. The older man grew to love Doc's visits, and would bring out his fiddle and play old-time tunes for hours to the boy's guitar or banjo accompaniment. Doc recalled, "Me and Gaither sat down there, under a big hemlock there, and played, gosh, a bunch of tunes. I thought he was a good old time fiddler; I really enjoyed that."[2]

Doc's daughter Nancy remembered Gaither's house years later: "The aged-wood smell of Grandpa Gaither's old house again fills my nostrils; the sweetish aroma of pinto beans and fatback simmering on the woodstove; the crackling of the fire... Grandpa would sit in a straight wooden chair by the fire, his hands clasped together over the bib of his Jack Rabbit overalls, and I would sit on the floor, legs crossed, completely entranced as he sang 'The Miner's Child' or 'Little Bessie'... He would play the fiddle for me too, and I would dance a jig for him. He played banjo for me, and even the Jew's harp. His music and his kindness seemed to blend as one."[3]

Gaither and his wife, along with their two oldest daughters, also often visited Doc's cousin Willard Watson when Rosa Lee was still a small girl. Rosa Lee came to spend time with her friend Pansy, Willard's daughter, and paid Doc, Willard's young cousin, little mind at the time. The little Carlton girls sang a few songs, however, and Doc remembered, "I don't know if Rosa Lee noticed me [but] I thought, 'Why, she's got a pretty voice.'"[4]

Doc did not see Gaither again for the next few years, until Gaither moved with his family to Deep Gap in 1944. Around the same time the Americans stormed the beaches at Normandy, love invaded Doc's heart and never left.

21-year old Doc recalled visiting his new neighbors with his brother Arnold shortly after the Carltons moved to Deep Gap: "Me and Arnold, we [went] out there... And that's when I noticed Rosa Lee as, well, you know, a beautiful woman, you know, a girl. Somebody that would really attract your attention. Somebody might as well have hit me with a brick."[5] Rosa Lee recalled the early visits Doc made with his brother Arnold: "[When] I was 13...we moved over close to where Doc's folks lived. And he and Arnold came over and played with Daddy all the time."[5]

Doc quickly developed a crush on Rosa Lee: "I didn't have a lick of sense. I thought, 'Well, if it'll be, that's the girl for me'."[4] Doc thought of Rosa Lee as a beautiful woman, though she was still just a young girl. Every time Doc walked past the Carltons' house, his heart skipped a beat, and he hoped that she would be there.

Doc always talked in interviews about the song "Shady Grove" being one of his favorites, and it is clear that there is some personal significance for him to the line from the traditional song, "little girl, barefoot on the floor..." Rosa Lee was just a teenager, with a pure small voice when she sang, and the coy charm of an Appalachian country girl. In remembering the meaning of the song "Shady Grove", Doc wrote about his courting days: "'Shady Grove,' to me, means my wife, Rosa Lee, and my memories of going to see her when I was a boy. She was a sweet country girl, and very often I might go to her house unexpectedly, and she might be barefooted, you know. To me, she was the best thing God ever created, there wasn't any use in talking about it. That's what 'Shady Grove' means to me; happiness."[6]

Rosa Lee had been unpacking dishes with her friend Pansy, Willard Watson's daughter, when Doc first thought of his future wife romantically. Her voice caused handsome young Doc to go weak in the knees, and soon he came courting. Doc thought about her every waking minute, and visited whenever he could. He recalled, "Every breath of every day was her name."[1] He began to teach her how to play guitar. And they fell in love.

Rosa Lee remembered her music lessons with Doc: "Daddy [had] bought me a little guitar when I was 12 and I just knew how to play a few chords and sing a little bit... Doc showed me chords and helped me some with it..."[5] Rosa Lee continued to play the guitar with Doc, and after their children were born, they spent many evenings playing music and singing songs as a family. Rosa Lee even sang on stage in various places with Doc and Merle, but once they went out on the road for hundreds of days each year, Rosa Lee quit. She had little interest in it any more. In a 1984 interview, she said, "They're gone all the time picking – I don't care to keep it up playing by myself – couldn't play much anyway... Just lost interest I guess... I couldn't keep traveling with them either, 'cause they were flying. Their music reached much farther than mine. I didn't sing nothing but the old stuff."[5]

When Doc and Rosa Lee first were courting, they were quite the handsome pair. Doc had chiseled high cheekbones and a windswept haircut, his face, neck and arms browned by the sun. He had just a hint of rebellion behind the way his eyes squinted tightly, his face in a smile, as he would pull on his cigarette. Rosa Lee was a sweet country girl, still slightly round in her youth; she wore homemade dresses and bows in her hair. Doc embodied one portion danger, a second portion charm, and a third portion old-time music and values. He was blind, which brought out the natural caretaker in Rosa Lee. Doc's disability brought out the natural caretaker in her, and she looked forward to the times she could touch him, and act as his guide, into a room, across a field. Doc found a sweetness in her that he had never felt before, and he knew immediately that she was the one for him.

Even though she loved Doc, in hindsight, Rosa Lee, through the years, began to realize that she had been very young when she became pregnant with Doc's baby at the age of 15, marrying him soon thereafter. Rosa Lee recalled: "I was just a child. I mean, I liked him and his music, but I was just a child. Some people, I don't know why, when their children reached teenage years, their parents expected them, I reckon, to get married and go on their own. But at the time I didn't know the difference; that is just what people did. Doc is nine years older but he wasn't real grown up."[7] Doc agreed: "She had more sense than I did when we started dating, even though she was just a kid, a girl – a whole bunch more."[5]

Rosa Lee Carlton was certainly already very mature for her age, but there are few girls who, in this day and age, would be considered "old enough" to become pregnant as a 15-year old, or to become married at that age. Let alone to a man who, however charming, would require a great deal of service and care for the rest of her life. Rosa Lee was signing on to be her husband's eyes to the world. She took over Doc's mother's role, though she was only a girl. Hence the difference in the way Rosa Lee and Doc described their early days together. In remembering their courtship, she said, "I was just a child,"[7] and he said, "Every breath...was her name."[1]

After two months, Rosa Lee's pregnancy started to show, and the young couple was hurriedly married at the courthouse, on June 8th of 1946. Doc's mother Annie was present for the ceremony, but her parents were not. Doc applied for the marriage certificate, and he printed a white lie on the form, because Rosa Lee's father Gaither was not present to give permission. She had to lie about her age, saying that she was 18 years old, the age required to legally marry in North Carolina. On the form, Doc, or whoever was helping him write the form, wrote that Rosa Lee was 18 years old, though she was in actuality only 15.[8]

Just under five months after their marriage, Rosa Lee went into labor early (after seven months of pregnancy), and their baby girl was delivered stillborn by a midwife.[9] Nowhere in any interview have Doc or Rosa Lee talked about this child, whether due to the fact that the child was conceived before they were married, or whether it was simply too painful a memory for either to bring up in public.

Their small unnamed daughter was born and died on the same day, October 28th, 1946. On the newborn child's death certificate read the simple words: "Watson not named (F)." The parents were listed as: "Watson – Arthur *(sic)* Lane / Rosa Lee." Doc was listed as 23 years old, and his trade profession was listed as simply: "Blind." Rosa Lee's profession was listed as: "Housekeeper."[9]

Surely the stillbirth of their first child was crushing to the young parents. Thankfully, both Doc and Rosa Lee had strong and supportive families around them, and they simply began to pick up the pieces and start over again.

In an interview with Nick Spitzer, Doc recalled the sparse income he received from the state and from odd jobs here and there in the late 1940s and 1950s: "I was married, and Rosa Lee and I had two children, and we had just moved out on our own, and except for tuning a few pianos and splitting my own stove wood, I was accepting charity from the state of North Carolina as Aid for the Blind, which is available if you need it. And they were helping my kids a little bit, when they were old enough to start with school."[10]

In the early days of their marriage together, times were especially good for Doc and Rosa Lee. They had a chance to spend a great deal of time together, and they both worked hard around the house to make their simple life function like a well-oiled machine. Doc would chop wood for Rosa Lee, with which they heated the house in winter, and cooked all year long. Doc also tinkered around the house, helping to put a roof on the garage, planting trees, and fixing things like the sink and the radio. His daughter Nancy, in a 1984 article, wrote how Doc had just been up on the roof of her two-story home, "mounting a TV antenna, and hooking it up for a very clear picture on several channels."[11] He famously was even written up in the local electric corporation's monthly newsletter in 1957 for having rewired his home's electricity. The company inspected Doc's home and it passed the test, which astounded the inspector. Ralph Rinzler later heard that story, then spread it around the music business, and it became part of Doc legend. Musicians still buzz to one another, "Did you hear that he wired his house for electricity?" amazed at their blind guitar hero's skill and courage. Doc remembered: "Some joker had put pennies behind the fuse plugs."[10]

Rosa Lee tended a large garden, and canned food for the often-cold winter months. In an interview with Mark Humphrey, Doc remembered that "Rosa Lee grew the awfullest* vegetable gardens you ever seen every summer to help feed us."[12] Doc recalled fondly the hard work of those years, and also the struggles in an interview with Tom Alesia in 2003: "It was [a tough life]. But, you know, the first years we lived out on our own, I'd give every bit of my savings if I could live those four years over. There's something about peace and contentment that no financial security can ever cover. I'm getting philosophical with you. But I know. I've been there. The only thing that I regret is that I was handicapped and couldn't help with the hard work that my little sweetheart did to help us along through those years."[13]

Even once Doc started to get high profile gigs in New York City, Los Angeles and Chicago with the Clarence Ashley Group, his family still lived in poverty.

---

* The superlative "awfullest" was used here by Doc Watson to express its exact opposite meaning, possible definitions being: "most incredible" or "most wonderful."

Doc remembered: "We were poor folks. Rosa Lee and I had a rough time making ends meet. Just recently we were talking about those days, and she said, 'Honey, I remember when I hunted the house over to find enough pennies to mail you a letter on the road.' We were from a totally different culture, and people in New York didn't understand the meager fare that some of us here in the mountains had to get along on."[14]

One of the greatest moments of Doc's life was when he and Rosa Lee were able to buy their own home with the savings they had been able to cobble together over the first seven years of their marriage. Rosa Lee was now into her twenties, and Doc had just hit 30 years old, and they had two little ones with bare feet on the floor. Merle was four, and Nancy was a toddler of two. They moved into their new home in 1953. Years later, Sam Bush, the world-famous mandolinist and singer-songwriter, remembered a conversation when Doc told him that, "one of the happiest days of Doc's life was when he and Rosa Lee could buy their own house."[15]

Doc thought back to that first winter in their new home, in 1953 and '54: "Back when me and Rosa Lee first moved out on our own, we heated the house with coal, but she cooked on a wood stove, and I cut all the wood we used that winter. There was two or three paths through the woods up above where we lived, and I'd carry me a walking stick. I could tell by the echo where the trees were, and I could tell by tapping on the tree if it was dead or not. I only cut the dead ones, eight and ten-inch poplar and pines."[11]

Doc's little boy Merle often went with his father to chop wood: "Merle...was four or five, [and] he'd go with me and if a tree had woodpecker holes, he'd always say, 'Daddy, don't cut that 'un. It'll be wet.' And sure enough, if I did cut it, water would run out when it fell and it'd be sopped and wouldn't burn. He was a smart little feller."[11]

Doc related a story that would scare any mother or wife to death, but truly shows his fearlessness, as well as his close relationship to his son: "One time I cut a dead chestnut tree about fifty feet tall. No way to tell the top was rotten. When it started falling it hit some limbs of a nearby pine tree and that rotten part broke off...hit me right between the shoulders! Knocked me flatter than a fritter and the breath out of me too. [I] thought I was hurt bad, but I didn't even get skinned! Merle was back up the hill out of the way and he hollered, 'Are ye killed, Daddy?' I'll never forget that."[11]

Doc loved his children dearly, and he loved his wife. They lived together with a coal-burning heater, a wood-burning oven, and a garden. They listened to the radio, or sat outside at the picnic table on a beautiful day. His children were young, and adored their father, and they ran around his feet all day long as he tinkered with this or that. As far as Doc was concerned, it was the perfect life.

Maria Muldaur visited the Watson family just before Easter weekend in 1961. Doc and Gaither had both invited Muldaur to stay with them in North Carolina when they met her briefly a month earlier in New York, after the Clarence Ashley Group's first performance there. Upon visiting them, Muldaur had the good fortune to experience the true simplicity of the life that Doc and his extended family shared in the hollows of Deep Gap before Doc's life changed with the successes of the mid-1960s. Muldaur walked back into an earlier time, and into a place different than she had ever imagined. For a New York City girl, this was fascinating.

Though her experiences at Doc's home took place eight years after Doc and Rosa Lee had moved out on their own, and after Doc had played his first concert in New York at PS 41 in Greenwich Village, Doc was still not famous in the folk world or anywhere else; his life had changed little, except that his children were now bigger. At 12 years of age, Merle was a quiet boy who walked with a slight limp as a result of polio that had permanently injured him at age six. Nancy was a sweet nine-year old, and wore a little pair of glasses. Both children were very curious about their northern visitor. They had heard all of the tales their father had told them about his trip to New York City the month before, and they had met Ralph Rinzler and Eugene Earle the previous year, but they were surely stunned by Muldaur's beauty and charm.

Muldaur recalled that she and her boyfriend Walter, along with Allan Block, a well respected old-time fiddler in New York's folk scene, and his two daughters (one of whom was Rory Block), had made a plan to go to North Carolina to the Union Grove Fiddler's Convention: "Allan wanted to enter it, and we wanted to just go there to see all the music and stuff. The plan evolved that we were going to stay with Doc for a while, because we'd been really warmly invited to do so."[16]

Muldaur remembered the drive to North Carolina in their VW bus: "It was still snowy up on the Blue Ridge Highway. I remember getting to Doc's house... I just felt transported into another world. Before this, I'd never been further away from Manhattan than basically Jersey or Long Island. I was a little Sicilian girl who grew up in the heart of Greenwich Village in Manhattan. Traveling all through the South was fascinating to me but when we got to Blue Ridge Mountains, it was like I was stepping back in time. On these snowy mornings, you could see all these cabins with smoke curling up from the chimneys. Real rural life from a bygone era. It was exquisite."[16]

Doc and Rosa Lee truly did live a dream, though they had none of the "luxuries" of modern life: no television, no indoor plumbing, no fancy games and toys. They valued songs, food, wood smoke, birdsong, and the taste of hot tomatoes, picked right out of the garden on a summer day.

Muldaur recalled driving up to Doc's small wooden home: "We drove up to Doc's house. They knew we were coming. That was when I first met Rosa Lee, who was very sweet, and their two children, Nancy and Merle. It was the tail end of winter, still pretty cold down there. And just off the main road on a dirt road, there was this house with white shingles or sideboards. And there was a little porch. It was small. Downstairs there was a living room and kitchen, and upstairs were a couple of bedrooms. And they gave us one of the bedrooms. The kids might have ended up sleeping with their parents. I'm not sure."[16]

Muldaur continued: "They just put on quite a spread for us. They treated us so wonderfully. I think we stayed down there a good week that first time. And after dinner, the different relatives all walked down some path and ended up on the front porch and in the parlor, and all started singing hymns. I thought I had died and gone to heaven. As a kid I had read *Little House on the Prairie*, and many books about life in America a hundred years ago. And this was like they were living it."[16] Muldaur remembered every detail of Doc's home: "The kitchen was remarkable. There was a huge wood-burning stove in the kitchen and then a family table under one window. There was this huge stove that was totally wood-burning. They had electricity but they didn't have running water in the house. They had electric lights but they didn't have gas or central heating or anything."[16]

Muldaur was amazed by Rosa Lee's ability to do almost anything on a wood stove. Surely that tickled Rosa Lee, and made them fast friends. Muldaur recalled: "She cooked on the stove, and what was interesting was, on the side of it was a tank, and there was a spigot in front of the stove. So there was always hot water, because as long as they were burning wood for their cooking and their heating, there was hot water to do dishes and so forth. I was just fascinated by how she was cooking and what she was cooking, and I said to her, 'God, you do that all on a wood stove?'"[16]

Rosa Lee, in great pride at what her husband was able to do around the house, answered Muldaur with something she was not expecting. Muldaur remembered: "She said, 'Yeah, it gets pretty hot in here in the summertime, but old Doc fixed me up with a fan,' and she showed me an exhaust fan set up in the window at one end of the kitchen. He'd taken a motor from an old washing machine and turned it into an exhaust fan to cool off her kitchen when it was warmer. I imagine cooking for four people or more on a huge wood stove could get pretty warm in the summer. I was just blown away that Doc could take apart an old washing machine motor and turn it into an exhaust fan and set it up."[16] Doc was truly a genius at taking modest means and turning them into luxury.

Muldaur was rightfully amazed by just about everything that she saw during that visit to Deep Gap: "And then, the other thing was they didn't have refrigeration, but they had a springhouse. And almost everything we ate came out of their garden. And then, up on the hill was an outhouse. I had seen outhouses before, from my various other adventures in the country, but this was the cleanest, most pleasant double-seater I had ever seen. It was just the sort of thing that would make a city girl shudder normally, but it was so well-kept and maintained and taken care of that it didn't seem like a hardship at all. And guess who built that? Doc!"[16]

Doc and Rosa Lee had created a comfortable lifestyle for themselves and their children. What more could they need? Doc was very proud to get off of State Aid to the Blind in later years, but he always regretted leaving that idyllic lifestyle behind. He truly loved those first years he spent alone with his wife and children in their little house together.

Eddy Merle Watson was Doc and Rosa Lee's first surviving child, and their firstborn son. He was born at Doc's parents' home to a midwife on February 8th of 1949, at ten in the morning, just over two years after their first (stillborn) child. Doc waited in the living room of his parents' home while a midwife was birthing the baby in a back room. According to the Watson family, Merle's legs were kicking as the midwife brought the newborn baby to his father for the first time.[17]

On Merle's birth certificate, Doc's occupation was listed as a musician.[18] Only two years before, Doc's occupation on the death certificate of his unnamed daughter had been listed as simply "blind." Clearly, things were already changing for the young musician. Perhaps dreams had entered his mind of supporting his family with music. But surely, he never would have guessed the heights to which he would someday rise with his music.

Doc and Rosa Lee named their son Eddy Merle. From the liner notes to *Southbound*, Doc recalled choosing his boy's name: "We named him Eddy Merle for Eddy Arnold, the Tennessee Plow-Boy, and who else but Merle Travis."[19] Doc would later famously have a conversation with Merle Travis himself about having named his son after him on the *Will the Circle Be Unbroken* album.

Doc's daughter was born two and a half years later, and they named her for her two grandmothers; Nancy Ellen. She was born on July 11th of 1951, and this time, Rosa Lee decided to go through labor in a hospital bed at Watauga Hospital in Boone instead of with a midwife. On his daughter Nancy's birth certificate, Doc is described as a 28-year old farmer.[20] Though he did many things around the home for Rosa Lee, he was hardly a farmer.

Rosa Lee was only 20 years old when she had Nancy, and that would be the end of her childbearing. But there would always be children running around the Watson home. By the age of 35, she was already a grandmother; by her fifties, a great-grandmother, and today she is a great-great-grandmother.

Rosa Lee was always very attached to her children: "I had two children that I dearly loved and I enjoyed being a mother and housewife and taking care of the family. I enjoyed the job, I reckon. And Lord, I worshipped my young-uns and [I was as] happy as I could be, taking care of them. I never got to go nowhere, but it didn't even bother me. I didn't even want to go if it was somewhere I couldn't take my kids."[7]

The memory of those first several years that Doc and Rosa Lee spent in their little cabin with their two small children is like no other for the blind musician. Though they had little, he truly cherished every day of his simple life with his love Rosa Lee and his beautiful children.

Merle still lives on in Doc's memory, standing as a small boy at the top of the hill, out of the way of any falling trees, shouting to his father which trees are the best to chop down.

# CHAPTER NOTES

1. *Wolmuth, Roger, After Years of Hard Traveling, Mountain Maestro Doc Watson Looks to Find Some Easy Pickin' At Last. People Weekly, August 10, 1987: p. 57-65.*
2. *Holt, David and Doc Watson, Doc Watson and David Holt: Legacy, Audio CD, High Windy Audio, 2002.*
3. *Watson, Nancy E., A Glimpse of What It's Like to be Part of 'The Watson Family' (liner notes to The Doc Watson Family: Songs fom the Southern Mountains), 1994.*
4. *Dawidoff, Nicholas, In the country of country: people and places in American music. 1997: Pantheon Books.*
5. *9-Master Doc and Merle: Doc's House, Doc, Merle, Rosa Lee. 1985, Ralph Rinzler Folklife Collection, Smithsonian Institution.*
6. *Watson, Doc and Ralph Rinzler, The Songs of Doc Watson. 1971, New York City: Oak Publications.*
7. *Holt, David, Liner Notes to Doc Watson and David Holt: Legacy, High Windy Audio, 2002.*
8. *Marriage Certificate for Arthel L. Watson and Rosa Lee Carlton: June 8, 1946.*
9. *Death Certificate for Watson Not Named. 1946.*
10. *Spitzer, Nick, Interview with Doc Watson. 1987, Smithsonian Institution, Ralph Rinzler Folklife Archives: Washington D.C.*
11. *Watson, Nancy, Doc Watson: A Closer Look. Bluegrass Unlimited, August 1984. 19(2): p. 8-11.*
12. *Humphrey, Mark, Liner Notes from Doc Watson: Rare Performances 1963-1981, Vestapol/Rounder, 2002.*
13. *Alesia, Tom, A Good Audience Makes an Old Tune Fresh. Wisconsin State Journal, March 6, 2003.*
14. *Siegel, Peter K., Liner Notes from Doc Watson at Gerde's Folk City, Sugar Hill Records, 2001.*
15. *Gustavson, Kent, Telephone Interview with Sam Bush. April 9, 2009.*
16. *Gustavson, Kent, Telephone Interview with Maria Muldaur. April 1, 2009.*
17. *Doc Watson Biography. 2005, MerleFest.*
18. *Birth Certificate for Eddy Merle Watson. 1949.*
19. *Watson, Doc, Liner Notes from Doc Watson: Southbound, Vanguard Records, 1988.*
20. *Birth Certificate for Nancy Ellen Watson. 1951.*

Photo by John Cohen ©
*Gaither Carlton playing fiddle at a house party near Deep Gap, early 1960s.*

Photo by John Cohen ©
*Doc Watson playing guitar at Annie Bird's apartment in NYC, March 1961.*

# CHAPTER EIGHT
## Williams & The Rail-Riders

*"I remember in the early '50s I already knew that Doc Watson was the best guitar player in this damn country. I heard that from one person telling another, and it made it twenty miles over to where I lived. And soon we were sneaking over here to see if we could steal a lick or two on the guitar."*

- Joe Wilson[1]

In his earliest local appearances as a teenager, Doc was known by his given name *Arthel*. But a short while into his amateur career, he began to employ the moniker that later followed him to fame.

In the early 1940s, Arthel occasionally played a little show on the radio station WHKY with his friend Paul Greer, broadcast live from O.P. Loot's furniture store in the nearby town of Lenoir. Doc wrote about the live broadcast in which he first acquired his nickname: "The young man I worked with played the guitar and sang some, and his name was Paul Greer. They called him Paul, which was nice and short over the radio. The announcer came to me before we were on the air and said, 'Your name's Arthel.' He pronounced it kind of slow and said, 'That's too long. What's a good short name for the radio? Let's think up a good name right here.' There was a young lady there – she must have been fourteen or fifteen – and she yelled out, 'Call him *Doc*.' I never found out who she was; she was just back in the audience in the furniture store. The name *Doc* has come in very handy to me as a professional name because it's easy to remember."[2] Doc's musicianship and amicable personality was more memorable than his name, but the nickname certainly granted him a memorable mystique in the folk world.

Doc was one of the best guitar pickers in the entire Boone area in the late 1940s, but he wasn't able to make a living at it; hot guitar picking wasn't what people came to see on Friday night at the local juke joints. He knew that he had talent, but his blindness stood in the way of his winning many contests, and getting any kind of recognition as a front man. In an interview with Jean Stewart (who was also blind) for *Sing Out!* magazine, Doc remembered how he, at times, felt angry and bitter because of the way he was treated: "Yeah, it happened a couple of times back in the '40s when I tried to get into radio and things. I'd get refusals because of the handicap. Yeah, it [hurt]. I'd be bitter and sulk for a long time, for a month or two, then I'd get an audition."[3] Doc spoke about the difficulty he had especially with radio: "It's kind of hard for a fellow that's visually handicapped to get on any kind of radio show."[4] But it wasn't long until Doc had a small taste of the stage career that was to come.

Bill Monroe came to town with his Bluegrass Boys, including the young Earl Scruggs tearing up the five-string banjo, and Lester Flatt singing lead and playing guitar. Doc wouldn't miss the concert for the world. However, Bill Monroe was ill, resting in his car while the remaining members of his band were trying to figure out how to play an entire show without him. Doc and his friend "Frog" Greene, with whom he often played on the streets of Boone, as well as on various radio programs around the area, went to Bill Monroe's car to pay to tribute to him, as many young players would do when they saw a master play in their local area.

When Frog led Doc to Bill's car, and they were introduced to their childhood hero, they shook hands. Because Doc and Frog had heard Bill wasn't feeling well, Doc remembered saying boldly to the bluegrass pioneer, "Bill, they tell me you're feeling pretty bad, my friend." Monroe replied to him, "I'm pretty sick...I think I got hold of some bad sausage."[5]

Doc and Frog saw the opportunity in Monroe's misfortune, and they went to the back of the tent and found Lester Flatt. Doc shook his hand, likely telling him how much he enjoyed his music. Then, citing Bill's sickness, Doc asked him, "Lester, could me and my buddy here play a tune on the show? Seems like you're shorthanded a little bit."[5] According to Doc, Flatt thought it was a good idea; he thought that the audience would certainly enjoy seeing some local boys on stage, and it might lengthen a show that had been shortened without Bill. Flatt and the others backstage quickly found two guitars for Doc and Frog, and they passed a quick audition. The pair went on stage before The Bluegrass Boys, playing a few Eddy Arnold songs.[5]

In 2003, Earl Scruggs and Doc Watson teamed up to play a concert for National Public Radio's *All Things Considered* after the release of their album with Ricky Skaggs called *The Three Pickers*. They had a conversation about their first meeting backstage after that Boone performance. Doc said, "First time I heard Earl play, he was with Bill Monroe's tent show, and he and I both were pretty young then." Earl responded, "What – did we come through Boone or something?" Doc continued, "Yes, it was at Boone, Earl, and I got to come backstage, and me and you picked a few."[6] Allegedly, after the concert, Doc had the chance to play with Scruggs backstage: the opportunity of a lifetime for the excited young guitarist.

Despite this brief glimpse into stardom when he and Frog were lucky enough to help cover for Bill Monroe that day in the late 1940s, Doc otherwise only occupied amateur and minor professional stages until the spring of 1961.

Doc's first professional job was at the American Legion Hall in Boone, where he played square dance music for hours on end with fiddler Uncle Charlie Osborne. Jerry Wilson, a barber from Boone who had let Doc play in front of his shop for many years, was often the caller for many of the dances, and sets could go as long as 30 minutes without stopping, giving the young guitarist plenty of practice. Musicians and audiences started to notice Doc's virtuosity, and soon, one of his neighbors put a little band together to feature Doc and get him a few dollars to help support his family. Jack Williams put the band together, and they called themselves Williams and the Rail-Riders.

The first time Jack Williams met Doc was through Uncle Charlie Osborne. Jack recalled: "Around about 1952…[I] went to see if Charlie Osborne had moved. Charlie was a piano picker. I mean, he was dandy. He says, 'Let's go down here, and I'll introduce you to a guitar picker.' And we were going down to Doc's. And on the way down there, he told me, he says, 'Now this boy's blind.' And I said, 'Well, is he picking the guitar, or is he just chording the thing?' And he said, 'Well, you listen in, and you tell me what he's doing…' When [Doc] played all that Merle Travis stuff and all that stuff picking the guitar, I just had to sit there in amazement, how he was doing that, not being able to see anything. And after we'd picked there for a pretty little spell, well, we started talking about forming us a little group, you know, [to] make us a little money."[7]

Doc became the lead guitar and singer for Williams and the Rail-Riders when he was 29 years old in 1952, one year before he and Rosa Lee were able to purchase their own home in Deep Gap.

Jack Williams had a full-time job working on the railroad, and didn't need to play music with the group in order to earn income. However, he enjoyed their gigs very much, and he knew that he would be helping his neighbor, Doc, support his young children. And of course, Williams heard the incredible virtuosity that came from Doc's flat pick, and thought that someday, someone would pick up on his greatness: "I recognized the boy's talent. I knew that if he ever went somewhere where somebody heard him who could help him, why, he was on his way."[8]

Jack and Doc ended up working together until 1960. They performed, according to Doc, "sometimes with a five-piece band and sometimes four,"[9] playing at clubs and organizations in eastern Tennessee and western North Carolina, including a Rod and Gun Club picnic or two as well.[9] Doc recalled the different halls they played in a 1976 interview with Bert Lloyd: "Well, we did the VFW, Moose Lodge, and a lot of different lodge halls that they'd have around, and we did just some straight clubs, like Frontier Club for instance in the Bristol/Kingsport area, where I guess that was a – it wouldn't be counted a lodge, but it was a club and we did some country clubs. Actually dances was the whole music we played. From 8 to 12, you know, on Friday or Saturday night. We'd get about a 30-minute break in the middle of that, [if one of us] wanted to get a cold beer or a cup of coffee or something."[10]

During the week, Doc worked hard to be the best lead guitar player he could be, listening to the radio each day, and picking up a half dozen songs.[11] Williams and the Rail-Riders would then play at various venues on Friday and Saturday nights, and Doc would be able to try out the tunes he had learned with the band.[10]

Doc and his band played fiddle tunes, jazz tunes, big band pop music, and old standards. Williams encouraged Doc to play the melodies, allowing the band to have a clean sound, since Williams was already chunking away on the chords of the song on the piano. Doc would also then be able to play along with Williams' group without having to learn all of the complex chords in each jazz tune, which Williams, of course, could read off of a lead sheet, but which obviously Doc could not. From that period on, Doc honored the melody above all else, whether in rockabilly, modern folk music, or old-time singing.

Williams and the Rail-Riders also played some gigs for charity from time to time, Doc remembered in an interview with Jon Sievert: "Every first Thursday night in each month, we played free for the veterans at the Mountain Home Veteran's Hospital in Johnson City, Tennessee… That was a rewarding thing too, because they enjoyed the music much better than the people that came to dance. They listened."[12]

Local audiences were mostly interested in dancing and having a good time, far different than the folk music audiences. Doc would later have in New York and around the country in the folk boom. The locals in the 1950s were raucous, and as Doc remembered, "there were the people who...really didn't know or care that much about music. It was just the *beat* that they wanted, and to have a good time on [Friday or Saturday] night, you know. After a hard week's work they wanted to relax a little, have a few drinks and dance... They weren't really there [to listen]... Occasionally you would have someone that would sit and listen to a good song if you put one in, you know, but mostly it was just for fun."[10]

Doc got, as he remembered, eight solid years of technical practice playing his electric guitars. He came out on the other side a skilled and fluent 37-year old guitarist by the time he was "discovered" by Ralph Rinzler in 1960.

## CHAPTER NOTES

1.  Wilson, Joe, *Doc Watson: Just One of Us*. Muleskinner News, June 1974: p. 10-14.
2.  Watson, Doc and Ralph Rinzler, *The Songs of Doc Watson*. 1971, New York City: Oak Publications.
3.  Stewart, Jean, *A Conversation with Doc Watson*. Sing Out!, January/February 1981. 29(1).
4.  Watson, Doc and David Grisman, *Doc Watson and David Grisman - In Concert (1999)*, DVD, Vestapol, 2001.
5.  Smith, Richard, *Can't You Hear Me Callin': The Life of Bill Monroe, Father of Bluegrass*. 2001: Da Capo Press.
6.  *Three Pickers in Studio 4A*, from *All Things Considered*. 2003, NPR.
7.  Murphy, Joe, *Doc and Merle -The Lives and Music of Doc & Merle Watson (1985)*, VHS, Vestapol, 1996.
8.  Wolmuth, Roger, *After Years of Hard Traveling, Mountain Maestro Doc Watson Looks to Find Some Easy Pickin' At Last*. People Weekly, August 10, 1987: p. 57-65.
9.  Watson, Doc, *Liner Notes from Doc Watson: Southbound*, Vanguard Records, 1988.
10. Lloyd, Bert, *Interview with Doc Watson*, Audio CD, Ralph Rinzler Folklife Archives, Smithsonian Institution, 1976.
11. *43-Master Jack Williams Interview*. 1985, Video Recording, Ralph Rinzler Folklife Collection, Smithsonian Institution.
12. Sievert, Jon, *Doc Watson: 'Like Some Kind of Fine'*. Frets, March 1979. 1(1): p. 20-26.

# CHAPTER NINE
## Ralph Rinzler

*"I'd sat on the back of a pickup truck...and thumped on the banjo and talked with Ralph about the old-time music and how I grew up. By the time we got over to the house, Ralph was all excited and thought he'd discovered somebody. I had a lot of misgivings about it."*

- Doc Watson, 1975[1]

*"As a young man recently at college, I had no real sense of how to talk with Doc about a fresh career on the folk music circuit."*

- Ralph Rinzler, 1993[2]

*"Ralph, this may sound silly, but when I talk with you I feel like I have a place in the world worth bragging about."*

- Doc Watson to Ralph Rinzler, 1963[3]

A young Jewish mandolin player from the suburbs of New York City would change Doc Watson's life forever. Ralph Rinzler turned Doc Watson into a household name among acoustic musicians, and put him on the path towards music stardom and legend. But Doc has often said he would have much preferred a simple life, and not the one his fame soon brought. In a conversation captured by Joe Murphy on the 1985 film *Doc and Merle*, Doc said to his old friend, "I wouldn't go through that again," to which Rinzler quickly replied, slightly misunderstanding Doc, "I wouldn't take anything for it either."[4] As their conversation continued, Doc explained his reasoning: "I don't know how to put this. I love you as good as every brother I've got, buddy, but let me tell you this right now... If I knew what I know about this when you came down [to Deep Gap the first time], I'd have made the decision, 'Buddy, I can't do it...' No, you could have come back any time you wanted to, and we'd have picked the hell out of it, but [I would have told you], 'I ain't going on the road.'"[4]

Ralph Rinzler succeeded in convincing Doc to go on the road, never imagining that such an opportunity might disrupt the idyllic life Doc had enjoyed with his wife and kids. But he made it possible for Doc to proudly earn a living for his family in the only way he knew how. Rinzler opened every door he could reach for his blind friend, starting him out on a half-century career in the music business.

Ralph Rinzler was born in 1934, the son of Russian-Jewish parents Harry and Beatrice Rinzler. Even as a child he was fascinated by the diversity all around him in New York City, and he would ask his mother, a school teacher, to take him with her to all of the shops, so that he could see the butchers, bakers and grocers from different cultures. As he grew older, he was allowed to do something special on his birthday each year, so he would ask his parents to take him to New York's ethnic neighborhoods to look around and experience different worlds right within the same city.[5]

Rinzler was given a set of Library of Congress records as a child, after which he became hooked on traditional music. He taught himself how to play the banjo, guitar and mandolin, and was one of the founding members of the folk club at Swarthmore College. He was a French language major in college, and after he graduated in 1956, he traveled through Europe, making friends that would last a lifetime, including folklorist Bert Lloyd.[5]

Returning home from his travels, Rinzler located to New York City, where he reconnected with the folk music scene there, including Pete, Mike and Peggy Seeger, John Cohen and many others. He soon joined a traditional music ensemble, the Greenbriar Boys, traveling the country with them from one college to another, often sharing the bill with Joan Baez. Rinzler also began to make journeys to the south, inspired by Alan Lomax and his friends and colleagues Mike Seeger and John Cohen, who also travelled south to record traditional musicians.

Then, only a few years out of college, without a record or a contract to his name, Rinzler struck traditional music *gold* in 1960. He traveled down to Union Grove, North Carolina over Easter weekend for the Union Grove Fiddler's Convention with his Greenbriar Boys bandmates. Together, they entered one of the old-time band competitions, and won it; they were the first band from the north that had ever won a competition at the large regional festival. After winning the competition, Rinzler's secondary goal was to record a few interesting old-time musicians who happened to be at the festival. He did this with his friend Eugene Earle, an engineer and 78-record collector who had already been planning to collect some records in the area that weekend.

Rinzler hoped they might get lucky enough to meet a musician from Harry Smith's 1952 6-LP compilation on Folkways Records called *The Anthology of American Folk Music*, which had become like a bible for the New York folk music movement with its eclectic mix of 78-recordings from the 1920s and '30s. Rinzler had acquired the record set in 1952 when it first came out, and had listened to it over and over again, mining it for traditional music repertoire and techniques. It was a long shot, but Rinzler knew that many of the recordings on the *Anthology* had come from the North Carolina area, and if any of the featured musicians on the *Anthology* were still alive and active, they might show up at the largest fiddler's convention in the area.

One state away, in eastern Tennessee, Clint Howard and Fred Price had prepared for months with their coach and mentor Tom Ashley, an old-time musician who lived down the road from them near Mountain City. He had taught them the tricks of the trade, hoping to help the group secure one of the $150 cash prizes awarded for best band. Price and Howard also enlisted their banjo-playing friend Jack Johnson from Pilot Mountain, North Carolina to round out the group. The musicians did not win the contest that day, but they did win a great opportunity; a young gentleman with dark hair and a big smile wandered into their practice room, and enthralled by the music, he stayed. The young man was Ralph Rinzler.

Years later, Rinzler remembered hearing the old-time trio rehearse one of their songs: "At the fiddler's convention... Clint, Fred and Jack were rehearsing ["Footprints in the Snow"]. The sound was enigmatic; it held me there. The song said *bluegrass* but [the] fiddle and the banjo carried another message."[6] Rinzler did not yet know it, but he would soon be seeing a lot more of these three men and their coach. And five months later, they would also first introduce him to Doc Watson.

Fred Price's fiddle playing, in particular, excited Rinzler; Price was playing old-time fiddle in the context of bluegrass. Rinzler went up to Price and asked him, "What do you call what you're doing?"[7] Price's response was, "Old-time music."[7] Rinzler was very surprised, because nearly every other group in the contest was playing something akin to the more contemporary bluegrass sound of Bill Monroe. He further probed the fiddle player, "Why are you playing that instead of what everyone else is playing?"[7] The fiddle player then explained to Rinzler that they had come to the contest with their coach, Tom Ashley. Rinzler immediately thought of the *Anthology of American Folk Music*, knowing that another man named "Ashley" had recorded two of the most riveting songs on Harry Smith's *Anthology of American Folk Music*. Rinzler then asked Price if he had heard of a *Clarence* Ashley. According to Rinzler, the group's coach, whom they knew as *Tom* Ashley, overheard the conversation; he looked up and said, "Well, that's me!"[7] Rinzler initially did not believe him, thinking that the elderly musician was trying to trick him. After all, not even his own bandmates knew him as Clarence. But, according to Rinzler, Ashley said, "On RCA Victor I was Tom, and on Columbia I was Clarence, but they're both me."[7]* Rinzler recalled how amazed he was when he realized that this man actually *was* the Clarence Ashley he had listened to for years on the *Anthology*. In 1990, Rinzler said: "I couldn't believe I was standing there looking at this guy that I thought had disappeared from the face of the earth before I was born, who had played that incredible [version of the song] 'Coo Coo Bird' on the *Anthology*."[7]

Tom Moore, the grandson of Clarence Ashley, related his grandfather's version of the meeting: "Ralph met my granddad at the Union Grove Fiddler's Convention. He was talking to him, and he said, 'Do you know Clarence Ashley?' My granddad said, 'Oh, yeah.' They talked a bit more, and then my granddad said, 'Well, I'm him!' From that point on, of course they grabbed onto Granddad and wanted to get him recording again."[8]

Clint Howard, a great storyteller, embellished the tale: "This tall slim fellow came up and said, 'You wouldn't happen to know a fellow by the name of Clarence Ashley over at Mountain City, would you?' I said, 'No I don't know Clarence Ashley,' but I says, 'I know Tom Ashley. I bet he knows him. Right out there he stands.' I hollered and I says, 'Tom, do you know a fellow by the name of Clarence Ashley over home?' And he said, 'No....'" Ashley was playing a joke on his young friend and the northerner. He then

---

* *In the interest of clarity, for the rest of the book, Clarence "Tom" Ashley will be referred to as Clarence Ashley, the name he went by on both the Harry Smith* Anthology *in 1952, his 1961 Folkways record,* Old-Time Music at Clarence Ashley's, *as well as the 1991 CD compilation of Ashley/Watson material,* Clarence Ashley And Doc Watson: The Original Folkways Recordings.

shouted, "Hell! *I'm* Clarence Ashley,"[9] surprising Clint, who had only known him as Tom Ashley to that point.

Rinzler told Ashley that his 1929 recording of "Coo Coo Bird" was beloved in the New York folk scene, and because of his own passion for the song, he had even himself attempted to write to Clarence Ashley in Mountain City, only for his various letters and telegrams to come back, stamped *Return to Sender*. Ashley explained to Rinzler that he was known as Tom Ashley to everyone locally, and that was why the letters had probably been returned.[10]

Rinzler persuaded the group to be recorded by Eugene Earle, so the group recorded "Footprints in the Snow" and a couple of other songs. Ashley wouldn't play the banjo or sing "Coo Coo Bird," but they did manage to coax him into singing one song with the backup of the small band: "Put My Little Shoes Away." Rinzler asked if he and Earle might come back south sometime in the near future to record a few songs so that Ashley would have the time to brush up on his banjo playing, since he had not performed in many years. Ashley said he would consider it, and Rinzler took that as a hopeful sign.

Mike Seeger, himself an old-time music legend, recalled that his old friend Ralph Rinzler had been immediately aware of the importance of his discovery: "Ralph was just beyond being elated... To find somebody like [Ashley] who was so special was incredible. It was just one of those major revelations."[11]

When he was a young man, Clarence Ashley had been able to make a decent living by playing music and performing on stage, but in later years he worked at any jobs he could find. His son started a place called The Dairy Bar on the outskirts of Mountain City, Tennessee, and Ashley would help him with the fruit stand next to the restaurant. Ashley's grandson Tom Moore remembered: "My granddaddy would drive a truck to Georgia, maybe even Florida some, to pick up some fruit to haul up there to the fruit stand. And I worked in there a couple of years in the summertime, just about a week or two weeks at a time."[8]

In between odd jobs, Ashley had still played music at land sales and other varied local venues when he could until he permanently injured the index finger of his right hand when a heavy shed fell on it. He stopped playing the banjo, and did not pick up the instrument again until after the first recording session with Earle and Rinzler in late 1960. The widely-imitated *clippety-clop* sound of Ashley's clawhammer technique in the 1960s that sounded a bit like soft horse's hooves came as a result of his stiff finger.

Photo by John Cohen ©
*Fred Price, Clarence Ashley and Clint Howard in Galax, Virginia.*

Eugene Earle was a beloved figure in the 1960s folk scene in New York though he was not a musician himself, and had not really been all that interested in folk music until the New Lost City Ramblers started breathing life into some of the old-time music that he had collected on record.

Someone told Earle about the Ramblers, and he showed up at their second or third concert. John Cohen of the Ramblers recalled, "Earle didn't look like anybody in our audience. He said, 'I've got these old 78 records; you're welcome to come to my house to listen.'"[12] Cohen was intrigued, and soon visited Earle: "I remember in those days I had a little Vespa motor scooter and the West Side Highway in New York was cobblestone in those days. And I would ride up that freeway, across the George Washington Bridge, and visit Gene Earle. I think the first time I went, he said, 'What do you want to hear?' And there were more than 10,000 records on the wall. He had them catalogued by serial numbers, not by name. But he did have lists. So then he gave me a copy of his list."[12]

Eugene Earle was a music collector, not a folklorist; Cohen spoke about what that meant in the context of the times: "Back then, folklorists collected songs and information and so forth and wrote books. But collectors were not folk singers; collectors just collected series of things. 'Columbia 15000, Columbia 16000. Here's a rare Okeh, here's a Brunswick,' finding a whole series of something and even going looking for ledger sheets; looking for old catalogs. He collected primarily southern hillbilly music."[12]

Cohen remembered the deal he and Earle struck: "I started going out to his place with this relatively portable Pentron tape recorder, which I'd strap to the back of my Vespa and bump up the highway with all these cars, cross the George Washington bridge to his house. And suddenly there's 10,000 records, and he would ask me, 'What do you want to hear? I'll let you record anything you want.' We had some kind of set up."[12] The opportunity Earle presented to Cohen was certainly not lost on him. Much of the Ramblers' later repertoire came from the records on that wall.

In preparing for the Labor Day weekend recording session with Ralph Rinzler and Eugene Earle, Clarence Ashley told his young friends Fred Price and Clint Howard that, since Howard could only play rhythm, their group needed a lead guitar player. At the Union Grove festival, the young men had used Jack Johnson to play banjo, but since he lived far away, Ashley thought of Doc Watson, with whom he purportedly played a few land sales years before. He also likely was thinking of more contemporary country music, and wanted the sound of Doc's electric guitar in the group in order to impress the men from New York. Most importantly, with Doc's help, Ashley would be able to record for Rinzler without having to pick up the banjo again.

Clint recalled, "When Ralph Rinzler came over to Mountain City to record me and [Clarence] and Fred, we needed a lead guitar player because I only play rhythm guitar. [Clarence] said he knew a feller over in North Carolina named Watson that was pretty good on the guitar, so [Clarence] and I went over to Deep Gap to find him. We didn't know where he lived, but I looked up and saw *Watson's Garage*, so we went in there and asked them if they knew a feller by the name of Doc Watson. And the man said, 'Yes, I know him,' and pointed across the road and said, 'He lives right up there.' We went on up to the house and Doc and two teenaged boys were putting down a linoleum rug and Doc was showing them how to cut it. And we asked him if he wanted to play with us."[13] And of course, Doc agreed.

They never practiced together as a group; Doc asserted that he would be able to play with the group without practice. They agreed to meet at Ashley's home on September 3rd when the northerners would arrive. Little did Doc know that he would be bringing Rinzler to meet his family only two days after that, recording all of their family songs for the world to hear.

Eugene Earle again accompanied Ralph Rinzler to North Carolina on the first weekend of September 1960, five months after their first meeting with Clarence Ashley. Rinzler remembered: "To make good on my promise, I traveled to East Tennessee with Eugene Earle... On arrival at Ashley's home, we were introduced to Doc Watson. Ashley had not taken up the banjo again. Instead he had asked Doc to join him and agreed to sing to Doc's electric guitar accompaniment."[14] Rinzler was understandably frustrated. He had wanted to re-create the magical acoustic old-time recordings he knew so well from the *Anthology of American Folk Music*, and take them back with him to New York with him as a treasure to show the New York folk crowd.

Rinzler recalled, "I heard a wisp of electric guitar, and I didn't really register it, except to be put off... After all, I was going down there to reconnect with a very extraordinary banjo player and singer who represented something absolutely, diametrically opposed to anything that could happen with an electric guitar."[15] Ashley had not picked up his banjo again after meeting Rinzler five months previously, and was fully expecting to be recorded with the accompaniment of Doc's electric guitar. Rinzler, rather brusquely, asked Doc to put down his Telecaster and pick up an acoustic instrument. Rinzler said: "Gosh, couldn't you get an acoustic?"[16] Rinzler remembered: "Doc replied, politely but rather firmly, that this was his guitar and that's what he was used to playing."[16] Doc refused to submit to the northerner's request to lay down his electric guitar and pick up an acoustic instrument.

Doc had worked hard to create a reputation as an electric guitarist in his local community, and he was stymied as to why Rinzler did not want him to play his instrument of choice on the recording with Ashley. After all, in the words of T. Michael Coleman, "it was not the traditional mountain music that we associate with Doc that he was playing, but America's other traditional folk music rockabilly... music that transformed Doc Watson from a street musician selling pencils and picking songs for whatever it would bring, to a professional musician who could support his family on his own with pride."[17]

Rinzler recalled that, in this first meeting with Doc, "recording under such circumstances appeared to be unacceptable to both of us."[15] Rinzler had decided that Doc wouldn't be recording with Ashley on the sessions, since Doc wouldn't play acoustic instead of electric guitar.

Rinzler, deciding not to even stay around long enough to hear the first rehearsal by the group on September 3rd, 1960, got in his car and drove three hours up to where Jack Johnson lived in North Carolina. Johnson was the banjo player who had played so wonderfully with Fred Price and Clint Howard at the Union Grove Fiddler's Convention that spring. Johnson's playing would, in Rinzler's mind, be far more acceptable on a recording of old-time music than Doc's electric guitar.

Rinzler returned late at night with Johnson, the banjoist from North Carolina. Early Sunday morning, September 4th, Rinzler was surprised to see that Doc had arrived for the session, since he had no interest in recording the young guitarist and his electric instrument. All of the musicians then piled into a pickup truck in order to drive to Clarence Ashley's daughter's home in Saltville, Virginia, where they had agreed to record.

The group drove northward through the mountains. Doc sat in the cab of the truck, and Rinzler, wanting to enjoy the fresh mountain air, took a seat in the truck's bed. Rinzler recalled: "Since I was alone out there and had about an hour and a quarter to ride, I started to play the banjo."[16] Suddenly, the truck stopped, and the passenger door swung open: "Doc jumped out, walked to the back and said, 'Let me see that banjo, son.' Then he played Tom Dooley and played the hell out of it."[16] In a 1988 interview with Richard Harrington, Rinzler recalled Doc's picking in the back of that truck as "some of the best pure mountain picking imaginable."[15]

Doc entranced the tall northerner as he sang and frailed out, in old-time style, the song "Tom Dula," (or "Tom Dooley," as it was known in the folk world because of the Kingston Trio's version) to Rinzler's utter amazement and delight. Rinzler remembered, "I got to hear Doc play banjo... I was dazzled that the same person who played that electric guitar was playing five-string banjo in an archaic style with extraordinary skill."[15]

Emerging from this 37-year old blind man's adept fingers, Rinzler heard an old-time sound that he had previously only known from old records and old men. Mountain music came alive in the frailing hands and baritone voice of this man he had previously thought could only play Nashville-style licks on his Fender electric. Rinzler remembered, "Those were the first few tunes I had ever heard him play and I knew immediately that a man who could pick a banjo as Doc did would understand what kind of music we were in search of some six hundred miles from New York."[18]

Rinzler was amazed by Doc's version of "Tom Dooley," which had been a national hit by the Kingston Trio. He recalled, "The Kingston Trio's 1958 hit record was still resonating across the nation. Doc's version, unlike theirs, would have been compelling to anyone enlightened by Harry Smith's *Anthology*. In fact, I had brought the six-record collection with me to give to Ashley as a way of making clear to him why I understood his importance. Doc and I reviewed the list of performers and songs on the album covers. To my astonishment, he was familiar with many of them, having heard the recordings and some of the performers themselves in his childhood and having known others as neighbors. We talked about the growing audience for this music in colleges across the nation. He told me about his occasional radio shows and public performances with...Jack Williams and his rockabilly ensemble. He talked of his family version of Tom Dooley and then reeled off a host of old-time songs still current in the area. This seemed to me remarkable. An electric guitar player who was also deeply versed in the repertoire and styles of the *Anthology* and the Lomax Library of Congress recordings. Doc was only eleven years older than I, but this was his living tradition. For me it was an archival treasure; hardly the music I expected to hear from a near contemporary who played Nashville hits on an electric guitar."[14]

Rinzler recalled their conversation in the back of the pickup: "When [Doc] proceeded to talk to me, he was articulate, charming, witty, profound – as much as you could be sitting in the back of a truck bumping along the road. I was completely astonished by him, as an intellect, as a personality and as a musician... I knew the styles of the music but had never really connected with the people who played it. I knew it as a sound, not as an expression of a thinking, functioning person sitting in front of me. I had no idea what kind of people played this music. I just had the sound ringing in my ears of this beautiful, pentatonic, archaic-sounding music sung in a vocal style that left Frank Sinatra far behind. Doc was the first traditional musician I ever became a close friend of. And what astonished me was that the people who are great musicians in traditional music are as profound as great artists in any kind of art. He is an extraordinarily warm, compassionate and witty human being with an incredible breadth of knowledge."[15]

Now that Rinzler had made friends with Doc, he tried to convince him to abandon the electric guitar, and to join the recording sessions with Ashley. Doc did not agree, but he said that he would try to simply turn the guitar down. When they began recording again, Doc tried turning down his amplifier, but it did not work. Doc recalled the situation: "I had to be persuaded in my own mind [not to play the electric guitar]... I wanted to play it and turn it real low. We tried that on a couple of tunes and Ralph didn't have to tell me that it didn't work... I borrowed an acoustic guitar to play on the rest of them."[15] And from that moment on, Doc became known as an *acoustic* guitarist.

Ralph Rinzler was so enamored with Doc after their conversation in the back of the pickup that he arranged to record the next day (September 5th, 1960) at the Watson home. Doc's daughter Nancy, who was only nine years old at the time, recalled the first visit that Ralph Rinzler and Eugene Earle made to their home on Labor Day 1960: "Ralph Rinzler and Eugene Earle came to the little two-story, wood-frame house where we lived...[and] neighbors came from miles around, just to sit very quietly around the walls of our living room and listen. In the middle of that small room, a homemade, echo-proof recording studio had been set up. Daddy and Ralph had cleverly devised it by drawing Mama's quilting frames to the ceiling, and hanging four of her handmade quilts from the frames for walls. Then they placed a few scatter rugs on the studio floor to absorb the foot tapping. I don't believe the actual floor space was much bigger than a queen bed quilt, but I don't reckon anybody got gouged by anybody else's elbows. At least no one mentioned it."[19]

Rinzler and Earle, amazed by Doc's ability to play and sing any number of old-time tunes, asked him to play "Cannonball Blues," but he could not remember all of the words. Earle then put on the 78-record of the song, after which Doc was immediately able to perform it. His raw talent amazed both Earle and Rinzler. Much to Earle's excitement, Doc also knew the Frank Hutchinson songs: "Train That Carried My Girl From Town" and "Worried Blues," two of Earle's favorite 78s.[20]

Rinzler and Earle brought with them a copy of the *Anthology of American Folk Music* when they visited the Watson family for the first time, in order to explain the importance Appalachian music held to the traditional folk music scene in New York. When Earle put the needle down on the song "Omie Wise," Rinzler recalled, "All listened intently. Gaither, in his denim bib overalls, had come straight from his garden. As the song ended, tears were streaming down his face. No one spoke. Gaither sighed and said quietly, as though to himself, '[Makes me think of] old times.'"[14]

"Is that you a-playin' that?" listening to this Record of these carpenters ~~Doc~~ Gaither
"yep" Tom
"makes me think of old tunes." ~~Doc~~ Gaither

"DOC" ARTHEL ~~L.~~ L. WATSON
GAITHER WILEY CARLTON  father-in-law of Doc
~~the~~ Arthel L. WATSON
called the OLD MEEKS.
ARTHEL WATSON BOX 34 DEEP GAP, N.C.
TAPE #III DJ SEPT. 1960
DEEP GAP, WATAUGA CTY N.C.

1. Pretty Polly - fiddle + guitar; Gaither + Doc 4:13
2. Willow Garden - same as 1 2:50
  2 false starts
3. Rubens train - Doc, guitar + vocal; Gaither, banjo 1:38
4. Jimmy Sutton - banjo in E chord tuning
5. Down the Road - Doc, guitar + vocal; Gaither, banjo 2:07
6. Ground Hog - 1.
7. Old Rattler - Tom, vocal; Gaither, banjo; Doc, guitar
8. Brown's Dream (2 takes) Gaither + Doc 1:15
9. Fiddler's Dram - Gaither + Doc CUFFY 1:33
  SIDE 2 2:45
10. Merry Go-round (miss meecard) - ~~Cuffy~~ in the woodpile - Sally Goodin
11. Sally Goodin - CUFFY IN the Woodpile + Merry-go-round 2:18
12. Kitty Wells - Doc WATSON - vocal + guitar
13. The LAWSON FAMILY TRAGEDY - DOC
14. I'm going back to Jericho - Doc, Gaither, Ralph 1:50
15. SKILLET GOOD + Greasy: Doc + Ralph 2:05 2:20 2 takes
16. LORD THOMAS - ROSALEE CARLTON WATSON
17. CLAUDE ALLEN - 3.34

Gaither Carlton Box 92 Deep Gap, N.C.

*Notes in Ralph Rinzler's notebook from the September 5th 1960 recording session with Clarence Ashley, Gaither Carlton and Doc Watson in Deep Gap.*

Doc was very excited by the recording session, but, as he told Colin Escott in a 2002 interview, "Ralph heard me play, and told me that I had something to offer the public. It scared the thunder out of me."[21] The men were attempting to show Doc and his family how important the old-time music was, and what it meant to the folk music world. Because of Doc's incredible ability to interpret old-time music, Ralph Rinzler wanted him to stick with that music, and with the acoustic guitar and banjo, and not play the electric anymore. And Rinzler knew that, if he could somehow bring Doc to New York, the folk community would be amazed by his incredible ability to breathe life and virtuosity into this music they had all only known from 78 records.

In a 1988 letter to the Department of Cultural Resources for the State of North Carolina, Rinzler wrote: "Though he was attempting to make a living at the time by performing commercially popular country music, I discovered that he held a vast repertoire of traditional songs he had learned over the years at family and community gatherings. I encouraged Doc to perform the songs and tunes that had been passed from generation to generation, and, as I listened, I knew I was hearing a great American folk artist. As you may know, I devoted several years of my life to helping Doc [and the Clarence Ashley Group] reach the kind of audience [they] deserved."[22]

Ralph Rinzler's struggle to get Clarence Ashley and his fellow musicians an audience began directly after that first visit: "Once back home, Gene Earle and I collaborated on editing and documenting the recordings. I approached several record companies. One record company owner[*], a friend, smiled apologetically saying of Doc's material, 'It's nice, but it won't sell.' There was no interest in the tapes, except at Folkways, where Moses Asch agreed to issue the edited material promptly. In retrospect, the existence of a record producer like Asch was of decisive importance. Via Folkways, he provided what the major labels no longer did: access to old-timers like Ashley and to brilliant younger artists like Watson."[14]

Rinzler was enthralled by Doc Watson's performances on the recordings he brought home, but within his folk music community in New York at the time, the great treasure he had discovered was *Anthology* artist Clarence Ashley. As expected, once Rinzler revealed his discovery and subsequent recording of

---

[*] *Most likely Maynard Solomon, owner of Vanguard Records.*

Ashley, the response he received was highly favorable. Though the recording of Doc's family might have been equally or even more important to Rinzler personally, it was on the back burner to the Ashley recordings because of the interest of Rinzler's peers in this shadowy character from the *Anthology*'s past. *Old-Time Music at Clarence Ashley's* was released in early 1961, just before the Clarence Ashley Group played its first live concert at PS 41 in March of that same year.

While Rinzler was focused on Ashley and the first Friends of Old-Time Music concert, he played the tapes of his Ashley and Watson recordings for his 15-year old friend David Grisman. Grisman remembered visiting Rinzler in his kitchen just after he had returned from his Labor Day trip: "I noticed Doc's playing on the newly-recorded tapes that Ralph Rinzler brought back from the sessions for *Old-Time Music at Clarence Ashley's*. It was in the kitchen of Rinzler's home in Passaic, New Jersey; Ralph was playing the tapes and upon hearing Doc's amazing flatpicking solo on 'Pretty Little Pink,' I asked, 'Who's that incredible guitar player?' Of course that was only my introduction to Doc, whom I soon came to know through Ralph."[23]

Rinzler took note of Grisman's interest and that of others, when they heard Doc on the recordings, and then began including Doc to a greater extent in his larger plan. He recalled: "I considered Ashley and Watson to be on par with The Carter Family and Uncle Dave Macon. My strategy for attracting an urban audience for Ashley and Watson had two parts. The first was to legitimize them by demonstrating the historic links and relationships between the two of them and musicians already acknowledged to be our nation's prime recording artists in their field. The second was to validate the *folkness* of their roots through detailed biographic notes and articles. The strategy was successful and attracted the attention of journalists such as *New York Times* music critic Robert Shelton, and others in similar positions."[2]

Ralph Rinzler also had a plan for the *kind* of music that he thought would be successful within Doc's career. He acted as Doc's agent for nearly a decade, and worked hard to establish his presence as a traditional musician in the folk music scene, though Doc was far more progressive than Rinzler allowed him to show on stage or recording.

Doc remembered in a 1981 interview that Rinzler had worked with him extensively at the beginning of his career so that he would not sing rockabilly or other non-traditional genres. According to Doc, Rinzler said, "Now Doc, the main thing is to emphasize your musical heritage, the good old traditional and ethnic music of this area, until you get your foot in the door, and then you can expand into a lot of other music...The songs will be your own versions, of course, your own emotions…but until you get started, you'll have to really lean on the old-time music because that's what people want to hear."[24]

Mike Seeger also remembered Rinzler's coaching of Doc: "Of course Ralph tried to encourage Doc to do traditional music as much as possible. But he had a great respect for Doc, of course, and friendship, and I think that they both knew one another's beliefs pretty well."[11]

Although Doc did understand the importance of appealing to the New York folk fan base, he later realized that Rinzler had been overly narrow in his pigeon-holing of Doc's career. In a note Rinzler typed up on November 18th, 1989, after listening through parts of a lengthy interview of Doc, he acknowledged that he had given Doc strong advice to stick to purely folk music, and that Doc had struggled under that advice. Rinzler wrote, "He spoke of the tension of his first solo concert at Urbana 1964…But then he said something matter-of-factly, not judgmentally, that at the beginning of his career under my guidance he had abandoned entirely a kind of music that he liked. He didn't say it, but it was obvious to me that it was because it didn't fit into my notion of his repertoire. I encouraged him not to sing songs like 'The Sheik of Araby' because of the narrowness of my conception of folk music based on what the Library of Congress issued, which didn't include pop music."[25] Based on this note that he wrote to himself, Rinzler had finally realized that Doc might not have appreciated how forcefully Rinzler had pushed traditional music on Doc, a very diverse musician.

Ralph Rinzler practiced what he preached. He was simply teaching Doc to be a musician like he was; one who valued traditional music above all else. His work in the 1960s with the Greenbriar Boys was revivalist, and breathed life into older, traditional styles, and in part inspired the young Bob Dylan, Joan Baez, and many other folk-era stars.

Grammy-nominated banjoist Tony Trischka was a big fan of Rinzler and the Greenbriar Boys when he was a teenager. In his words, "They were my heroes. I would just stare at Ralph Rinzler's F5 Mandolin on the cover of the Greenbriar Boys' album *Ragged But Right*. I loved his mandolin playing and his singing. I remember seeing them do a half-time hootenanny at the Syracuse Chargers football game. There were like 40 people in the stands, 20 people for the game and 20 people to see the Greenbriar Boys. That was probably '64, '65, something like that. And I remember we went to a party afterwards and I jammed with them a little bit."[26] Rinzler was an important figure in the burgeoning New York City folk music scene.

Jean Ritchie, the dulcimer-strumming folk singer who had been in the New York folk music scene since the late 1940s, remembered how important Rinzler was in the early 1960s: "He was always doing something; he was always into something in music. He was interested in everything, and at the same time he didn't go on about it. But you could tell that he was deeply interested and he was looking for ways to promote music all the time and help people get started. I think he could realize when he heard people sing whether or not people were going to accept them and like them, and he would push them and get them jobs, and he was really just so much of a help to everybody."[27] Ritchie recalled that Rinzler soon stopped playing with the Greenbriar Boys, devoting his career instead to supporting others: "He didn't sing much. When I knew him, he didn't really perform much at all. And once he left the Greenbriar Boys, he would play at a party or something like that, but he never really performed again."[27]

Rinzler's contribution for the rest of his career was largely unseen by the world, but it was felt in every direction. He worked tirelessly in support of folk music and traditions around the world, and he was instrumental in preserving those traditions. Among other achievements, just before his death, Rinzler secured the Smithsonian Institution's acquisition of Folkways Records, including countless Pete Seeger, Leadbelly and Woody Guthrie recordings. He was also largely responsible for the creation of the vital new record label called Smithsonian-Folkways that would release much of the Folkways material, including the original Ashley/Watson sessions.

Rinzler had an immense impact on the world of folk music in the United States, but his interests did not stop there. He was highly influential in other regions of cultural preservation, and even ran a store in Cambridge, Massachusetts for a time called Country Roads, where he sold traditional arts and crafts.

Peter Rowan, a vocalist and guitarist best known for his lead vocals and guitar in the band Old and in the Way with Jerry Garcia, spoke of Rinzler's great appreciation for tradition, illustrating this appreciation with what he called a *secret story* about Ralph. Rowan came to truly understand the character of his mentor when he vacationed with him off of Cape Cod. Rowan said, "We were out on an island off of Cape Cod where his wife's family had a place. And we went and we visited a woman who was old, and I think she was blind. Her house was all outfitted in the most ancient Cape Cod style. It was full of the wondrousness of the trade in handmade goods and furniture and this and that from days gone by. These older sisters were living together there. I sang a song or two there, and Ralph kind of gave me the eyebrow, like he was saying, 'You're being a little too original.' Soon thereafter, he picked up the banjo as if to say, 'Songs are fine, but this is what I want this lady to hear.' And he sang 'The Fox and the Hounds' or something; one of those real crooked weird old tunes, and he played it on the banjo. And this woman just lit up with the sound. That was Ralph. He truly appreciated tradition."[28]

Ralph Rinzler, the great protector of folk traditions, worked hard for the causes he believed in. In 1963 he became the Field Programs Director for the Newport Folk Foundation, and in 1967, he started the Smithsonian Institution's Festival of American Folklife and became its first director. The Festival of American Folklife is still active today.

Alice Gerrard, a good friend of Ralph Rinzler's, as well as a well-known bluegrass musician, and the long-time editor of the *Old-Time Herald*, remembered Rinzler's first days in Washington: "Ralph was just an amazing person with this huge energy. He was a visionary kind of a person. He loved traditional music, and he really wanted to do something. The festival was one way of doing it and so was his management of Doc Watson and Bill Monroe."[29]

Mike Seeger remembered Rinzler's dedication to his career: "Ralph had rock-solid beliefs in being useful for people's culture. And he worked with Archie Green, who's just recently passed, and basically he and Archie and a small group of like-minded people are the reason that the American Folklife Center is there, and that the National Endowment for the Arts has a folk arts program. And also the Smithsonian, and the National Council for the Traditional Arts, was reinvigorated by these other developments. So it was an amazing time; that all happened in the early '70s."[11] Ralph Rinzler, behind the scenes, pulled thousands of tiny strings that made the continuation of folk traditions into the 21st century possible.

Ralph Rinzler died in 1995 of AIDS. Mike Seeger, who also passed away shortly after his 2009 interview for this book, spoke about his friend Rinzler's early death: "It was a real, real loss when he died. It was very obvious in the last days, by 1990 I would say. But it's really, really sad."[11]

Rinzler's friend George McCeney remembered, "At the end, I didn't know he was as sick as he was. And then just all of a sudden he was gone."[30]

In a touching memorial to Rinzler within his book on Bill Monroe, Richard Smith wrote, "On July 2, 1994, the Festival of American Folklife was in colorful blossom on the Capitol Mall when a colossal thunderclap punctuated the afternoon and rains swept the area. In one performance tent, a Caribbean musician told the jittery audience that in his country, such a heavenly display signified that a great man had died."[5] The reality of Rinzler's death was, however, far more private and personal, and his diagnosis and death from AIDS shocked those who knew him closely. Rinzler was 11 years younger than Doc, and the blind musician was especially heartbroken by the sudden death of his friend Ralph only nine years after losing Merle.

In his last conversation with Rinzler a few days before his death, Doc said, "Well, old friend, if I don't see you anymore here, I'll see you over there."[5]

# CHAPTER NOTES

1. Ward, W.H., *Watson of Deep Gap: A Retrospective*. Appalachian Journal, 1975: p. 102-110.
2. Rinzler, Ralph, *Liner Notes from Bill Monroe and Doc Watson: Live Duet Recordings 1963-1980*, Off the Record Volume 2, Smithsonian/Folkways Recordings, 1993.
3. Watson, Doc, *Letter to Ralph Rinzler "when I talk with you, I feel like I have a place in the world worth bragging about..." January 1963*.
4. Murphy, Joe, *Doc and Merle -The Lives and Music of Doc & Merle Watson (1985)*, VHS, Vestapol, 1996.
5. Smith, Richard, *Can't You Hear Me Callin': The Life of Bill Monroe, Father of Bluegrass*. 2001: Da Capo Press.
6. Rinzler, Ralph, *First draft of Liner Notes for Doc & Clarence album*. 1991, Smithsonian Institution, Ralph Rinzler Folklife Archives: Washington D.C.
7. Cohen, Ronald, *Interview of Ralph Rinzler (transcript)*. 1990, Smithsonian Institution, Ralph Rinzler Folklife Archives: Washington D.C.
8. Gustavson, Kent, *Telephone Interview with Tom Moore*. Oct. 6, 2009.
9. Holt, David, *Liner Notes to Doc Watson and David Holt: Legacy*, High Windy, 2002.
10. Miller, Minnie M., *Tom Clarence Ashley: An Appalachian Folk Musician*. 1973, ClarenceAshley.com: East Tennessee State University.
11. Gustavson, Kent, *Telephone Interview with Mike Seeger*. May 23, 2009.
12. Gustavson, Kent, *Personal Interviews with John Cohen*. April 8 & August 6, 2009.
13. Howard, Clint. *Oft Told Tales*. 2009 11/1/2009 [Last accessed; Available from: http://www.mountainmusicrecording.com/OftToldTales.html.
14. Rinzler, Ralph, *Liner Notes from The Original Folkways Recordings of Doc Watson and Clarence Ashley 1960-1962*, Smithsonian Folkways Records, 1994.
15. Harrington, Richard, *Doc Watson, Strumming Home*. The Washington Post, January 25, 1988. Washington D.C.: p. C1,C8.
16. Wolmuth, Roger, *After Years of Hard Traveling, Mountain Maestro Doc Watson Looks to Find Some Easy Pickin' At Last*. People Weekly, August 10, 1987: p. 57-65.
17. Watson, Doc, *Docabilly*, Audio CD, Sugar Hill, 1995.
18. Watson, Doc and Ralph Rinzler, *The Songs of Doc Watson*. 1971, New York City: Oak Publications.
19. Watson, Nancy E., *A Glimpse of What It's Like to be Part of 'The Watson Family' (liner notes to The Doc Watson Family: Songs fom the Southern Mountains)*, 1994.
20. Metting, Fred, *The Life Work And Music of the American Folk Artist Doc Watson*. 2006: Edwin Mellen Press.
21. Escott, Colin, *Liner Notes to Doc Watson: Songs from Home*, Capitol Nashville, 2002.
22. Rinzler, Ralph, *Letter to Dr. Lawrence J. Wheeler Regarding North Carolina Award: May 8, 1984*.
23. Gustavson, Kent, *Email Interview with David Grisman*. March 25, 2009.
24. Stewart, Jean, *A Conversation with Doc Watson*. Sing Out!, January/February 1981. 29(1).
25. Rinzler, Ralph, *Notes on Omnibus Interview*. 1989, Smithsonian Institution, Ralph Rinzler Folklife Archives.
26. Gustavson, Kent, *Telephone Interview with Tony Trischka*. April 27, 2009.
27. Gustavson, Kent, *Telephone Interview with Jean Ritchie*. May 6, 2009.
28. Gustavson, Kent, *Telephone Interview with Peter Rowan*. June 1, 2009.
29. Gustavson, Kent, *Telephone Interview with Alice Gerrard*. June 2, 2009.
30. Gustavson, Kent, *Telephone Interview with Annie Bird*. April 24, 2009.

# CHAPTER TEN
## The Watson Family

*"I remember sitting around the living room and listening to his family sing the most wonderful hymns and songs, as various people played various instruments. And I was just soaking it all up. And I would look up, and down the stairs would come creeping two kids who were supposed to be in bed. I remember Merle in his blue seersucker pajamas. And then his little sister Nancy with her little glasses in her little flannel nighty sneaking down behind him. And they were just peering through the railing, sitting on the top stair. They saw that I saw them, you know, and they were going kind of like, 'Shh, don't tell.' It was like they couldn't bear to be in bed when all this music was going on, and there was company from up north and all that going on."*

- Maria Muldaur[1]

Something about Doc Watson's second record with Folkways in 1963, *The Watson Family*, has kept Doc Watson fans enthralled for generations. The album's popularity is due not to fast licks and smooth sounds, but rather its intimate portrait of Doc Watson's family. The listener is transported into Doc's extraordinary world through field recording-like scratchy breakdowns, ballads and hymns. But the content is not raw; the songs are anchored by Doc's rock-solid bass harmony and metronomic rhythm. Little did Doc or his family members dream of the wide audience that would eventually listen to the performances they recorded in the simplicity of the Watson home in Deep Gap.

In 1963, *New York Times* reporter Robert Shelton spoke about the interest that had already grown up around Doc Watson because of his records. Shelton wrote, "One Southern mountaineer, Arthel (Doc) Watson, has in the last two years become almost the object of a cult among city folk fans. Watson is a featured performer on the recent album *The Watson Family*...and the earlier *Old Time Music at Clarence Ashley's...* Both give a hint, if only that, of why Doc Watson is being lionized for his guitar playing and singing."[2]

Rinzler waxed eloquently in the liner notes to *The Watson Family*: "The smell of wood smoke on the clear mountain air, the crackle of leaves and twigs under foot, the sound of a Sunday evening hymn sing drifting across the valley – all are among the treasures of Doc's childhood and present life. His love of these treasures of country life, his understanding of the people who surround him and their distinctiveness...all these pour out in his speech; no difference if he sits before thirteen thousand at the Newport Folk Festival or in the company of a few friends in New York, Chicago or Los Angeles."[3]

Every musician who listened to *The Watson Family* record not only saw a window into the Watson family's musical tradition; they also felt connected to the family. Others felt a desire to have a family and/or lifestyle like the one they heard on the album.

Abigail Washburn, the singer-songwriter best known for her work with the band Uncle Earl, talked about her own desire to want to *be like* Doc: "I kind of resented my upbringing, which of course my parents worked so hard to give me. I had a comfortable upbringing in the suburbs, in a nice house, with our own little plot of land, our own lawnmowers, and the ability to go to McDonald's and Roy Rogers whenever we wanted... I was surrounded by strip malls, and I went to fine public schools, and my parents worked really hard to give that to me. I went off to college, and I resented being a product of this modern, contemporary age of living in suburbia on these little plots of land and isolated from each other and from anything other than mainstream culture. So I felt really envious of what Doc is, and I wanted to be a piece of that. I wanted to have that kind of earnest tradition be a part of my life, rather than this socio-economic longing for something better. Doc came along, and all of a sudden...at first I wanted to be able to be the kind of things that Doc is. But of course I can't. I can learn great lessons from Doc, but one of the lessons that came along as a result of wanting to be like Doc, was that...being from suburbia and having the influences that I have is just as cool as Doc Watson is, for everything that he is. And I started to appreciate just exactly what I am because everything Doc is, is so right."[4]

Washburn's desire to be like Doc turned her towards finding her *own* true identity and her own musical styles. In others, however, the desire turned them directly towards Deep Gap, North Carolina, where they would wander around knocking on doors until they found Doc's family home.

Vermont guitarist Paul Asbell recalled making a pilgrimage to Doc Watson's home as a kid: "My dad knew that I was really gaga over this guy, and he was doing a magazine article about a guy named Billy Barnes who worked in Asheville, North Carolina, during one of the very early Lyndon Johnson War on Poverty programs. At any rate, my dad would be driving down to North Carolina in the summer of 1964, and he basically said to me, 'Paul, I'd love to have you come for the trip. We'll be gone for about four days...' So it was half a day of driving and he didn't tell me where we were going, but he dangled these little hints. And finally, we were driving on this honky little dirt road and I'm just thinking, 'What the hell?' And then he pointed to a sign, and he said, 'Do you see that sign there?' And this tiny little sign said, 'Welcome to Deep Gap.' I said, 'Deep Gap? Dad! This is where Doc Watson lives!' He said, 'I know, and we're going to drive up to his house and we're going to have him sign your record.'"[5]

Asbell recalled, "I have to say, Doc was not enormously welcoming, but I think he must have had ambivalences about the whole thing in a way. But he signed it, and I still have that record. We didn't spend more than maybe 15 or 20 minutes there. I think my dad would have loved it if we'd have been able to spend an hour, but that wasn't really in the cards. But you know, Doc was gracious enough about signing the album."[5]

When it was not music fans visiting Doc to get his autograph, musicians came down to visit him and play a few tunes. Alice Gerrard remembered visiting the Watson family with Ralph Rinzler in the 1960s: "We went down there and visited Doc and Rosa Lee, and that was when I think Gaither was still alive. And it was just amazing, that visit. Doc's family was totally friendly. And I remember there was lots of music played, and singing, and Ralph might have been recording stuff, too."[6]

Maria Muldaur described the food that Rosa Lee served in such a way as to start even the weakest taste buds salivating: "The thing I remember most was her breakfast, which happened very early in the morning. Honest to God there were fresh-made biscuits with amazing butter, blackberry preserves, wonderfully fresh eggs, and biscuits with sausage gravy, and then there were sausage patties. It was breakfast beyond what a little Italian girl from New York City would ever have dreamed a breakfast could be. And she just whipped this up every morning on the stove. And for lunch and dinner, there would be some of her canned string beans, or whatever the vegetables were that came out of her spring house, and it was just amazing."[1]

George McCeney recalled visiting Doc in 1963, when Doc's 14-year old son Merle was courting his future wife: "I remember Merle went courting one night when we were there. Doc and Rosa Lee went over to these people's home." He described the teenage boy further: "Merle kept kind of to himself. I wouldn't say he was an unhappy kid, but he impressed me as sort of solitary. He wasn't really interested in what his father was doing and all that." In fact, McCeney remembered vividly Merle's current musical fad was not a guitar, but a drum set: "Merle was playing the drums at that point. I remember his drum set really well. It was painted speckled blue. And he would wail away on those things, and I thought, 'My God, Doc must really love his children.' I mean he was a horrible drum player!" He also recalled little Nancy, who was "just a really cute gal then," and who certainly did not cause many ripples for her parents.[7]

Maria Muldaur was moved by her visit: "These were people living such a pure lifestyle. They were just so naturally spiritual as opposed to religious in some phony way. Their faith was very real, very natural. They were so grounded in their environment. They were living within their means. Growing their own food. This was way before it became fashionable to grow organic food."[1] In the Watson home, she was surrounded by the blanket of tradition, and when they would sing, she was amazed: "Just to hear the music seemed quite exotic to us. We listened to it in New York on the scratched up 78's, but to see that music completely integrated into the lives of people, being a natural expression of their lives, that just brought so much richness and depth to my love of this kind of music. I've pursued it ever since."[1]

Annie Bird recalled her first trip down to visit Doc and his family along with Maria Muldaur, "We went to visit Doc in North Carolina, and they wanted us to go over to Gaither's house. So of course it was across the mountain or something, I don't know. We were just taking hairpin turns and everything else. And we had to walk up the side of a mountain, and they kept saying, 'Oh, watch out for the rattlesnakes.' I wasn't too happy about that, but then we finally got there and he had a piano way up there… And finally we got back, and Doc Watson was mad. He was really upset because he was afraid that we had been killed on the road. He's kind of an…he had anxiety about it, you know, thinking that we were kind of stupid city people."[8] Doc was concerned about his guests, knowing that it was just as complicated to get around the mountains for city people as it might have been for him to navigate New York as a country boy.

Bird was excited to see Doc and Gaither again, because they had stayed with her at her apartment in New York, and the trio had become friends. But even having met Doc and Gaither prior to her arrival in Deep Gap, Bird recalled that she was unprepared to see the world that Doc lived in. Doc was still living in poverty in 1961, supported by State Aid to the Blind, not yet earning a living from music. She recalled, "Of course we never thought that he was living like a poor person and we should have been bringing food and stuff like that, because that wasn't exactly in our vocabulary then. We weren't too sensitive. I think after a few times like that, Doc kind of put the *kibosh* on that kind of thing. He said he couldn't support everybody coming down there."[8]

In a 1968 interview, Rosa Lee spoke about the frequent guests they had received over the past 7 years since the first concert in New York City: "We enjoy them all, except for the beatniks… They make you nervous because they ask all those questions you don't understand. But we don't want to hurt their feelings."[9]

Doc and Rosa Lee always did their best to be good hosts to friends and pilgrims alike. In the early years of Doc's career, though the young couple had little, their family life was rich, and all of Doc and Rosa Lee's friends and relatives would come to see the northerners, and they would often make music while the children played games outside until it got dark on the mountain.

From the beginning of Doc's career, his family was in the spotlight along with him. On *The Watson Family* LP, just about every member of Doc's family sang or played. They later joined him on stage at the Newport Folk Festival in 1963, and Gaither had accompanied Doc to New York in 1961. And of course, Merle later accompanied his father for two decades on the road.

Doc had eight siblings, and Arnold was the oldest, born on the first day of 1912. His brothers Otis, Jerome and Linney, respectively, were all spaced every two years after that. In 1921, General and Annie's first daughter Ruby was born, and two years later, along came Doc. His brother David was two years younger, his sister Jewel was four years younger, and his youngest sister, Ethel was born 11 years after Doc, when Annie was 39 years old. Doc's cousin Willard was also close to the family, and was like an uncle to Doc. He was born 18 years before Doc, in 1905.

Willard would always show up in later years if guests arrived from somewhere out of town, much to the delight of Peter Rowan years later, who recalled

Doc's older cousin's profane sense of humor: "Willard Watson was a tremendous guy. He made the little toys that kind of, fornicated. Wooden fornication. Guys [screwing] mules. He had a great sense of humor, man."[10]

In 1961, the year that Doc first played a concert in New York City, his father turned 70 years old and his mother Annie was four years younger. She participated in a number of concerts and a few recording sessions through the years. At the Newport Folk Festival in 1964, Doc proudly announced her from stage: "I'd like to introduce...a lady that's milked more cows and rocked as many babies as anybody in the audience, I guess. My mother, Mrs. General Dixon Watson."[11]

Many of Doc's admirers feel that his career did not begin in 1961 in New York City, and it did not begin with *Old Time Music at Clarence Ashley's*, released the same year. The Ashley record probably had a circulation of only a few hundred, and the concert in New York was only held in an elementary school in Greenwich Village. The Newport Folk Festival in 1963 brought Doc to a larger audience than ever before. Even young Bob Dylan was rumored to have been secretly holding hands and talking with Joan Baez at the back of the Doc Watson concert during the '63 Festival. Doc spoke about the festival in an interview with Jon Sievert: "That Newport Festival was something... We'd go on stage and 8 to 10,000 people would go dead quiet and listen to the music. Man, you couldn't believe the ovations... You knew the people were there to hear the roots of their music."[12]

Tony Trischka was a big fan of Bob Dylan as a teenager, and went to the Newport Folk Festival in 1963 to see his hero perform. That is when he, and thousands of others, first happened upon Doc Watson. According to Tony: "I remember seeing Doc at the Newport Folk Festival in 1963... It seems to me that, for most people, that festival was when Doc really hit it. That festival was the first time anyone heard him play 'Black Mountain Rag,' or 'Doc's Guitar.' People were just like, 'Where did this guy come from?' It was amazing. He sort of set the whole folk world on its ear, I think, at that point. Again, people in the know were aware of *The Watson Family* record, I suppose, but for your average listener, which I was at that point, that was the first anyone had heard of him."[13]

The concert so inspired Trischka that he went home and started learning "Doc's Guitar" and "Black Mountain Rag" on his guitar. Trischka, known around the world for his virtuosic and beautiful banjo playing, still plays a little guitar, thanks to Doc: "I can still only play about five things on the guitar, and 'Deep River Blues,' 'Doc's Guitar,' and 'Black Mountain Rag' are in that number."[13]

In a contract dated July 26th, 1963, Doc allowed Vanguard to record all of his performances at the Newport Festival from July 26th to 28th. The release showed that Doc would get a sum of $50 for each solo performance released by Vanguard.[14] After the incredible success of Doc's performances at the festival, Rinzler had little trouble negotiating with Maynard Solomon, the head of Vanguard who had at first passed on *The Watson Family*, and within a year, Doc recorded his first album for the record label.

## CHAPTER NOTES

1.     Gustavson, Kent, *Telephone Interview with Maria Muldaur*. April 1, 2009.
2.     Shelton, Robert, *Bountiful Area: Southern Highlands a Bottomless Well For Recordings of Folk Music*. New York Times, June 2, 1963. New York: p. 126.
3.     Rinzler, Ralph, *Liner Notes to Doc Watson*, Vanguard Records, 1964.
4.     Gustavson, Kent, *Telephone Interview with Abigail Washburn*. June 8, 2009.
5.     Gustavson, Kent, *Telephone Interview with Paul Asbell*. March 16, 2009.
6.     Gustavson, Kent, *Telephone Interview with Alice Gerrard*. June 2, 2009.
7.     Gustavson, Kent, *Telephone Interview with George McCeney*. May 22, 2009.
8.     Gustavson, Kent, *Telephone Interview with Annie Bird*. April 24, 2009.
9.     Wren, Christopher S., *Doc Watson: Musicmaker from Appalachia*. Look, 1968: p. M6,M8.
10.    Gustavson, Kent, *Telephone Interview with Peter Rowan*. June 1, 2009.
11.    Watson, Doc, *Treasures Untold*, Audio CD, Vanguard Records, 1964.
12.    Sievert, Jon, *Doc Watson: 'Like Some Kind of Fine'*. Frets, March 1979. 1(1): p. 20-26.
13.    Gustavson, Kent, *Telephone Interview with Tony Trischka*. April 27, 2009.
14.    *Contract to Record at Newport Folk Festival July 26-28 1963*, Smithsonian Institution, Ralph Rinzler Folklife Archives.

Photo by John Cohen ©
*Doc's older brother Arnold at a house party near Deep Gap in the early 1960s.*

Photo by Mark Reid ©
*Doc Watson onstage in the 1970s.*

# CHAPTER ELEVEN
## The Friends of Old Time Music

*"I'm really a mountain country boy... I sure was green when
I went to the city... Lord, I was scared to death."*
- Doc Watson[1]

W hen Doc Watson stepped off of a Greyhound bus in New York
City in mid-March 1961 only weeks after his 38th birthday, he had
little idea that he was starting a professional career that would take
him across four continents and millions of miles on the road. In fact, this was by
far the furthest away from Deep Gap he had ever been, and stepping off the bus
into Manhattan felt like visiting another planet. He was grateful to have his
father-in-law Gaither with him to help navigate. He never would have guessed
that just over a year later he would make the same trip all by himself.

John Cohen was with Ralph Rinzler when the bus that was meant to be delivering Clarence Ashley arrived from North Carolina: "From what I can remember,
we went to the Port Authority bus station, and a bus came in. All of a sudden, we
were saying, 'Oh, here's Clarence Ashley...Who's this guy? Who's that guy?
And who's this blind man?' They were leading Doc off the bus... It was
Clarence Ashley, Clint Howard, Fred Price, Doc Watson and Gaither Carlton.
Five of them. And what do you do with five guys in New York? Where are they
going to stay?... There was a woman who sang on the concert, Annie Bird, and
her boyfriend was a guy named Dave Levy. The two of them had an apartment
up on the Upper West Side on the edge of Harlem, pretty high up."[2] Maria
Muldaur remembered: "Unlike most of us who were living in tiny little cold
water flats in Greenwich Village or Little Italy, Annie lived in a real *grown up*
apartment with an extra bedroom, somewhere on the Upper West Side."[3]

Annie Bird recalled the visit: "It was just Doc and his father-in-law Gaither
Carlton; they both stayed at my house. I can't remember why I was asked.
Probably because I had an apartment with spare bedrooms, and I was involved
with the group that was going to sing."[4]

Maria Muldaur was good friends with Annie Bird: "Annie was the genuine article. She was from Virginia and played auto harp, and sang. She had a boyfriend

named David Levy, who played passable rhythm guitar. And she knew every Carter Family tune. Every Monday night people would go to Gerde's Folk City, and that would be *hootenanny night* back in those days. And there'd be anyone... Dylan was there; that's where I first met Taj Mahal. And then the old guard; people like Josh Logan, Peter La Farge, and Cisco Houston, all of the guys that had hung with Woody Guthrie and been part of the social protesting of the '40s and '50s, from the days of The Weavers, Pete Seeger and so forth. I met Annie first at Gerde's, and we took a liking to each another and hooked up, and decided to have a Carter Family duet together. I played the fiddle, and also strummed out some real rudimentary guitar, and we learned tunes together."[3]

Annie Bird recalled her housegues Doc's sensitive stomach: "The funny part about the time when Doc and Gaither stayed at my home was I thought I'd just cook southern, you know, and have corn bread and beans and all that kind of stuff. But when Doc got out there, he said, 'Oh, I can't eat that; it gives me heartburn,' or something. I forget what he said exactly. So I had to kind of go and make a steak dinner or something, I can't remember what I did. It was pretty funny. Never heard of anybody from the south that didn't eat cornbread and beans. We'd all eat that. I still do to this day. That was really...I was shocked! I thought, 'What am I supposed to do? What's my next act here?' Fortunately I had other things I made, but after that I was pretty careful. I mean, Gaither had to be there, because Doc was blind, of course, and he needed help, you know, getting around the apartment and stuff like that."[4]

As well as playing wonderful duets with Doc in the course of the upcoming PS 41 concert, Gaither Carlton was also Doc's guide in the strange city. On future visits to New York, Ralph Rinzler would arrange to have young musicians take Doc around when he or a friend could not. David Grisman recalled being one of Rinzler's such assistants for several of Doc's visits to New York: "I became friends with Doc during his many early trips to New York. I would help him get around the city and hang out with him as one of Ralph's willing assistants."[5] But on this first visit, Rinzler and Cohen worked hard themselves to keep their guests comfortable.

John Cohen recalled an amusing story about the group and their taste for a certain brand of tobacco: "Either Clint Howard or Fred Price would send me out to get a few things for them, and besides sandwiches, one of them would ask me, 'Would you get us such-and-such brand chewing tobacco?'"[2] Cohen had no idea where to find that certain brand of tobacco, but he said he would try, and as he recalled, "Fortunately we were on the edge of Harlem. The first little grocery store I walked into, I asked for that brand of chewing tobacco and they had it."[2] Cohen was highly amused that the kind of chewing tobacco they preferred was only available in the "impoverished part of New York City."[2]

Mike Seeger, Ralph Rinzler and John Cohen all spent a great deal of time at Annie Bird's apartment during Doc and Gaither's, preparing songs with Clarence Ashley and his band; helping them map out the repertoire they thought the New York audience would enjoy.

Seeger remembered recording the group: "[The musicians from North Carolina] came to New York City several days early, and Ralph wanted me to record them. And I think we had a hard time recording; I didn't have a decent recording machine. I think we had to borrow something. As I recall, we just gathered people around the microphone as well as we could, and recorded them in what seemed like a fairly normal New York apartment. It wasn't as small as some of the downtown apartments are, though."[6] To help absorb unwanted noise, they hung up blankets around the recording area.

Cohen also described the sessions: "For three or four days, maybe more, in preparation for this concert, we spent time with [the five southern musicians] at Annie Bird's apartment. We went through their entire repertoire, or as much as we could. 'Let's use this in the concert,' 'Let's not.' And so on. We knew the tunes, between Ralph and myself, and Mike was there as well." Cohen recalled that it was quite an interactive process between the northern folk musicians and this southern group that had only played together a few times. They knew certain tunes, and they listened to records to recall others. Then the northerners would give their opinions as to which songs they should use, and what instrumentations and arrangements to try. Cohen said, "They would throw out tunes for us to listen to, and we would respond to certain ones more than others." Cohen remembered that the mood was relaxed: "If they were nervous, you couldn't tell."[2]

By the time Doc Watson stepped off the bus into New York City, folk music had been well rooted in Greenwich Village for nearly two decades, since the end of the Second World War.

The two main centers of folk music activity in the "Village" (as Greenwich Village is known to New Yorkers), were The Folklore Center, which was located on MacDougal Street, and Washington Square Park, a city park with a fountain in the center, surrounded by the campus of New York University. Throngs of young folk musicians and folk music enthusiasts from children to advanced players, stood, walked and sat all around Washington Square on Sunday afternoons, playing instruments of every size and shape. Additionally, at Israel (Izzy)

Young's Folklore Center were rooms filled with books, records, and acoustic instruments, and musicians would congregate and play music, talk about music, and make connections.

John Cohen recalled the New York City folk music environment in the early 1960s: "The scene around Washington Square and the scene around Folklore Center *was* the scene. It was the scene from which the folk music movement emerged. It was also the same scene that attracted Tom Paxton and Bob Dylan and folks to come to New York. There was something happening there. There were a lot of NYU students at Washington Square: David Grisman among them, and Maria Muldaur, a Village kid."[2]

Maria Muldaur remembered, "Every Sunday in Washington Square Park you could walk around the big fountain there in the middle of the park. There'd be clumps and clusters of bluegrass musicians and old-timey musicians, there'd be Italian guys playing mandolins and singing... There'd be blues-picking people; delta blues, ragtime blues. I mean, it was wonderful, and you just walked around it like a rotating hootenanny. People would stop playing with one bunch of people and go over and start playing with another bunch of people. It became fascinating for me right about my senior year of high school in 1959."[3]

Muldaur, like so many other folk musicians, met the members of her first band around the fountain at Washington Square: "In 1962 I ran into a young mandolin player in Washington Square Park one day named David Grisman. His mom was still bringing him from New Jersey to the park to play, and we formed a group called Maria and the Washington Square Ramblers. We actually got a little gig every Sunday at a funny Italian restaurant on Long Island whose owners had decided that folk music was the new biggest thing, and they wanted to present what they called 'folk music' to draw people into the restaurant. Wow! Our first paying gig!"[3]

The Village music scene was wonderful for folk musicians at any level, because professional players hung around in the same circles as amateurs. Southern musicians would mix with northern, white with black, and rich with poor.

Tom Paxton, who was a young folk singer from Oklahoma at the time, recalled: "Washington Square was a big deal. All around the fountain there'd be people either standing or sitting on the fountain playing different kinds of music... You'd go around and you'd hear Jimmy Rodgers songs on the autoharp or you'd hear some Israeli folksongs going on, or you'd hear a bluegrass group, or a blues singer, or someone singing God knows what. It was a *smorgasbord*."[7]

Jean Ritchie, southern singer and dulcimer player, went with her young family each Sunday to the park: "We used to live on Bleeker Street and 7th Avenue

South and we'd walk over to the park and sing every Sunday. I had a baby in a carriage, so I never sat down and played a dulcimer or anything, and I never was really photographed as one of the people to come and hear, but we were very much a part of the Village and we all saw each other get started."[8] Jean Ritchie had of course been singing traditional Appalachian music in the New York City music scene for a decade by the time Doc set foot in Manhattan, and she released her 14th album in 1961.

The Village was a great draw for folksingers from around the country, and soon overflowed with eager young musicians, hoping to see Woody Guthrie, Bob Dylan or Pete Seeger, happy to live in relative poverty and participate in the liberal, artistic, melting pot of culture that hovered around Washington Square. Maria Muldaur was luckier than most: "I ran away from home right about then, and since I lived in the Village, I didn't see the need of running more than six blocks away."[3]

John Cohen and Ralph Rinzler reveled in the diversity of the music around them, and both participated heavily in the folk music scene heavily in the early 1960s. They had also led and taken part in hootenannies for many years by the time the Friends of Old Time Music came about.

The word *hootenanny* was originally a nonsense word, used in the Appalachian Mountain region to mean something like *whatchamacallit* – when someone did not know the name for something. Pete Seeger has said in several interviews that he first heard the word in the 1930s on the west coast, and he was part of the small group of musicians who adopted the word as a name for their rent parties in New York. In a 1959 *New York Times* article, Seeger told interviewer John S. Wilson that hootenannies had been around for 18 years, and had originated as "afternoon rent parties" hosted by the Almanac Singers.[9] When any member of the New York folk singing community was short on rent (which was apparently a very common occurrence), they would have big music parties where everyone would come and play and sing for hours on end.

Jean Ritchie recalled: "Somebody would have a loft that they lived in and they wanted to make money to pay their rent, so they'd invite everybody in and pass the hat. Then they'd all sit around and sing, and then they'd pass the hat again. And because nobody had any money, people would only give them a little, but it would amount up to enough to pay their rent. That's how that kind of thing started."[8]

Maria Muldaur also spoke about hootenannies in New York: "I remember hootenannies on Saturday night at some YMCA on 23rd Street. You'd look around in a circle, and there'd be Pete Seeger, Odetta, Johnny Herald, and a handful of old-time musicians... There was just a potpourri of different factions of folk music. There were the disciples of Woody Guthrie who picked up guitars to mostly get across a message or a social commentary. Bob Dylan hit the scene about that time as well. And then there were the Clancey Brothers singing pure Irish music in there. And then there were a huge number of beautiful girls strumming nylon string guitars, singing English ballads and other songs they'd written themselves, songs that to this day I call 'Dear Diary' music. People of all kinds would come together, and parties would spontaneously happen, and jams, hootenannies, whatever you want to call them."[3]

Many times as part of the larger hootenannies, well-known musicians would perform their music, and it would be an event not unlike a music festival in later years. But it was not common for traditional musicians such as Clarence Ashley to participate in these events until Pete Seeger and a few others featured such musicians within their own concerts. John Cohen remembered another performer to do that: "There was a wonderful guy named Frank Warner, who was something of a good collector. I remember going to some of his concerts, and he would hold up a photograph of the person he learned the song from and talk a little bit about them."[2]

Once they had spent some time in the south, listening to true southern and Appalachian musicians, Cohen and Rinzler wanted to transmit the music to the public unfiltered. They wanted to see what would happen if traditional musicians were to sing on stage by themselves, instead of Pete Seeger or another folk "musician having to be there to *interpret* the song for a northern audience.

Cohen explained: "The need to feature traditional musicians was there long before The Friends of Old Time Music started."[2] Cohen believed that he and Rinzler could help to fulfill that need, and indeed they did. Cohen remembered, "This kind of concert had never been done before."[2]

When John Cohen was nearly 18 years old, the seed for the Friends of Old Time Music was first planted within his mind. He remembered being at the memorial concert for Leadbelly in Town Hall at midnight of January 28, 1950. The concert had been paid for by the Leadbelly Memorial Concert Committee and was headed by Alan Lomax, the American folklorist and field collector, as part of his Folk Music at Midnight series in Carnegie Hall. Many musicians played their music that night to pay tribute to their old friend, including Brownie McGhee, Pete Seeger and Woody Guthrie, as well as jazz musicians Sidney Bechet and W.C. Handy.

John Cohen remembered the concert very well: "The Weavers were there; that was the first time I'd seen them, and Oscar Brand. Woody Guthrie was there, and he was playing with this young guy Tom Paley; that was the first time I'd seen Tom." Of course, Paley later became Cohen's good friend and musical partner at Yale, leading the hootenannies with him, eventually creating the New Lost City Ramblers with him and Mike Seeger. Cohen continued, "And actually, another incredible moment was between the first half and the second half, they brought this blind man out who played two songs, and then left. And I couldn't believe what I was hearing; it was Reverend Gary Davis. But they didn't say anything about him. There was nothing in the program about him. And of course I didn't know what I was hearing, but eventually I pursued him and made recordings of him."[2] Although it is now very common for traditional musicians to have their own concerts, and to even put out their own recordings, it was highly uncommon in the 1950s, and this appearance by Reverend Gary Davis was remarkable for young Cohen.

In December of 1960, only three months before Doc Watson first came to New York City, and three months after Rinzler had returned from recording Ashley the first time in Tennessee, Cohen and Rinzler thought up the Friends of Old Time Music series.

Cohen recalled, "In December 1960, the New Lost City Ramblers did a concert at 13 Astor Place and our guest was Elizabeth Cotton."[2] Elizabeth Cotton had, of course, been a maid for the Seeger family. While Mike, Peggy and Penny were growing up, she became very close to the musical children, and she revealed to them that she had played guitar decades earlier. Young Mike began to record her on his tape recorder for the first time in the late 1950s, and he began to do concerts with her in 1960. This concert in New York was one of the first at which she had ever performed. Cotton was incredibly well received, but she was just an opening act or guest with the Ramblers. Cohen and Rinzler had a discussion a few days later about what would happen were she able to headline a concert with only her music, without the support of the Ramblers.

Mike Seeger recalled that the idea behind the Friends of Old Time Music concerts was to "get the traditional musicians themselves heard. This was a new idea then. Prior to that time, everybody in the city thought that, or nearly everybody, thought that there needed to be an interpreter and they had to interpret this kind of music for city people to take it."[6] Seeger was taken with Rinzler and Cohen's idea: "In the early '60s, we learned…that people didn't need any help at all; people loved them the way they were. That was major, and the Friends of Old Time Music had a big part, and Ralph had a major role in that mission."[6]

John Cohen recalled the first discussion he had with Rinzler about the Friends of Old Time Music concept: "A few days after the concert with Elizabeth Cotton, Ralph came over to my loft, which was right nearby, near Cooper Union, and he said, 'Wasn't that wonderful? Don't you think we should be able to put on concerts just out of the traditional musicians? Even without you guys serving as the introducers?'"[2] Cohen knew immediately where Rinzler was going with this. He responded, "Oh, yeah, that makes sense, how can we do that?"[2]

Rinzler was always the one with a mind for details; as Cohen remembered, Rinzler spoke in clauses and sub-clauses. He knew how to get things in order, and how to put spin on it. That helped him later do a great deal of incredible non-profit work. He also had excellent connections. Rinzler continued planning out loud: "Well, let's see. Izzy puts on concerts, he can get a hall and do publicity, and people can buy tickets at the Folklore Center."[2] Of course, he was referring to Israel Young, the owner of the Folklore Center, who had his finger on the pulse of the Village folk music scene. Cohen recalled that Rinzler then went immediately into action, and said, "Maybe we could get a non-profit status,"[2] and "Where can we find a hall?"[2]

That same night, they even discussed a name for their budding non-profit organization: "I think Ralph told me that, at the Library of Congress, they had something called 'The Friends of Music.' So I said, 'Yeah, well, we could call our organization 'The Friends of Old Time Music.' That would be good.'"[2]

Because Rinzler had trouble getting "Friends of Old Time Music" as a legal name, Cohen remembered telling Rinzler, "All right, look, that'll be like our logo."[2] Of course, it was certainly not easy for Rinzler to put the non-profit together, but nevertheless, he put it through in record time.

As part of starting up the non-profit corporation, Rinzler had to choose a board of directors. The members of the board included Cohen, Rinzler, Jean Ritchie, Izzy Young and Margot Mayo, who had founded the American Square Dance Group in New York City, and was very involved in the folk revival movement. Rinzler had, of course, strategically chosen each of the members for their various interests and connections.

Mere weeks after obtaining the non-profit status, and only three months after that day he and Cohen had first discussed the possibility, Rinzler and Cohen started the wheels turning towards the first concert of the Friends of Old Time Music.

In addition to having a good following, and many friends in the folk music world at the time, board member Jean Ritchie also had a nice house. Many of the meetings meetings in which the Friends of Old Time Music discussed future concerts took place at her home in Port Washington, just east of New York City on Long Island. She recalled: "At the meetings, they would mostly just talk; planning who would come, and about who was going to do what, and who was going to ask to do what, and so on. I didn't work too hard on the Friends of Old Time Music, I really didn't. All I did was to provide a place to meet, and of course I was interested in it."[8]

Cohen and Rinzler knew that if they pooled their resources and connections, they would easily be able to arrange a few concerts that would feature old-time musicians, a concept that excited both of them, especially since each of them was grooming a traditional musician for the public stage. Rinzler had Clarence Ashley in mind for the concert series, and Cohen immediately thought of Kentucky musician Roscoe Holcomb, whom he had discovered and recorded in 1959.

John Cohen had taken Holcomb under his wing, and was deeply inspired by Holcomb's workman hands playing both banjo and guitar, and his "high lonesome sound," a term that was coined by Cohen in attempting to explain Holcomb's incredible singing. Holcomb was later a large influence on Bob Dylan among countless others who heard his music. In a conversation with John Cohen for *Sing Out!* magazine, Dylan said that Holcomb's music had "an untamed sense of control."[10]

In the same way that Holcomb had great freedom within his music, Clarence Ashley had a carefree nature to his humor and personality. He was immediately at home in front of an audience, and was able to entertain with his old-time humor in a way that was fascinating to admirers of the folk movement. However, Ashley did not express Rinzler's ideology behind traditional music as well as Holcomb expressed Cohen's.

John Cohen believed that Roscoe Holcomb's music was beautiful precisely because it came from the hands of a man who had worked his whole life. Ashley's music, on the other hand, was largely contrived, and was part of a show put on for the audience. Ashley did not show his true personality very often on stage, unless he sang a solemn-faced hymn with the rest of the musicians present. Nevertheless, Ashley was the find of a lifetime, because in Rinzler's circle of friends and colleagues, the *Anthology of American Folk Music* was extremely popular. Yet it was Doc Watson who would later be the pearl in Rinzler's oyster shell: an unexpected treasure. Rinzler would soon find that Doc's humility, humor, hard work, and incredible musicianship met his own ideal of what a traditional musician should be. He also loved the softness of Doc's voice and personality, just as Cohen craved the high lonesome sound that Holcomb so embodied.

The first Friends of Old Time Music concert took place on Saturday night, February 11th, 1961 in the auditorium of PS 41, an elementary school in Greenwich Village. The tickets sold for $1.50, and were available from the Folklore Center. The concert nearly sold out. Cohen remembered: "The hall was pretty packed, considering that we had no mailing list. We had to do it through word of mouth, and little posters."[2]

Cohen recalled designing the posters in preparation for the concert: "I did all the posters one letter at a time, with press type," and then he and Rinzler printed them, and Izzy Young handed them out at the Folklore Center. Cohen continued: "We didn't have any budget. I mean, I spent some money to print them, 500 or 1000 copies, whatever it was. But since we didn't have a mailing list...it was only the Folklore Center where you could hand them out, and Washington Square. And then word of mouth."[2]

PS 41 stands on 11th Street and the Avenue of the Americas, in Greenwich Village. It is an elementary school for children from kindergarten through fifth grade, and it has a wall of windows along its front. PS 41 was originally built in 1867, and remodeled in 1957, only four years before the Friends of Old Time Music concert series used its auditorium. John Cohen remembered the hall: "It was a nice little auditorium. I was amazed that we were able to get it so cheaply, and that's because we were non-profit."[2]

The first two concerts of the Friends of Old Time Music in New York not only introduced two obscure musicians to the northern stage, they also very much embodied the musical philosophies of two close friends, both of them passionate enough to devote their entire lives to traditional music and art.

**The Friends of Old Time Music**
**present**

# ● CLARENCE ASHLEY ●

### Country recording star of the 1920s & '30s

**GAITHER CARLTON**......fiddle
**FRED PRICE** ...............fiddle
**CLINT HOWARD** ..........guitar
**DOC WATSON** .............banjo

### Farmers & musicians of Tennessee & North Carolina

# &

# ANNE BIRD

## SAT. MARCH 25, 1961

John Cohen talked about the organization of that first concert, "The first concert was a miracle. Somebody pointed out recently that [around the] end of December...we had our first meeting, and by the second week of February we had our first concert. Roscoe Holcomb was the first. And the way we got people in was that Jean Ritchie and the Greenbriar Boys and the Ramblers would play... Roscoe was totally unknown, so our following - people who knew us - would hopefully come to this and then be exposed to him."[2]

Maria Muldaur recalled her first impression of the Friends of Old Time Music concert series: "Ralph Rinzler and John Cohen started going to the rural south, where they were discovering that a lot of these people, who to us were these mythical mystical mysterious voices from some misty past on these scratchy 78s that were put on Folkways record compilations, were actually quite alive and well, playing on their back porch somewhere in North Carolina or Alabama or wherever. They started to bring them up north to do concerts."[3]

The concerts took the folk scene by storm, and were the talk of the town. And the musicians from distant states who came to perform in the concerts would also interact with local musicians during the day at the Folklore Center and on Washington Square. The concert series was more than just the performance. It was an experience for the entire community.

Tom Paxton recalled the buzz about the Friends of Old Time Music concerts: "There was a real love for the music, and excitement about the event, and of course you'd have your little cliques of someone who knew or thought they knew more about the artist than others, and they would have all this kind of showing off. But mainly they were musical events and people were happy about them and excited about hearing this particular artist."[7]

In order to promote their new organization, and hopefully build up a following, Cohen spoke to the packed audience: "I remember at the first Friends of Old Time Music concert, I jumped off the stage, right into the audience, and I said, 'People are asking, "How do I join The Friends of Old Time Music?" The way you join Friends of Old Time Music is you come to a concert, and you pay your admission, and you sign up on the sign up sheet, and then you're a member of The Friends of Old Time Music.'" I remember clearly leaving the stage so it wouldn't be somebody above announcing to the people how they should do it; I just got out there... I was just part of the gang, so to speak. That was my mindset. And from that we got a mailing list. The audience was mostly made up of people who played music."[2]

The Roscoe Holcomb concert went spectacularly well, and quite a few of the audience members signed the mailing list to find out about upcoming concerts.

At the time, however, there had not yet been a second concert planned. John Cohen recalled, "The concert was received well enough, so we decided to do a second concert, which was the Clarence Ashley concert."[2] They set a date of six weeks after the Holcomb concert, leaving little time to prepare the details.

Rinzler was quickly in touch with Ashley, and Ashley set about pulling a band together. He was able to convince Fred Price, Clint Howard, Gaither Carlton and Doc Watson all to travel north for their debut in New York City. The group would quickly put together whatever music they could, and upon their arrival in New York, Ralph Rinzler and John Cohen would work with them to arrange their program.

On the evening of March 25th, 1961, the Clarence Ashley Group waited nervously backstage at PS 41 for their concert to start. The small auditorium was filling once again with music fans from around the city, coming to see this legend who had recorded on the *Anthology of American Folk Music*. The concert's 450 seats sold out quickly, and the audience was electric.

Maria Muldaur remembered that night very well: "I went to the concert with my boyfriend Walter. We'd heard about them, and we really wanted to go, and we got there a little late. The place was full, so we got seats at the very back. And from the first minute, I was spellbound. Of course, Clarence Ashley was his usual charming, funny self. I loved all the songs they were doing, you know, 'The Coo Coo' and all the wonderful songs."[3] Muldaur was especially entranced by the smiling old man who played several duets with Doc on the old-time fiddle: Gaither Carlton. She admitted, "I loved Doc and I loved everything that was going on, but Gaither's fiddle playing just captivated me. It was very simple, very primitive, but so sweet. It was just wonderful."[3]

Clarence Ashley did not stand out much to Muldaur, who was looking for depth and emotion more than showmanship. The older gentleman snapped his suspenders and smiled broadly while telling country jokes, while Doc was humble and simply played tunes with mountain purity, and sang in his steady baritone. Muldaur remarked, "Clarence Ashley was cute, but Doc Watson was deeply profound! He was on a whole other level!"[3]

Yet it was not Doc's guitar work that astounded Muldaur and the rest of the audience that night; it was his solid, strong voice, singing; "those haunting old ballads like 'Hick's Farewell' with Gaither playing his fiddle accompaniment."[3] Muldaur admittedly "fell in love" with what she said was a "spiritual purity that emanated when he sang."[3]

*New York Times* reporter Robert Shelton also singled Doc out for both his instrumental and vocal ability in his Monday review of the concert, writing that Doc Watson was "a pleasant singer and sure-fingered guitarist who, as accompanist, was the work-horse of the evening."[11]

In fact, Doc's guitar playing that night was so stunning to the audience that Rinzler recalled: "Although Doc performed as a part of the group, doing only a few solos on the program, he was immediately singled out by the audience and each guitar break was followed by a spontaneous burst of applause."[12]

Robert Shelton's *New York Times* article that was published on Monday, March 27th began with a description of the group's material: "Quintet From the Blue Ridge Offers Program of Ballads, Spirituals and Hoedowns,"[11] and then described the group as, "five farmers from the Blue Ridge Mountains [who] brought a ripe harvest of traditional music to the city Saturday night."[11] Despite the amusing pun, the article was well written, and a boon to the Friends of Old-Time Music. Shelton additionally gave the organization high praise, saying that the Friends of Old Time Music were, "a sort of Anglicized, folk-oriented *Pro Music Antiqua*."[11] Shelton was essentially legitimizing the intellectual importance of the group, and he further did so in his comment that Ashley and Watson's version of "The Coo-Coo Bird" that night had, "whispered a sensitive colloquy that was almost reminiscent of fine chamber music."[11]

Rinzler and Cohen were overjoyed at the positive review they had received from Shelton, and it did wonders for their reputation. Soon, their concerts would be held at New York University, and not in the elementary school auditorium, though it had been a fittingly humble place for Doc Watson's first northern performance. Shelton wrote in his article, "[The Friends of Old Time Music concert series] deserves to have its guests heard in some midtown auditorium with more than the 450-seat capacity and the soggy acoustics the school auditorium provides."[11] Shelton knew that this was only the beginning of the Clarence Ashley Group's time in the limelight.

There were many in the crowd that day who were impressed by the musicians, and after the final applause had died down, Rinzler recalled that, "two invitations were extended to the group: The University of Chicago Folk Festival for February 1962 and the Ash Grove (a Los Angeles coffee house/cabaret) for March-April 1962."[13] This was the beginning of a long series of engagements for the Ashley Group, and of a long career for Doc Watson.

Clarence Ashley was amazed by the renewed interest in his music. John Cohen recalled visiting Ashley in the summer of 1961: "The concert came, and then the review came, and a few months later, Mike Seeger and I did a little tour in the south. And we stopped off at Ashley's right away. I remember him looking up at us while standing at his kitchen sink, and saying, 'Well, you know, my life is like a rose. I bloomed in the spring, and then I bloomed again in my late life, just before the winter.'"[2] Clarence Ashley died only six years later, after having traveled across the country several times, and after a brief tour of Britain.

After the Clarence Ashley Group's first concert that night in March 1961, there was a large party at musicologist Alan Lomax's house. Annie Bird recalled, "The parties were wild. Everybody did their own thing. A lot of people smoked and did all kinds of things in those days, and we had a good time."[4]

Jean Ritchie recalled working the entire night with her husband George Pickow on a 16mm film: "My husband George shot the pictures, and I did the sound; they had me on the dials all night; I couldn't go to sleep or anything. We were there, up at Alan's house. We have film footage of that; there's a little movie. Alan Lomax always claimed it, and he got his daughter to finish it, and she didn't do a very good job; she was just a young girl at the time. We were always mad about that."[8]

Ritchie recalled filming Maria Muldaur at the party: "Maria was also at that party. I've got a picture of her dancing; she had black shiny boots on. George got a lot of shots of her boots. This was before she started singing anything hardly. She was just a young girl."[8]

Muldaur was with her friend Annie Bird at the party that night, and because Bird knew Doc and Gaither well after having them as houseguests for the last week, Muldaur asked her if she would introduce them: "I begged Annie to introduce me. I was just so in awe of them, and what their music sounded like, and the purity of their spirit and everything. So she introduced me to them. She said, 'This is my friend Maria; we sing some Carter Family stuff together.' They were all very nice. And I went up to Gaither and told him how much I loved his playing. I said, 'Oh I just wish you lived here. I would really love to learn to play the way you play. I just love it.' And he just looked at me with these twinkly blue eyes, and he said, 'Well, come on down to North Carolina. I'd be happy to show you how to play; it ain't hard.' From that grew our friendship, and I wrote to them, and he wrote back. Again, he offered, 'Come on down we'd love to have you.'"[3] Of course, a few months later, Muldaur did visit her new friends in North Carolina, and a lifelong friendship began.

Muldaur recalled Lomax filming Clarence Ashley that night: "They had a big floodlight all set up, to interview Doc, Clarence and everybody. A funny thing happened when they were filming; I remember it like it was yesterday. Alan Lomax kept saying to Clarence Ashley, 'So, Clarence, what is the meaning of 'She doesn't warble cuckoo 'til the fourth day of July.' What is the significance of that?' So Clarence would say, 'Well, the cuckoo, we call it a rain bird, and it don't start to sing until it's going to rain,' or something like that. Because something was the matter, or somebody was talking, or the lighting wasn't right, Alan made him do it about four times. And this was supposed to be a natural, off the top of the head kind of thing. Alan would start over, 'Well, Clarence, we need to do that again. Now tell us again what exactly is a cuckoo.' After four times of doing this, and by now it's 12 or 1 in the morning, the party is in full swing, and he had just done a long concert, and this is all really new to him. After the fourth time being interviewed with the same questions, and trying to come up with the same responses, Clarence said, 'Well, the cuckoo is a kind of a reindeer.' And at that point, we said, 'You know, Alan, enough!' Give him a break! He's not even remembering what he's supposed to say! So that was kind of funny and I've always remembered that."[8]

Muldaur also recalled seeing Woody Guthrie at the party, and then realized that he had also been at the concert earlier that night: "These two people came in to the concert, and they were kind of making a bit of a commotion. I turned around and saw that it was Jack Elliott and somebody else. I was quite annoyed, and I thought, 'God, don't they have any respect? Why can't they be quiet?' After the concert, word was there was going to be a party over at Alan Lomax's house. We get to Alan Lomax's house, and the party's just jam-packed full of people. Mike Seeger was there, and John Cohen, of course, and I remember clog dancing with Johnny Herald. So, in walked Jack Elliott, and who do you think was with him? It was Woody Guthrie! He'd sprung him out of the psychiatric hospital he lived in. Woody had Huntington's Disease, and so it hadn't been that they were drunk... I had thought that they were drunk back there making all that commotion, but it was just that he was kind of spastic, and just not totally in control of his motor reflexes and so forth. I didn't say anything, but at the concert, I was looking around, annoyed, and going, '*Shh*, can't you people shut up and listen.' I didn't say it, I just kind of gestured it. Then when I saw them at the party, I felt so bad! Anyway, he sat in the corner and seemed to have a good time, and that's who was hanging out at the concert and party!"[8]

If Woody Guthrie was indeed at the concert and party, he would surely have enjoyed the sound of the string band; he, like Doc, had grown up with the records of the '20s and '30s, and with radio from then on. He was only 11 years older than Doc, and as his career tragically ended, Doc's was just beginning. Larry Long, the founder of the first Woody Guthrie Festival in Woody's hometown of Okemah, Oklahoma in 1988, speculated as to what Woody might have thought of the music that night: "Like everyone else in attendance, I think Woody would have been humbled to be in Doc's presence."[14]

The audience might, in part, have felt humbled in Doc's presence, but Doc *certainly* felt humble in the audience's presence. It was the first concert he had ever given where the audience had truly listened to each and every nuance, reacted to every word he sang, and observed every lick on each instrument. A new world was opening up to the talented bard from North Carolina, and he was ready for it. Doc stepped on stage and sang and played his heart out.

## CHAPTER NOTES

1.   Edwards, Bob, *Doc Watson Interview*, from *Morning Edition*. 1989, National Public Radio: USA.
2.   Gustavson, Kent, *Personal Interviews with John Cohen*. April 8 & August 6, 2009.
3.   Gustavson, Kent, *Telephone Interview with Maria Muldaur*. April 1, 2009.
4.   Gustavson, Kent, *Telephone Interview with Annie Bird*. April 24, 2009.
5.   Gustavson, Kent, *Email Interview with David Grisman*. March 25, 2009.
6.   Gustavson, Kent, *Telephone Interview with Mike Seeger*. May 23, 2009.
7.   Gustavson, Kent, *Telephone Interview with Tom Paxton*. April 14, 2009.
8.   Gustavson, Kent, *Telephone Interview with Jean Ritchie*. May 6, 2009.
9.   Wilson, John S., *Hootenanny Fills Carnegie Hall as Eighteenth Season Begins*. The New York Times, September 21, 1959. New York.
10.  Cohen, John, *Conversations with Bob Dylan*. Sing Out!, 1968. 18(4): p. 6-23,67.
11.  Shelton, Robert, *Folk Group Gives 'Village' Concert*. New York Times, March 27, 1961. New York p. 26.
12.  Watson, Doc and Ralph Rinzler, *The Songs of Doc Watson*. 1971, New York City: Oak Publications.
13.  Rinzler, Ralph, *Liner Notes from The Original Folkways Recordings of Doc Watson and Clarence Ashley 1960-1962*, Smithsonian Folkways Records, 1994.
14.  Gustavson, Kent, *Email Interview with Larry Long*. June 30, 2009.

# CHAPTER TWELVE
## The Clarence Ashley Group

*"It was just mind-boggling to play a few good old tunes; I mean in the real old time way, with all the nicks and scratches like antique furniture's got; and have a whole raft of folks stand up and give you an applause like that. It was really a heart-warming thing..."*

– Doc Watson[1]

With the rousing success of the Friends of Old Time Music concert in New York City, the Clarence Ashley Group quickly became a sought-after traditional music act on the folk circuit. They soon played stages across the country, and Doc Watson's career was born. Though Ralph Rinzler had told the group over and over again that New York audiences would enjoy their music, they had never truly believed it until their first appearance at PS 41 was over. The men watched from backstage in astonishment as the audience gave them a standing ovation.

Clint Howard initially thought the audience felt sorry for them: "I know that when Doc Watson, and Tom Ashley and Fred Price and myself went to New York, we got up on the stage and played, and they began to holler and cheer us... I thought they was sorry for us. I said, 'They don't like this old music. They just feel sorry for us 'cause we're from down there in the mountains.'"[2] In another interview, Howard said that he gave Doc a friendly punch in the shoulder backstage, and said to him, "They know we're out from the old mountains and we ain't got good education, and they're sorry for us."[3] Howard remembered that Doc reassured him, saying, "Clint, I believe they like this music."[3]

Both men soon realized that these New Yorkers liked their mountain music better and in a different way than people did back home in the mountains. Doc explained the phenomenon succinctly in an interview with Bert Lloyd: "City kids liked old-time traditional folk, and country kids wanted a 'citified music.'"[4] Much as J.S. Bach was an anomalous musician when he wrote in the older *chorale* music form in the early 18th century, these musicians were lifting up an older musical form, breathing life into music that this New York audience had to this point only heard on scratchy old 78 records and on the *Anthology of American Folk Music* compilation.

Doc's version of the backstage story differed slightly from Howard's. In Doc's telling of the tale, he was the one who heard the applause and said, "I believe they like that music."[5] Howard then replied to him, "No, they just feel sorry for us mountain people."[5] Doc then repeated, as if to confirm it for himself as well, "No, I do believe they like this old-time music."[5] Doc recalled that Clarence Ashley then said to him, "Well, son, I'll tell you – I don't understand it. But ain't you tickled that they like us that good?"[2] Doc responded, "Yes, sir, I really am, Tom.'"[2] Then they went back out on stage and did an encore.

Regardless of the precise details of the event, the southern musicians spoke among themselves in amazement about the audience's positive response to their mountain music. Doc called it an "absolute thrill" they all felt when they stepped off stage and heard the thunderous response in the small auditorium. Though they were "in total disbelief at first,"[2] the musicians soon realized that they had something to offer the folk music world, just as Ralph Rinzler had assured them.

Ralph Rinzler had been amazed at the breadth of repertoire Clarence Ashley and his fellow musicians were able to come up with during the September 1960 Saltville recording sessions. Therefore, upon returning to New York, his first impulse, because of the importance and quality of the sessions, had been to find a record label that would release the music. Eugene Earle had agreed to help him shop the album around to different labels, and assured Rinzler that he would assist in the production of the upcoming album.

Rinzler had scrawled a brief to-do list in the notebook he had brought with him to the Ashley session for note-taking *(list follows, unedited)*:

1. *One copy tapes for Each*
2. *Folkways 1st rights*
    a. *If not F.ways – others*
3. *IF Folkways*
    (1) *– contract to Tom for tapes*
    (2) *copyrights: copyright Claude Allen / – Mary & Marthy*[6]

Thirty years later, Rinzler wrote of his initial attempt to get the audio from Clarence Ashley and his fellow musicians picked up by a record company: "In 1961, after an unsuccessful attempt to get the material released by mainstream record companies, a recording including some of the material on Disc II of the present set was released by Folkways Records."[7] Rinzler certainly never would have expected both of the albums that began with that weekend's sessions to sell thousands of copies, and stay in print and on music store shelves for the next 50 years.

There was a loose sheet of paper clipped simply to the inside cover of the Swarthmore notebook that Ralph Rinzler took with him to the Labor Day recording session. At the top of the sheet of paper, Rinzler wrote "Tape I: Side I" and listed the songs they recorded during that session. It represented the humble beginning of Doc Watson's career. Even though Rinzler had enjoyed his conversation with the blind man in the back of the pickup truck on the way to Saltville, the New Yorker only referred to Doc's playing in his notes once, after the third tune of the day. In that song, Doc had used his electric guitar with the volume turned down to accompany Clarence Ashley. Rinzler noted "3. Poor Ellen Smith – 2:25 (electric guitar)."[6]

After recording 13 usable takes during the long day in Saltville, Doc asked to do another take of "Pretty Little Pink" with the group. He had now warmed up on the acoustic instrument, and felt he would be able to play a better version. In 1991, Ralph Rinzler remembered recording this version of "Pretty Little Pink" at the end of the first day's session: "On this closing hoedown, everyone was cooking, so Doc discreetly stepped forward for the only hot flatpicking break he was to offer that first day."[8] Doc actually took two breaks in that version of the song, which was later released at the end of the 1961 *Old Time Music at Clarence Ashley's* LP on Folkways Records.

While little 13-year old Tommy Moore played washboard in the background, Fred Price kicked off the tune with a rich fiddle line, supported by the two-finger backup of Jack Johnson in an arpeggiated old-time banjo style. Doc Watson and Clint Howard played solid backup guitar, and Howard began to sing. During the first instrumental break, Fred broke out into a solid version of the melody, and Doc began to do backup runs in the style of Riley Puckett. After another sung verse, Doc nervously filled in a break with arpeggiated guitar lines filling out the simple melody. Howard then sang the next verse, "Every time that I go home / I do my best to please her / The more I try the worse she gets / And I be darned if I don't leave her," followed by the chorus.

After Howard finished singing, Doc Watson began his career as the king of the acoustic guitar. At that moment, he finally felt free enough, after an entire day of recording on a borrowed acoustic instrument, to take a nine-second break that would change the rest of his life. Capoed on the fifth fret of his borrowed guitar, Doc played, in the key of G, one of the guitar breaks that will go down in history. Although, in hindsight, knowing the entirety of Doc Watson's virtuosic guitar catalog, the break was quite modest and reserved, this was the lick that made Rinzler do a double take when he listened again to the song. And this was the tune that Rinzler's 15-year old friend David Grisman heard before commenting to Rinzler that Doc was an amazing guitarist.

In the nine seconds of Doc's second solo break, Rinzler first realized that Doc Watson might have a chance at a solo career in the folk music industry. But Rinzler was at first blush primarily interested in the folk music *treasure* he had discovered in Clarence Ashley of the *Anthology of American Folk Music*. It was with observations about Ashley that Rinzler filled up most of his brown Swarthmore Ethics notebook. He wrote a few notes about each of the other musicians, including a brief line about Doc: "DOC WATSON – DEEP GAP, N.C. 37 yrs old (near Boone),"[6] but he took far more extensive notes about Ashley's childhood, career, and family, fascinated by this character of legend who had come to life before his very eyes.

Clarence Ashley was born in Bristol, Tennessee in 1895, and at age four, he moved near to Mountain City, Tennessee, where he remained for the rest of his life, and where Rinzler eventually visited him in 1960. He attended school until the age of ten, and lived with his grandparents, who both sang but didn't play instruments.[6]

Ashley's mother Rosie-Belle had married a fiddler named George McCurry, only to find out soon afterwards that he had another marriage and family elsewhere. McCurry was run out of town, and little Clarence Earle McCurry came along a few months later.[9] He was never known by his given name, and was nicknamed "Tommy Tiddy Waddy" by his grandfather. As he grew older, the "Tiddy Waddy" was dropped, and he was known as Thomas Clarence Ashley (taking the name Ashley from his maternal grandfather).[6] Later, Ashley used both of his names to his benefit when he recorded for different record labels in the 1920s and '30s.

When Ashley was eight years old, he began playing the banjo. His first instrument was a peanut banjo given to storekeepers who purchased peanuts. And around the age of twelve, he picked up the guitar. He immediately began playing his instrument wherever he could, much as Doc Watson did with his guitar nearly 30 years later. He played for quiltings, where groups of women would gather around, as well as apple-cuttings and bean-stringings, where beans (called *leather britches*) were dried, along with peaches, corn, pumpkins and blackberries. He also played for log-rollings, *'lassy-making* (molasses-making), and also for house- and barn-raisings.[6]

At 16 years old, Ashley started working at his first medicine show as a banjo player and singer, alongside a traveling "doctor" named Doc White Cloud, and a comedian. They sold colored water and Doc White Cloud convinced local townspeople that it could cure their assorted ailments. Ashley worked with the medicine show until 1943, under various owners, traveling from town to town in a prairie-schooner covered wagon with the stage rigging, platforms, lanterns and all the rest, while Doc White Cloud traveled in luxury in a horse-drawn carriage out front. Ashley would of course entertain during the shows, but he was also responsible for feeding the horses and hauling water.[6] Little did Ashley know that he would be traveling on the road with *another* Doc four decades later.

Ashley was married at 17 years old to Hettie, a local 14-year old beauty, and soon started playing accompanying guitar with the legendary blind fiddler G.B. Grayson. They would play on the streets, near carnivals, and outside of mines on payday.[9]

Ashley also played with several other groups, including a group named the Blue Ridge Mountain Entertainers with whom he made his first commercial recordings, for the Star Piano Company.[6] After that, he recorded 78s with various groups for both Victor and Columbia; he recorded as *Tom* Ashley for Victor, and *Clarence* Ashley for Columbia. Soon, he also played with a trio called Byrd Moore and his Hot Shots, with whom he also recorded for Columbia. After his session with the Hot Shots in October 1929, Ashley offered to sing a few *'lassy-makin'* (molasses-making) tunes for Columbia, which is when he played his version of "The Coo Coo Bird" that was later chosen from among thousands of 78 recordings to be part of Harry Smith's *Anthology of American Folk Music* in 1952.[9] If it hadn't been for those few 'lassy-makin' tunes that Clarence Ashley played for Columbia in 1929, Doc Watson would never have had a career in folk music.

The next rung up the stepladder of success for Doc Watson and the rest of the Clarence Ashley Group was their two-week engagement at the Ash Grove in Los Angeles, California, a small club with a loyal following and an incredible lineup of musicians on their schedule. The Ash Grove was the west coast equivalent of the Friends of Old Time Music in New York City. Even the acts that were booked at the Ash Grove were to a great extent organized by Mike Seeger, John Cohen and Ralph Rinzler, who suggested their favorite acts to Ed Pearl, the club's owner, who would subsequently book them for concerts.

Ed Pearl was only 21 when he started the Ash Grove in 1958. He recalled how it all began: "I had heard the Harry Smith *Anthology of American Folk Music* in 1956. That was one of the first times I lived with a woman, and she happened to have that record set, so we spent a lot of time listening. To me those records were a real eye opener. And right after that, after the woman went back to her husband, my dad told me I should get out of town, so I took a job. I got a job up at Edwards Air Force Base, and I was doing data evaluation from the first supersonic jets, in '56 and '57. I stayed up near the base most of the time, and I was rooming with a whole bunch of hillbillies and blacks. I had been playing the guitar for a while, and I joined a square dance band. I was working and playing with those guys for a year, really country-sounding fellows, and they accepted me. Actually I started going with a hillbilly girl and everything like that. So I mean I really liked those guys. It was part of my world. I'm Jewish, but I was born in the part of Los Angeles that was about half white, mostly Jewish, and Mexican-American; and I came from a working-class family with five kids, and my dad was a toolmaker, not a businessman or anything."[10] Pearl's interest in all kinds of cultures and all kinds of music started early, and after his exposure to Harry Smith's *Anthology*, he became interested in all forms of American traditional music.

Pearl continued, "I started the Ash Grove because I met somebody and I was sort of wooing her. I met her at The Flamingo Club on Sunset Boulevard. If there were one figure of flamenco in the 20th Century, it would be her; Carmen Amaya. She was a great singer, dancer; a great artist of the last century. And so Carmen had brought her troupe to Palm Springs. And when they arrived there, the nightclub folded. So there she was, a gypsy with no money who had to go back to Spain, and the entire troupe was cut loose and stayed in cheap hotels throughout Los Angeles and of course hung around this one flamenco club. The guitar playing and so on was so much better than anything, you know, in the folk circles, that I wanted to put on a show for the folk people. But the flamenco guitarist was a gypsy, and he wouldn't play unless he got either $50 or $100, I forget what exactly. Which meant we had to charge money, which meant that we had to do a commercial thing. We were just going to do it for the gang, but this changed everything."[10]

Pearl looked for a concert hall to house a flamenco concert, and ended up speaking to the owner of the Los Angeles Jazz Concert Hall which he rented for $50. He remembered the theater, "This was a beautiful 700-seat theater, and I filled it up. So then I put on two more shows, and each one was a full house, with different kinds of things." He began to book more shows, and had nightclub owners approach him, wanting him to book their clubs. He checked out the nightclubs, and did not trust the clientele and ownership, so he decided with his girlfriend at the time, Kate Hughes (who later became Kate Rinzler), to open his own concert hall, the Ash Grove.[10]

Pearl and his girlfriend worked hard to set up the new music space: "We converted a big furniture display room and work area into the foyer and concert hall. In the middle were the office and the bathroom. So it was really easy to do the front and the back, and the division was obvious." Soon they filled it with excited guests for the first time. He recalled that the club would not seat many people: "The Ash Grove was relatively small. Theoretically it was supposed to seat something like 200, but we got up to 250 when we had to. But it was well planned, so there was rarely a time where people were actually packed in like that. I mean, nowadays in the same space, people would be standing a lot, and there would be far fewer tables. The room capacity would now be between 300 and 400."[10]

The most unique feature of the small concert hall was the counter that surrounded the stage. That counter helped spawn countless musicians over the generation the club was in existence. Pearl described the stage and counter in the front of the room: "The stage was built deliberately a foot and a half elevated, high enough so that the musicians could see to the back row. And then there was a counter right around the rim of the stage so people would sit right there next to the musicians; the lip of the counter was higher than the stage. That place quickly became the property of Ry Cooder, David Cohen, Taj Mahal, and all of the people who were learning how to play."[10]

Soon these young musicians would watch in amazement as Doc Watson played the guitar in a manner that none of them had ever seen before. In 1991, Rinzler wrote: "One of my clearest recollections from Doc Watson and Clarence Ashley's first appearance at the Ash Grove in April 1962 is a young Ry Cooder's rapt attention and interest in them and their music."[11]

Roland White, of The Kentucky Colonels, the White Brothers, and the Nashville Bluegrass Band, recalled that Ed Pearl always made sure that they would come to see the amazing musicians that came into town: "Anything and everything that came at the Ash Grove, if it was something that he thought we should see, Ed Pearl would call us and say, 'You need to come see this act,' or 'this guitar player,' or 'this singer...' And then we would go."[12]

Roland White's first band, The Country Boys, known mostly for having played on the Andy Griffith Show, also played some of their earliest gigs on the Ash Grove stage. White remembered, "A friend of ours in Southern California by the name of Walt Pittman told us about the Ash Grove in either '58 or '59. And that's the first time we ever played in that sort of environment. It was a place where people were listening to music, not where people were dancing or something like that. It was kind of scary."[12] This was not a club that was interested in music for some other purpose. It was a place where listeners came to really listen to the music that was being performed. White continued: "The audience members were actually looking at us, you could see their faces. It wasn't totally dark. They were actually looking at us and listening. The Ash Grove was just a different thing."[12]

Following their successful concert in New York in March 1961, the Clarence Ashley Group performed in February 1962 at the University of Chicago Folk Festival, shortly after which the group was invited at the last minute to play at the Ash Grove in March 1962. Doc and his Blue Ridge farmer cohorts played concerts night after night together in various configurations and with various guests, all in the relaxed but exciting atmosphere of the small club. Rinzler wrote of the Ash Grove's importance to the group: "It was the Ash Grove booking that permanently changed their performing style."[7] Indeed the Clarence Ashley Group's two-week long tenure at the Ash Grove was what firmly established them within the folk music world.

Ed Pearl remembered the Clarence Ashley Group's first visit to the Ash Grove: "I truly loved Clarence, Fred, Clint and Doc. I honestly felt extremely close to them as I did to many other artists. I really enjoyed being with them... When they first came, I took Doc, Fred, Clint and Clarence on a tour of Los Angeles, and we went out to Knott's Berry Farm. That was a particularly memorable visit because when we were out there, Ashley wouldn't leave his banjo in the car, so he carried it with him. Anyway, Knott's Berry Farm used to be a total distinction from Disneyland, which is right down the road. And it was very down home at the time. That was, of course, before they put in all the rides and all that. The main attractions were the streets that were in an 1880s, 1890s style. And so they had an old apothecary and this and that, and of course they had a saloon and a shoot out with a wagon and horses and all of that kind of thing. They had a lot of that. The thing that was great about that visit was that this actor got up and was supposed to be selling some elixir. And Ashley, after a while said, 'Son, let me show you how to sell that stuff.' He picked up the banjo and he sold. He was so good I was surprised. It turns out that was his profession. All these years when he wasn't making a living by recording, he was out hustling Dr. Brown's Elixir or whatever. He really knew how to do it. It was really fine to see. He was so good, and all the guys loved it; they saw Tom do his whole act and all that."[10]

The southern musicians all shared Ed Pearl's small beach house for the weeks they played at the Ash Grove: "I rented a little beach house in northern Santa Monica that actually belonged to the Ocean Bay Beach Club or something like that. They rented them out, and they were really cheap. The Dillards remember that little house, The Kentucky Colonels went down there…I mean, everyone was hanging around the beach house. But I never stayed there with Clarence and Doc and the others. While they were staying in the house, they took up the whole thing. It was very small."[10]

All four of the eager musicians worked on their repertoire in the small cabin that they occupied on the beach, and each night, their sets got better and better. Ralph Rinzler typed up a set list of 59 songs on Ash Grove paper for them, so that they would know what songs they could play, with whom, and when. He taught them how to run the sets, and how to work the folk audiences. He also started grooming Clint and Doc to run the show in case Ashley wasn't feeling well enough to run the sets. The set list Rinzler typed up included the following tunes, written in this order on the set list *(unedited list below)*:

## FRED'S FIDDLE TUNES:

*Lee Highway / Cumberland Gap / Sally Goodin / Humpback Mule / East Tenn. Blues / Carroll County blues / Cackling Hen / Girl I Left Behind / Turkey in the Straw / When You and I were Young Maggie / Fire in the Mountain / Chicken Reel / Pretty Little Widow / Lonesome Indian / Cindy*

## CLINT HOWARD:

*Sally Ann / Richmond blues / Ellen Smith / Maggie Walker / Run Jimmie Run / More Pretty Girls than One / Willow Garden / Honey babe blues / Old Man at the Mill / Rock little John the baby / Cabbage head Song / Lonesome road blues / Rosewood Casket / Rubens train / Roving gambler*

DOC, CLINT, FRED:

*Home Sick for Heaven / Looking toward Heaven / Streets of Glory / Lonely Tombs / Banks of Old Tenn. / Lonesome Valley / Short Life of Trouble /*

TOM ASHLEY, CLINT, DOC, FRED:

*Amazing Grace / Old Account / Circle be unbroken / Daniel Prayed / Sunny Tenn. / Banks of Ohio / Faded Roses / Blue ridge Mountain / Old time Religion / No Telephone in Heaven / Free at Last / Maple on the hill / Free little Bird / Woa Mule / Cluck old hen*

CLINT & DOC:

*Way down in town / Correna / Crawdad Song / Walking Cane / Sweet Heaven When I die / Greenback dollar / New River train*[13]

There is no question that in that first series of concerts in Los Angeles, Rinzler intended Clint Howard to lead the group. Howard played in every song on Rinzler's set list. He played backup to Price's fiddle tunes, and supported Doc and Ashley on the songs they sang lead.

Ed Pearl remembered the way that Howard, with Doc's help, was able to lighten up the concert with jokes and lead the group from stage: "Clint and Doc had this repertoire going, where they really knew each other, and they could make jokes and make references and bring up the culture – I mean just help the audience to get a better sense of the culture that they were there sharing with us."[10]

An example of the banter that the crowd got to enjoy from Clint and Doc is the following conversation that took place on stage in Seattle several years later, during the taping of the *Old Timey Concert* LP: Clint said, "While Doc's getting that thing ready, I'd like to tell you a little tale on him and Fred."[14] Doc quipped, "Hush..."[14] Clint continued, "I ain't gonna hush. I was down there at home one day, and I picked up an old boy, was a going down the road in a little truck, you know. And I picked this old boy up and I said, 'Son, you want a ride?' He said, 'Yeah, I believe I do,' and he got in the truck. And I said, 'Son, I believe you're about the slowest talking person I've ever seen.' He said, 'I ain't near as slow as my sister is.' I said, 'Well, how slow is she?' He said, 'Doc Watson and Fred Price picked her up the other day... [and] Doc asked her if she'd ever been kissed, and before she could tell him she hadn't, she had!"[14] Doc responded, "Well, now, I don't care if you tell that one on me, buddy... It ain't been too long ago since that might have been the truth!"[14]

During their first series of concerts at the Ash Grove, though Clint Howard emerged as the string band's leader, Doc Watson emerged as a wizard on the guitar. Guitar players all over the area heard about him after the first few nights, and they came to see his fingers move, and they allowed their minds to dream about someday playing guitar as well as Doc.

One of those musicians was Clarence White, who would soon become one of the greatest trailblazers on the acoustic guitar of the 21st century, revolutionizing phrasing on the flattop guitar forever with his innovative patterns.

In fact, White had his first chance to play music with Doc at an Ash Grove event organized by Ed Pearl. Clarence White's brother Roland, a legendary mandolin player in his own right, recalled, "Ed Pearl, or somebody that worked at the Ash Grove would have an afternoon lunch or something with whomever was playing there that week, and he would invite the *in* people, which we were some of. And we'd go to his or her house, and sit around and pick. Clarence got to play with Doc the first time at one of those little events there, and swap licks and stuff."[12]

The atmosphere at the Ash Grove was informal, and that was the beauty of the club. Young musicians could sit in the crowd, and as their favorite musician walked by, they could reach out and touch them if they liked. The musicians had to walk right through the audience to reach the stage.

Ed Pearl remembered, "The artists had to walk through the place and say hello. The only bit of film on The Ash Grove that still exists is a Muddy Waters concert in 1972, and you see Muddy walking through the audience. And one person after another came up to shake his hand, so it took him like five minutes to get onstage because of everyone like that. And then the audience would just hang around with the staff and people that they met there. It wasn't like a regular nightclub."[10]

There was another way that Ed Pearl's Ash Grove was unlike other night-clubs. It appealed to many different kinds of people, and became a melting pot of sorts; it offered a very wholesome and educational environment, without any kind of violence or trouble.

Pearl recalled, "We never had any problems at all, with anything, ever. I mean, the Hollywood police used to send kids from the Sunset Strip to The Ash Grove because they knew it was a good thing. I mean there were other police that had a negative image of me politically, which they didn't like. But most of them liked what I did. In '68 it was not popular to be a policeman in Los Angeles. I mean, the movement was huge because people were upset and all that. Well, the L.A.P.D. couldn't get any recruits in L.A., so they opened up a recruiting station in Saigon, and as the guys were being checked out of the Army, they signed them up for the L.A.P.D. They hired for the most part southern whites. Well, of course, they gravitated towards The Ash Grove because that was their music. And so I had all these southern white cops that would tell all these kids, 'What are you doing up here, smoking all that dope? You ought to go out to the Ash Grove.'"[10]

Paul Chasman, who has since become a guitar legend in his own right, first saw Doc Watson at the Ash Grove with Fred Price and Clint Howard, and recalled the energy of the venue: "In the Ash Grove they had this little practice room that was just off of the lobby, so you could hear the musicians in the practice room warming up and playing their tunes, and, oh my God, it was incredible what was coming out of there the night I first heard Doc Watson at the Ash Grove. We were all sitting in this little coffee house, and Doc Watson, Fred Price and Clint Howard just filed through the aisle, with Doc's hand on one of their shoulders. They stepped on stage and they were just a bunch of country boys. It just felt like they could be in your living room."[15]

The musicians seemed to invite the audience into their world with their fiddle tunes, ballads and hymns from the mountains. But there was also some-thing else; there was the virtuosity of this blind guitarist who stood out from the rest of the musicians. There was some spark that Doc Watson had that enthralled his audience then, and continued to enthrall audiences from the White House in Washington D.C. to the concert halls of Washington state and every-where in between.

Paul Chasman's eyes were glued to Doc's hands, and he was mesmerized. Indeed, the audience was soon filled with aspiring guitarists who watched every move the blind guitarist made. Chasman recalled, "When I saw Doc at the Ash Grove, I learned really quickly never to let my eyes leave his hands. I don't know what they were playing, maybe 'Way Downtown,' and all of a sudden I heard this rocket shot of a lick between one of the phrases. Where did that come from?

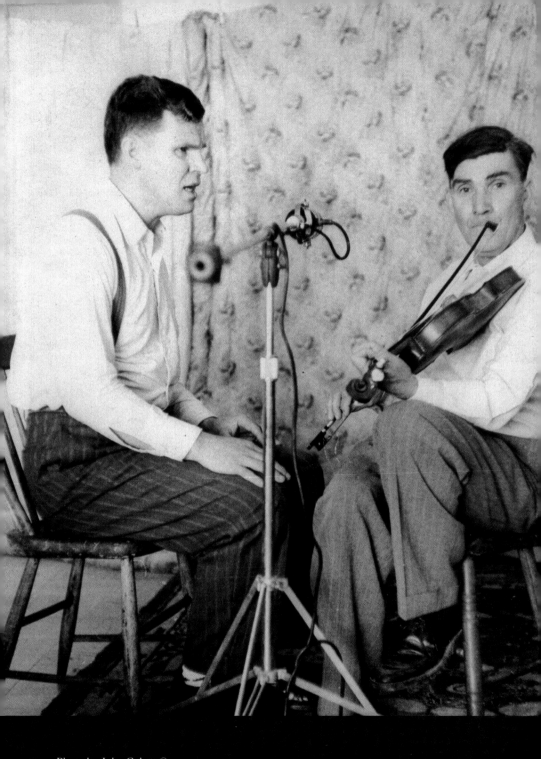

Photo by John Cohen ©
*Gaither Carlton & Doc Watson recording at Annie Bird's apartment in New York City, March 1961. Quilts were hung on the wall to dampen the sound.*

Ralph Rinzler

Mr. Brandt
Ralph Rinzler

**Swarthmore College Book Store**

Ask for No. 760CM

Spiral Binding—U. S. Patents 1516032-1942026. Other Patents Pending.

Digital scan by Stephanie Smith.
Reprinted with permission of the Ralph Rinzler Folklife Archives, Smithsonian Institution.
*The Swarthmore Ethics notebook Ralph Rinzler brought with him to the Labor Day
1960 recording session with Clarence Ashley & Doc Watson.*

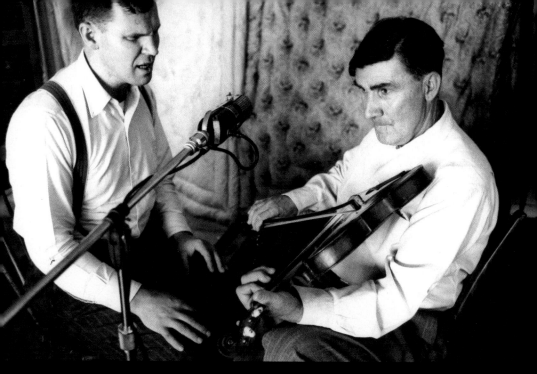

Photo by John Cohen ©
*Doc Watson & Gaither Carlton recording a fiddle and voice duet at Annie Bird's apartment, March 1961.*

*Annie Bird & Doc Watson on stage at the first Friends of Old Time Music concert in March 1961 at PS 41 in New York City.*

*Fred Price & Doc Watson backstage at the Chicago Folk Festival 1962.*

*Clarence Ashley & Doc Watson backstage at the Chicago Folk Festival 1962.*

Photo by John Cohen ©

*Clint Howard, Clarence Ashley & Doc Watson
backstage at the Chicago Folk Festival, 1962.*

Photo by Peter S. Shenkin ©
*Doc Watson onstage at Fincastle Folk Festival, 1965.*

Photo by Nic Siler ©
*Rosa Lee and Nancy Watson backstage.*

Photo by John Rocklin ©
*Doc Watson & David Holt at MerleFest.*

Photo by Tony Cartledge ©
*David Holt & Doc Watson at MerleFest.*

Photos by John Rocklin ©

*Doc Watson & his grandson Richard at MerleFest.*

Photo by Nic Siler ©
*Merle Watson, Doc Watson & T. Michael Coleman on stage.*

Photo by John Rocklin ©
*Rosa Lee & Doc Watson at MerleFest.*

Photo by Nic Siler ©
*Merle Watson playing slide guitar on stage.*

Photo by Bob Voors ©
*Doc Watson & Jack Lawrence at MerleFest.*

And then I started watching what he was doing, and I was blown away by his economy of movement."[15]

On their first trip to California, Ralph Rinzler drove the Clarence Ashley Group the entire way from eastern Tennessee to Los Angeles. Actually, most of the group slept in the back seat while Doc Watson stayed awake in the front of the station wagon with Rinzler, who recalled the unforgettable trip in a 1988 interview: "I'd drive through the night, and while the others slept, Doc had to keep me awake... He'd entertain me with stories, songs, jokes and reminiscences and he was an incredible raconteur."[16]

Later, in 1994, Rinzler added: "On the road to Los Angeles, Doc made a significant commitment to share the automobile driver's responsibility. He kept me awake and attentive for forty-eight hours at the wheel by singing unaccompanied songs and regaling me with stories of his family and music. We rolled straight through from Dallas to Los Angeles, barely arriving in time to climb on the stage for the first night's performance. After that, I felt as though Doc and I had grown up together from early childhood."[7]

Sometime in the middle of the night, Rinzler remembered saying to his blind friend in a moment that changed their relationship forever, "Doc, what you do to keep me awake in the car is an infinitely more interesting and moving experience than any of the stuff Clarence [Ashley] and Clint Howard do on stage. They're canned performance and you're human integrity. Talk to the audiences if there was one person there driving across the country and you'll steal everybody's heart."[16]

Doc soon took Rinzler's advice and never looked back. That day in the car, Doc began to realize that he could become a leader, and despite his accompanying role in most of the Ashley Group's material, he began to take more risks on the guitar and to play more solo tunes. Rinzler described Doc's stage presence: "He got up there and he was just himself, like he always is, and he's been doing it ever since."[16]

Doc later gave Rinzler the credit he was due: "Ralph is responsible for, well, I'll say, most of my success because I didn't know a thing about stage performing or anything, and was scared more than a kid when he sees a big Holstein bull with spiked horns coming at him to get on the stage. And Ralph set me down, and gave me a good lecture on that I had something to offer and all I needed was a little self-confidence."[17]

As Rinzler rushed his musicians across the country to barely get them to Los Angeles in time for their gig, Jean Ritchie was also arriving in the city. She remembered pulling up to the Ash Grove that afternoon: "In '62 I was out in California, and I had gone out to headline for Ed Pearl at the Ash Grove. When we pulled down to where we could see the marquee, there it said, *Jean Ritchie* in big letters, and underneath in smaller letters was *Clarence Ashley and His Friends*. I think Ralph Rinzler booked us at the same time on purpose, because he told Tom, 'She's a good person to sing with because she doesn't try to hog the spotlight.' Anyway, we had a two-week run out there together. And they were just so great; I loved all of them. It was a very small place, but it was always filled with people when we were there."[18]

Doc was very observant of all that happened around him at the Ash Grove, and Jean Ritchie was a great influence on the development of his solo repertoire. From backstage, Doc listened to Ritchie sing a capella songs and tell stories about her upbringing in the mountains. They were both talented musicians who could play songs solo, sing unaccompanied, and tell stories about family, childhood, and mountain home. He was fascinated by her ability to lead a concert from stage, and the two of them quickly became friends.

A few days after they had arrived in California, Doc asked Clarence Ashley if he would ask Jean if Doc could *see* her. Ritchie remembered that Doc ran his hands across her face and over her shoulders, and then told her, "You are a very pretty girl."[3]

During the first concert series at the Ash Grove, Clarence Ashley came down with laryngitis due to the heavy smog in Los Angeles, and he stayed home for a few back-to-back nights.

Clint Howard was the natural choice to lead the show from stage in Ashley's absence. He led the group in a very old-time way, just as Ashley had always done. However, though Clint was the natural leader for the group, Rinzler wanted to see Doc eventually step into a leadership role because of his easygoing charisma, and saw something greater in the cards for Doc than being a simple accompanist. So Rinzler did something that changed the rest of Doc's career: "Knowing that Doc could read braille, I went to the local institute for the blind and purchased the necessary equipment. That night, Doc went on stage with the program card stamped out in braille taped to the top of his guitar. He spoke on the stage much as he would with a few friends gathered about him in his house and he and the audience just sat back and enjoyed the show together."[19]

Ralph Rinzler was certainly not upset that Clarence Ashley was ousted as the leader of the quartet. From what he had seen, John Cohen recalled that everyone in the group was, "kind of contentious about Ashley because he was an old man, and impossible to get along with; demanding and cranky."[20] Cohen spoke also about the fact that Rinzler had found a "parallel universe thing in Doc," and therefore wanted to support Doc more than the others. Rinzler became even more frustrated with Ashley when he heard him lampoon Doc onstage, saying: "Now Doc, he's the workhorse of the crew. He's blind, but he can do anything a ten-year old boy can do."[20] Rinzler explained that away in a 1988 interview with Richard Harrington by saying that Ashley had been a blackface comedian, and that was his sense of humor, but it had really rubbed Rinzler the wrong way.[16]

As if directly juxtaposed with Clarence Ashley's cranky demeanor, Doc was polite and entertaining as a houseguest and he was charming and welcoming on stage. Like nothing else, his incredible humility and friendliness helped Doc to gain friends in the business and to get through the lean years of his career.

Ellen Harper-Verdries, the mother of popular musician Ben Harper, and the daughter of Dorothy and Charles Chase who owned a little folk music club called The Golden Ring not far away from the Ash Grove in the 1960s, recalled Doc, Clarence, Fred and Clint all staying at her home when she was a child. She remembered that Doc was really interested in her and the other kids, which she was not used to; most of the musicians who came through were too busy to talk to them. But Doc was different, possibly because he also had young children at home whom he missed.

Harper-Verdries recalled: "One of my clearest memories is that Doc Watson and Clarence Ashley had played a concert here, and then come to our house to sleep for the night. They got up in the morning, and they came down to the breakfast table. They were sitting around our breakfast table in the morning, and my mother made plates of eggs and bacon. And she made these great big, fluffy, golden biscuits that she was very proud of, and she put it all on the table. Doc picked up a biscuit, and he said something like, 'Whoa, this is going to be good.' And she said, 'Yes, and here's the butter and the maple syrup to go on it.' And he replied, 'Why would I want to ruin a perfectly good biscuit with maple syrup for?' He said, 'Don't you have any gravy?' She said, 'Gravy?' And then, it was very funny because Doc started saying, 'Well, here we go, it's the North and

South all over again,' you know, 'what we fought the war over.' And she said, 'Well you just wait a minute.' And she went in the kitchen and she mixed up what was left, the bacon fat and some butter and flour and water and mixed up this big pitcher of gravy and brought it out and he said, 'Well, I'll be darned, that's the best gravy I've ever had. I guess the North and South can work it out.' They had quite a bit of fun with that."[21]

Doc's charm and his virtuosic talent soon began to take him around the country, both with and without the other members of the Clarence Ashley Group. By the mid-1960s, in the words of folk singer Greg Brown, "the folk boom had boomed."[22] The folk music craze had dried up. With ever fewer festivals and venues asking for folk musicians, Doc would have a hard enough time making a living by himself, let alone if he had to split the take at small venues across the country with three other bandmates.

Clint Howard remembered Rinzler coming to speak to him: "Ralph came to me and said, 'Clint, something I want to ask you and Fred. There's gonna be some jobs come up that I can get Doc. Some people can afford to pay him but they can't afford to pay all of you. Like, in some of the little festivals and clubs. I don't want to make you all mad at me or hurt your feelings, what do you think about it?' I said, 'If you don't want to make me mad, you better get him them jobs.' Because you know that's just the way he had of making his living. So he got to getting Doc jobs when they couldn't afford to hire all three of us."[3] So Clarence Ashley, Clint Howard, and Fred Price went home again, back to their farms and daily lives. It was time for Doc to go on the road by himself.

# CHAPTER NOTES

1. Spitzer, Nick, *Interview with Doc Watson*. 1987, Smithsonian Institution, Ralph Rinzler Folklife Archives: Washington D.C.
2. Murphy, Joe, *Doc and Merle -The Lives and Music of Doc & Merle Watson (1985)*, VHS, Vestapol, 1996.
3. Holt, David, *Liner Notes to Doc Watson and David Holt: Legacy*, High Windy Audio, 2002.
4. Lloyd, Bert, *Interview with Doc Watson*, Audio CD, Ralph Rinzler Folklife Archives, Smithsonian Institution, 1976.
5. Dawidoff, Nicholas, *In the country of country: people and places in American music*. 1997: Pantheon Books.
6. Rinzler, Ralph, *Notebook from Research/Recording Trip to Deep Gap*. September 3-5, 1960.
7. Rinzler, Ralph, *Liner Notes from The Original Folkways Recordings of Doc Watson and Clarence Ashley 1960-1962*, Smithsonian Folkways Records, 1994.
8. Rinzler, Ralph, *First draft of Liner Notes for Doc & Clarence album*. 1991, Smithsonian Institution, Ralph Rinzler Folklife Archives: Washington.
9. Miller, Minnie M., *Tom Clarence Ashley: An Appalachian Folk Musician*. 1973, ClarenceAshley.com: East Tennessee State University.
10. Gustavson, Kent, *Telephone Interview with Ed Pearl*. May 29, 2009.
11. Rinzler, Ralph, *Letter to Bonnie Raitt, draft 1 Regarding Re-Release of Old Time Music at Clarence Ashley's: August 18, 1991*.
12. Gustavson, Kent, *Telephone Interview with Roland White*. June 12, 2009.
13. Rinzler, Ralph, *Setlist for Ash Grove*. 1962, Smithsonian Institution, Ralph Rinzler Folklife Archives.
14. Watson, Doc, *Old-Timey Concert*, LP Record, Vanguard Records, 1967.
15. Gustavson, Kent, *Telephone Interview with Paul Chasman*. April 13, 2009.
16. Harrington, Richard, *Doc Watson, Strumming Home*. The Washington Post, January 25, 1988. Washington D.C.: p. C1,C8.
17. Cherry, Hugh, *Interview with Doc Watson*, from *The Many Faces of Folk Music*. 1968, Armed Services Radio: USA.
18. Gustavson, Kent, *Telephone Interview with Jean Ritchie*. May 6, 2009.
19. Watson, Doc and Ralph Rinzler, *The Songs of Doc Watson*. 1971, New York City: Oak Publications.
20. Gustavson, Kent, *Personal Interviews with John Cohen*. April 8 & August 6, 2009.
21. Gustavson, Kent, *Telephone Interview with Ellen Harper-Verdries*. July 3, 2009.
22. Gustavson, Kent, *Email Interview with Greg Brown*. April 1, 2009.

# CHAPTER THIRTEEN
## One Man Band

*"As a young man recently at college, I had no real sense of how to talk with Doc about a fresh career on the folk music circuit. Our experiences were very different, but with a little innovation, within 2 years, Doc was making an impact on the college folk song and urban coffee-house circuit."*

— Ralph Rinzler[1]

D oc Watson, throughout his career, has always had an uncanny ability to put an entire show together, with jokes, banter and conversation, ripping guitar licks, incredible singing, and every genre under the acoustic rainbow. No one in the history of acoustic music has had the ability that Doc Watson had, especially in his prime, to entertain an audience. In his guitar workshops at universities in the 1960s, Doc was also able to demonstrate rock and roll, country, blues, country-blues, bluegrass, Travis-picking and every other style imaginable on the acoustic guitar, as well as banjo, mandolin, auto harp and any other instrument someone would press into his hand.

Ricky Skaggs, a bluegrass mandolinist who has picked up Bill Monroe's torch in support of traditional bluegrass and recording album after album of musical gold, spoke about Doc's solo music, and how diverse it was: "When he started doing his own stuff... He was still bringing that stuff out of the mountains, but he had to have something that was kind of his, so he was doing these old hobo songs, he was doing these old country tunes, and he was doing Merle Travis as good as Merle Travis, and playing, singing, and then he'd drag the banjo out, he'd drag the harmonica out, you know..." Skaggs then went on to imagine what it would have been like to have seen Doc live in his early years: "He was just a one man band, and it was just so incredible to hear these recordings, you know, I've seen some of that stuff of what he would do, some of it live, you know. But I can't imagine what it would have been like to see him in the '60s and early '70s. My God, that would have had to have been just the greatest. Thank goodness we've got some recordings from that period in time."[2]

Photo by Peter S. Shenkin ©
*Phil Zimmerman and Doc Watson backstage at Fincastle Folk Festival in Virginia, 1965.*

Because of his ability like no other living musician to entertain audiences, diehard Doc Watson fans always secretly hope Doc will leave his entourage behind; whether his son Merle and bassist T. Michael Coleman in the 1970s, or David Holt today. Many fans long for the times that Doc steps out on stage all by himself to play a few songs with just his guitar, recalling his solo gigs of the '60s.

Mandolin innovator and legendary acoustic musician Sam Bush remembered the first time he ever saw Doc play live: "In 1965 I first saw Doc play at what was arguably the first Bluegrass Festival that was ever held; at Fincastle, Virginia, at Cantrell's Horse Farm. Carlton Haney was the promoter. It was a Friday night, getting kind of chilly, and the way I recall it, Merle was supposed to play but had gotten sick, so Doc went on by himself. I have chill bumps now thinking about hearing Doc come on and play by himself. It was awesome."[3]

A few great recordings were made early in Doc Watson's career, and among the most highly coveted and respected was the recording called *Jean Ritchie and Doc Watson at Folk City*, an LP that came out on Folkways and quickly became a favorite among folk musicians and fans. Ritchie remembered that her husband, George Pickow, recorded the entire concert using only one microphone, standing in front of Ritchie and Doc, moving the microphone from one to the other while they were performing in order to feature a certain voice or instrument. The recording still sells after more than 40 years, and is one of the favorite albums of Doc Watson fans. Clearly Pickow had a good ear for on-the-fly mixing.

Jean Ritchie enjoyed singing with Doc: "I think we had something in our singing in which we leaned on each other. We knew that we could lean on each other. Not physically, but in the singing. And we always knew what to do at a certain place and how to sound. It just sort of came naturally, because both of us were in the same pitch and all, and had the same feeling. We really were great respecters of each other's music and I think that helped a lot. Doc was charming. He was always friendly and always had a smile, and always had good things to say to you..."[4] Pickow's recording of the night they shared the stage was a crucial documentation of both the beautiful duets they made together, but also of the night that started Doc's solo career.

For the second time, Doc had traveled to New York City on a pioneer's voyage, but this time, he was alone on the Greyhound bus, arriving in the city at the beginning of December 1962. In October, he had returned to the Friends of Old Time Music with his brother and father-in-law to perform songs from *The Watson Family* LP, but he had never come to the city all by himself, nor truly traveled all alone, until this trip. Ralph Rinzler's cousin Richard Rinzler hosted Doc in New York, because Ralph was away on a tour with the Greenbriar Boys, and would only be home several days later. Richard met Doc at the Port Authority Greyhound Station, and brought him onto the subway, where he took him to the apartment he shared with his cousin Ralph at 87 Christopher Street in Greenwich Village. Their apartment was eight blocks away from Gerde's Folk City, where Doc had two weeks of concerts scheduled. Doc had borrowed a Gibson guitar from his friend Ray Handy in North Carolina, because he still didn't have an acoustic guitar of his own.[5]

Ritchie recalled how their joint gig at Gerde's Folk City had been organized: "A few months after I saw Doc in California, he wanted to drop out and be on his own. I guess maybe Ralph talked him into that, too, because he was so good. And there were so many things he could do. When they were playing together, Clarence Ashley would just give him about one song throughout the set, you know. So he wanted to play more and have people enjoy his music more and so on. At the Ash Grove, we sang some songs together. 'Storms Are On The Ocean' was one of our duets, and some others went very well. Then, Ralph wanted Doc to go to Gerde's Folk City, and I'd been singing there fairly regularly. So Ralph said, 'Will you come in when Doc does his first solo gig? Because you know, that'll keep him from being nervous.' I don't know why Doc would ever have to be nervous, but Doc thought it was a great idea, so I came in and did the other half of the program. We did one short-ish set each, and then we did a set together. And that went very well."[4]

Doc was still unknown except in the very small circles of the folk music world, and had only made a few dollars from his blossoming folk career. His family was still living below the poverty line, and these trips to New York were full of pressure for 39-year old Doc. Joe Wilson recalled, "He was instantly famous but not instantly affluent. The club dates paid very little and Doc often returned home with only a few more dollars than he had when he left."[6] Soon everything would change, but for now, he tried to sleep at night, sirens blaring and people shouting, serving as constant reminders of the distance between Doc and the mountains of home. Doc also knew that this would be only the beginning of a long career of lonely voyages away from home, which certainly didn't detract from his homesickness.

Gerde's Folk City was a small club located at 11 West 4th Street at the corner of Mercer Street, where countless folk musicians got their start, including Bob Dylan, only two weeks after Doc's first concert at PS 41, opening up for John Lee Hooker on April 11, 1961.

There was a humble entrance to the beloved Village folk club in front of the Gerde's restaurant and bar, proclaiming "N.Y. Center – Folk Music," with its folk music venue in the basement. The restaurant and club were run by Italian immigrant Mike Porco beginning in 1952, and he began hosting Monday night hootenannies in the basement in 1959, which quickly became a happening, attracting the cream of the crop within the folk movement. The Greenbriar Boys were regulars at Folk City, alongside The New World Singers, Odetta, Pete Seeger, Phil Ochs, Peter, Paul and Mary, Simon and Garfunkel, and countless other performers.

Mike Porco recalled first meeting folk singers at the restaurant: "In 1952, my cousins bought a restaurant in the Village, an old place called Gerde's... One day, in late 1959, two guys walked in – Izzy Young and Tom Prendergast. They told me they were folk fans. I said, 'What's folk music?' Izzy ran the Folklore Center and they kind of tried to explain to me the popularity of people like Pete Seeger, Joan Baez and Odetta... So, the folk tradition at Gerde's – which was renamed The Fifth Peg at Gerde's – was begun..."[7] Young remembered the deal the three men struck: "We would pay all the publicity, we would pay all the singers, and we would keep the gate. He would sell drinks and food. He couldn't lose. We couldn't win." Admission was $1.50 per person, and they struggled to make ends meet. The makeshift club opened in January 1960 and closed by May. But the idea of a folk music club was not lost on Porco. The next month, with help from talent booker Charlie Rothschild, he reopened the club as Gerde's Folk City.[5]

Porco was looking for something that could bring in more customers, and be more lucrative than The Fifth Peg had been. Thinking about all of the young folk musicians who regularly came to his restaurant, he thought that he should try out an amateur talent night. He spoke about it with Rothschild and with his friend, New York Times reporter Robert Shelton, and they both suggested that he capitalize on the term "hootenanny" which was popular at the time. Porco remembered: "The hoots went on all night and attracted many of the younger professionals who were still perfecting their craft – Judy Collins, Tom Paxton, Jack Elliott, Dave Van Ronk, even a very young Arlo Guthrie... [And] one day, this young boy came in asking to play. He said his name was Bob Dylan..." Porco later signed on as Dylan's legal guardian because the boy wasn't yet allowed to sign for his own union card.[7]

The meanings of Gerde's Folk City within Doc Watson's career were manifold. First, the two-week long engagement helped him first develop solo material in front of an audience that he would use for the rest of his career. Second, it allowed him to play with other folk musicians from within the New York City folk music scene. Third, it allowed him to promote his own name, and not be an accompanist as he had been for the last two decades. The last point was the most important. Doc had never been a headliner before. He had played some amazing gigs, but he had never been the headliner: certainly not in front of such a consistently packed and interested audience. During those two weeks in 1962, Doc forever endeared himself to the city that never sleeps.

One of the musicians who played with Doc for several nights during that first series of concerts at Gerde's was John Herald, a member of the Greenbriar Boys with Ralph Rinzler. James Reams, a New York City old time musician and long time friend of John Herald, remembered, "Ralph Rinzler set it up for him to play with Doc. I think he was just flabbergasted at Doc's abilities, and it was probably one of the biggest thrills in his life."[8] Herald also then recorded with Doc the next year on his first self-titled album with Vanguard.

Another influential musician who first played with Doc Watson on the stage of Gerde's Folk City was David Grisman. For young Grisman, playing with Doc on stage was a major rite of passage. He remembered, "I was 17 at the time...and I think Ralph's younger cousin Richard put a bug in Doc's ear about me having a mandolin with me. In any case, Doc invited me up on stage to play a song or two. I remember playing 'In the Pines' and perhaps another tune. It made a profound impact on me because I had never been asked by a pro to sit in before that. It was then, and still is today, a great thrill to play with Doc."[9]

That was the first time that Doc had the opportunity to share the stage with up-and-coming musicians, but certainly not the last. Playing with Doc on stage has been a rite of passage for generations. He played with the young flatpicking guitar wizard Clarence White on stage at Newport in 1963, brought Sam Bush, Marty Stuart and countless other instrumentalists along with their tours in the 1970s and 80s, played fiddle tunes backstage with blind fiddler Michael Cleveland in 1993, and shared a stage with young mandolinist Chris Thile at MerleFest in 2003. Playing with Doc on stage is a rite of passage, and the musicians of every decade who are lucky enough to join him on stage go on to become the innovators in their field.

Photo by John Cohen ©
*Ralph Rinzler & John Herald at the Gaslight Café, 1962.*

Mark D. Moss, editor of *Sing Out!* magazine since 1983, remembered being in the audience to see Doc play at Gerde's Folk City: "We walked down a few steps to get into the club's tiny room, which certainly didn't hold more than a hundred people. It was kind of like being in like a cellar all painted black, then there were spotlights, and black and white pictures on the wall of folk revival stars that all played there. And when Doc played, it got pin-drop silent because there were a lot of guitar players in the room and transfixed eyes were trying to see how he was doing that so fast, but so smooth. Just the sound of what he did, I'd say that really opened my mind to a lot of things in that kind of way; the breadth of material that he was doing and how he could bring it together. It was almost like you were sitting in the guy's living room or kitchen and having him sing with you."[10]

Doc recalled the Gerde's Folk City concerts very well, especially how focused the audience was on his music: "I could not believe the attentiveness of the little audiences there. I was under the impression for a long time that a man had to be able to see and put on a big act on stage to get people's attention. It was unbelievable how people would sit intent and listen to those old-time tunes. In those days I never really thought that I would become an entertainer in the public's eye in this country and all over the world. It was the most amazing thing in the world, when people applauded and hollered and yelled for more."[5] Doc spoke about Gerde's as practice for the rest of his career: "I thought, 'Did I really do that good?' I'm sure that was the beginning, like laying down a groundwork, learning how to do something. That had a lot to do with whatever style happened later."[5]

Doc began to gain a foothold in the folk music world, and guitarists began purchasing his recordings and attending his concerts in droves. At the same time, well-known musicians began to hear about him, including Bill Monroe. When Ralph Rinzler began managing Monroe in the early 1960s, it was natural that the two musicians should meet.

Doc and Merle first met at the Ash Grove in Los Angeles in 1963, and a life-long friendship was forged between the two men; a friendship that later culminated in a career-high performance in front of President Jimmy Carter on the White House Lawn in 1980. Doc also shared the stage with Bill Monroe at Newport in 1963 in front of thousands. At the same festival, Doc played as a member of the Clarence Ashley Group, the Watson family group, and solo. This was just the break Doc needed, and at Newport, he reached a wider audience than he ever imagined would be possible.

Tony Trischka remembered of the 1963 Newport Folk Festival: "The whole protesting thing was big that year, because Dylan was there, Phil Ochs was there, Tom Paxton was there, Pete Seeger was there, and Peter La Farge and some other slightly less well-known folks. And then Bill Monroe was there that year, and I remember loving that. I remember wondering, his banjo player had this very strange style, and I couldn't figure out what it was, and it turns out it was Bill Keith playing melodic style. And then of course all the old blues guys were there, like Mississippi John Hurt. I don't think Skip James was there that year, but Sonny Terry and Brownie McGhee were. Peter, Paul and Mary, who were also there that year, were big, much bigger than someone like Mississippi John Hurt in a commercial sense, but I think there was a reverence for these older names. I kind of remember that everyone was sort of on an equal plane, which is what Newport wanted."[11] Trischka recalled the important structure that the festival's organizers had put into place for that year's festival: "I remember Newport paid everyone the same amount of money, whether you were Peter, Paul and Mary or Doc Watson. I still have the program books from back then, and it said that in there, in their credo statement. Everyone was getting the same amount of money. Which was a great leveler. I think that was a pretty cool way to do it."[11] The great leveler of equal pay for all musicians brought musicians like Joan Baez and Bob Dylan together, as well as Doc Watson and Bill Monroe. It allowed Mike Seeger to conduct a workshop on banjo with the help of Clarence Ashley, Doc Watson and Dock Boggs. It brought together acts like Peter, Paul and Mary, who were major commercial successes, with musicians like Doc and his family, who still lived in poverty.

If Doc could have looked out at the sea of people who hushed to hear the sounds of his old time singing and blistering flatpicking, Doc would have seen that the audience hung on every note. But he certainly heard the hush, and knew they were listening intently. Doc was now *somebody* in the world of folk music; he was mentioned in sentences alongside Bob Dylan and Mississippi John Hurt, young artists and traditional music legends.

Doc looked calm and collected on stages in front of audiences both small and large. At Newport '63, he had been in front of tens of thousands of people, and at the Ash Grove, he'd been in front of 200. Regardless of the venue, Doc made his audiences feel like they were on his front porch. And it wasn't hard for Doc to imagine; he would just squint his sightless eyes tighter, inviting his audience back home with him to Deep Gap through his singing and playing. Despite Doc's rock-solid rhythm and relaxed banter on stage, he admitted his fear to Eugene Earle in a 1988 interview: "Gene, that first solo concert tour

I did…buddy, I'm going to tell you what's the truth. I was scared out of my senses, on the stage by myself."[12]

Doc told Earle that the Ash Grove concerts in 1962 and 1963 hadn't scared him, but that solo engagements were a different story: "The concert stage… scared me to death."[12] Doc especially had a hard time knowing that the audience could hear all of his faults, and that, since he was playing solo, his playing was very exposed to scrutiny: "That was what really floored me – [the audience was] gonna hear all my mistakes. But, boy, once you realized that they really cared about it, and if there was… If you want to look at a piece of antique furniture – if there was a nick and a scratch here and there in the music, they didn't mind at all. They wanted to hear you play the old things. So I got in there and worked on it, things like 'Matty Groves,' the ballad. That was a tough one, but I did my guitar arrangement on it, and worked it out. That thing's five minutes and thirty seconds long, but it tells the tale…"[12] Doc remembered that, even out in front of thousands of people, "you could hear a pin drop sometimes, unless there was city noise."[13]

It didn't take long before Doc started to relish going on stage in front of an admiring audience, but he never got used to the traveling and loneliness of the road: "The music itself and the shows on the stage I loved… That, plus the fact that I was earning a little living while poor little Rosa Lee was doing back-breaking work at home and keeping the home fires burning. I was trying to do my part, and the lonely hours was the interest I had to pay…on the money I earned."[14] Guy Clark, Texas singer-songwriter and great admirer of Doc Watson, recalled, of his own dues-paying years: "Just about everybody gets to pay their dues. It's just part of it. If you want to keep doing it, you've got to start somewhere. And it's usually not at the top. You gradually keep doing it and hopefully get better at it, and hopefully get paid more."[15]

There were times when Doc felt that he wouldn't be able to keep up the weeks of travel, sleeping on couches and fending for himself. He specifically remembered one moment in his early solo career that he almost quit everything: "In '63, I was playing at a place in Philadelphia at a place called the Second Fret… It was in the center of the city, and I was going to have to stay in a little motel across the street, and if I did that, it was going to eat up what I could earn in the two weeks I was opening for [Clarence White's band, The Kentucky Colonels]. I wasn't going to clear but about, oh, maybe 50 or 60 dollars a week, and I couldn't see that, 'cause it was hard work. It was 5 nights a week, and I made up my mind, at the end of that two weeks, I was going to go home and I was going to stay there."[14] Doc had been all around the country, with the Clarence Ashley Group and now solo. He'd been on the largest stage for folk music in the country, and he'd played small clubs and everything in between but he wasn't able to make any significant earnings, and he started to doubt that the benefits could outweigh his doubts. And most importantly, he missed his family and home terribly: "I was one homesick boy for my wife and children. I still begrudge those years that I had to be away from them. That's a hard thing to do, [no matter how much you] love music; as [much] as you love a good audience."[16]

Doc recalled that his new friend Jerry Ricks provided the solution to his problem, leading to his decision to stay on the road: "I almost did quit in '63... [But] there was a young fellow, Jerry Ricks, who worked for Manny Rubens at the 2nd Fred in Philadelphia; he was working in the kitchen; I guess he was cooking. And I went in there and was going to stay in a little hotel right across the street, and I'd be by myself all day long and as I had a two-week engagement there..."[16] However, when Doc finished his set, Ricks came up to him and said, "Doc Watson, there's a good clean room over at my house with a nice bed in it and your name is on the door – I want you to come stay with me for these two weeks. You don't need to stay at no fleabag [motel]."[14] Doc agreed to stay with Ricks, but only if he would allow him to share the grocery bill, and they'd play music together as some kind of additional payment. Ricks recorded their sessions together, and learned a great deal from Doc, and Doc learned a few blues licks from his friend. Doc remembered that the men ate "like kings," and they only spent $35 each for the entire time.

Before Doc met Jerry Ricks, he would have cleared just $50 for the entire two-week engagement, but due to his new friend's generosity, Doc was able to make $200 and bring home some money to Rosa Lee. With Ricks' help, Doc had found a way to make a lucrative living. He could enjoy Ricks' company, pay for his groceries, and still earn a good income for his tenure at the folk club. He decided not to quit. And Doc also kept getting along in the industry, slowly learning how to make a good living at it; soon reaching heights he couldn't have imagined.

Doc made young, admiring friends on every stop along his path, and one of the first to meet him was Peter Rowan, who lived in the same building as Ralph

Rinzler and met Doc in 1963: "I was living with Bill Keith and Jim Rooney in Cambridge, Massachusetts, and Ralph Rinzler lived just downstairs. And so we hung out a lot, and that's how I met Doc. He would come up and stay at Ralph's place and we would have parties upstairs and everything. We'd sit around in the evenings and pick, up at Bill Keith's. Doc would play all kinds of things, including banjo. Mostly he'd play guitar, but at the time Ralph was coaching him to show all his talents. Did I feel like the luckiest guy in the world? Yes."[17] Indeed, every one of Doc's young musician friends who had a chance to hang out and pick with him felt lucky.

Tom Paxton was another young musician who had befriended and was deeply inspired by Doc. He recalled many times at the Gaslight having the opportunity to watch the septuagenarian country blues legend Mississippi John Hurt and Doc Watson pal around: "Since I was kind of on the permanent staff at the Gaslight – I played there once for nine months straight – I got to hear Doc every night he played there, and I got to hear John Hurt every night when he played there. That was the irreplaceable time of experience in my life. I recall seeing Doc and John Hurt sitting there talking and nodding heads and laughing. John was a very old man by then, and Doc was still very young. But they sure got along well together." Paxton recalled that Doc carried around a tape recorder: "Doc would be backstage at the Gaslight with his tape recorder recording everything. That's how he learned a lot of songs – off the tapes that he made."[18] Doc made friends with and learned from every musician he encountered, regardless of age, both inspiring and taking inspiration.

Doc's friendships also started opening opportunities for him, though he could not accept all of them. John Cohen remembered that he and Mike Seeger greatly respected Doc Watson, and that, when Tom Paley quit the New Lost City Ramblers in 1962, they had to choose a replacement for him. Before they decided on Tracy Schwarz, they auditioned the idea of asking Doc to join the group. Cohen remembered: "Tom Paley announced he was leaving the Ramblers, but couldn't say when. So we couldn't really replace him right away. And we had the idea that Doc, having sung with us in New York and the University of Chicago festival, might be able to reach out and join the group. It would even satisfy our program more; it would be meeting of country and city. And so I remember, when I was in the North Carolina area for some reason, I drove over to Doc's to talk to him about this. And then I got this letter back from Doc. The letter thanked us and all of that, but he said, 'I don't think I want to travel very much. I'm not up to that.' But he also wrote, 'If there's ever a big festival or something like that, a big high paying job, I'd be glad to join you boys; I just have to come up early and we can rehearse some.'"[19]

Since Doc Watson left the Raleigh School for the Blind, Doc had lived as a charge of his home state, and with his state support and his meager income from playing square dances, he had supported his two children and purchased a modest home. And now, just after his 40th birthday, Doc Watson finally would be able to earn a living for his family without any help from the state. Even today, around 70% of the blind population in the United States is unemployed.[20] Doc was breaking the mold, and he couldn't have been happier.

In April of 1963, only two years after he had brought Doc Watson to New York with the Clarence Ashley Group for their first performance, Rinzler received a letter from the Watauga County Department of Public Welfare in North Carolina. Frances Walker, a caseworker for the blind, wrote:

*Re: Arthel Watson*
*Deep Gap*
*North Carolina*

*Dear Mr. Renizler (sic):*

*The above named person receives Aid to the Blind through our department. He tells us that you have been scheduling him for appearances with "The Friends of Old [Time] Music" band.*

*We would like to know how much Mr. Watson earns from these appearances. This information is necessary for our records. We will appreciate your sending us a statement verifying Mr. Watson's wages.[21]*

Shortly thereafter, knowing of this event's importance to Doc and his family, Rinzler wrote back to Miss Walker, "With regard to Mr. Watson's earnings on these appearances, I can only say that his fee varies with the individual booking. At my request, he has kept a detailed account of both his earnings and expenses since January 1st, 1963. On his return to Deep Gap at the beginning of June, Mr. Watson will provide you with a copy of his records."[22] And when the welfare worker contacted Doc and confirmed his earnings, he went off state assistance permanently. Doc remembered, "My daughter was so proud of that – bless her little heart... She was the proudest young-un I've ever seen."[23]

WATAUGA COUNTY
## DEPARTMENT OF PUBLIC WELFARE
BOONE, NORTH CAROLINA

April 12, 1963

Mr. Ralph Renizler
87 Christopher Street
New York 14, New York

> Re:  Arthel Watson
>      Deep Gap
>      North Carolina

Dear Mr. Renizler:

The above named person receives Aid to the Blind through our department. He tells us that you have been scheduling him for appearances with "The Friends of Old Country Music" band.

We would like to know how much Mr. Watson earns from these appearances. This information is necessary for our records. We will appreciate your sending us a statement verifying Mr. Watson's wages.

Thank you.

Very truly yours,

WATAUGA COUNTY WELFARE DEPARTMENT

*Dave P. Mast*

Dave P. Mast,
Director

*Frances Walker*
rhc

(Miss) Frances Walker,
Case Worker for the Blind

FW:rhc

cc

15 May 1963

Miss Frances Walker
Watauga County Dept. of Public Welfare
Boone, North Carolina

Dear Miss Walker:

With reference to your letter of April 12th, I should
like to offer an apology for the delay in my answer;
the letter was recently forwarded to me here in Los
Angeles.

I have, in fact, been acting as agent and manager for
Mr. Watson booking appearances throughout the country.
With regard to Mr. Watson's earnings on these appearances
I can only say that his fee varies with the individual
booking. At my request, he has kept a detailed account
of both earnings and expenses since January 1st, 1963.
On his return to Depp Gap at the beginning of June, Mr.
Watson will provide you with a copy of his records. Should
you require any further information from me, please do
not hesitate to write to me at my New York address, and
I shall endeavor to provide you with the material at my
disposal as promptly as possible.

Very truly yours,

Ralph C. Rinzler

Digital scan by Stephanie Smith.
Reprinted with permission of the Ralph Rinzler Folklife Archives, Smithsonian Institution.
*Letter from Ralph Rinzler to Dept. of Public Welfare, May 15, 1963.*

Interviewing Doc Watson in 1974, Joe Wilson asked Doc about most
important moment in his career; Doc answered Wilson, smiling: "One day
I came home from a trip, sat down and wrote to the people with the state, and
told them I wouldn't be needing their help anymore."[6]

When Maynard Solomon, the owner of Vanguard Records, heard about Doc's popularity at Newport '63, as well as his diverse talents, he began speaking with Ralph Rinzler about signing Doc to Vanguard for his solo material as well. This would lead to Doc's first major income from his efforts as a folk musician. In December of 1963, Doc signed a contract with Vanguard to record his first solo album, and was given an advance of $1000. That was just the beginning for Doc, but it was an important step for him towards supporting his wife and kids with his music.

Doc Watson's self-titled first Vanguard album sold nearly 9,000 copies in 1964, and in its second year posted similar numbers. Rinzler wrote to Doc in the postscript of a November 1964 letter: "Just remembered what I wanted to tell you. Maynard and I checked the figures on your record...it has sold 5,000 copies to this date. This is far better than Maynard had anticipated in these first few months. It has paid for itself or almost paid for itself by now, and you will go into royalties by about the first of the year [1965]. How about that?"[24] Doc's record wasn't the label's bestselling album by any stretch, but these were reasonable figures, and Vanguard continued to support Doc's music for years to come.

Vanguard was a record label not unlike Folkways, in that both were willing to release material that other labels wouldn't touch. Folkways, for example, released Pete Seeger's entire catalog during his time on the blacklist in the 1950s and early 1960s, and Vanguard released the Weavers' catalog (of whom Pete Seeger was the lead singer) in the same period. Joan Baez later liked the Vanguard record label because it allowed her to be outspoken in her political activism; after releasing her first two albums in 1960 and 1961, Baez embarked on a controversial tour of the south, encouraging integrated crowds at her concerts, soon after to be featured on the cover of *Time* magazine for her outspoken actions and views. Largely because of Baez's records, Vanguard was at the peak of its power in the music industry when Doc signed with the label in 1963.

Sam Bush recalled getting his copy of Doc's first Vanguard LP: "I'll never forget when Doc's first record came out on Vanguard, just that photograph is so stunning to me, the black and white photo of Doc sitting there with a Martin D-18. When I first heard that record, I loved his voice, and the playing was so clean, and, obviously, he's known for flatpicking, but what a great fingerpicker he is, too. Also overlooked is his singing, and definitely overlooked is what a great harmonica player he is. He also played some banjo on 'Come All You Good Time People.' It was just so beautiful and straight to the point; not one wasted note anywhere."[25]

As the numbers began to pour in for 1964 sales, Rinzler had indeed done good work on Doc's behalf, and Doc got his first royalty check in early 1965. And more important than income or initial numbers, the reviews that came in from various national newspapers were incredibly positive, and made it easy for Rinzler to book Doc around the country at various folk clubs and universities for higher fees. In the *Chicago Daily News*, Joe Haas reported, "Here is perhaps the best solo album by the most talented singer and instrumentalist today, with an authentic background in both American folk and country music. Doc Watson is an amazing instrumentalist, perhaps the best folk and country guitarist around and a fine fiddler and banjo-picker, too. In his pleasing North Carolina tenor, he sings a fine selection of songs including 'Omie Wise,' 'Tom Dooley,' 'Intoxicated Rat,' and 'Talk About Suffering,' and you won't hear a better fingerpicking guitar solo than 'Doc's Guitar.'"[26] And there couldn't have been a much better review for Doc's record in a major Chicago newspaper. A similarly stellar review was written for *The Sunday Standard* in Washington D.C. by Herman Schaden: "Doc Watson is as natural as the Blue Ridge Mountains he comes from. A master of the guitar, banjo, and harmonica, he sings with the unabashed zest of a fellow who learned it all as a boy, and doesn't hanker for new-falutin' ways..."[27]

Doc recorded his first Vanguard album over just a few days in New York City shortly after the contract negotiations with Vanguard were completed. During that same extended visit to New York, Doc also played his first large concert in the city, double-billing Town Hall (1100-capacity sold out audience) with Bill Monroe. Robert Shelton, who had so favorably reviewed the Clarence Ashley Group's concert in 1961, waxed even more effuse about Doc's talents in his review of the concert: "Mr. Watson is a blind singer and instrumentalist whose almost legendary guitar technique has won him a cult of admirers... Mr. Watson's talents are more than virtuosity. Few singers out of the Southern Appalachians are so able to evoke another time, another place, and another set of aesthetic standards. Whether in playful ditties or spirituals, his grainy, emotion-laden voice transports one into the 'folk life' of the south. His incredible finger dexterity, the economy of statement and a rhythmic mastery turn Mr. Watson's flatpicking, as his style is called, into dazzling showpieces. Occasionally, the single-note melody line will seem to be moving the fluidity of country fiddling to a guitar. On banjo, harmonica, guitar or singing unaccompanied, Mr. Watson is a complete country music titan."[28] The review from the *New York Times'* premier folk music reporter, combined with his first "official" recording session for Vanguard, certainly didn't dampen Doc's spirits about the possibilities that lay ahead for him in the music world. And this was the first time of many that a reporter used the word "legendary" to describe Doc.

A year after his first album was recorded, Vanguard began arranging for Doc to record a live album. It was to be titled *Doc Watson in Concert*. Ralph Rinzler was hoping that Doc would continue to support the traditional persona he had helped him to develop over the past few years. Rinzler wrote Doc a letter on November 25th, 1964 that outlined the details: "There is a chance that Vanguard will start to record your concerts in the very near future so that your next album can be an all live recording *Doc Watson in Concert*. I am not certain that they will be at the two concerts in January, but you can be certain that they will be recording you by early spring at your concerts. With this thought in mind, you should start to work on a few new songs so that you will be singing material that you would like to see on a third record at your concerts." Rinzler wanted Doc to develop additional material so that concert audiences would continue to want him to show up; he could play new music each year, much as popular musicians did. He wrote, "Try to get as much as you can from Gaither in the way of verses to old songs and tunes as well. Especially try to get together a version of 'Georgie.' Then there is the version of the 'Dying Cowboy' that Mrs. Waters sang. Perhaps you and Rosa Lee can leaf through *The Christian Harmony* and find another hymn which you heard way back when.... You can get verses to 'Stay in the Middle of the Road' or 'Everybody's Leaving This Town,' whichever one was sung, and pick that on the banjo. Also there is 'Cousin Sally Brown' which you pick the fire out of on the banjo. There should be another tune in the finger-style blues vein like 'Deep River Blues' and 'Weary Blues.' I think that for this third record, you could easily do that Tom Paxton tune 'Wonder Where I'm Bound' if you feel you'd like to record it. One or two comic pieces like '50 cents' or something in that line would be good and then a guitar instrumental, either finger style, like 'Doc's Guitar' or flatpicking style on some fiddle tunes will fill it out."[24]

Rinzler had serious ideological positions on the music that he thought Doc should record on his upcoming album, and he told him so. Rinzler wrote: "Doc, this may seem like a tall order to fill, but along with a measure of success such as you have attained comes a responsibility to yourself and your past reputation. We both have talked about the way folks will talk of a performer and say, well he was o.k. when he started out on his first few records, but then he started doing all that other stuff. What they are usually saying reflects the fact that a performer works hard to get somewhere, and as soon as he's recognized and successful he gets lazy or gets an image of himself as a SUCCESS. It's easy enough to say that you don't think that way, because you surely aren't that sort of person, but it's sometimes hard to see the connection between the hard work that goes into learning songs and the importance of maintaining the level of your material and performance as high as it was at the outset. In your case it is all the more important because you are not simply an entertainer...people get more of a message from you than they do from an entertainer, and they believe in you. Now, you can say amen and forgive the sermon."[24] Rinzler truly believed that Doc would be more successful if he stayed within the confines of the folk paradigm, and he hoped that Doc had left his electric guitar days behind him.

Doc really relied on Rinzler's guidance through the early years of his career, and he also allowed Rinzler to program his albums and sets in his first few years on the road. Doc remembered putting together his repertoire: "I didn't throw away the old music. I kept it in the repertoire. I learned a lot of later things too. I hadn't forgotten the old music; I had to brush up on it. If I liked a song, I'd learn it... People would give me records or tapes. Most of the music I brushed up on I got from Eugene Earle, the collector. He would send me lots of recordings on tape off the old records. In the '60s when I was learning old, new material, some of it was new to me, and some of it was stuff we had on records at home when I was little."[29]

Rinzler remembered going on collecting trips with Doc in his local area: "Doc was active in the quest for repertoire. Together we visited and recorded numerous members of his immediate and extended family. Doc refreshed his memory on verses through these family visits and recording sessions, and through our joint review of major folksong collections, which we perused while on the road or visiting each other's homes. Independently, Doc established productive relationships with record collectors and discographers who sent him tapes of vintage recordings, some of which he had heard as a child; others were either new or only vaguely familiar to him."[29]

John Cohen remembered that it took a long time for Doc to admit that these songs weren't all from his family members or even from his community. He also learned a great number of the songs off of records: "For years Doc wouldn't acknowledge that Ralph played him song after song off the Harry Smith *Anthology*. I mean, he gave him the whole thing. That was not known for a very long time. And Doc certainly didn't talk about it." Rinzler's goal was that Doc would appear to have an immense traditional music background, and they would collect music together in order for it to happen. Jack Lawrence, Doc's longtime road partner and stellar flatpicking guitarist, remembered, "Coming into the folk music boom was a real effort for Doc. He went back to relatives, to Cecil Sharp's book of Appalachian folksongs... Doc went back and studied the old songs.

Ralph told him to play the folk revival for what it was worth. Play the old songs first, he said, and then you can do what you want to do."[30]

In thinking about Doc Watson's diverse musical tastes, Jonathan Byrd, a North Carolina folk singer who is often compared with Doc, said, "Doc was a true traditional musician, in the sense that he took in what his community gave to him and gave it back in a way that represented his best effort. He rearranged verses so that the songs made more sense, brought Travis-style picking in to set more of a stage for a story (rather than a busy dance-rhythm), and used a capo for better positions and keys. He was being of service to his audience, rather than re-producing an intellectual idea of authenticity."[31]

While Doc was constantly on a quest for new material to record, Rinzler wanted Doc to remain a *purist*. Rinzler would often become infuriated by musicians who would do jazzy versions of ballads and bluegrass versions of modern pop songs. Rinzler's friend Neil Rosenberg remembered that Rinzler especially hated The Country Gentlemen because they would do this.[32] He didn't want Doc's music to turn into the kind of music that the Country Gentlemen made, and he did everything in his power to keep Doc traditional by his own aesthetic.

After Doc released his first album with Vanguard, he spent a great deal of time on the road. In late January of 1964, only several weeks after he had finished recording the album, he left home to play the first dates in a busy year with Ralph Rinzler. Chicago, New York, Boston, Minneapolis. And then, on March 19th, 1964, Doc went on tour by himself for the first time. He had played solo engagements before, but this was a six-week long tour. He remembered: "The first concert [was at Purdue University in Indiana]. I had a tape of it for while, but it was actually...so bad that I erased it. I kept the second one, I've got it somewhere, it was [at the University of Illinois in Urbana]. And I sounded little better the next night and so I'd better keep that tape."[33] Each night, Doc improved and was a little less nervous than the previous night, and only five days into the tour, his father-in-law Gaither would be joining him for nearly two weeks in Chicago. Doc then played gigs through the Midwest, and stayed on the road until the 6th of May. That was the longest Doc had been away from home since he'd been at the Raleigh School for the Blind as a boy. But he survived the experience and he made good money, and of course he enjoyed the audiences.

Ralph Rinzler, who acted as Doc's manager until the late 1960s when Manny Greenhill took over, in later years realized that the road had been extremely difficult for his blind friend. Rinzler thought back in a 1988 interview: "It took a terrible toll on him... The stomach ulcers for the first few years just ground him up."[34] Doc recalled: "If I had to travel by myself again like I did in the early '60s before Merle started, I would have quit a long time ago... Son, that's hard. For a green country man not really used to the city, it was a scary thing to come to New York and wonder, 'Will that guy meet me there at the bus station, and will the bus driver help me change buses?' and all that stuff, people not knowing you're blind and stepping on your feet. It's just scary, the road is."[34] But Doc braved the road, and he made a good living for his family. He even traveled to England in 1966, where Rinzler accompanied him on the journey and on stage. In the Ralph Rinzler Folklife Archives in Washington D.C. are still all of the receipts from the Buchanan Street Station Hotel and Restaurant in Glasgow where Mr. R. Rinzler and Mr. Watson stayed in Room No. 49, and spent 3 pounds 70 for the room and breakfast on November 21st, 1965. And there is the receipt for the draughtsman and diving knife that Doc bought as souvenirs at an antique shop.[35] But what isn't in the written record is Doc's exhaustion.

Doc had now been on the road solo for two solid years, and he was a middle-aged blind man. He always was very pleasant and polite, but road-weariness was easy to see around his eyes. Peggy Seeger, the wonderful singer, folk musician, and sister of Mike Seeger, was living in Great Britain at the time with her husband Ewan MacColl, playing and singing within the English traditional music scene; they made eight albums together between 1960 and 1964. She recalled Doc's visit to England with Rinzler: "Doc came over there...Doc came to England. I remember Ralph Rinzler brought him around, and he came to our club. And he was exhausted. Ralph had arranged a literally night after night after night after night tour. Doc was exhausted, but he did a beautiful show. He did a lovely show. Really. There's an English style of guitar playing now, but I remember there weren't very many really good guitarists then. And when Doc came over, people flocked to hear the guitar playing. They loved it."[36] It was the experience of a lifetime for Doc to visit England, and his career in the states was really starting to take off as well. But his health was deteriorating, and he was also smoking more cigarettes than he should have been, as many folk singers did at the time.

Traditional, blues and popular singer Ben Harper, on the road all over the world in support of his bestselling albums, spoke about his own touring schedule and his family life, identifying with Doc's troubles on the road: "It's a non-negotiable thing that as you get older, you have to find a better way to balance out. The challenge is to balance out home life with the road to your advantage, and to your children's advantage. It's easier said than done, but it is doable, it's possible. I'm turning 40 this year, and this is the first time in my life I feel like I am reaching a fair place. It has been more about me to date, I will admit, not to say that I haven't been at every parent/teacher conference and that I haven't been there for every first day and every last day of school and every birthday. I mean, I've structured it responsibly, but yet still with the narcissist that it takes, the single dimensional, the uni-dimensional focused narcissism it takes to be a touring musician, I have just this year, for the first time, gotten a great balance that favors family over work, and I'm really proud of that and I look forward to making that stick for years to come."[37] At age 40, Harper has learned to handle the pressures of the road. But he has already been on the road for nearly two decades, and at age 40, Doc had just started out.

Rinzler helped Doc when he could, and he successfully figured out a way for Doc to spend more time at home, now that his records were selling better, and he was able to get a little more money for each live concert he played. In a letter to Marlena Langston on December 19th, 1965, Rinzler detailed his plans to shorten Doc's tour for the next year. He said that, "Doc finds that traveling is beginning to take a toll on his stamina and wishes to cut down on the length of his tours. Thus I have to cut a week out of his West Coast tour..."[38] Doc needed to find some way to stay healthy. The answer might not have been what he was expecting. His son Merle soon agreed to come with his dad on the road full time.

There's no way that Doc could have continued to make a lucrative career in the ensuing years if Merle hadn't joined him. The folk scene was drying up, and Merle enabled him to reach a younger audience that he wouldn't have been able to otherwise reach. Merle also allowed Doc to have a family member with him all the time, to lead him in terrain he'd never seen before, to lead him onto stage, to cut his steaks and tell him if a pretty girl was walking by. Doc had toured for a few years all by himself, but it was very hard on him, and he didn't want to do that anymore.

Among the first things Merle influenced was his father's smoking habit. As a 50-percent business partner, Merle had gotten more powerful in what he was able to say to his father, and he saw how cigarettes damaged Doc's health and voice. Little did Doc know then, Merle probably made it possible for his father to live as long as he has; still traveling and playing concerts at age 87.

Doc quit smoking in 1967. He recalled in a 1974 interview: "I quit cigarettes seven years ago... I think I was up to two packs a day. I told Merle, 'Son, I'm gonna quit these dadburn things.' He said, 'You ain't got the nerve.' That really struck me. They had my voice almost as bad as it is now [with laryngitis]. I had let a little thing like a cigarette take over my whole life."[39]

Merle Watson didn't want to follow in his father's footsteps. He chose the drum set when his parents gave him a choice of instrument. For Christmas in 1963, following a year of great news for Doc and a thousand dollar advance from Vanguard Records, Doc and Rosa Lee purchased a new baby blue drum set for their 14-year old son. Merle played around on the drums for a couple of months, but never got much of anywhere on them. When Doc went out on the road in March of 1964 for six weeks, Merle, perhaps wanting his father to be proud of him, picked up the guitar. Merle's sister Nancy remembered: "It was on a night in April, when Merle was barely fifteen, that he said, 'Mama, I've decided what I really want to do.' 'What is it, honey?' she asked. He'd received a set of drums at Christmas, so I was sure that he was going to say he wanted to play the drums. But [he said], 'I want to play the guitar.'"[40]

While Doc was touring the Midwest, Merle picked up the guitar and learned a few chords from his mother, and was able to accompany her on a number of tunes. When Ralph Rinzler came down to visit the Watson family a few weeks later, to see how they were holding up without Doc for the nearly two months he would be on tour, he was amazed to find that Merle was able to play the guitar. In an interview with Bert Lloyd, Merle recalled that he got a lot of practice when Rinzler came to visit: "Ralph Rinzler was responsible for me [really being able to play the guitar] in the beginning I guess... He came down and spent some time with us when Daddy was on a tour once, and I learned a couple of chords and we went around the house for a couple of weeks picking, and that started it."[41] Rosa Lee recalled Rinzler's visit: "Ralph Rinzler come – I guess it was Easter weekend – and Merle sat down and backed everything up that he played. [Ralph] got so excited, he didn't know what to do; he was running all over the place..."[42]

Before Doc Watson ever saw his son play the guitar, Merle had already been featured in newspapers around the country: a picture of him playing guitars with his mother. One caption under the photograph, printed in the May 16th, 1964 Miami Herald, read: "Eddy Merle Watson's Mother Sings Ballad of Murder... he accompanies North Carolina song on a guitar." And so began Merle's music career at the tender age of 15. In the article, Winfrey even wrote, "[Merle] has Doc's gift for the guitar; after seven weeks of practice, he already plays better than a teacher I once had in Miami..."[43]

Doc remembered the first time he heard that Merle had started playing the guitar: "[Ralph Rinzler] called me, and he said, 'I've got a surprise for you. I got some news for you.' And I said, 'If it's bad, then lay it on me.' And he kind of laughed, and he said, 'Merle has started playing the guitar.'" By the time Doc arrived home on the 22nd of May that year, just over two months after he had left home on tour, Doc recalled that Merle could pick "Never on Sunday" and a few other "fingerstyle things."[13]

Doc was so amazed at his son's ability to back him up on just about any tune that he decided to ask his boy to come with him to a festival. Merle was thrilled. Doc recalled asking, simply, "Son, I believe you're ready to play some back-up with me on stage. Would you like to go with me to Berkeley?'... [And] we went to the Berkeley Folk Festival in 1964. That was the first trip that Merle made with me."[44]

Despite Merle's accompaniment of his father on the road and onstage, the strain of travel and the pressures of business weighed heavily on Doc, and he ended up fighting for his life in Nashville after his appendix ruptured in 1966. Besides good doctors and his family members around him, Doc also was visited by bluegrass legend Earl Scruggs in the hospital. The men were already friends, but Scruggs' support of Doc and his family in their time of need cemented that friendship forever.

Doc's friendship with Earl Scruggs went back to one moment over Christmas in 1963 when Scruggs stopped by for an unannounced visit. George McCeney, who had installed bathroom plumbing into Doc's home the year before, was visiting Doc again with Ralph Rinzler and his friend Gary; Rinzler had to take care of some business with Doc, and had invited the others to come along. McCeney remembered: "We didn't stay at [Doc's] house, because there were three of us, which would have been a little too much, so we stayed at a hotel in Boone and just went out to Doc's every day. One day we were playing, the four of us at Doc's house, and I was playing guitar and Doc was sitting on the couch playing the banjo. Gary played the bass, and when Ralph was with us he played mandolin. Looking back at playing the guitar at Doc Watson's house, I mean, you'd have to be a 25-year-old fool to do that. There was this knock at the door right at the end of a song we were playing. So I was closest to the door, and so I went over and opened the door. And there was this sort of diminutive guy there in a leather jacket. He said, 'Is this Doc Watson's house?' And I said, 'Yes, it is.

Can I ask who's calling?' Well, just as I said that I realized who was calling, it was Earl Scruggs standing there."[45]

If there were only a few figures in music that Doc could have listed whom he admired most, Scruggs would have been on that list. Little did he know the great banjoist was directly outside his door. At the time, Doc was still holding his own banjo in his hands, waiting to start the next tune with his friends. Scruggs said to McCeney at the door, "Do you think I could come in and visit with Doc?" And McCeney replied, "I think he'd be delighted." Scruggs then walked down the hill to tell his wife that it was the correct home, and McCeney closed the door and walked back to the living room where the musicians were gathered.[45]

McCeney continued: "Doc was sitting on the sofa still holding the banjo. And he'd heard none of this exchange. I turned to Doc and I said, 'Doc, you will never believe who's at the front door.' He said, 'Who, George?' I said, 'Earl Scruggs.' Well, they say the shortest interval of time is a nanosecond. Really, the shortest interval of time is the time it takes Doc Watson to get a banjo off from around his neck into a case and back under the sofa when somebody tells him that Earl Scruggs is at the door!"[45] Of course, Doc was known by that time mostly as a guitarist, though he was an excellent banjo player. He even played Scruggs-style banjo at times on stage, as well as clawhammer style and other various methods. But at that moment, in the presence of *the* banjo player, he did *not* want to be holding a banjo.[45]

McCeney recalled that Doc was a bit "star struck" when Earl Scruggs came in; Doc had of course listened to his music for a good part of his life. But McCeney also noticed that Scruggs had a "real affection for Doc," and had wanted to meet Doc because he had admired his music. Scruggs told McCeney and the rest of them that they only took one week off per year, over Christmas, and he and his family would come up to a resort in Blowing Rock, North Carolina to ski at a local resort. Scruggs had heard Doc lived in the vicinity and had found his way to Doc's home.[45]

Earl Scruggs remembered flying Doc home in his airplane: "I used to fly a lot – I had an Aztec airplane... And Doc came over to Nashville to do an album with Lester Flatt and me, and he had appendicitis, and we [just about] lost Doc Watson. But he finally pulled through with it. And he was really wanting to go back to Deep Gap... [So] I said, 'Doc, I'll take you back to Johnson City, [Tennessee]; that's as close as I can get you to Deep Gap.'"[46]

Doc also recalled the flight: "I was in the co-pilot's seat, and Randy, Earl's middle son, was behind us. And when we got out away from the traffic around Nashville airport, Earl said, 'You want to fly this apiece?' And I said, 'Gosh, Earl, I might goof up and kill us all!' He laughed and he said, 'No you won't,' he said, 'You've got to set the controls, and I'll tell you where to put your feet and how to hold it, and then that stick will take you up or down...'"[46] And Earl Scruggs let his blind friend Doc Watson fly his plane. Earl remembered explaining to Doc how to fly the plane: "I was wanting to see if he could hold it straight and level, which is hard with an airplane. You get the nose down, you get into a bank or a climb..."[46] Doc continued to reminisce: "And I guess I flew 25 minutes...or something like that – and he kidded me and said, 'Doc, you're flying by the seat of your pants, and doing a good job!'"[46]

Doc said about his friend Earl, "My friendship with Earl will last as long as I live. And if he outlives me, I hope he'll still think of me as a good friend. I won't go into detail on this. He'd be embarrassed if I did, but when I was in the hospital over there, we were flat broke, as far as finances, and Earl, I think, realized that, and he took my family into his home just like they were his own folks. Earl was just like a brother, that's how much of a friend. And I feel that way about him yet – that friendship has not grown old in any book."[46]

Earl Scruggs not only brought Doc into his family circle, both musically and personally, he also gave his blind friend the experience of flying. Again, Doc felt the joy he had felt as a child on the edge of the cliff with his brothers gathered around, as he swung on the vine and released at the highest point, believing he could fly. Now Doc was *actually* flying; navigating only by his sound radar, holding the controls tightly as Scruggs instructed, so that the plane wouldn't crash down into the Blue Ridge foothills below. Empowered with new courage and resolve, Doc soon went back out on tour, tightly gripping the controls of his career and hitting the road once more.

# CHAPTER NOTES

1.  Rinzler, Ralph, *Liner Notes from Bill Monroe and Doc Watson: Live Duet Recordings 1963-1980*, Off the Record Volume 2, Smithsonian/Folkways Recordings, 1993.
2.  Gustavson, Kent, *Telephone Interview with Ricky Skaggs*. April 29, 2009.
3.  Bush, Sam, *"This is What they Said" Poster*. 2000, Doc and Merle Watson Museum.
4.  Gustavson, Kent, *Telephone Interview with Jean Ritchie*. May 6, 2009.
5.  Siegel, Peter K., *Liner Notes from Doc Watson at Gerde's Folk City*, Sugar Hill Records, 2001.
6.  Wilson, Joe, *Doc Watson: Just One of Us*. Muleskinner News, June 1974: p. 10-14.
7.  Porco, Mike, *Talkin' New York*, in *Conclusions on the Wall: New Essays on Bob Dylan*, E.M. Thomson, Editor. 1980, Thin Man: Manchester.
8.  Gustavson, Kent, *Telephone Interview with James Reams*. April 9, 2009.
9.  Gustavson, Kent, *Email Interview with David Grisman*. March 25, 2009.
10. Gustavson, Kent, *Telephone Interview with Mark Moss*. March 23, 2009.
11. Gustavson, Kent, *Telephone Interview with Tony Trischka*. April 27, 2009.
12. Earle, Eugene, *Interview with Doc Watson*, Audio Cassette, Southern Folklife Collection: Eugene Earle Collection, 1988.
13. Watson, Doc and David Grisman, *Doc Watson and David Grisman - In Concert (1999)*, DVD, Vestapol, 2001.
14. Holt, David and Doc Watson, *Doc Watson and David Holt: Legacy*, Audio CD, High Windy Audio, 2002.
15. Gustavson, Kent, *Telephone Interview with Guy Clark*. March 18, 2009.
16. Spitzer, Nick, *Interview with Doc Watson*. 1987, Smithsonian Institution, Ralph Rinzler Folklife Archives: Washington D.C.
17. Gustavson, Kent, *Telephone Interview with Peter Rowan*. June 1, 2009.
18. Gustavson, Kent, *Telephone Interview with Tom Paxton*. April 14, 2009.
19. Gustavson, Kent, *Personal Interviews with John Cohen*. April 8 & August 6, 2009.
20. Gustavson, Kent, *Telephone Interview with Donna Hill*. May 6, 2009.
21. Mast, Dave P. and Frances Walker, *Letter to Ralph Rinzler from Watauga County Department of Public Welfare*. 1963, Smithsonian Folklife.
22. Rinzler, Ralph, *Letter to Frances Walker, Watauga County Dept. of Public Welfare*, F. Walker, Editor. 1963: Boone, NC.
23. Holt, David, *Liner Notes to Doc Watson and David Holt: Legacy*, High Windy Audio, 2002.
24. Rinzler, Ralph, *Letter to Doc and Rosa Lee Watson Regarding Contract, Commission and Bookings: 25 November 1964*. 1964.
25. Gustavson, Kent, *Telephone Interview with Sam Bush*. April 9, 2009.
26. Haas, Joe, *Records in Brief*. Chicago Daily News, August 28, 1964. Chicago, IL.
27. Schaden, Herman, *Folk Singers Making It Big These Days*. The Sunday Standard, August 16, 1964. Washington, D.C.
28. Shelton, Robert, *Country Singers Present Concert: Doc Watson and Bill Monroe Win Applause of 1,000*. New York Times, Nov. 30, 1963. New York: p. 18.
29. Rinzler, Ralph, *Liner Notes from The Original Folkways Recordings of Doc Watson and Clarence Ashley 1960-1962*, Smithsonian Folkways Records, 1994.
30. Dawidoff, Nicholas, *In the country of country: people and places in American music*. 1997: Pantheon Books.
31. *University of Chicago Folk Festival Schedule of Events*. 1964, Smithsonian Institution, Ralph Rinzler Folklife Archives: Washington D.C.

32.      Smith, Richard, *Can't You Hear Me Callin': The Life of Bill Monroe, Father of Bluegrass*. 2001: Da Capo Press.

33.      Lloyd, Bert, *Interview with Doc Watson*, Audio CD, Ralph Rinzler Folklife Archives, Smithsonian Institution, 1976.

34.      Harrington, Richard, *Doc Watson, Strumming Home*. The Washington Post, January 25, 1988. Washington D.C.: p. C1,C8.

35.      Rinzler, Ralph, *1965 Eng. Tour Doc Exp. Rcpts*. 1965, Ralph Rinzler Archives, Smithsonian Institution: Washington D.C.

36.      Gustavson, Kent, *Telephone Interview with Peggy Seeger*. July 1, 2009.

37.      Gustavson, Kent, *Telephone Interview with Ben Harper*. June 4, 2009.

38.      Rinzler, Ralph, *Letter to Marlena Langston "Travelling is beginning to take a toll...": 19 December, 1965*. 1965.

39.      Jaynes, Gregory, *The Blind Musician from Deep Gap*. The Atlanta Journal and Constitution, 1974: p. 8-9,16,19.

40.      Watson, Nancy E., *A Glimpse of What It's Like to be Part of 'The Watson Family' (liner notes to The Doc Watson Family: Songs fom the Southern Mountains)*, 1994.

41.      Lloyd, Bert, *Interview with Merle Watson*, Audio CD, Ralph Rinzler Folklife Archives, Smithsonian Institution, 1976.

42.      *9-Master Doc and Merle: Doc's House, Doc, Merle, Rosa Lee*. 1985, Ralph Rinzler Folklife Collection, Smithsonian Institution.

43.      Winfrey, Lee, *Doc Watson Makes It Using 'Natural Resource'*. The Miami Herald, May 16, 1964. Miami, FL: p. 1A,3A.

44.      Murphy, Joe, *Doc and Merle -The Lives and Music of Doc & Merle Watson (1985)*, VHS, Vestapol, 1996.

45.      Gustavson, Kent, *Telephone Interview with George McCeney*. May 22, 2009.

46.      Watson, Doc, Earl Scruggs & Ricky Skaggs, *The Three PIckers*, Rounder Records, 2003.

# CHAPTER FOURTEEN
## Pete & Doc

*"As Woody Guthrie said, 'Left-wing, right-wing, chicken-wing. It's the same thing to me.' What matters is what's in the heart. When I headed out on the road years ago, looking for a job, hitchhiking, not sure where my next meal might come from, and feeling low, I was always lifted back up through the grace of human kindness. Quite often by people completely different from me... No matter where you start out on your path you will be drawn to others with shared values, regardless of politics or religion."*

- Larry Long[1]

When Doc Watson came to New York in March of 1961, the political climate was very heated, and he was unknowingly stepping directly into the middle of it. Pete Seeger was convicted at the end of the month by a jury trial and sentenced to ten years in prison for Contempt of Congress; having refused to submit to the demands of the House Un-American Activities Committee. The next month, the Freedom Riders in Alabama were firebombed by the Ku Klux Klan. These were tumultuous times.

This was not the world that Doc Watson knew and loved in Deep Gap. At home in the mountain hollows of North Carolina's Blue Ridge Mountains, there was no need for much political or racial struggle. Most people in his hometown looked the same, spoke the same, and if they had a guest of another race or culture, they weren't prejudiced. Doc remembered: "We knew a few black folks well enough to sort of get acquainted with their pattern of speech – the dialect – because my father was very good friends [with] an old time mountain black preacher that lived in Boone, and he used to get him about every other summer to run the revival meeting. He was a good preacher. And he spent the night a lot of times at our house, so we were familiar to a great extent with black folks, and had some visits from other people. I met a lot of them when I'd go to Boone as a boy with my dad, in his Buick Touring Car."[2] Doc recalled that he wasn't familiar with overt racism: "There never was [racists] – except for just a few people – there were some racists in any one area you go to, I don't care if it's north or south. For the most part, the mountain folk were tolerant and not [racist], if you want to put it that way, toward the black folks – they were friends..."[2] Indeed, some of Doc Watson's best friends in the mid-1960s when he was on the road were the black blues musicians with whom he shared the stage: "I really enjoyed meeting Mance Lipscomb, Son House, and Lightnin' Hopkins, all those guys. Once they got to know you and realized you weren't a racist or something, they were really nice folks. They were great fellows, good people to meet..."[3] However, Doc's home state of North Carolina was also the home state of the Ku Klux Klan, and all of the progressive folk singers in Greenwich Village knew it. They had heard about the lynchings. They knew about the social segregation. And these white southern Appalachian musicians coming to New York City did not know the negative connotation their fiddles and banjos might have for the northern audience.

In an interview with Ray Allen in 2005, John Cohen spoke about first realizing the impact that bringing southern white musicians to New York City in the heat of the Civil Rights Movement might have, when he overheard a conversation at the Folklore Center preceding the first Clarence Ashley Group concert at PS 41. The young folk musicians Cohen overheard were wondering out loud whether the upcoming Friends of Old Time Music concert would be featuring "those southern white guys in the white sheets."[4] This discussion alarmed Cohen, but it informed his and Rinzler's decision to *interpret* from the stage. Cohen did that for the first concert with Roscoe Holcomb, just as Ralph Rinzler did with the Clarence Ashley concert six weeks later. Cohen recalled: "the act of finding linkages between people who would otherwise be opposed to one another was interesting and political. We were putting our stamp of approval on these white guys who until that time had been stereotyped as racists, lynchers, and all those nightmarish things about the South."[4] They wanted to put a friendly face on the southerners whom they brought to the New York audiences, but in doing that, they also would have to train the musicians to exclude the portions of their repertoire that might be perceived as racist.

According to Ray Allen: "Cohen and Rinzler worried that Ashley and other artists might slip into their old vaudeville and blackface minstrel routines."[4] In the context within which he lived, Ashley's blackface minstrel *Rastus* persona was acceptable and funny, but within the charged surroundings of an active Civil Rights struggle within the New York City progressive community, such a performance would have been understood as a blatantly racist act. The young northern musicians explained to Ashley and the others that they needed to be careful not to fall into the roles that the audience was expecting them to fall into. They were representatives of their culture, and they didn't want the musicians to be seen as the bigots that many audience members were expecting.

After showing the Greenwich Village community a new face of Appalachian culture and music, the Clarence Ashley Group left for home on the Greyhound Bus, just missing the biggest folk music demonstration that had ever taken place in Washington Square. The city of New York had started to crack down on "beatniks,"[*] and Washington Square was one place they always came on Sunday afternoons, along with the musicians. In the *New York Mirror* the day after the protests in Washington Square, headlines read, "3000 Beatniks Riot in Village."[5] The city recently had begun requiring permits for public performances, and they wouldn't issue a permit to the folk musicians who had, for more than a decade, always peaceably assembled around the fountain in the park.

Izzy Young, who had worked over the last several months with Cohen and Rinzler to create and publicize the Friends of Old Time Music concert series, was also very involved in the politics of the folk music movement. He remembered: "I tried all of March to get a permit for our folksings in…Washington Square Park during April, and I couldn't get any answer out of the Parks Commissioner's office… We couldn't get the permits by April, so the first Sunday in April I personally went all around the park and told the kids not to sing, not to play anything. I thought it would be a demonstration of our good faith… So the next day the Commissioner said he was denying us a permit because we brought what he called 'itinerant singers and unsavory characters' into Washington Square Park… Well, we decided to hold a protest meeting in the Square the next Sunday, which was April 9, [1961]. We got together in the park, about five hundred of us around the fountain. I stood in the center [of the fountain, which was] dry this time of year—and cautioned our people not to cause any physical disturbance; you know, no violence or anything. Then we sang songs. Besides us,

---

[*] *The word "beatnik" comes from the term "Beat Generation" coined by Jack Kerouac in 1948, and the Russian suffix "–nik", and was first invented by Herb Caen for a 1958 newspaper article. The "Beat Generation" represented an artistic and cultural movement, whereas "beatnik" was a largely stereotypical term often applied to anti-conformist youths by the media.*

there were maybe four thousand other people in the park: onlookers, people passing by, and who knows, maybe a few people looking for trouble."[6]

The Parks Commissioner in New York City had not issued a permit to the folksingers for many reasons. As Young pointed out, the Commissioner had refused the permit because of the "unsavory characters" and "undesirable elements" that were attracted to the park by the folk singing, though the Washington Park Sunday afternoon folk music crowd was largely made up of a family-friendly audience; many parents allowed their children to go to the park with instruments in tow, and other locals rolled their babies in strollers to listen to the various musicians. Izzy Young believed that the Commissioner had not allowed them a permit because of racial bias, since the park, and the folk music scene in general, was a place for racial mixing.

Although Doc was largely color-blind in his life and in his music, he didn't get involved in any kind of overt activism in support of Civil Rights, and he certainly never got involved in the politics of folk music. He was a southerner of conservative heart and mind in a sea of northern liberals.

As Pat Donohue, the house guitar player for Prairie Home Companion, after his disclaimer, "I'm really the least political guy you're ever going to run into," said about the political world of folk musicians: "I've never met a single person in folk music who was not a liberal or democrat. I'm serious, other than maybe Doc and Chet Atkins."[7]

There is a reason why Doc never raised political or social issues in his music, on stage, or in public conversation; if he had been interested in sharing his right-leaning political views too much during his career, he would probably not have been embraced as readily by the folk music world that made up his base.

Unlike country or bluegrass singers in today who lend their voices or faces to one political campaign or another, Doc never got into that game; he was only interested in entertainment. Because he kept political discussions at arm's length, Doc was able to enter many doors in the music business. He has been accepted by country and folk music, and both conservative and liberal listeners. He couldn't have done that if he had been overtly political. And now, at the end of his career, Doc has been acknowledged by organizations and individuals across the spectrum of political belief, from the Country Music Hall of Fame to

Bill Clinton's White House. Doc became a true American hero precisely because of his *apolitical* presence in the world of music.

Doc's friend and contemporary Pete Seeger was his opposite regarding social and political activism. Although the two men played a strikingly similar repertoire of American folk music, their intentions were dramatically different. The two men first met in the early 1960s, and have been friendly ever since, but their politics could not have been more disparate.

Pete Seeger was one of the most controversial figures of the 1950s and early 1960s, having stood up to the House Un-American Activities Committee in 1955 with his famous statement, "I am not going to answer any questions as to my association, my philosophical or religious beliefs or my political beliefs, or how I voted in any election, or any of these private affairs. I think these are very improper questions for any American to be asked, especially under such compulsion as this."[8] Basically, he refused to lie, and was held in contempt of Congress for that refusal, later being sentenced to ten years in prison. Though his conviction was later overturned by an appeals court, Seeger was required to tell the government anytime he traveled outside of New York in the late 1950s and '60s. He was blacklisted. And the nationally famous lead singer of the Weavers struggled for many years to make ends meet.

Jean Ritchie remembered going to a hootenanny at Pete's apartment during that time: "I remember when Pete and Toshi lived in a tiny little apartment in Greenwich Village, and I guess they had their oldest girl there. I remember having to go to the bathroom, and I went upstairs and saw Toshi there, who was taking care of the baby. We were all singing downstairs. And Pete was just having people in to sing because he liked singing, and he wasn't doing too much because he was blacklisted. He was having a hard time getting places to play."[9] Seeger carved out a circuit of colleges and schools across the country who would still hire him to come in and sing folk songs, inspiring those campuses to create folk music clubs, and eventually opening up the college circuit to folk musicians like Doc Watson who made his living in the mid-1960s playing and conducting workshops at those schools.

Pete Seeger was also blacklisted in the media for many years. But when the early 1960s rolled around, the ABC network moved to break that blacklisting and bring Seeger onto their show Hootenanny was a wildly popular television program that capitalized on the hootenannies that had started in New York City and spread with the folk music movement to the college campuses of the nation. ABC had groomed Jack Linkletter to be the host, and the show quickly gained popularity, with up to 10 million viewers each week. ABC knew that if they were able to bring Seeger onto the show, who was widely viewed as the godfather of folk music, countless younger acts would follow suit. They sent him a letter with the following text: "ABC will consider Mr. Seeger's use on the program only if he furnishes a sworn affidavit as to his past and present affiliations, if any, with the Communist Party, and/or with the Communist front organizations. Upon so doing, the company will undertake to consider his statement in relation to all the objective data available to it, and will advise you promptly [whether or not] it will approve the employment of Mr. Seeger."[10] The network executives were asking him to sign what was called a *loyalty oath*. This felt too much to Seeger like his meeting with the House Committee, and he refused. Soon, Seeger's manager released the details of that letter to the public, and many well-known artists began to boycott the Hootenanny show immediately thereafter. John Cohen recalled, "It split the folk music world."[11]

Tom Paxton remembered the specifics of the Hootenanny boycott: "Groups like the Chad Mitchell Trio that were very political and very liberal, were nevertheless on Hootenanny many times. Judy Collins was on many times. However, Joan Baez said that yes, she would appear on the show, but only if Pete were on the same show with her. And Peter, Paul and Mary did the same thing."[12] Ralph Rinzler, whose band the Greenbriar Boys was on tour after having released their first album the year before on Vanguard, had been excited about the Hootenanny show, and had booked his own group as well as Doc Watson and Bill Monroe on the show, but now he wanted to back out of the commitments, and he hoped that Doc and Bill Monroe would follow suit.

Doc's appearance on Hootenanny would be a great opportunity for his career. He was being asked to play on national television while he was still having trouble making ends meet in Deep Gap, and his family was still living in poverty back home. He was excited to perform on the show, and was happy that his first Vanguard album was selling well. He was very hesitant to back out of the Hootenanny engagement, because he saw the huge television audience as a boon to his career. He wrote a letter to Rinzler on March 19th of 1963 regarding the show (*edited here for spelling*):

> "...Ralph, in writing my opinion concerning the contracts we signed, I may sound a little selfish but I don't think we should break them. My reasoning is, that if we refuse to play on the

*festival it may do us a lot of harm, even if they don't bring a suit against us. Even though I disagree completely with most of Pete's political views, I would have thought twice about signing the contracts if I had known about this at the time.*

*Maybe I'm being over-cautious, but the way I see it people like Joan Baez can afford to boycott places where they refuse to hire Pete. But a fellow like me who is just getting started in the profession can hardly afford to break a contract, not even a little one. Ralph I hope you are not angry with me for deciding not to break the contract because I have to be honest with myself, and if you, Johnny, and Bob still wish to break your part of the contract, please don't let my decision influence you in any way. For I realize that every person has to think for himself."[13]*

In this letter to Rinzler, Doc uncharacteristically slipped out of his apolitical nature regarding music. He understood Rinzler's loyalty to Pete, but Doc didn't agree with Seeger's politics, and to lose the kind of exposure the gig would bring him when his family was still living in poverty wouldn't make sense. Interestingly, Pete himself would probably have told Doc *not* to boycott the show. Seeger was far more interested in the young people of the country being exposed to traditional American folk music than he was in playing out his vendetta against the ABC network. Mark Moss, the editor of *Sing Out!* magazine, remembered that the boycott was "not something really endorsed or encouraged by Pete."[14] Tom Paxton recalled Pete attending a gathering of the boycotting musicians: "Pete came to this big [meeting] we had down at the Village Gate. And he actually tried to talk us into dropping the boycott because he thought, as bad as it was, the show was helping to get folk music out into the world. I mean, he was putting himself second and he thought that anything that helped spread folk music was great."[12]

Although he was frustrated by his continued lack of performances due to his blacklisting over the next two years, Pete certainly didn't hold Doc's performance on the national program against him, and they remained good friends, seeing one another at festivals around the country. And in 1965, when Pete got his own public television show called Rainbow Quest, he invited Doc to come onto the show with Fred Price and Clint Howard. Pete had a big heart, and a history of not holding grudges; something that supported him in his long career. His half-sister Peggy Seeger remembered that Pete even forgave the people who informed on him in the 1950s: "Pete doesn't have an enemy in the world. Pete has forgiven people who informed during the House Un-American Activities

Committee. I mean, not forgiven, but he works with them. He doesn't turn his back on them, never turned his back on them. He said they did what they had to do. Even though a lot of them affected his income and his life."[15]

March 19th 1963

Hi Ralph,

It was sure nice to hear from you, and to hear you say that you miss us. I'll tell everyone hello for you, but I'm a little indoubt about ringing Merle's Jaws since he is getting so big. I might get my own jaws rung. (Haha.)
Rosa Lee says to tell you thanks a lot for helping to make her visit to New York such a pleasant one. She says she enjoyed every minute of it.

Ralph, in writing my openion concerning the contracts we signed, I may sound a little selfish but I don't think we should break them. My reasoning is, that if we refuse to play on the festaval it may do us a lot of harm, even if they don't bring a suit against us. Even though I disagree completely with most of Pete's political vews, I would have thought twice about signing the contracts if I had known about this at the time.

Maybe I'm being overcausious, but the way I see it people like Joan Baez can afford to boycott places where they refuse to hire Pete. But a fellow like me who is just getting started in the profession can hardly afford to break a contract, not even a little one. Ralph I hope you are not angry with me for deciding not to break the contract because I have to be honest with myself, and if you Johnny, and Bob still wish to break your part of the contract, pleas don't let my decision influence you in any way. For I realize that every person has to think for himself.

In your letter you mentioned getting a copyright on the song Lone Journey. It will surely be O. K. with us, and we will gladly pay the cost of getting a copyright on it.

Boy Merle and Nancy sure are excited about the fact that might get to come to New York this summer. I'll have to admit that Rosa Lee and me are a little bit excited too.

Let me hear from you when time permits.

A friend,
Doc.

*Letter from Doc Watson to Ralph Rinzler, March 19, 1963.*

Ketch Secor of Old Crow Medicine Show made a brilliant conclusion about the difference between Doc Watson and Pete Seeger in the world of folk music: "It's as if Doc is the subject and Pete is the scholar. You know, Pete couldn't do what he does without all of the Doc Watsons of this world. Pete required Brownie McGhee and Sonny Terry. Pete needed Cisco Houston and Woody Guthrie. He needed their authenticity, because Woody came out of the dust bowl, and Doc came out of the holler... Pete's very much part of a musical family that's totally the opposite of Doc's, yet inextricably linked."[16]

Pete Seeger, despite his humble lifestyle, simple dress and traditional songs, was the son of a professor, and hadn't grown up in poverty. He went to an Ivy League university before dropping out early. He learned the songs of the country by listening to records and tagging along with Woody Guthrie and other amazing folk singers as a young man. Doc Watson was born poor, had a limited education, and when he met Seeger in the early sixties, he was *still* poor. They shared the same songs, but the songs had dramatically different meanings for both musicians. When Pete sang the song "Groundhog," he was singing a song that made him think and feel the country nature of the tune. When Doc sang the song, he thought of the tough groundhog skin that his father had stretched on the maple frame of the little banjo he had made for his boy, or the taste of groundhog from when his brothers had brought home fresh meat for the family.

Michelle Shocked spoke about the difference between the two performers, and the two audiences: "In the folk revival, middle class folks were following their own ideology. They loved the underclass, it was just hillbillies they didn't like."[17] Indeed, the urban crowd loved Doc Watson, but they were never really able to connect to Clarence Ashley or Clint Howard. Doc was able to appeal to them with a certain smoothness and virtuosity that didn't appear *hillbilly* to them. Other singers within the 1960s folk movement also tended to *improve* the rough-edged mountain music. Joan Baez did beautiful versions of songs in her clear-as-a-bell soprano that that had previously been sung simply in nasal tone. Shocked said, "Pete Seeger's crowd liked the *idea* of the underclass, but they didn't like the *actual* underclass. People would rather have romantic notions about the underclass; that helps keep them at an aesthetic arms distance, rather than having to meet and confront those folks."[17]

Both Pete and Doc worked hard to bridge the gap between classes, and between different elements of society. Their audiences ranged from educated upper middle class to the underclass. For Doc, the mixing was most apparent in the 1970s on the festival circuit. Mike Marshall, the innovative mandolinist and composer said: "One of the things that drew me to the music, when I go back to that first festival that I was at, was that both cultures were colliding. I mean you had the rural people who owned this music; whose grandpappies taught it to them. They were out at those campsites jamming. But right alongside them were these longhaired hippies of the early 70's. That represented to me that music was the common ground that brought these people together. That meant that, even as a 13-year old kid, I could see social implications that this was a connecting point. It enabled all of us to bridge across these waters."[18]

Joe Crookston, award-winning singer-songwriter from upstate New York, described political beliefs in music using the image of a Venn Diagram: "If there is anything I believe in this world, this is what it is. I am standing here in my kitchen and on the wall is this huge circle painting that I did, and I'm actually looking at it right now. It is Venn Diagram, which is where you have many different circles, and there's a place in the middle where all the circles intersect. Every one of those circles represents something. One represents Christianity. One represents liberals. And one represents gun-toting conservatives. You have all these different circles, and then there is this place where maybe two of the circles intersect, then maybe three of the circles. And then there is a place; a common little shape they all share in common. When I'm writing music, or standing on stage, whether it's in New York, or in Boone, North Carolina, I sing directly to that common little shape in the middle of the Venn Diagram. That's what I think Doc Watson's thinking is, too. I am political in that I believe that the shape in the middle of the diagram is a place where humanity intersects. I refuse to exist solely in one of those circles. Every one of those circles is flawed in its own way."[19] Both Doc and Pete have always been able to find the place where humanity intersects, bringing people from disparate communities and backgrounds together through their music.

In the early 1960s, the idealism of Ralph Rinzler and John Cohen with the Friends of Old Time Music concerts, and Ed Pearl of the Ash Grove in Los Angeles, helped to propel the traditional music underclass into the spotlight. Rinzler never intended to look down on Doc Watson's family, and indeed the Watsons effectively adopted him as a member of their family, which was an important part of his life in his ambitious and turbulent thirties. Pearl also connected with the musicians who played at the Ash Grove, and probably because he had grown up in the working class himself, he never presented the musicians in a way that would demean them. Pearl said of his own childhood,

"I grew up poor. And that's something that many of us shared in common, and probably why we enjoyed the music so much."[20]

Pearl continued: "With the Ash Grove concerts, I always tried to show the music of black people and of white country people in the context of their entire culture, and sort of as a representation of it. And so I would try to show newspaper articles about the society where they came from on the board outside the hall. And that included everything. I wanted to show the religion; I wanted to show the children; I wanted to show what people do with 80-percent of their waking hours, which is making a living. I would always show the bulletin board with the articles, pictures, and information to the artists and say, 'Well, is there anything here that's wrong or that you don't want me to show?' And I never got anything other than them saying, 'No, you got it right.'"[20] Bill Monroe, according to Pearl, supported the information written on the board by announcing from the stage, "Now I want you to go outside and I want you to look at what Ed put up there. That's the truth. You're going to see how our people live and that's good."[20]

One amazing thing about the audiences at the Ash Grove was also symptomatic of both Doc Watson and Pete Seeger concerts everywhere at the time; the audience was very diverse racially and socially: "The greatest thing about The Ash Grove was the audience. It included people that were from Appalachia and lived in Burbank, who lived in Bakersfield, and who lived in the country parts of Southern California. And at the same time, African-Americans who moved from the Delta to southern Los Angeles would show up. And very often the audiences were mixed. Whatever differences Ash Grove audience members had were subsumed by the great art and the great artists we put onstage. In terms of religion; in terms of children; in terms of how they made their living; in terms of the socioeconomic status of the communities they came from; those things were not that similar. And people understood that, and yet people appreciated their differences, and we never had a racial incident in the Ash Grove."[20]

Sam Bush spoke about Doc Watson's inclusive ideology: "Doc doesn't see age, race, color, or gender." Bush remembered the audiences at the beginning of his own career, how diverse they were, and how varied the performers were, and what Doc's reaction was to the differences between the people: "I remember once we were talking about long hair, or people not liking long hair, or beards and this and that. And Doc just said, 'Well, from where I sit, it all looks the same.

I don't feel any difference...A good person's a good person.' I think Doc just enjoyed hanging with good people. I think if you respected Doc, he respected you back."[21] Doc respected everyone, regardless of politics, class or race.

Tom Paxton, who is known for his often outspoken politics, remembered: "When I was with Doc it was purely music that we talked about, or just people. It just didn't occur to me to go into any kind of political thing."[12] Paxton was further amazed how well Doc was able to get along with musicians who outwardly appeared so different from him: "I don't think there was a racist bone in Doc's body.... In Newport I remember there was always a late night party over at George Wing's place, which was a big Newport kind of house. It was fabulous. You'd have these old Appalachian guys and the black blues singers, thick as thieves. They had music to talk about, and hard times. There wasn't one of them that hadn't known hard times, and they could talk about farming, mining and stuff."[12]

Ellen Harper-Verdries, mother of bi-racial singer Ben Harper, remembered her parents Dorothy and Charles Chase speaking about Doc and his race-blindness: "One of the things I can remember, you know, was my parents talking when they didn't know that their children were eavesdropping on them. And I recall a conversation about how amazing it was that Doc could sit in a room; there could be black people, brown people, or whatever...and there didn't seem to be any blatant racism at all, you know. I'm sure my parents had their own stereotypes of the south."[22]

Folk singer and activist Si Kahn told a story about how traditional music brings people together: "Without calling names, a friend of mine said about a mutual acquaintance in music, he said, 'You do know he's a real right winger?' I said, 'Oh yeah, I know that.' He said, 'And he knows you're a real left winger.' And I said, 'Well, kind of hard to miss, isn't it?' And he said, 'Yeah, but he loves you, because you respect the tradition.' I was really honored. And I think that there's a common ground, an agreement to disagree, a respect for people who honor the tradition and the different ways in which the tradition plays out in our lives. I think you have to learn to live together."[23] Both Pete Seeger and Doc Watson transcended each political or personal morass with which they were confronted by turning to tradition.

Mike Seeger recalled that his parents (Pete Seeger's father and step-mother) "had a very strong mission and belief that effort needed to be made to counter the popular music takeover of media, and efforts needed to be made on both books and broadcast radio to try to keep the old songs alive that had been alive for millennia."[24] Pete carried that torch onwards, keeping traditional music alive in the hearts and minds of millions.

Doc also believes in the importance of traditional music. He said in a 1978 interview: "When Merle got into the business with me, we expanded, but we didn't throw away the roots. It's like finding a real pretty plant. When the flower starts lookin' good, [if] you chop it off and throw away the roots...pretty soon the top wilts. That's what happens to a lot of commercial music. It doesn't retain enough roots to sustain it."[25]

Performing largely traditional material also allowed Pete and Doc both to stay out of the songwriters' rat race. They both cheered on Tom Paxton and Bob Dylan, but then they returned to the well of tradition for their own performances. This also allowed both men to stay just outside the celebrity spotlight for most of their careers, each of them in their country cabins; Pete's, overlooking the Hudson in New York, and Doc's, overlooking the Blue Ridge Mountains in North Carolina. Both men have since been honored by just about every honoring body, from presidents to Halls of Fame and all sorts of committees, but they both remain humble, always returning to their simple lives in the hills.

Because both of their devotion to the performance and dispersion of traditional music, the two men have made their mark on American culture, and inspired generations of musicians to pick up an instrument and/or sing a song. Mike Seeger used the words of country legend Grandpa Jones to describe Pete and Doc, and their contribution to the world of music: "I remember standing backstage with Grandpa Jones once, and I said, 'I'm amazed you've been able to do all that, Grandpa.' And he said, 'And I did it all without a hit record.'"[24] Pete Seeger and Doc Watson had a few flashes in the pan, but they will be remembered for the tunes they passed on to their audiences, and for the enjoyment they inspired.

Both Pete Seeger and Doc Watson have shared their honesty and songs with the world for the better part of a century, and they're both still playing concerts and passing along the gift of traditional music to the world.

Singer-songwriter and traditional musician Abigail Washburn spoke about the importance of traditional culture in a political world: "I think cultural discussion needs to get a lot louder than political discussion. I'm concerned about the power of politicians in the discussion of globalization and what the world's going to look like. We need honest voices to speak up about who they are, and to get big and loud and converse and encourage other people to discover themselves in the midst of what's happening, in the midst of globalization, and in the midst of these larger robust political conversations that are always happening. We need to change how we think about power."[26] Pete and Doc have just such honest voices. Just think what Doc's version of "Amazing Grace" and Pete's version of "We Shall Overcome" have done for the world…

Washburn continued, "The more we are able to change how we think about power, the more the shift will happen. And that's what I do. I go all around China and I play music in universities and clubs, in orphanages and disaster relief tents. I go all over and I play traditional American music. I play traditional Chinese music, I play original music, and I do it with as much honesty as I thought I heard in Doc. And I think that'll change the world."[26]

# CHAPTER NOTES

1.  Gustavson, Kent, *Email Interview with Larry Long*. June 30, 2009.
2.  Spitzer, Nick, *Interview with Doc Watson*. 1987, Smithsonian Institution, Ralph Rinzler Folklife Archives: Washington D.C.
3.  Menius, Art, *Doc Watson: Roots of Mastery*. Bluegrass Unlimited, 1997. 32: p. 30-38.
4.  Allen, Ray, *Staging the Folk: New York City's Friends of Old Time Music*. Institute for Studies in American Music Newsletter, 2005. XXXV(2).
5.  *3000 Beatniks Riot in Village*. New York Mirror, Monday, April 10, 1961. New York.
6.  White, Ted, *Balladeers & Billy Clubs*. Rogue, 1961.
7.  Gustavson, Kent, *Telephone Interview with Pat Donohue*. March 11, 2009.
8.  *Pete Seeger to the House Unamerican Activities Committee*, from *The House Unamerican Activities Committee*. 1955: Washington D.C.
9.  Gustavson, Kent, *Telephone Interview with Jean Ritchie*. May 6, 2009.
10.  *ABC Finally Puts Itself on Record Re 'Hootenanny'*. Variety, September 11, 1963.
11.  Gustavson, Kent, *Personal Interviews with John Cohen*. April 8 & August 6, 2009.
12.  Gustavson, Kent, *Telephone Interview with Tom Paxton*. April 14, 2009.
13.  Watson, Doc, *Letter to Ralph Rinzler "Even though I disagree completely with Pete's political views...": March 19, 1963*.
14.  Gustavson, Kent, *Telephone Interview with Mark Moss*. March 23, 2009.
15.  Gustavson, Kent, *Telephone Interview with Peggy Seeger*. July 1, 2009.
16.  Gustavson, Kent, *Telephone Interview with Ketch Secor*. March 19, 2009.
17.  Gustavson, Kent, *Telephone Interview with Michelle Shocked*. March 12, 2009.
18.  Gustavson, Kent, *Telephone Interview with Mike Marshall*. March 26, 2009.
19.  Gustavson, Kent, *Telephone Interview with Joe Crookston*. March 25, 2009.
20.  Gustavson, Kent, *Telephone Interview with Ed Pearl*. May 29, 2009.
21.  Gustavson, Kent, *Telephone Interview with Sam Bush*. April 9, 2009.
22.  Gustavson, Kent, *Telephone Interview with Ellen Harper-Verdries*. July 3, 2009.
23.  Gustavson, Kent, *Telephone Interview with Si Kahn*. May 26, 2009.
24.  Gustavson, Kent, *Telephone Interview with Mike Seeger*. May 23, 2009.
25.  Escott, Colin, *Liner Notes to Doc Watson: Songs from Home*, Capitol Nashville, 2002.
26.  Gustavson, Kent, *Telephone Interview with Abigail Washburn*. June 8, 2009.

# CHAPTER FIFTEEN
## Doc & Merle

*"Doc and Merle were independent. They were as independent as Phish and the Grateful Dead, before any of that kind of thinking ever started. They were doing their own thing. They went from town to town, dropping off eloquent music in their presence, and then they would disappear back into the mountain. And they did it in a very dignified, independent way when everybody else was scrambling just to be a part of the big parade. They had a parade of their own."*

- Marty Stuart[1]

*"We got used to each other. [Merle] was...the best friend I ever had, and it showed in the music. He could feel what I was going to do; he could anticipate it. The same way with me. It was that way between us when we were on stage."*

- Doc Watson, 1995[2]

L ike the progeny of many entertainers, Merle Watson heard the siren call of the road early in his life. As a boy growing up in small town North Carolina, Merle hadn't experienced much outside of his narrow world, and when he heard of his father's great adventures in New York City and across the country, he quickly became entranced, and when the chance came for him to travel with Doc, he jumped at it.

Instead of finishing high school, 15-year old Merle went out on the road in 1965 with his father. In later years, Merle finished high school by correspondence, and he learned guitar at the feet of such masters as Mississippi John Hurt; the best schooling a musician could have. His mother Rosa Lee wasn't ready for her son's departure from home, and in June of 1965, when her men left to tour together, she was inconsolable. She wrote of her loneliness to Ralph Rinzler, who was still Doc's manager at the time:

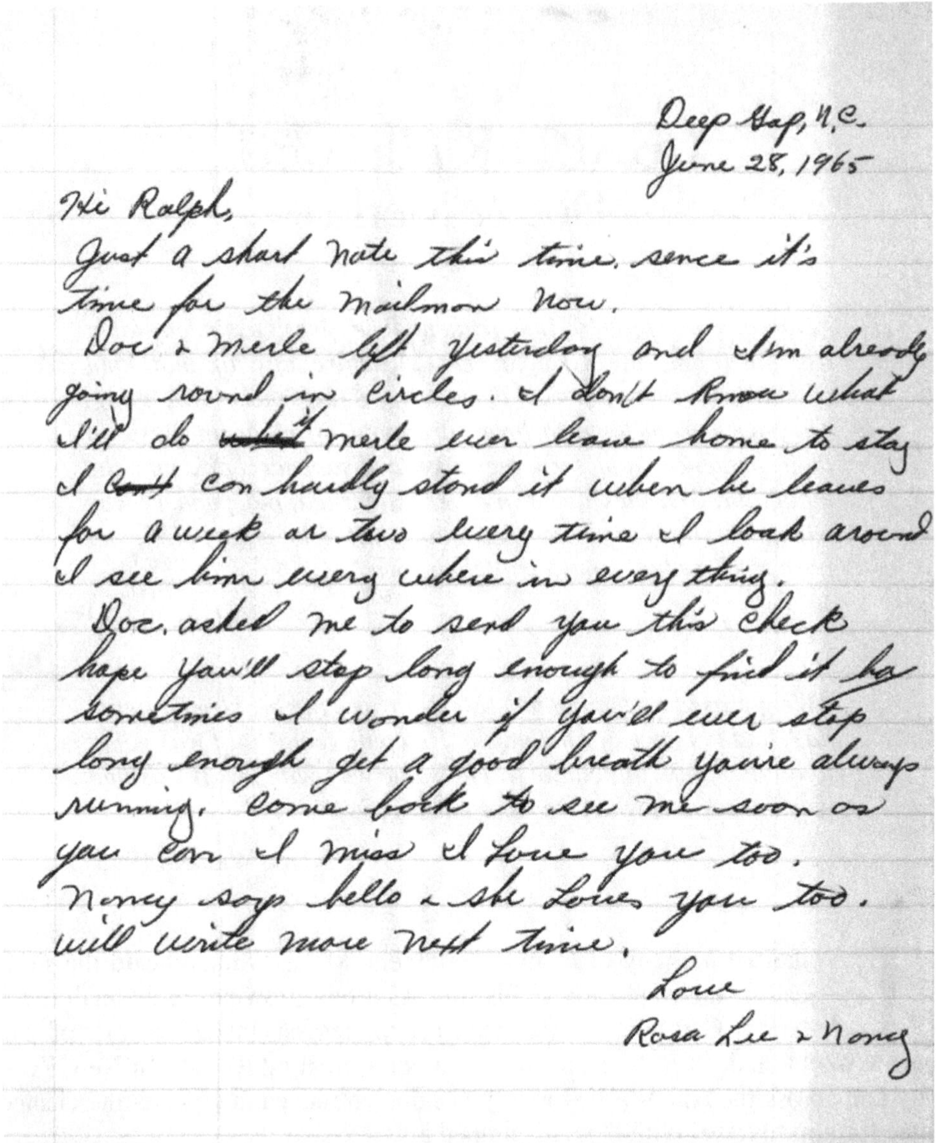

Deep Gap, N.C.
June 28, 1965

Hi Ralph,

Just a short note this time, sence it's time for the mailman now.

Doc & Merle left yesterday and I'm already going round in circles. I don't know what I'll do if Merle ever leave home to stay I can't can hardly stand it when he leaves for a week or two every time I look around I see him every where in every thing.

Doc, asked me to send you this check hope you'll stop long enough to find it by sometimes I wonder if you'll ever stop long enough get a good breath you're always running. come back to see me soon as you can I miss I love you too. Nancy says hello & she Loves you too. will write more next time.

Love
Rosa Lee & Nancy

Digital scan by Stephanie Smith.
Reprinted with permission of the Ralph Rinzler Folklife Archives, Smithsonian Institution.
*Letter from Rosa Lee & Nancy Watson to Ralph Rinzler, June 28, 1965.*

*Deep Gap, N.C.*

*June 28, 1965*

*Hi Ralph,*

*Just a short note this time, since it's time for the mailman now.*

*Doc + Merle left yesterday and I'm already going round in circles. I don't know what I'll do ~~when~~ if Merle ever leave home to stay I ~~can't~~ can hardly stand it when he leaves for a week or two every time I look around I see him every where in every thing.*

*Doc asked me to send you this check hope you'll stop long enough to find it <u>ha</u> sometimes I wonder if you'll ever stop long enough get a good breath you're always running. Come back to see me soon as you can I miss I love you too.*

*Nancy says hello + she Loves you too. Will write more next time.*

*Love*

*Rosa Lee + Nancy[3]*

Rosa Lee didn't only miss her boy because he was going on the road with Doc. She also missed him because he was soon to be married, and in nearly every way, Merle would be leaving her nest. When he came off of the road, he would soon either go out partying with his friends or go home to his wife and small children. Rosa Lee wrote the letter to Rinzler as if she were mourning the loss of a loved one, and indeed that might have been the last time she was able to truly be a part of her son's life.

The early years on the road together were wonderful for both Doc and Merle. Merle was exposed to a world he could never have imagined, with screaming fans and late night parties near his hotel, all night jam sessions with the greatest musicians he had ever heard, and advice from old-timers both black and white. And he was able to bring a good living home to his own young bride and small boy. And Doc now had a companion on the road with whom he could eat breakfast each morning, with whom he could travel, and with whom he could at times sit in silence. He didn't have to entertain Merle as he had always felt obliged when sleeping on hosts' couches. Merle also brought new energy to Doc's playing; from the very beginning, the younger Watson was the consummate accompanist, never stepping into the spotlight except to take occasional tasteful solos. He made his father sound good, and he freed him up to play some of the most blistering flatpicking guitar ever played.

Doc recalled Merle's enjoyment and fear during their first performance on stage together at the Berkeley Folk Festival in 1965: "He was so proud he about busted his shirt buttons when he walked onstage. He could play several finger-style things, and I asked him if he wanted to play lead guitar and he said, 'Oh, God, no.' And boy, he didn't miss a chord even when he played the banjo. I told him, 'Well, son, you did great. How do you feel in front of 12,000 people?' He said, 'Well, I wanted to run.'"[4] One thing that helped Merle feel less afraid, Doc recalled in a 1988 interview, was seeing Mississippi John Hurt, a diminutive old man with incredible charisma and stage presence, walk on stage at that same festival: "He said what helped him as much as anything was, he said…'John Hurt come out there just like he owned the place.'"[5] And Merle began to walk on stage with that same kind of calm confidence. He became his father's personal and musical anchor. Doc would hold his son's upper arm while walking onto stage, and Merle would always be there to lean in towards after a great song, shouting to him off microphone about the details of their next song.

Merle gave Doc a much greater freedom to travel than he had ever had before, and father and son even made a trip to Africa in 1968. Merle was still only 19 years old, but he led his father around to all of the villages, and made sure that they caught all of their (complicated) international connections. Doc recalled that the people in Africa loved their music, and compared him to Jimmie Rodgers, whom they had heard on their radios for years. He remembered in an interview with Stephanie Ledgin: "Some of the kids would come and put their hands on [my] arms and say 'Jim-mee Rah-jah.' I couldn't believe that!"[6] It was a trip of a lifetime for young Merle. Doc remembered, "He got to meet a lot of people and go to a lot of places that he never would have gotten to go. For instance, one example is a tour we did in Africa for the State Department. I was going to turn that down… [But then Merle] told his mother… 'I do hope Dad'll go because I'll never get another chance to go and see it.' So when I found that out, I called Manny, and I said, 'Yeah, Manny, I'll take that tour for the State Department in Africa because Merle wants to do it awful bad.' Merle was a champ on that trip. He was just a kid in his late teens. He had a birthday when we were over there, in fact. I'll tell you one thing; that was an adventure. It was like boot camp in the Army. We lost 15 pounds. Each one of us did. It was so hot over there, and the food you got to eat, half of it you couldn't eat, and you had to survive on the parts of it you could stand."[7] Doc and his boy traveled through Kenya, Malawi, Zambia, Botswana, Lesotho and Swaziland, playing for excited audiences at each stop.[8] "We got back to Johannesburg, South Africa, and this [guy who] was sent to us as a guide by the State Department, he just came into the hotel room and sat down and said, 'Merle, son, do you think you can get you and your dad back home from here?' And Merle said, 'Sure can. All I have to do is look at the ticket.' And he did, buddy... Merle didn't have a bit of problem with it. That's just an example of how good he was out there on the road."[7]

By 1969, Doc and Merle had not only traveled the country and the world together, but they began to really get inside one another's musical styles. Merle had learned to play driving backup to his father's virtuosic flatpicking breaks, and he had learned to take solos himself when his father wanted to take a break. Larry Long remembered seeing Doc and Merle in 1969 in St. Cloud, Minnesota at a small club called The Coffeehouse Extempore. He remembered their onstage chemistry: "The affection between Merle and Doc was clearly very deep. They were the right and left hand of each other. Their humor was infectious. There were only a hundred people in the room, because that's about all it could hold. I was seated only a few feet from Merle and him. Doc's fingers moved like lightning – as effortless as taking a breath."[9]

Just as the two musicians complemented one another on stage, so too did they fit into separate roles on the business side to their career. Doc was the leader on stage, and Merle was the leader off stage. Doc, who was outgoing and energetic on stage, became quite reserved and was not fond of socializing. As Jerry Douglas recalled, "after the concerts, Doc would be talking to people that he knew, and Merle would work the crowd. And onstage Merle never said anything. Doc did all the talking."[10] Pat Donohue confirmed that Doc and Merle reversed their roles on stage and after the concert: "One of the times I remember opening for Doc and Merle was in Boulder. I was in a duo at the time, and we shared a dressing room with them. I just remember they were very quiet with each other. Merle was ebullient and talked to us quite a bit, and Doc was a little bit more reserved. Moreover, I just don't remember them talking to each other very much at the time. Merle was friendly and outgoing, which kind of surprised me after watching him on the stage all those years. He's the quiet one on stage, so I remember thinking to myself, 'Oh, that's a surprise!'"[11]

Because Merle was so quiet on stage, he fell into the role of accompanist. It was to Doc's credit that he always did his best to bring his son up onto the pedestal with him as an equal, just as Merle did for his dad socially. When asked in 1994 about his desire to allow his son to shine on stage next to him whenever he could, whether on slide guitar or fingerpicking, Doc replied, "Well, I tried to give Merle the credit, let him earn the credit that was due him, credit that he never got from most of the record producers. Somehow or another, if you look at the earlier recordings, they'll say 'Doc Watson, arrangements.' Merle played as big a part in the arrangements as I did. That still irks me about those people, why they didn't see that..."[12] Though largely uncredited, Merle indeed helped to shape his father's sound dramatically starting in the late 1960s, helping to usher in a new era of plugged-in acoustic music.

In 1965, the live album *Doc Watson and Son* came out on Vanguard, and in 1966, Doc and Merle recorded *Home Again*, and *Southbound*, and *Strictly Instrumental*, Doc's album with Flatt and Scruggs, was released on Sony's country music label in 1968. This flurry of albums, culminating in the collaboration with Flatt and Scruggs was the big break Doc had been looking for, and Doc and Merle began to get more appearances than they could handle. Over the next two decades together, they rarely stopped for air, touring on an often-rigorous schedule and recording more than a dozen studio albums together.

Ralph Rinzler, attempting to keep Doc within the traditional mold he had created for him, wrote the liner notes to Doc's second Vanguard release, *Doc Watson and Son*, shortly before handing over the job of agenting Doc to Manny Greenhill. He wrote: "There isn't a song on this record that Doc didn't know twenty-five years ago. Most of them he has known for thirty or more. What has he been doing all this time? Pretty much the same thing he is doing right now; enjoying the way of life, the country, the friends and family that surround him."[13] That statement couldn't have been further from the truth, though the illusion satisfied fans and the record label. Change had been brewing in Doc's style since he had started in the business; he loved many kinds of music, not just traditional, and he wanted to integrate some of those tunes into his recorded work. Merle encouraged him, and together they widened the traditional music genre into what Doc would later name *traditional plus* music.

The record *Southbound* was heavily influenced by young Merle Watson. He had only really played a background role on their first album together, but on this new record, Merle wrote the words to the title track, and his ideas about the production of the album and songs on it changed Doc's music for the rest of his career. The words to the song "Southbound" expressed the sentiments of the two country boys who now spent most of their lives on the road:

> *I've been here a month or more stuck in this ol' city,*
> *Folks that have to call this home, they're the ones I pity,*
> *Lord I'm homesick and blues are the only tunes I ever seem to pick,*
> *I go out and walk the streets 'til I get blisters on my feet,*
> *I'm southbound.*[14]

Doc wrote about the origin of Merle's title track: "A few years back, we were working in New York for a few weeks. I think we had done a couple of recording sessions, and maybe a couple of weeks at the Gaslight. Anyway, Merle, from the first time he had been to New York City, had decided he didn't like the place. There was just too much noise and not enough fresh air, and you know how that appeals to a country boy. He got to sitting around there doodling with the guitar, like with a pencil on a piece of paper, and all at once he began to come up with some pretty good-sounding things. He didn't come up with words right away, but just thought a lot about them. He'd go out and walk the streets because he was so lonesome, and he actually blistered his heels just loafing in the city during the day. 'Southbound' is a good example of a homesick country boy in a big city somewhere, wanting to go home; he just wanted to get out of there."[15] The guitar playing and chord patterns are directly related to John Hurt's playing, and have just a hint of the style Merle was to develop on the road with his dad for the next two decades, with a lot of blues and a lot of stride fingerpicking. The lyrics were simple and to the point; brilliantly constructed, and full of the frustration Merle felt at being "stuck" in New York in 1966 on his first extended trip away from North Carolina.

On the *Southbound* album, Doc recorded all of the songs that he had never felt able to record before. He opened the album with sustained bowed bass notes and a strong, "I was born one morning..." as if straight off of a rhythm and blues or blues record from the day. The song, of course, then swung into a backbeat, and Doc sang "Walk on Boy," a lyric written by the 33-year old country singer Mel Tillis; a song that inspired him because of it's message, "There ain't nobody in this whole wide world gonna help you carry your load."[16] This was a bold opening for an album within which Doc Watson broke with the strictly traditional image he had maintained so well since his career began in New York City only five years before.

Doc apologized to his traditional music following in the liner notes to *Southbound*, and with that, broke with his traditionalist past, and ventured forth to record any tune that he came across, regardless of its origin. Doc's apology in the *Southbound* liner notes reads, "You will find this album a bit different from those I have previously done, but you will also find that it is closely related in many ways with old-time country music. It is a sort of bridge between the old and the new, including one of the Carter Family tunes, a tune by the late Jimmie Rodgers, a Delmore Brothers tune, one of my own compositions, a composition by my son, Merle, and a whole lot of other things that I hope you will enjoy." At the end of the liner notes, Doc, as if someone desperately pleading with the listener wrote, "I hope this album won't lead you folks to thinking I'm forsaking American traditional music, because I'm NOT!"[17] The liner notes spoke to a great fear that Doc had at the time of alienating his audience; something he certainly didn't want to do. But he also hoped that he could stop neglecting the part of his musicianship that honored modern southern country music, popular music, jazz, and all of the other forms of music that he loved and had neglected on the public stage since 1960. And with this album, Doc and Merle ushered in a new generation that would be marked by innovation in acoustic music. Merle, quietly and behind the scenes, as a teenager in Vanguard's New York studio, said to his father, "Dad let's make another kind of record."[17] And they did.

Sam Bush remembered the first time he played on the same stage as Doc and Merle: "I'll tell you how that all kind of got started. There was a tour that started in Winfield, Kansas at the festival there, in the fall of 1974 that New Grass Revival did where we would open up for Doc and Merle. And at that time, Merle had his band called Frosty Morn. New Grass Revival would open the show, and then Merle's band Frosty Morn would play a set, and then Doc and Merle would play a set and then incorporate maybe a few members of Frosty Morn into the set. And then our banjo player Courtney Johnson, and Curtis Burch, our Dobro player, and I would then get to sit in with Doc at the end of the show. I think I probably sat in a little bit more than they did, and I ended up most often playing fiddle with Doc over the years." The young musicians did several shows that first trip with Doc and Merle: "On that tour we started in Winfield, Kansas, went through Colorado, down to Southern California, all the way up to Northern California, and I think there were probably about 14 shows we did. That was when I got to know Doc and Merle better for the first time. Especially Merle."[18]

Sam Bush and all of the young musicians particularly hit it off with Merle. Of course they looked up to Doc; he was already a legendary musician, and fun to hang out with, but Merle was their age, socially liberal like they were, and enjoyed talking with them about just about any kind of music. Bush recalled: "Merle and I discovered that we both loved to listen to Duane Allman's guitar playing, so he and I would sit and listen to the Allman Brothers together."[18] As Bush and Merle listened to different kinds of music, their styles developed, and though they were playing primarily acoustic instruments on stage, their performance on those instruments was heavily influenced by the rock and roll, blues, and other electric styles around them as well as by the traditional acoustic techniques that had been resurrected within the folk music movement only a few years previous. Sam Bush remembered Merle's slide guitar playing as a sum of many different styles: "Merle had become really proficient on the slide guitar by then, and Doc was loving the slide that Merle was playing. Merle was his own man on the slide, even though he had his influences. Merle also took Doc's fingerpicking style and made it his own. Doc always told me that he felt Merle was the better fingerpicker of the two of them. And Merle was quite great at it."[18]

Both Doc and Merle enjoyed musical exploration, and always did their best to support groups that were at the cutting edge of acoustic music. Doc had himself played all kinds of music on the stage, from rockabilly to old-time, and he watched around him as young players began to embrace every kind of music, fusing elements into their own new unique styles. David Grisman created music that was a fusion of jazz and bluegrass called Dawg Music, the New Grass Revival founded a kind of music called New Grass, and many other groups spread their own experimental sounds. Tony Trischka recalled the electricity in the music of the time: "There was a lot of excitement in the air because, in retrospect, I think during that time period, the history of acoustic string music in the United States in particular was making its biggest transition. And if I had to single out the biggest, most radical transition made, it was probably the David Grisman Quintet, using essentially bluegrass instruments to play a type of string jazz, or to play a type of music that even to this day you can't really categorize. But that, I think, was a catalyst. I don't remember specifics other than it just being generally good camaraderie. The players, there were a few times out of the year where there would be events where I would be playing there with J.D. Crowe, and the New Grass Revival would be on the bill, and John Hartford and Vassar Clemens and Doc and Merle Watson. Those were exciting days, you know; they really were. We all played together onstage in jam sessions, and Doc would call me out to play some tunes with him and Merle, and there was just excitement in the air."[19]

Jerry Douglas, the king of the Dobro and long-time member of Alison Krauss' band Union Station, as well as a brilliant solo artist, remembered how Merle would bring young players to Doc's attention while the two Watsons were on the road, and how Doc would subsequently take the young players under his wing: "I think they had a trade going on. I mean, think of all the things that Doc brought Merle into, and how much Merle owed to Doc for that. But then there was this other draw from younger musicians who would go to Merle instead of go to Doc. Merle would introduce them to Doc. There are a lot of people who came down the highway that are known for playing with Doc Watson who wouldn't have been there if it hadn't been for Merle. Merle introduced these people to Doc and said, 'Hey, Dad, you should hear this guy play. This is something.' And so Doc as a musical student would be open to hearing this, otherwise he would never have heard those young musicians. And he might never have reached the younger audience as well without him. Everybody wanted to hear Doc Watson play, but Merle was the connection." Douglas went on to list a few of the major connections he saw Merle make for Doc: "Merle was largely responsible for bringing Vassar Clements to Doc, and Marty Stuart, Mark O'Connor, you know, all of those kinds of people. You know, they never would have known Doc Watson, other than just had been fans and been enamored with him. Merle said, 'Hey Pop, we need to let this guy sit and play with us, or go out and do this tour with us,' and that brought a lot of people to Doc Watson that normally wouldn't have come along."[10]

Marty Stuart recalled how he first met Doc and joined him on the road: "I knew of Doc through Lester Flatt, and that's where we kind of became buddies; by way of that camp. And after Lester died, I spent the summer of 1979 just kind of jobbing around. Vassar Clements gave me a job for a minute. And then I ran into Doc and Merle at the New Orleans Jazz Fest. Merle offered me a gig, just to come along for the rest of what was left of the summer. And that's how we hooked up for real. We'd jammed a little bit here and there, but it kind of became a formal invite at that point. And I only stayed there for the duration of that summer. But we played more music in that six or eight-week window than I've played with most folks in a lifetime, and it was some of the most eloquent, wonderful, heartfelt music I've ever been a part of. I played the mandolin on tunes most of the time. Me and Doc played guitar head-to-head on some things, and I think I probably murdered and butchered 'St. James Infirmary' when I played the fiddle. But that's the stuff I remember. I've played alongside some of the greatest musicians of our time. And I don't know that anybody comes any closer to being just an absolute genius of greatness than Doc and Merle Watson."[1]

Sam Bush recalled that the New Grass Revival got a big break from Doc: "I feel that Doc and Merle were very generous to include the New Grass Revival in the show, because I really doubt if we contributed that much to the draw of the show, but I think it was more for musical love, and a real sidebar to Doc and Merle's generosity." And he spoke to the "legion" of musicians who would come out to see Doc and Merle, who of course, eventually, also began to follow the New Grass Revival, jump-starting his career: "You'd see a lot of musicians in the audiences while out there on tour with Doc and Merle. Of course, there'd be a whole legion of young guitarists that, you just can't imagine the admiration that they would have for Doc."[18]

A young longhaired bass guitarist named T. Michael Coleman did sound for Doc and Merle at Appalachian State University in Boone every time they came through. He would soon travel with Doc and Merle for more than a decade before going on to play bass for the Seldom Scene. Coleman had grown up in nearby Leaksville, North Carolina, and was two years younger than Merle, but had little experience with professional music before Doc and Merle hired him in 1974. Soon he was on the road with Doc and Merle in a 23-foot Winnebago at age 23, going to all of the big stages in the country, and having a wild time with Merle and all of the young and brilliant musicians in the music scene at the time.[20]

Doc and Merle began to log serious hours on the road, often with T. Michael Coleman and others. Doc said in a 1980 interview: "We did 108 playing nights just last year. Still, it robs you of the intimacy of the family life at home. Something that, I guess, I don't know, maybe there's city people that feel this strongly about it, that have grown up in the city. But us mountain folk feel pretty strong about families, and the close-knit family life of home, fireside, being at the supper table and the breakfast table in the morning with your wife and your children. To me, it means a whole lot. And I reckon that ain't nothing to be ashamed of, by no means."[21]

While on the road Sam Bush remembered an enlightening meal with Doc, Merle, and fiddler John Hartford: "Out at the Strawberry Bluegrass Festival, I remember eating a meal with Doc and Merle and John Hartford. And we were finishing up the meal, and everybody was getting out their money to pay. So Doc reaches into his wallet and he says, 'Here, Merle, here's a twenty.' And Hartford just looked at him and said, 'Doc, can you feel the difference in that money?' And Doc started laughing and he said, 'No, John, I just know where I put them,' he said, 'I'm not that good.' He said, 'I just know which one's where.'"[18] Doc's innate sense of good music was similar. Once he heard these young musicians (after Merle pointed him the right direction), Doc mentored and fathered them, and treated them all as if they were his sons on the road with him. And Merle treated them all as if they were brothers.

A wonderful article written by Gregory Jaynes in 1974 for the Atlanta Journal and Constitution described the festival scene of which Doc and Merle were such an integral part. Jaynes wrote, "At 5 o'clock, a…white Winnebago Brave pulled next to the stage and parked beneath three loblolly pines and a sweet gum. Merle Watson was at the wheel. The crowd immediately lost interest in the Country Grass, a group which gamely played on. Several dozen people circled the Winnebago, swatting away gnats and peering into the windows. Doc Watson was in the back, sleeping off 12 hours on the road."[22] Merle was the road manager, and there he was, making sure that they arrived at the festival on time, while Doc tried to sleep off laryngitis so that he could sing that evening.

Although life on the road held many surprises, and allowed Doc and Merle to make a great living for their families, it was very difficult to spend each day and night traveling, and then keep up the stamina required to step on stage in front of thousands of fans and entertain them. On this particular night, Doc not only faced his own sickness and road-weariness, but he stepped onto stage in the middle of a thunderstorm. Jaynes wrote, "At 10 minutes after 6, Watson walked to the stage on the arm of his son, Merle. The long applause was mixed with real thunder. Two songs later, a torrential rain had pared the faithful to 2,000. 'Are we covered?' Watson asked his son. Assured, he played one more song while the wind whipped the rain on the stage in sheets."[22] The road was unpredictable, and Merle was Doc's rock. Though Merle didn't speak much on stage, what he did say held everything together.

Doc and Merle weren't always lucky enough to stand in front of thousands of fans. At the beginning of their career together, they played small clubs and tried to make a few dollars with each appearance. And before Merle met the scores of brilliant young musicians with whom he would work to change the face of folk, bluegrass and acoustic music, he hung out with essentially just his dad on the road. That is a period in time that Doc treasured for the rest of his life. In a New York Times article from November 1970, Mike Jahn wrote of the father and son musicians spending time together; Merle was 21 and Doc was 47: "Between sets [Doc Watson and his son] can be found drinking beer in front of the jukebox in the bar above the Gaslight, listening to a continuous stream of Creedence Clearwater Revival records."[23]

Doc and Merle's experimentation with both traditional and modern music had gained them much attention in the music community of the early 1970s, and when Earl Scruggs suggested to the Nitty Gritty Dirt Band that they enlist Doc to play guitar on their planned *Will the Circle Be Unbroken* LP, a collaboration between old-time conservative country musicians and modern, long-haired neo-traditional musicians, they thought he would be a great addition to the album. But the band didn't want both Doc and Merle; they only wanted Doc.

Doc recalled the offer he received from John McEuen of the Nitty Gritty Dirt Band: "It must have been '69...We were in California at the time, working the Ash Grove, and we were at Dale Zimmerman's, some friends of ours who lived out there. And John came in at the birthday part of it Miss Zimmerman had set for Merle. It was in February, and John got me off in the corner and told me he wanted me to work on that *Will the Circle Be Unbroken* album. And I said, 'John, I'd like to do it – have you invited Merle?' He said, "No." Well, he didn't turn around and go over and talk to Merle, and I won't go into this any more, and I just said to myself, 'I'm not going to do it.'"[24]

Doc soon changed his mind after Merle encouraged him. In a 1983 interview, Doc recalled: "Merle got me off in the corner and said, 'Dad, it did hurt my feelings, but do it. It will get us in audiences that have never heard us before.' He had a good head on his shoulders, buddy. Let me tell you that. He said, 'Do it.' He said, 'I believe you ought to. It will help us out in the long run even if they didn't invite me.' Now, that was being a man."[25] Merle knew how important it would be to both of their careers. Doc affirmed that Merle had been correct: "Well, I did it, and he hit it right on the head. It really helped us."[25]

The *Will the Circle Be Unbroken* album, recorded in six days in Nashville in August of 1971, then released in 1972, became wildly popular, and immediately gained unprecedented acclaim. Doc recalled the quick but effective way the album was recorded in Nashville; Most of the tracks were recorded in one or two takes. Doc remembered, "Think about this: most of that was unrehearsed... We just fooled around a little bit with a tune, and then did it. I can't believe how well that thing turned out."[26] The three-record set sold platinum received two Grammy nominations. The album was a watershed for acoustic music, opening the door to a whole new generation of musicians and listeners.

Musician John Pushkin recalled the impact of the album on the music world: "Huge. Huge. For everybody. I already knew about people like Doc, and I knew about Earl Scruggs, but a lot of people didn't. That album really opened up that kind of music to a lot of young people who hadn't heard it before. They had only heard people like the Nitty Gritty Dirt Band playing, but they hadn't heard where that music really came from." Pushkin remembered that *everyone* knew the *Circle* album: "When I was in college everybody had that record. Everybody was listening to it. I think because of that, Doc went up to a whole different level, as far as people who were aware of him, and people who liked his music."[27] Hal Crowther wrote the song "Tennessee Stud," Doc's hit from the *Will the Circle Be Unbroken* album, into his novel *Cathedrals of Kudzu*: "New England had never seen anything like Doc... Preppies from Connecticut with expensive Martin guitars were trying to lower their voices and flatpick their own way through "Tennessee Stud." A year earlier, half of them had been listening to Fabian."[28]

Singer-songwriter Michelle Shocked remembered the impact the *Circle* album had on her father, and eventually her own musical beginnings: "My father, who I did not grow up with, developed an interest in The Nitty Gritty Dirt Band and their album *Will the Circle Be Unbroken*. My best understanding of him is that he was a late blooming hippie, though I was young at the time. He kind of veered away from the straight and narrow. At the time he was working as a schoolteacher, his friends all started growing their hair long and he grew his hair long. They started smoking pot and he started smoking pot. Then shortly after the Nitty Gritty Dirt Band album, they all started saying, 'Let's go to bluegrass festivals.'"[29] Around this time, Doc and Merle began to find a huge audience and a loyal following. Their music no longer only appealed to folk music fans. Doc and Merle adapted to the new world of acoustic, bluegrass, folk, jam band music, and embraced new sounds, young players, every political belief, and every hairstyle into their fan base and entourage of musicians.

Shocked continued to describe her father's newfound obsession with traditional and acoustic music, and how that brought her to the music for the first time: "My father was a schoolteacher and loved books. And he was teaching himself to play bluegrass out of a Mel Bay *How to Play the Mandolin* book. And at the same time, a lot of his friends were teaching themselves to play guitar. My dad would take my brother (who is ten years younger) and me, and load up the van. My dad had custody of my brother in the summer, so I would come and stay with them, and he'd take us to Winfield, Hugo; places like that. I'm pretty sure that I first saw Doc Watson at Winfield, Kansas in '78."[29]

Tony Trischka spoke about the *Circle* album serving to bring an entire new generation into the world of traditional and acoustic music: "The *Will the Circle* album certainly spawned a whole new generation of people listening to that music... I think it was also great for Doc and Merle."[19]

Mandolinist Mike Marshall was one of the young musicians who first heard Doc Watson on the *Circle* album in 1972. Because of the vibrant music festival scene at the time, and because Doc and Merle were on the road so many days per year, Marshall soon after had a chance to see them live in concert. He remembered, "I first saw Doc at the Georgia State Bluegrass Festival in July of 1972 at the Shoal Creek Music Park in Lavonia, Georgia, where he was playing with Merle. I was very young. The festival was life-affirming. And it was life-changing to see Doc. I knew I was experiencing something really special and really important to me. That one weekend or that one ten-day period set me on my complete career path. I even bought a mandolin out of the back of a truck that weekend.'"[30]

Because of the widespread popularity of the *Circle* album, and in the recent aftermath of Woodstock, Doc and Merle had great success in the early 1970s on festival stages. However, many of the venues they were booking were not the kind of places that either of them wanted to play. In a 1988 interview with Fresh Air's Terry Grosz, Doc remembered: "I sure was glad when my son Merle started on the road with me, because if we went to a place and they didn't treat me too good, 'Dad, we won't come back here no more,' and that was the end of it. I'd tell Manny, I'd tell Mr. Greenhill, don't book there no more. We didn't hit too many places that weren't really decent to us, but once in a great while, there, 'course I won't call any names because we're on nationwide radio. But we were in a few places where they treated you like pieces of used equipment. And that was the end of playing there, we just didn't do it again. That's the best thing you can do, you know, is not tolerate that, just move away."[31]

Merle would also make sure that his musical contemporaries in their various groups would get paid on time. Jerry Douglas remembered how Merle helped them out: "Anytime we were all at a festival, Doc and Merle pulled in the big crowd, and they would get paid first. Doc and Merle could easily have just walked off with everybody's money. I remember Merle once telling a promoter that had told us that there was no more money, 'I know there's more money left, and I'm not leaving here until you pay them.' So we all got paid, and Doc and Merle then waited for the rest of their money to come later. That just doesn't happen. At that point, it became more of a family affair than a business agreement between a bunch of people. And I'm sure that Merle made that guy pay. But he made sure we were paid first. He was taking care of his buddies."[10]

Sam Bush recalled a similar situation: "It got to a point in the tour, I remember we were in Berkeley, California. I think New Grass Revival had a van and two cars, because we had a drummer at the time. At any rate, by the time we got to Berkeley, California, we ran out of money, and we didn't have any money to buy rooms. Merle talked to Doc, and I don't know how it came up, because we didn't want to admit it. But Merle found out we didn't have any money for rooms, and I remember he and Doc bought our rooms for two nights in Berkeley, California. That's what kind of guys they were."[18]

Merle and Doc made it possible for generations of future musicians to benefit from the innovative playing of Sam Bush and Jerry Douglas among countless other young players. And Merle was only a few years older than these musicians himself, but he had an old soul, and had already been in the music business on and off for nearly a decade, almost as long as his father, and he had quickly become in charge of more than just notes on the guitar; he was in charge of their entire operation. Jerry Douglas remembered: "Merle was also the conductor on stage. If you sat in with them onstage, he would conduct everything while Doc did his thing. Doc ran the show, and Merle would nod at you to take the next solo, and then Doc would yell out your name. Merle would always tell Doc who was there, and that job was passed down to Jack after Merle died. Merle was always the conductor and the band leader, and Doc was the star."[10]

Long before Merle met Sam Bush and Jerry Douglas, Merle proved himself to be a great friend to musicians, and the honest, kind and caring partner who would be invaluable to his father on the road for the next two decades. Doc recalled, "We were playing a festival and the promoter was questionable. Merle found out that this fellow wasn't going to pay Sonny Terry and Brownie McGhee... So Merle walked up and said, 'If you pay Doc and me what you owe us, I would appreciate it.' The guy said, 'Oh, sure,' and paid us the rest of what he owed us. Sonny was standing close by, and Merle turns around and says, 'Sonny, here is your money.' Merle turned back to the promoter and said, 'Now pay me,' with a little chuckle that meant, he better do it. And the guy was livid but he paid us what he owed us."[32]

Doc, with great pride, continued the story about legendary blues musician Sonny Terry: "Sonny comes to where I am standing and bumps my shoulder and says, 'Doc Watson, you got a fine man for a son.'"[32]

# CHAPTER NOTES

1. Gustavson, Kent, *Telephone Interview with Marty Stuart*. May 18, 2009.
2. Ide, Stephen, *Doc Watson: Nostalgia and Pleasure*. Dirty Linen, 1995(64): p. 33-43,115.
3. Watson, Rosa Lee, *Letter to Ralph Rinzler "Doc and Merle left yesterday and I'm already going round in circles.": June 28, 1965*. 1965.
4. Rowe, Jeri, *Doc Watson - in his own words*. 1997, Greensboro News and Record Online.
5. Earle, Eugene, *Interview with Doc Watson*, Audio Cassette, Southern Folklife Collection: Eugene Earle Collection, 1988.
6. Ledgin, Stephanie P., *Father and Son*. Acoustic Guitar, 1993: p. 49-57.
7. Menius, Art, *Doc Watson: Roots of Mastery*. Bluegrass Unlimited, 1997. **32**: p. 30-38.
8. Sievert, Jon, *Doc Watson: 'Like Some Kind of Fine'*. Frets, March 1979. **1**(1): p. 20-26.
9. Gustavson, Kent, *Email Interview with Larry Long*. June 30, 2009.
10. Gustavson, Kent, *Telephone Interview with Jerry Douglas*. April 10, 2009.
11. Gustavson, Kent, *Telephone Interview with Pat Donohue*. March 11, 2009.
12. Reamy, Margaret, *The Real Thing: Doc Watson*. The Record Exchange Music Monitor, April 1994: p. 1.
13. Rinzler, Ralph, *Liner Notes to Doc Watson and Son*, Vanguard Records, 1965.
14. Watson, Merle, *Southbound*, Vanguard Records, 1966.
15. Watson, Doc and Ralph Rinzler, *The Songs of Doc Watson*. 1971, New York City: Oak Publications.
16. Tillis, Mel and Wayne P. Walker, *Walk on Boy*, 1960.
17. Watson, Doc, *Liner Notes from Doc Watson: Southbound*, Vanguard Records, 1988.
18. Gustavson, Kent, *Telephone Interview with Sam Bush*. April 9, 2009.
19. Gustavson, Kent, *Telephone Interview with Tony Trischka*. April 27, 2009.
20. Coleman, T. Michael, *T. Michael Coleman's Biography*. 2002, Doc and Merle Watson Museum at Cove Creek.
21. *Doc and Merle Playing at White House*, Video, Ralph Rinzler Folklife Archives, SI-FP 1990-VTR-29 #65, 1980.
22. Jaynes, Gregory, *The Blind Musician from Deep Gap*. The Atlanta Journal and Constitution, 1974: p. 8-9,16,19.
23. Jahn, Mike, *Doc Watson and Son Present Folk Songs*. The New York Times, November 15, 1970. New York: p. 81.
24. Holt, David and Doc Watson, *Doc Watson and David Holt: Legacy*, Audio CD, High Windy Audio, 2002.
25. Gartner, Rick, *Doc Watson*. Frets, 1983(8): p. 33-35.
26. Nitty Gritty Dirt Band, *Will The Circle Be Unbroken, Vol. 3*, Audio CD, Capitol, 2002.
27. Gustavson, Kent, *Telephone Interview with John Pushkin*. June 10, 2009.
28. Crowther, Hal, *Cathedrals of Kudzu*. 2002: Louisiana State University Press. 192.
29. Gustavson, Kent, *Telephone Interview with Michelle Shocked*. March 12, 2009.
30. Gustavson, Kent, *Telephone Interview with Mike Marshall*. March 26, 2009.
31. Grosz, Terry, *Interview with Doc Watson*, from *Fresh Air*. 1988, National Public Radio.
32. Holt, David, *Liner Notes to Doc Watson and David Holt: Legacy*, High Windy, 2002.

Photo by Mark Reid ©
*Merle Watson playing slide guitar on stage.*

Photo by Nic Siler ©
*Merle Watson playing banjo on stage.*

# CHAPTER SIXTEEN
## Midnight Rider

*"Well, I've got to run to keep from hiding,*
*And I'm bound to keep on riding,*
*And I've got one more silver dollar,*
*But I'm not gonna let them catch me, no,*
*Not gonna let 'em catch the midnight rider."*

- Greg Allman and Robert Payne[1]

I n the early 1970s, Doc and Merle played concerts wherever they could, gradually expanding their audience throughout the decade, with great assistance from the success of the *Will the Circle Be Unbroken* album. In a rare interview in 1976, Merle said: "We are doing more work than we have, of course, in the past, and we are playing for noisier outdoor things now than we have before, and [it's] really helpful to have the [Frosty Morn] band, because a lot of times now you just can't play just traditional music for the audiences because they want to hear more up tempo things [and] you kind of have to have a band for that."[2]

In the early 1970s, in order to save time and effort, Doc and Merle started plugging in their guitars at every venue, bringing their own preamps, and controlling most of their sound from the stage. Soon after that, they also brought T. Michael Coleman, an electric bass player, into the group. The electrification of their instruments allowed them to perform on bigger stages and in more varied environments without sacrificing clarity and volume, and it also helped them to avoid any trouble working with sound people at different venues. They pretty much had it down to *plug and play*, and they easily took their show on the road in their Winnebago.

Photo by Nic Siler ©
*Doc Watson & T. Michael Coleman on stage.*

Though Doc and Merle were playing bigger stages than ever before, and exciting fans from coast to coast, the thrill of the road had legally left both of them. Ever since he had spoken with his father in 1967 about getting off the road, Merle longed go back to the Blue Ridge and do something closer to home. He wanted to be near his kids, his friends, and his own home and tractor.

Doc also never really liked the road, and though it was much easier for him with Merle, he still hated to be away from home: "I never did get used to touring, and it was awfully hard on Merle because I couldn't share in the driving. He drove God knows how many miles. It's a shame there wasn't enough money to hire a driver. I was trying to earn a living for my family, and Merle stuck by me, bless his heart."[3]

Merle's marriage was soon on the rocks, as he was nearly never home, and returned from the road a tired and different man. Jack Lawrence remembered how touring took its toll on Merle, and how his own first marriage was affected by life on the road: "Of course life on the road took its toll on Merle, and it also took a toll on my first marriage. I was gone constantly. I missed the births of my two youngest children because I wasn't really making enough money that I could take off and be there and still pay for it all. I was making a living on the road."[4]

Merle was a great business manager and logistics organizer: "Merle...was so good at travel on the road. As good as he was with music. He could memorize a dag blame city. He'd know right how to go back to it if it was a year later. And drove, if not hundreds of thousands of miles, but well over a million miles. I don't know how many miles that boy drove during the dues-paying days. Just he and I together...Traveling with Merle was one of the easiest things in the music that I've done. [The traveling] was hard...but it was easy [with Merle]."[5]

Merle was an easy-going fellow on the road with his father, although he took care of most of the hard tasks. He was in charge of the instruments, the sound checks, set lists, visiting musicians, opening acts, and all travel and accommodations. No wonder Merle loved returning home. When at home, he would rarely play with his father, and when he did pick up an instrument, he would pick up an acoustic or electric guitar and play slide in a local band or two. He also purchased a classical harp, and spent a great deal of time figuring out its complexities, learning a few tunes, and bringing the sounds of the large instrument back to his solo guitar playing. Ricky Skaggs remembered Merle's harp: "Merle had a harp in the living room at Doc and Rosa Lee's when I was over there, and he was playing the harp that day for me. It was so pretty to hear him play it."[6] Directly after that comment, as if to compare Merle's disposition to the tone of the harp, Skaggs followed up by saying, "He was very kind, very gentle."[6] Many of Merle's friends and colleagues remembered his gentle and warm-hearted nature.

However great his problems grew, he never had a cruel bone in his body. He was a great friend, and a gentle soul.

When Merle eventually decided to get off the road in the early 1980s, Doc was disappointed, but he certainly understood. His son had essentially served him for twenty years on the road, waking him up in the morning, leading him from venue to venue, and acting as his eyes to the world. Merle groomed his close friend Jack Lawrence for the role of accompanist; a role that Lawrence loyally performed for Doc for the next thirty years. Merle had decided to spend more time at home, hanging out with his mountain friends, and spending time with his children and grandchild. Merle lived a few miles outside of Lenoir, the small town where Doc had been given his nickname some forty years earlier. He worked at a local music studio producing records, and he started a modest construction company. One of his main projects was building a beautiful new home for his father on a plot of land overlooking Deep Gap, sandwiched between the Blue Ridge Parkway and the stretch of Highway 421 that is now called The Doc and Merle Watson Memorial Highway.

Ricky Skaggs recalled buying a house from Merle: "In the early '80s I came over to Doc's house. I had seen Merle somewhere and he told me about a log house that was on his property with straight 200-year old logs. And so I drove over one day from Nashville and I met with Merle and we went up in the woods and looked at this house. I bought that house from him; basically just the logs, you know. Then I got real busy, and my career just really took off, and one day I saw Merle and he said, 'Man, when are you going to come out to that house?' And I said, 'Oh, God, I've really got to do that.' And I sent a guy over to have them all numbered because I was going to have them taken down by number, log by log, so they could be put up the same way. And I was going to have a house built, and then just put those logs in a certain part of the house. But before he could take those logs down, the daggone house caught on fire! Those logs caught on fire in that house and all of them burned down. I hated it so bad, but there was nothing I could do about it."[6]

Not long after, Merle was also gone, leaving giant footsteps, and an empty chair on stage next to Doc. But Merle's death was unfortunately not entirely a surprise to anyone who knew him well. Like logs left to dry, it was just a matter of time before a spark would catch and everything would burn to the ground.

Merle, as one of the chief innovators of early acoustic music in the late 1960s and early '70s, pushed the envelope with his and Doc's music, and with the music he encouraged in the musicians around him. He believed in free expression, and helped many musicians to gain a foothold in the music movement that was sprouting. Mike Marshall, who first got into acoustic music in the early 1970s, to a great extent because of a Doc and Merle Watson concert he had gone to as a teenager, said about the music being made at the time: "This was the period coming *out* of the '60s. It was a freeing period for a whole generation; it was an explosively creative time. I mean when you look back on it, it was much more creative than in many ways what's going on now."[7] Not only were rock and folk intersecting, but blues, world music, classical music, and all genres were beginning to come together like never before.

By 1969 when the Woodstock music festival took place, the folk movement had already changed dramatically, even in Greenwich Village. Midwestern singer-songwriter Greg Brown traveled to New York in 1969, searching for a folk music scene that had already largely disappeared: "When I went to New York to try to be a working musician, it was 1969. The so-called folk boom had boomed, and what lingered was an echo. There was a little music fair advertised around the Village that summer up in a little town called Woodstock. I couldn't go; I had to work. But I was never really into rock and roll. I liked rhythm and blues, country blues, and the old hill tunes. New York exposed me to music from all over the world, though the folk scene as such did not amount to much at that point. I did not stay long – five or six months."[8]

Traditional folk music had gone largely out of style, and Woodstock had ushered in a new era of semi-acoustic music. The Grateful Dead, Crosby, Stills, Nash & Young, and many other bands that became hugely popular in the early 1970s often played with a mix of acoustic and electric instruments, and, though they rarely played traditional music, they cited as their influences the folk and traditional musicians of the 1960s. This brand of semi-acoustic music changed everything for folk and traditional artists who were still on the music festival circuit. Crowds no longer listened in rapt silence as they had done at Newport in the 1960s. Audiences longed to make each festival event into another Woodstock. This made it very difficult for artists who depended on *listening* audiences.

Michelle Shocked remembered the music scene at the music festivals of the 1970s: "The music festivals were very family-oriented, but there was an undercurrent of hippies, stoners, long-hairs. They would all be around, whereas at the same time, other bluegrass people would sit around on Sunday morning and sing bluegrass gospel hymns. The stoners would get together and sing John Prine songs like 'Plastic Jesus' and stuff like that."[9] Merle was in between both groups. He was all mountain, and all progressive. He was a long-hair from conservative country. He drank and experimented with *this and that*, but he showed up many times on Sunday morning, and he had some very personal conversations with his father about faith. He was deeply Christian underneath everything else. He partied hard, but he had a gentle soul. And in thinking back on his "highest moment" with Merle, Jack Lawrence laughed and quipped, "We're talking spiritually, not chemically?"[10] Merle had been Lawrence's good friend, whether stoned or sober, on stage, back stage, or at home.

One of the main features of the new Woodstock-era music festivals and music fans was their use of drugs. Some of the festivals were mild and family-oriented, but others were not. Musicians and audience members alike were filled with drugs from pot to cocaine and amphetamines, and it changed the focus of the music and the performance.

Tom Paxton recalled that there had been very little drug use in the 1960s folk scene: "The only drugs were pot and mescaline…And I'll never forget someone explaining to me about, I think it was mescaline, where you got these buds and everything and you ingested all these buds and everything and these buds, and eventually they made you puke, and then you got high. And I thought *[sarcastically]*, 'What a night out *that* sounds like.' And of course there was heroin, but that wasn't very common. A lot of guys were smoking pot, and I smoked it a bit, and I found that either it did absolutely nothing, or it completely paralyzed me. There I would be stretched out on the floor and everybody would be going down to Chinatown to eat, and I thought *[again, sarcastically]*, 'Am I having fun yet? No.' Pot was pretty much what you saw. And then toward the end of the '60s the amphetamines came in, and you'd find people who'd clean their house for three days. And I thought, 'Well, I don't think so.' I guess I was just too much of a tight ass to want to lose control. 'Why would I want to do that?' Control was hard enough won as it was."[11]

Although there was still heavy marijuana use in the late '70s and early '80s, the drug of choice was cocaine. Several anonymous sources spoke of Merle's experimentations with the substance and others. But that didn't make him anomalous. Many of the great singer-songwriters of the day experimented with cocaine and other similar drugs. In fact, in the early 1980s, many still denied the adverse effects of the drug, and millions of Americans had experimented with it. Cocaine also assisted musicians to play their music in all-night-long parties. In the hills of North Carolina, people who partied with Merle are still talking about his late night jam sessions. Musicians used drugs to aid in their perception of music, and to expand their consciousness and experience of life. Unfortunately, they simply didn't know the consequences of what they were doing to their bodies and minds.

Guy Clark recalled that Merle often hung out with their mutual friend Townes Van Zandt, a singer-songwriter known for his heavy drug use and brilliant though erratic behavior.[12] Van Zandt often went from couch to couch, and was known for using heroin, cocaine, and drinking alcohol in great excess. Like Merle, Townes went to rehab several times; some sources say that he might have been in rehab more than ten times in the later years of his life. Merle surely joined Townes on more than a few benders.

Alan O'Bryant, the brilliant singer and banjoist from the Nashville Bluegrass Band who lent his high harmony to some of Doc Watson's best records, remembered spending time with Merle near the end of his life: "You know, me and Merle would kind of pal around at some of these events when we got together. I think I even ran into him a couple times when I would be home on Christmas vacation. I'd run into him at parties or something like that, you know. But he was just one of the most straight-ahead guys. He'd just say, 'Hey dude, how you doing?' He was just one of the most unpretentious people."[13] O'Bryant noticed that Merle didn't want to be the star, and was quite happy to be sitting just stage-right of the spotlight: "He seemed like he was quite happy to hide out. You know, just a good ol' boy from where good ole boys come from..."[13] O'Bryant recalled Merle happily playing slide guitar at several of the parties, safely away from the spotlight.

Sam Bush had a close relationship with Merle that went back to Bush's early days in the business, and he had a great respect for both Doc and Merle. Bush remembered, in the early years, participating in wild times with Merle and others, but by 1984, he had gotten married, and had settled down. He remembered when Merle invited him to visit: "Merle would bring me over to North Carolina sometimes to play on records with them. But Merle would also bring me over when he would have a production project or something that he was doing. In 1984 Lynn and I had just gotten married. I was going to come over to North Carolina to record about a month after our wedding. And Merle said, 'We'll pay for Lynn's ticket so she can come too.' He said, 'There's a beautiful mountain cottage that we've got for you guys to stay in.' This was Doc and Merle's present to us, as a wedding gift. The funny part was, when we came there, yeah, it was a beautiful cottage, but what Merle forgot to tell us was that T. Michael Coleman would also be staying in the house with us." With a laugh, Bush recalled their friendship on stage and off: "I did have the pleasure many a time to go be the fourth wheel on the show with Doc and Merle and T. Michael. Those were some of my proudest moments."[14]

Bela Fleck also had a chance to get to know Merle just before his death, while working with him and Doc on their newest album: "The *Riding the Midnight Train* session was a bonding experience for me and Merle, because Doc asked us to do a couple of tracks with two banjos; in the clawhammer and bluegrass styles. This experience made us both very excited and we felt closer."[15] However, Merle wasn't the same gregarious musician that he had been, and years of hard living and hard traveling had taken their toll on him. During the same sessions, Fleck recalled: "Sometimes he was so quiet, I couldn't tell what I thought about him."[15] Merle, of course, didn't know that he was living his last few months, but he knew a change was coming. He was trying desperately to get off of the road completely, and several times simply didn't show up for concerts or recording sessions. He wanted a new start, whether through rehab or through staying home in the Blue Ridge, where he could spend time with his son, working on a few music projects, and building his dad's house in Deep Gap. Merle had served a long time in his father's service, and it was time for him to come home.

Merle had always been in his father's shadow. From not being invited to play on the *Will the Circle Be Unbroken* album to being omitted from just about every interview with Doc during their career as a duo, Merle got used to the neglect, but it surely never settled within him. Psychologist and bluegrass musician David Moultrup saw Doc and Merle in the early 1970s on tour, and experienced them close up in a workshop: "I think that that first opportunity that I had being close to Merle, now in hindsight, and frankly with the experience that I have in my office so often, I understand that when you have a parent who is a superstar, it puts an extra burden on you. It's like the sun is shining so bright that you don't know who you are relative to where the sun is."[16] Moultrup continued, "I was young at the time, I was either in college or barely out of college, and there's no doubt in my mind that me and all the rest of the kids in the workshop were thinking, 'I could play just as good as Merle, I want to be out there playing with Doc.' I'm quite sure that was going on. And my hunch is that Merle somehow was onto that drift and probably did not exactly want to be there. Likewise, I thought that it was significant that Merle developed his fingerpicking technique. And Doc tried to applaud him for that. But even there, it must have been hard to be sort of separate from the intensity of Doc's star that shone so bright."[16]

Tao Rodriguez-Seeger, the grandson of folk music legend Pete Seeger, said of Merle's experience: "I'm sure it was real hard being compared to Doc, I mean how could anybody feel good about themselves trying to take a break after Doc? But Merle could do it. If anyone could do it, it was Merle."[17] Indeed, Merle was one of the only musicians who could make Doc sound better by equaling his speed and tone. When Doc and Merle played twin guitars on fiddle tunes, they melded with one another's instrumental sound as if they were a vocal brother duet singing sweet songs. Many guitarists after Merle tried to twin with Doc on those tunes without nearly the same success. Jack Lawrence did some amazing playing with Doc, but he never was as intimate and as matched to Doc as Merle had been. The two Watsons not only matched one another in versatility and speed, but also in humility. They never stepped on one another's toes, and neither one of them competed with the other or showboated.

Rodriguez-Seeger, who never met Merle, spoke about Merle's quiet genius on the guitar: "I bet if Merle had lived, I think Merle would have stretched out more. I can't imagine he wouldn't have. One thing is never enough, I suspect, for the truly great and creative mind, and undeniably one of the great, great guitar players of the last century."[17] Beyond Merle's musical skill was his innovative approach to music and his encouragement of younger experimental players in the business. Rodriguez-Seeger talked about Merle as a kind of filter, bringing traditional music to an entirely new generation: "Artists and poets are just filters. You end up filtering the music through your own life, inevitably. And that's what Merle did. He ended up filtering this beautiful mountain music through his own life, giving it a younger perspective."[17]

David Moultrup thought about Merle's "younger perspective" against the backdrop of what acoustic music had been in the previous generations: "When I look at bluegrass, especially back in the '60s and '70s, it was very much sort of the embodiment of the male persona. It was tight-lipped, it was unemotional, it was testosterone-driven. It wasn't touchy feely. It wasn't insight-driven. It wasn't based on social relevance and consciousness. Every now and then you got a song that was socially relevant, but not to the degree that you did with the rock and roll or certainly folk music. And then what happened is that you'd get the leader standing there in one outfit, and then you'd get the rest of the guys were standing there in another outfit looking sort of like clones and I'm sure Merle was pushing against that."[16]

Peter Rowan remembered the tension deep inside his friend: "I think Merle appeared to be an extremely shy person, but he was pent up."[18] Rowan then went on to talk about Merle's eventual death: "Who can say why the tragedy occurred. You know, maybe it was because it was all given to him, you know. It was rough on him. When the father is that strong the kid struggles. Even if the father is totally giving and doesn't understand why the son should feel frustrated, you know. I mean, Doc was never anything but loving with Merle. That's a man you can be confident in; is a guy like Doc; totally confident in his presence."[18] Similarly, Doc had always been confident in Merle's rock solid accompaniment on the road and on stage.

Merle mastered a style of playing that complemented Doc's acrobatics on the guitar. He could play as fast as his father on the flatpicking tunes, but when it came to a blues or a ballad, Merle would bring out the classical guitar or his slide. He used a 5/8" Sears and Roebuck Craftsman socket wrench on his left fourth finger to glide across the strings like a hot knife through butter. The socket wrench was heavy, and Merle's touch was light, and the sound was uniquely his. Ben Harper, a master of the Weissenborn slide guitar, called Merle's slide playing "incredible,"[18] and Merle indeed impressed the greats of his generation with his technique, including Allman Brothers Band guitarist Dickey Betts. Doc remembered when Merle first started listening to the Allman Brothers' unique brand of southern rock: "[Merle] didn't start workin' on the slide guitar till the early seventies, when he heard, believe it or not, the hard blues rock Allman Brothers Band. He heard Duane Allman play electric slide guitar and he said to me one night, 'Daddy, do you reckon them licks could be turned to traditional music?' And I said, 'Yeah, if you put your mind to it you can do it.' That was all he needed. He grabbed a Craftsman socket wrench and stuck it on that finger and went to work on it!"[19]

Merle said in his 1979 interview: "I started in about 1973. I was definitely very influenced by Duane Allman's music. He was already dead, of course, but I had been listening to the Allman Brothers records. I know I've worked harder on my slide playing than anything else. That gave me a pretty hard time getting it down clean."[20] Merle talked about his technique: "[I use a] Sears & Roebuck

5/8-inch socket wrench... I think you really need that weight to get it clean... Well you have to have a real light touch on the strings – light but still firm. I keep my little finger just resting gently on the strings behind the bar. It takes quite a bit of practice to get the strength in your fingers to be able to move that bar around fast... There was a time when my hand would get very tired quickly when I switched over to slide, but I don't notice it at all now. Of course if I don't play for a week or two I'll really notice it."[20]

Jerry Douglas, a legend of the Dobro, said of Merle's slide playing: "I think Merle was really starting to hit his stride."[21] He talked about Merle's adoption of slide guitar as a way to have something a little different than what Doc offered, so as not to be compared all the time to his father's unmatchable virtuosity: "You know, if you're sitting there on stage with the best flatpicking guitar player alive, what are you going to do? When it comes time to take your solo, you're not going to blow away the guy who just played. So you better come up with something new, right?"[21] Douglas then described in slightly more technical detail the different sound that Merle brought to the slide guitar, using his Craftsman socket wrench: "He developed a slide technique that wasn't as noisy as that of most slide players; he didn't hit the frets. He was clean, and very soulful. But he had only really scratched the surface when he died. I think if he had lived he would have a totally different legacy as a slide guitar player. He was amazing, and it was too brief an experiment."[21]

Marty Stuart, Merle's friend and fellow innovator in the 1970s and '80s acoustic music scene, echoed Douglas' praise: "It was a divine experience to listen to what came out of that guitar. Merle had a socket wrench on his left hand when he played slide, and he was headed to a place where that particular style of guitar playing would absolutely belong to nobody but him. I know he admired Duane Allman, and certain other guitar players, but Merle was kind of like the rural version of that that nobody could claim."[22] Stuart believed that Merle's technique in fact went all the way back to his first festival performance in 1964, when he first heard Mississippi John Hurt play, after which the wizened old country blues singer give him private fingerpicking lessons. Stuart recognized that Merle used the unique opportunities that had been in front of him as a child, learning from masters of the guitar first hand: "I think a lot of that sound was rooted in his friendship with John Hurt and the old timers who took him in, and in the techniques that he adopted in the early days on the folk circuit. He came out of a deeper place with his playing."[22] Merle tapped into the rural styles of several musicians and blended them with Duane Allman's roaring blues guitar sounds to create a new guitar sound that was all his own.

Jack Lawrence recalled his old friend Merle's talent: "Oh, his live playing was just killer. I don't think it really got on record how good Merle was. He was able to do his finger-style alternating-bass kind of stuff in conjunction with playing the slide notes in there, like nobody I'd ever heard before. As if Mississippi John Hurt meets Duane Allman within him. And I still have not heard another slide player really play like that. And another thing he did that was different, and this all came about as a mistake from what I can understand, is that, when he was first learning to play slide, listening to the Allman Brothers' stuff, he asked somebody what tuning it was in. And somebody told him that Duane tuned in open A. But actually he tuned, of course, in G. So Merle's slide guitar was tuned in open A. That higher-pitched sound was also part of his style."[10]

Alan O'Bryant remembered that Merle's playing was consummately tasteful but reserved when he was on stage with his father: "I think that he was kind of understated in his slide playing, much the same way that Doc is in his approach to some stuff. I think that lots of times he would understate things for the sake of taste. But when he wanted to get out, when he wanted to get out there, he could. And I think that he was probably...at a somewhat early stage, a formative stage. And I think if he'd been able to continue... there'd be a lot more for us to witness along those lines. I mean, there's things about my playing now that I might have been reticent about before, but I'm a lot more confident about them now, as far as even banjo playing and things that I would attempt and things that I'll try just because I've had a lot more time to think them out, and kind of know where I'm coming from and where I'm going to..."[13] What nearly every musician who knew Merle agrees on is that he was just starting to come into his own when he died. He had started to venture into territory with his playing that would have blossomed into something new and extraordinary. After all, he died at age 36, which was a year younger than Doc Watson had been when Ralph Rinzler first recorded him in 1960 as part of Clarence Ashley's band.

Like O'Bryant, mandolinist Mike Marshall believed that Merle's greatest talent was in humbly and respectfully accompanying his father on stage. He made Doc's playing shine, not his own. In his few times hanging out with Merle, he remembered that Merle's personality was also incredibly charming and kind: "What can you say? Merle was a sweet, darling dude."[7] Countless musicians echo Marshall's sentiment, and miss Merle's presence in the acoustic music scene, even a quarter of a century after his passing.

Merle was certainly not only *darling* to his music colleagues, and he had no lack of luck with ladies on the road. For that and other reasons, his marriage split up not long after the birth of his two children, Richard and Karen. While on tour, Merle would respectfully bring his father to his hotel room, and then he would go out and have a good time on the town, often bringing a companion back to the hotel room with him.

In his 1974 article detailing a full day in the life of Doc and Merle at a Georgia tour stop, Gregory Jaynes wrote about the morning routine for Doc and Merle, gently hinting at Merle's inclusion of a female partner at the Sunday morning breakfast table at their Holiday Inn. When Jaynes called Doc early in the morning, he had not yet seen Merle, and told the reporter to call Room 154 to wake him up. They both agreed to share breakfast with him. Jaynes wrote, "Merle had been up for hours. He and a pretty bluegrass music fan got Doc and escorted him to the restaurant."[23] Jaynes wrote again later in the article about Merle's "friend," as well as T. Michael Coleman's "friend" at the breakfast table: "The place mats on the table carried a map of the United States, only the states weren't named and neither were the capitals. Merle and his friend and bass player Michael Coleman and a friend played a geographical game of fill in the states and capitals while Doc ate his Raisin Bran... Merle and his friend are trying to figure out whether Bismarck belongs to North Dakota and Pierre to South Dakota, or the other way around."[23] Merle used his "friendships" on the road in the same way as he used substances: to take his mind off of the day-to-day. Every day driving to a new venue and leading his father onto the stage, playing the same songs as his father's sideman.

Merle told Jaynes that they were on the road 22 to 26 days every month, and Doc then told the reader that he was thinking of retiring. In 1974, Doc was 51 years old, and the many miles had started to wear on him. Doc said, "In a year or two, I'm gonna cut back...I'm serious about that, too."[23] Doc then compared his eventual refusal to go on the road anymore with his earlier refusal to fly: "When I decide to, it'll be just like I was about flyin'. I quit it. I must have flown a half-million miles since '63."[23] Merle quickly quipped, in response to his father's statement about flying: "I've driven that far since you quit flying."[23] Doc then explained: "I won't fly unless it's absolutely necessary. Some kind of pressure built up inside me. I got an ulcer and I know flyin' was the cause of it."[23] Yet again, Merle had made it possible for Doc to stay on the road, and had driven millions of miles to make it happen. No wonder he needed to forget responsibility from time to time. He had been his father's business manager on the road since he was a boy of 15 years old, had neglected his own family and many other things in order to support his father's career. Mitch Greenhill, Doc and Merle's agent in the 1970s after his father Manny Greenhill's retirement, remembered: "Merle got tired of traveling. They had been doing it so long that it just didn't have any appeal for him [anymore].'"[23]

Despite Merle's great care for his father, Merle began, from time to time, to disappear. He would simply not show up where he was supposed to be. Rather than psychologically confronting the issues he might have had with his father, his wife, or his music career, Merle got out his frustrations and pent up emotions by, as he and his friends called it, "running in the hills." He would disappear for days and sometimes longer, and Doc would often have no idea where his son was. Doc supported his son through rehab several times, but it never took, and Merle always ended up with the same friends, running in the same mountains, as so many addicts do. Doc began to lose hope, and didn't know what to do for his son. He feared losing his son as his road companion and musical soul mate. And he also feared losing him completely, because there had been, according to anonymous sources, already several scares when Merle had narrowly escaped death.

Ketch Secor, lead singer of Old Crow Medicine Show, who lived only miles from Deep Gap with his bandmates before they were later "discovered" by Doc Watson's daughter Nancy while busking on the streets of Boone, said of Doc's boy: "I think that Merle was a burden for Doc to bear. Merle was always going to be a no show until the day he died."[24] Such a harsh statement is far off from the statements of praise so often showered on Merle after his death, but it represents the sentiment of the people who still live on the mountain who remember Merle; many locals remembered Merle as a young man who represented frequent trouble for his parents. One anonymous contemporary of Merle's from Deep Gap who had known the musician his entire life, recalled that young Merle was undisciplined, was his mother's sweetheart, and could "do no wrong" in her eyes, even into adulthood.

Secor concluded his argument in almost mythological terms, saying, "His daddy was always going to love him, and he was always going to hurt his daddy. And that tragic form, which was inescapable until the day he died, was such a part of the life of Doc Watson and everybody associated with Doc and Merle."[24]

Merle described his own unreliability in a 1976 interview with Bert Lloyd: "Well, I went out [to California] to do some sessions, I think it was going to be for a movie thing and I was getting expenses and all that stuff. And when we did some practice warm up with some musicians there it was just terrible, I don't remember who it was, it was just really bad. I just put my guitars up and decided that I had never been to Hawaii, so I just got on a plane and left, and spent the day and came home. It was just a real bad situation, I didn't enjoy it. I just can't play if it's pressured like that..."[2] And indeed, he would often simply disappear. Most of the time it didn't affect too many people, but at times, he neglected his responsibilities.

Marty Stuart remembered his friend Merle as a wonderful man plagued by demons: "He was probably one of the most deep-hearted people that I've ever met. He had an enormous heart when it came to people and musicians and his friends. On the exterior, he had this big ol' gruff bear appearance, but I think one of the things that may get overlooked is what a sensitive soul he was, and the artist side of him. He was a highly sensitive guy, as all great artists really are. But the thing that sabotaged it all was those little demons that haunted him. And the thing that was astounding to me was that sometimes he'd get off into a place where the ball and chain wrapped itself around his neck, and he couldn't get there for a tour. So me and T. Michael Coleman and Doc would go out and do the tour, and when he would show back up it was as if nothing had ever happened. No apologies, nobody spoke about it, and he hadn't probably touched his guitar in three or four or five weeks."[22]

Merle's downward spiral had begun. He began to let his addiction get out of control. Ketch Secor related a story that is told so often it is legendary in the music industry, though only talked about in hushed tones since it's thought of as something that might be disrespectful to Doc. But on the contrary, it's a testament to his strength as a father and a friend. He forgave his son everything, and did his best to move forwards, hoping that Merle would someday be healed of these afflictions. Secor said, "I'll tell you a story. It's probably second or third hand, but I remember someone telling me that Merle and Doc were out on a big road tour, and they couldn't find Doc. And Doc didn't show up for several events, and finally some managerial type figure, or maybe another member of the band found that Doc has been in the hotel room for like 35 hours, just stuck there with nowhere to go because Merle had been gone. Because Merle had been out on a tear."[24]

Shortly before Merle's death, he stopped touring with his father, and he even stopped showing up to the recording sessions for their next album, hiring instead his friends to go in his place. It seemed as though he knew he was going to die, and lined up the musicians with whom he thought Doc would be able to continue in the business. But in actuality, Merle didn't know that he was going to soon die; he wanted simply to get off the road, and out of the business, and each time he disappeared, he was closer to disappearing for good.

Some reports say that Merle had an abscessed tooth at the beginning of the sessions for *Riding the Midnight Train*, and that's why he had to back out of them. Alan O'Bryant remembered a different version of Merle's story: "Merle had hurt his hand doing something, and he wasn't able to play. And I'm not sure whether he wasn't able to play guitar altogether, or if he was only able to play slide, or what. But anyhow, Doc had me play rhythm guitar along while they were recording, while we were cutting these tunes. Of course I was singing with them on it, and I think that Bela Fleck was involved in some of that, too... Bela made the comment to somebody one time that I was the only banjo player he knew that had ever played rhythm guitar on a Doc Watson album. And I hadn't even thought about that until he said that. I didn't hardly think anything of it, except I couldn't understand why Doc wanted me to play rhythm guitar on his record."[13] In hindsight, it made a great deal of sense. Doc needed someone to play Merle's accompanying guitar part, because his son hadn't showed up. And Alan O'Bryant was a gifted musician who would be able to play the part required.

Merle stopped being there for Doc. Merle was a wonderful, sweet, loving son who cared more for his father than probably anyone else on the earth. But he let him down. He went on binges, and he neglected his responsibilities. Doc tried to help him, but he couldn't control his son's every movement, and so he stood by as his boy grew worse and worse, and then was gone.

Jack Lawrence filled in for Merle in the last few months of his life, both on record and on the road, and he later received what was something like a blessing from Merle to take care of and travel with his father, as if Merle knew he was on a downward spiral, and wasn't able to be there for his father as he would have liked to be. Lawrence recalled that he took the responsibility seriously, so much so that he stayed on the road with Doc for the better part of three decades, through thick and thin, taking over for Merle. Lawrence said: "Doc always knew I would be there. I don't think Merle was quite as on top of it sometimes as maybe I was in that regard. Doc always knew that I'd be there to get him to breakfast in the morning. No matter what kind of shape I was in, I'd be there."[10]

Lawrence would be there no matter what shape he was in partially because he was grateful for the great job he had with Doc. He was able to support his family for decades with the salary he took home from accompanying Doc. But he also had done his share of partying, with Merle and afterwards, though it never affected his career, because he was able to get himself out of bed in the morning and show up for work. Merle didn't have the same ability, whether more of an addict, or whether he knew it was "only" his father he would be disappointing, and not his "boss." Merle knew that, even if he disappeared, he would be welcomed back into his father's home and onto stages across the country to his father's right. If it had been a job that Merle could have lost, perhaps he would have respected it more, and he might never have gotten to the brink of personal destruction.

Lawrence remembered running in the hills with Merle: "Merle and I hung out whenever my rock and roll band played in the area up there. Merle would always come out and play with us. And there were always huge parties at somebody's house afterwards, though never at Merle's."[10] Lawrence was making his living at the time by playing gigs when he could get them; mostly rock in small clubs and bars. Merle would come and play on stage, happy to play a kind of music very different from what he had played on stage for twenty years with his father, and more like the kind of music he listened to for pleasure. Lawrence would also come to visit Merle in his little music studio in the years before his death: "Merle was producing some records at a little studio in Todd, North Carolina called North Star Productions. He would call me up, and I would end up staying at Doc's house while I was recording for him on whatever project he was working on... There were a couple different recordings that Merle produced and he would get me to go up and play guitar on. I remember one recording I came in on with the Smith Sisters, and Sam Bush was also on that session. And I remember sitting around with Merle and Sam just messing around afterwards. And there were other times when I'd be up there and Merle and I would have a tune or two together."[10]

Lawrence would then go on benders with his good friend Merle: "Of course we would spend hours and hours in the studio, and then we'd run in the hills afterwards. Which means there's people out in the hills that you knew, and you'd just go dropping around from place to place. And we'd go visiting some of his friends. And we'd do *this, that and the other*, if you catch my drift."[10] Lawrence only hinted here at Merle's experimentation with drugs, and few of Merle's friends have ever spoken about his drug and alcohol use.

Lawrence recalled with pleasure the times that he had a chance to play music with his friend Merle in the joyful atmosphere of the wild mountain parties: "I did more playing around at parties and stuff with Merle than I ever did on stage with him. And there were some cool musical moments. At the parties, we'd just pick up a couple of guitars, or we'd sit around, when I'd go up there and do recordings."[10] Ketch Secor reported that locals still talk about the incredible parties they had been to in the 1980s with Merle.

Secor's neighbors in the mountains near Merle's home talked about the 1970s and the "whole destruction of the good way,"[24] which came along with those parties of the 1970s and '80s. The old-timers in the mountains had watched Appalachian culture exploited for generations; mined for its songs, families mined for cheap labor, and mountaintops mined for their coal. Secor talked about what he saw as the destruction of the mountain culture: "The lifestyle of 'America's interest in the mountains' ruined the mountains, and it totally became *Dukes of Hazard* in a matter of ten years."[24] When Secor referred to the Dukes of Hazard television show, he was alluding to the lampooning of mountain culture in mainstream media as a place of superficial values (cars, guns and women) and little intelligence. Of course, the Dukes of Hazard television show was only the latest in a long line of television programs making fun of mountain culture, including The Beverly Hillbillies, Green Acres, Petticoat Junction, Gomer Pyle, and even The Andy Griffith Show, which didn't intend to lampoon mountain culture, but oversimplified life in the mountains so much that mountain people were thought to be *simple* and/or *gullible*, like Griffith's fictional sidekick Barney Fife.

The idyllic life depicted in fictional Mayberry, North Carolina, on The Andy Griffith Show may have been partially true during Griffith's youth in North Carolina in the 1930s and 1940s, and even in Merle's youth in the 1950s in Deep Gap, but was quickly disappearing, even as Griffith's show began to air on national television in 1960. And when heavy drugs came to Appalachia, they changed the landscape irreversibly. Secor continued: "I think that when cocaine made it to Deep Gap, once it got to the mountains, that was the destruction I'm talking about. We were living there 25 years after the fact, after the party was over. And the echo of the party was everywhere."[24] Secor asked countless locals about Doc's wild son: "Everyone remembered Merle, people that Merle would never remember. People that Doc certainly never knew. But everybody remembered partying with Merle."[24] Secor and the rest of his bandmates still felt the late musician's shadowy presence up in the mountain hollows, and he said of Merle: "He's a trickster. He's definitely the coyote if you were to put him into American Indian mythology."[24] He remembered, "For us, there was nothing quite like those stories. They had a kind of mythology. People had a reverence for partying with Merle. And for how wild things had gotten on the mountain."[24]

Secor spoke about the destruction of mountain culture at the hands of drugs and 1970s and '80s culture: "From the bizarre campy onslaught of tourists looking for Davy Crockett's cabin, all the way to people slinging dope and having orgies in octagonal foam domes on the side of the Blue Ridge Parkway, in a matter of twenty years. It's ridiculous, it's weird. And by the time we lived in the mountains, all of the youth were gone. All of the children had left, they all had gone to Johnson City or they'd gone to Charlotte or Winston. The undoing of the mountain culture has been going on for a long time."[24] Calm has long since returned to Appalachia, and the high times have ended on the mountain, but the memories always remain for those who partied with Merle.

The last conversation Merle had with his friend Jack Lawrence was a testimony to his deep troubles, and his hope that Lawrence would take care of his father if anything happened to him. Lawrence recalled the lead-up to their final conversation: "Doc and Merle were doing the *Riding the Midnight Train* record, which, if you go back and listen to it...Merle didn't have a whole lot going on in that record. It was a bluegrass record, and there wasn't a lot of room for slide guitar on it, and stuff like that. Actually, he'd not been traveling with Doc much that year, either. So I got a phone call from Merle, and he said, 'What are you doing this weekend?' I said, 'I'm off this weekend.' He said, 'Well, go, if you don't mind, go get a plane ticket on the band credit card to Nashville and just move in to my room here. I'm getting out of here.' And I think he told Doc he had a toothache or something, I'm not sure. And I'm not sure how true that was, actually."[10] Merle had actually just decided to disappear, and Lawrence had no idea where his friend was headed. Doc, presumably, was supposed to think that Merle had a toothache, but there's no telling what Doc actually knew about his son's whereabouts, or what he allowed himself to believe.

Under the circumstances, Jack Lawrence was understandably excited by the invitation Merle had extended to him, and he was excited to step in for Merle in whatever way he could. Lawrence recalled, "I went the next morning to get my plane ticket, and then I flew to Nashville and just moved right into Merle's room in the hotel."[10] That night, Lawrence received an unexpected call from Merle in that hotel room, which proved to be the last time he would ever speak with his friend: "Later that evening, right after I had gone to sleep, Merle called me and talked for about two hours about how he was tired, and he wasn't going to be doing this much longer."[10] This was the most intimate Merle had ever been with him, and Lawrence didn't know what to make of the call. But he knew Merle was serious: "I don't know what his reasons were at this point. I don't know if he was just feeling like he spent all his time in Nashville and wasn't really a part of this record, or if he was just flat tired of the whole scene, you know, going out on the road and playing music. He just said to me, 'I've got other things I want to do.' He wasn't very specific. I knew he loved doing the contracting work, and running bulldozers and putting together the subcontractors. I knew he loved doing that stuff, and he always had. That night, he just said, 'I want to do other things. I'm tired of playing music.' He just wanted to do something a little different musically as well as his contracting business and stuff."[10] As a 36-year old man, the father of two children, and a grandfather, Merle understandably wanted to get out of the rat race and spend more time at home, with his children, and doing the things he liked doing around his property and in the local community.

What Merle said next to Jack Lawrence that night was eerily prophetic: "Merle said, 'I'm not going to be around doing this much longer, and that's why I hired you. I'm glad you're hanging in there. You and Dad work well together, so I don't feel bad about this.'"[10] In hindsight, Lawrence realized the deep significance of that statement from Merle. It was a *charge* Merle was giving to Lawrence to take care of his father in his absence, which a few weeks later would be permanent. Merle told his friend that night, "I'm not going to be around much longer doing this. So I want you to promise me you'll take care of Dad."[10] For most of the rest of Doc's career, Lawrence has sat in Merle's chair, only an arm's length to Doc's right.

Lawrence told Merle, "Of course I'll take care of Doc,"[10] and from that moment forward, he took over from Merle: "When I came out on the road, T. Michael Coleman stopped taking Doc to breakfast, he stopped leading him through airports, and all of that became part of my gig."[10] Once Lawrence started taking Doc on the road, he understood how important Merle had been to Doc's survival on the road: "I could see where Merle was coming from. At that point he had spent 20 years playing music with his father, taking care of his father on the road and taking care of a lot."[10] At the end of the conversation, Lawrence assured Merle again: "Of course I'll take care of him."[10] He remembered sadly, "And I never saw Merle again. I didn't even talk to him again, because a month later he was dead."[10]

One of Doc's most treasured memories of his son was of a day he spent together with him at the Telluride Bluegrass Festival in Colorado only a few weeks before he died. Doc remembered that they both enjoyed the festival: "We could forget about everything and just play music."[25] And despite Merle's recent troubles with his health, Doc remembered: "I spent more time with him there than I ever had at a festival."[25] The usual routine was that they would play their concert, share meals together, and then Merle would drop his father off at his hotel room alone, where he would call Rosa Lee, listen to the radio, read, or relax. Usually he wouldn't hear from Merle until early the next morning. But this year at Telluride was different.

Merle knocked on Doc's hotel room door early one afternoon, and sat down next to his father. He spoke to him more honestly than he had in a long time. He hesitantly admitted to his father that he had shared his room with "a few too many friends."[25] Doc opened his heart to Merle at that moment, and in a fatherly way said, "Come and move in..."[25] Merle brought a few of his things to Doc's room, grateful for his father's company. Doc remembered that Merle was later preparing to head out, and he uncharacteristically asked Doc to come along: "At first I said no, but for some reason, I changed my mind."[25] And they spent the rest of the day together. The two men were not only family, they were best friends.

Every father makes mistakes from time to time, and Doc realized that he'd made his share of them. In an interview with Studs Terkel, Doc said: "When we're young fellas and newly married and the little ones come along, we don't think about how strict an example we need to set and the gentleness we need to instill in our offspring, rather than being a bossy daddy or mama and all that kind of thing. All of that has to come down, and it's a shame that it comes down too late in our lives most of the time."[26] Doc finally had time to sit with his son and speak with him about life and love. And only a few weeks later, his son was gone. Doc continued: "I look back and see so many things I left undone with Merle – little things that would have mattered so much. I could have done a better job of living rather than talking about it to Merle and things like that."[26]

Doc spoke of his son's struggles: "Merle, as far as his domestic life and his love life, had one hell of a rough time. And the road, because of his emotional depression and his load, was too hard on the boy. He was about to get mixed up in things that would have utterly destroyed him."[26]

Merle's close friend Carl Rudisill, owner of North Star Productions, the small studio where Merle worked locally, said, "I about had him talked into doing his own album. He was so good and people don't realize it. Everybody was just satisfied with it being Doc first and Merle second, and I wasn't. I think that that's what a lot of the problems were, a lot of the frustrations."[27]

Merle had lived in his father's shadow for twenty years, had weathered a divorce, and was struggling with substance abuse. He was a heavy partier, and liked to drown his troubles with alcohol. He also liked experimenting with guns, and he loved riding his tractor in precarious places. Rudisill said of Merle, the week after his death, "He had lived 12 of his nine lives... just living life to the fullest all of the time."[27]

Eddy Merle Watson died at 4:30 in the morning on Wednesday October 23rd 1985. His blue Ford tractor went over a steep embankment on Highway 321 near Nelson's Chapel, North Carolina, about ten miles from Lenoir and 30 miles from Deep Gap. The tractor overturned and pinned him underneath.[28]

Stories and rumors about Merle Watson's death still circulate in the hills above Deep Gap, and no one can say for sure what happened that night. The newspaper reported what eyewitnesses said about the accident, and people who knew Merle whisper off the record that Merle had been either high or drunk, partying until all hours, then driving home without his headlights at four in the morning in pitch darkness.

Although few details are known about Merle's death, local newspapers did a good job of covering the accident and the funeral, and conducted several inter- views with eyewitnesses. Together with the Watson family's version of Merle's death from the MerleFest website, the full picture begins to come into focus.[*]

According to the Watson family version of the story, it all began with late night restlessness. Merle was disquieted, and decided to wake up and work in his basement for a while. They reported that he had been working on trimming red beech paneling "that had been misgrooved," so that it could eventually panel the walls of his home's basement. The family reported that "the saw blade hit an undetected fault in the grain and a good-sized piece of hardwood splintered off, embedding itself in the muscle of Merle's upper arm."[29]

In the *Associated Press* article distributed the next day, many of the details of the accident were made public, corroborating this part of the Watson family version of the story. According to Caldwell County Sheriff Bliff Benfield, Merle had been "cutting wood on a table saw at a house he owned near Lenoir when a piece of wood struck his arm."[30] For indeterminate reasons, Merle decided not to either call an ambulance or drive somewhere in his truck. Instead, according to the Watson family's version of the story, Merle "grabbed his all-weather jacket [and] fumbled around in the pocket for the key to his farm tractor, and left to seek help."[29] He began to drive his blue Ford tractor into the moonless night.

In a story that seems almost biblical, uncorroborated in any news or eyewit- ness reports of the accident that night, the Watson family wrote that Merle was shunned by his neighbors: "Merle went to the houses of three of his neighbors, all of whom knew him well, but no one ventured forth from the comfort of their homes to help him."[29] In similarly flowery prose, the Watson family continued to describe the scenario facing Merle: "Finally, spotting a lighted house at the

---

[*] *MerleFest Executive Director Ted Hagaman confirmed that the Watson family authored the biog- raphy of Merle posted on the www.merlefest.org website.*

summit of a steep hill, he continued in that direction, praying he would not black out before he got there."[29] If Merle had been so weak, would he not have called an ambulance? Wouldn't his neighbors have? This version of the story might serve to comfort family and fans, but it raises more issues than it solves.

According to reporter Bo Emerson of the *Atlanta Journal*, Merle "rode his tractor up the steep driveway of his former brother-in-law, J.C. Hendrix, to seek help."[27] Nowhere in other versions of the story does it mention that Hendrix was Merle's brother-in-law, but even if he were a relative or a good friend, it would explain the most problematic questions surrounding Merle's death, namely, why would Merle not either call the ambulance or drive to his neighbors' homes in his truck instead of his tractor? Merle might have simply hopped onto his tractor to enjoy the cool night air as he drove to his friend's house for first aid.

Merle made it to his friend J.C. Hendrix's house early in the morning of October 23rd. Hendrix said to an *Associated Press* reporter later that day, "My driveway is very steep and I don't see how he was able to get up my driveway without any headlights."[30] According to the *Atlanta Journal*, Hendrix "bandaged his neighbor's arm and the two sat and sipped wine for about an hour before Watson headed back to his [own] house."[27] However, the Watson family version of the story says that Hendrix was "afraid to attempt the removal of the embedded wood from [Merle's] arm," forcing Merle to attempt getting the splinter out himself. The story printed on MerleFest's website alleges that Merle said to Hendrix, "Maybe I can get it out...I've got to have my arm. I have to pick the guitar. Have you got a knife and something for the pain?"[29] All they could offer was some wine, which they claim Merle drank "as an anesthetic" and in order to sterilize the knife that he then used to remove the "huge splinter." Hendrix and his wife then allegedly wrapped a bandage around his arm, willing to help once Merle had removed the splinter.[29]

According to both versions of the story, Merle had a few glasses of wine before mounting his tractor again as J.C. Hendrix looked on; the last person to speak to Merle before his death. Hendrix turned on the floodlights outside his home so that Merle would be able to navigate his steep driveway in the darkness, since he didn't have headlights. And he offered Merle a ride home, since it was the middle of the night, and both of them had consumed alcohol. Hendrix then remembered the last words Merle spoke: "He said he could make it."[30]

Only moments later, Merle's tractor slid down the steep side of Highway 321,[28] and turned over on top of him, pinning him underneath the blade.[30] J.C. Hendrix's neighbor Bobby Cline said, "[Hendrix] heard the tractor go off and knew that he had wrecked, and just as soon as he did he called the ambulance."[31] Cline recalled that Hendrix then ran to his home, shouting for help: "He [came] running over [here] to get the boys and me to help get it up."[31] Cline continued, remembering that they couldn't pull the tractor off of Merle: "We tried everything. We pried and we tried everything to try to get him out, but there wasn't any way."[31] Soon a rescue squad arrived on the scene, but it took them an hour to dig Merle out from underneath the tractor,[27] and by the time they were able to free him, he had died. According to rescue personnel, the weight of the tractor broke his back[30] and eventually killed him.[28]

The Watson family gives four reasons for Merle's death. All of them are possible answers to the question of why Merle ran his tractor off of J.C. Hendrix's driveway, but no one will ever know. Not even Hendrix witnessed the accident directly, and all anyone can do is conjecture what happened that night.

The first reason the Watsons gave for Merle's death is that he was weak from the pain of his injury and passed out, causing him to lose control of the tractor. This could very well have happened. The second reason they gave on the MerleFest website was that he had consumed red wine for the pain, and that had further contributed towards the alleged blackout. The third reason the Watson family cited on the MerleFest website is that his tractor brakes locked, causing him to lose control of his tractor. This could also have happened, but it's improbable that it would have happened at precisely the same time as a blackout.

And the final reason was not ever written on the MerleFest website, but Doc has spoken about it in recent interviews. He has alleged that Merle died of a brain tumor, or at least that the tumor had caused a stroke or a blackout, causing Merle to lose control of his tractor. In an interview in the year 2000, Doc told Michael Routh, "it hasn't been printed much and most people don't know. Merle had a brain tumor that very probably caused him to get killed. We found the diagnosis slip he was to give to the family doctor, but he never did... Rosa Lee found this in his files about six months after his death. It was inoperable. It probably caused him to black out or have a massive stroke according to the specialist."[32] Apparently, the unnamed specialist in this statement was willing to make a wild conjecture as to why Merle had died, since he hadn't had a chance to autopsy the body, and knew only that Merle had driven his tractor off of an embankment; nothing more.

A far more likely scenario is that Doc carefully shaped the story, hoping to turn Merle's death from a mistake into an inevitability. If he had indeed died of a brain tumor, Merle would go from being the victim to being a hero; sparing his parents the pain of his illness... Doc said, "He knew he was going to die, he didn't know for sure when, but he knew it as good as the Almighty knew it. He never told us. He didn't want to worry us with it – he was like that. He knew that we'd pamper and baby him, and he didn't want any part of that. He wanted to live as near normal as he could possibly with his load of problems. I understood that, though. It took me a while. I eventually said, 'Lord, I guess you knew it was time for him to check out and get out of this trouble.' But it sure left us with a load. Will I overcome it? It will be here as long as I am."[26]

As if protecting a family secret, Jack Lawrence referred in his interview, though rather weakly, to Doc's intimation that Merle had been suffering from a brain tumor before his death: "I don't know for sure, but some other health issues that he had may have contributed to his decision to get off the road. Now I don't know exactly how true that is, but it's been alluded to by Doc."[10] After brief prodding as to the truth of Merle's alleged brain tumor, Lawrence admitted, "I can't really say how true the story about the brain tumor is. I suppose it *could* be true."[10] But the skepticism was present in Lawrence's voice.

Although it is remotely possible that Merle died as a result of his brain tumor, having heroically kept his family in the dark, it is far more likely that, over 25 years, the story of Merle's death has evolved into a myth that allows Doc, Rosa Lee and the rest of the world to see Merle Watson as a hero; someone who had died while protecting his family. And Doc has certainly earned the right to see his son as a protector; his boy faithfully led him onto the great stages of the country, and protected him for most of his life.

The legends surrounding Merle's life and death will likely never be proven or disproven, but they will forever linger on the mountain. And with the immortalization of Merle through MerleFest, he lives on in the hills of North Carolina, and he haunts the world of acoustic music like no other figure; the tragic hero of American bluegrass and folk music.

Merle's close friend Jack Lawrence heard about the tragedy just over an hour after Merle was pronounced dead by the rescue workers on the scene. T. Michael Coleman called him: "Coleman called me at about 6:00 in the morning and told me what had happened. He said, 'Well, he's done it this time.' And my first thought was, *tractor*. And then I got the story, and of course it was the tractor."[10]

Merle had several near accidents on his tractor in the recent past, and his friends knew that he sometimes took unnecessary risks. Therefore the tractor was on the tip of Lawrence's tongue that morning when he heard the news.

Lawrence immediately thought back to that last conversation he had with Merle from his hotel room in Nashville. He realized quickly that morning what the significance of Merle's words had been to him. His duty would soon be to take care of Doc in Merle's stead, and he willingly accepted the role, and brought Doc back into the world of music. The three musicians, Doc Watson, Jack Lawrence and T. Michael Coleman, soon healed together on the road.

Lawrence was one of the first people Doc called that morning after he'd received the news that his son had died. Lawrence remembered that Doc said to him, "I don't know what I'm going to do."[10] Doc wanted him to come to Deep Gap, which he did, mourning along with the Watson family.

In their grief, Doc, Rosa Lee and Nancy did their best to pull together the funeral arrangements, and the service was held on Saturday, October 26th at two in the afternoon at the Laurel Springs Baptist Church, just down the road from Wildcat Creek and only a few miles from Merle's birthplace. Two local preachers, Reverend Hinkle Little and Reverend Gary Watson presided at the funeral.[28] Jack Lawrence was one of the pallbearers after the service, helping to carry the large ornate coffin supporting Merle Watson's burly 6'4" frame to his final resting place behind the still unfinished home built by Merle for his parents Doc and Rosa Lee, within sight of the kitchen window.

The morning after Merle's death, Doc woke up with the pain of loss that he would never again shake. The horrible knowledge that his son had died crept across his bed. Merle meant the world to him and Rosa Lee, and this loss would turn their world upside down.

Doc had not only lost his son, but his best friend, his road manager, his musical soul mate, and his *lead boy*. Ketch Secor used this term in a theory as to Merle's role in Doc's life: "There's this thing about people who lead the blind. They used to call them lead boys. Big Bill Broonzy used to be the lead boy, so I hear, for Blind Lemon Jefferson. So there was this relationship that young boys had to old black men that were blind and performers. And there was so much blind musicianship because music was something that the blind turned to. Look at Willie McTell, or Riley Puckett from the Skillet Lickers. All of these people had somebody to lead them around. And it's a relationship that itself is compacted into this folk mythology." Secor went on to describe the reciprocal nature of Doc and Merle's life together, and how Merle was in many ways might have been even "blinder" than his father: "The idea of the lead boy, the eyes of the blind, translates easily into the situation of Doc and Merle. But Merle was even blinder than Doc. It was the blind leading the blind. Merle had dazzling kaleidoscope acid eyes. I think he was really [screwed] up. I think he really struggled with his demons."[24]

Without his lead boy, according to Secor, Doc became cold and hard to anyone except his closest family and friends. Secor's band Old Crow Medicine Show was discovered by Doc's daughter Nancy, and will forever be linked with Doc Watson because of that event in articles and press releases, but Secor recalled that the only time he felt comfortable with Doc was the first day they met: "I've never been comfortable around him, except for that one time on the street corner."[9] He went on to explain that he addressed all of the band's letters to Rosa Lee, and that he saw Doc as a hard man,[9] something echoed by countless others after Merle's death.

Merle's friends immediately saw the change in Doc, even on the day of Merle's memorial service. Doc had retreated, in his hour of need, to the mountain. The funeral service was very traditional, and didn't include the music that Merle had loved so much. Perhaps Doc didn't want to pay tribute to the man his son had become; perhaps he saw that the demons had come along with Merle's love of modern music, or more likely, Doc simply didn't have the wherewithal to organize everything in his son's absence. But Merle's friends wanted to pay tribute to their old friend, and they gathered after the interment, once everyone had walked away, around the fresh soil at Merle's grave overlooking the Blue Ridge, and they summoned up the strength to sing their friend one last version of his favorite song, "Midnight Rider."

Peter Rowan remembered that moment well: "Merle was a very quiet kind of guy, but I guess he had a wild streak, and "Midnight Rider" was sort of his theme song. So when he had his terrible accident Jack Lawrence said, 'Let's sing 'Midnight Rider.'' There was a lot of grief and there was no way to really commemorate that moment. It was a tragic moment that afternoon."[33] Jack Lawrence remembered, "At this point, none of Merle's friends had been able to sing anything or play any music for him to say goodbye. And then, people at the funeral, there was Peter Rowan, and guys from the Nashville Bluegrass Band, and T. Michael Coleman and me, and all these great musicians. We could have really given him a nice musical send-off, but it just didn't happen that way. Mainly because it was Merle's funeral. If it'd been someone else and Merle had been there, he would have arranged for something like that to have happened. Without Merle being there, Doc and Rosa Lee were lost. They didn't know what to do. Without Merle they were lost. Anyway, people started leaving after the service, and so Peter Rowan and myself and Coleman and a couple other people stayed behind for a few minutes. Peter took out a little pouch and dropped something into the grave. I don't know what it was, and I never asked. Peter was the mystic...So we all stood around the grave after most people had left and sang 'Midnight Rider.'"[10]

Indeed, Merle had been a midnight rider, even until the end, driving his blue Ford tractor through the darkness with no headlights. All of his life, just as Doc had done, Merle had always looked head on into the night, and taken risk as it came his way.

Merle Watson was now "bound to keep on riding," and no one would be able to catch him anymore. By singing the song that Merle had loved while standing around his grave, Peter Rowan, Jack Lawrence and the other musicians sent his spirit away in a way of which Merle would have genuinely approved. The memorial service and funeral were stuffy and dark, crowded inside the small chapel in Deep Gap, and filled mostly with people who had never really known Merle for what he was. But these young men with their long hair and mournful faces sang Merle in their own way down his long road to a better place.

In an interview on the day of Merle's death, Ralph Rinzler spoke on National Public Radio about the boy he had known for 25 years. He remembered with a laugh: "Merle always did what he wanted to do... Couldn't nobody tell Merle what to do."[34] He said this in response to a question about Merle's guitar playing style, and whether Doc had influenced it at all. Rinzler continued, "The reason Merle's music was so evocative was that he was a powerful person, and the feeling for the country and for country life and value aesthetics was deeply set in him. So he was never going to change. You could influence him in talk and he would agree with you – but basically he was never going to leave the country."[34] And Merle never did leave the countryside. He always came home to the mountains he loved, and this time, he had come home for good. He didn't die on a distant mountain on the west coast, or in a hotel room in Nashville. He died in the Blue Ridge Mountains in the cool air of autumn, and was buried just across the mountain from the place where he was born.

Rinzler finished his memories of his old friend on NPR that afternoon with a comment about Doc and Merle's music and relationship: "I guess the first thing that comes to mind is the communication musically that you heard between Doc and Merle... [It] was a continuation of the kind of dialogue that a parent has with a child from the time the child is born. They were both so perfect together... [When they played together], it was like one person playing with four hands."[34]

Remembering his son three years later, Doc told a story: "We were at a restaurant in a motel once on the west coast. And Rosa Lee has a cousin who lives over on what they call Laurel Creek. He kept bees and some of the honey we got from them was the best that you could put in a jar. Merle liked that good sourwood honey and he liked it on his hot cereal for breakfast. He always had a little pint jar of it and if they didn't have honey, he'd sweeten his hot cereal with that. I think he ordered some oatmeal that morning and the gal comes to take our order, and he said, 'Do you have any honey in the place?' And she said, 'No, I'm sorry, we don't.' He said, 'Okay, go ahead and bring the oatmeal.' And he sets his jar of honey up there on the table. She brings the oatmeal and sets it down on the table and says, 'I'm sorry, but you can't eat that honey in here.' And Merle said, 'You just watch me.' When she left the room, Merle said, 'Did you hear her tell me I couldn't eat my own honey?'"[35]

After illustrating his son's headstrong nature as well as his gentleness, humor, and country ways, Doc closed by remembering his boy simply. He said, "Merle was a good friend, a good son and a good musician."[35] He was also a father and a grandfather; he had just celebrated his granddaughter's second birthday a month before he died.

# CHAPTER NOTES

1.  Allman, Greg and Robert Payne, *Midnight Rider*, Capricorn Records, 1970.
2.  Lloyd, Bert, *Interview with Merle Watson*, Audio CD, Ralph Rinzler Folklife Archives, Smithsonian Institution, 1976.
3.  Havighurst, Craig, *Living Legacy*. Acoustic Guitar, 2003. 13(12): p. 54-64.
4.  Murphy, Joe, *Doc and Merle -The Lives and Music of Doc & Merle Watson (1985)*, VHS, Vestapol, 1996.
5.  Watson, Doc and David Grisman, *Doc Watson and David Grisman - In Concert (1999)*, DVD, Vestapol, 2001.
6.  Gustavson, Kent, *Telephone Interview with Ricky Skaggs*. April 29, 2009.
7.  Gustavson, Kent, *Telephone Interview with Mike Marshall*. March 26, 2009.
8.  Gustavson, Kent, *Email Interview with Greg Brown*. April 1, 2009.
9.  Gustavson, Kent, *Telephone Interview with Michelle Shocked*. March 12, 2009.
10. Gustavson, Kent, *Telephone Interview with Jack Lawrence*. April 13, 2009.
11. Gustavson, Kent, *Telephone Interview with Tom Paxton*. April 14, 2009.
12. Gustavson, Kent, *Telephone Interview with Guy Clark*. March 18, 2009.
13. Gustavson, Kent, *Telephone Interview with Alan O'Bryant*. May 6, 2009.
14. Gustavson, Kent, *Telephone Interview with Sam Bush*. April 9, 2009.
15. Gustavson, Kent, *Email Interview with Bela Fleck*. April 24, 2009.
16. Gustavson, Kent, *Telephone Interview with David Moultrup*. April 27, 2009.
17. Gustavson, Kent, *Telephone Interview with Tao Rodriguez-Seeger*. May 20, 2009.
18. Gustavson, Kent, *Telephone Interview with Ben Harper*. June 4, 2009.
19. Stewart, Jean, *A Conversation with Doc Watson*. Sing Out!, January/February 1981. 29(1).
20. Sievert, Jon, *Merle Watson: Pickin' and Slidin' His Own Way*. Frets, March 1979: p. pp. 23-24.
21. Gustavson, Kent, *Telephone Interview with Jerry Douglas*. April 10, 2009.
22. Gustavson, Kent, *Telephone Interview with Marty Stuart*. May 18, 2009.
23. Jaynes, Gregory, *The Blind Musician from Deep Gap*. The Atlanta Journal and Constitution, 1974: p. 8-9,16,19.
24. Gustavson, Kent, *Telephone Interview with Ketch Secor*. March 19, 2009.
25. Lehndorff, John, *New interest in acoustic music pleases Doc Watson*. Greenville News, September 7, 1993. Greenville, SC.
26. Terkel, Studs, *Will the Circle Be Unbroken: Reflections on Death, Rebirth, and Hunger for a Faith*. 2002: Ballantine Books.
27. Emerson, Bo, *The day they buried Merle Watson: Tractor accident a tragic, early end for quiet guitarist*. The Atlanta Journal, October 29, 1985. Atlanta, GA: p. 17.
28. *A TRIBUTE: Memorial Obituary (Merle Watson)*. The Journal-Patriot, October 24, 1985. North Wilkesboro, NC.
29. *Doc Watson Biography*. 2005, MerleFest.
30. *Guitarist Merle Watson, 36, killed when tractor overturns*. The News and Observer. Raleigh, NC.
31. *Bluegrass musician dies in tractor mishap: Doc Watson's son dead at age 36*. The Atlanta Journal, October 23, 1985. Atlanta, GA.
32. Routh, Michael, *Doc Watson*. 2000, iBluegrass.com.
33. Gustavson, Kent, *Telephone Interview with Peter Rowan*. June 1, 2009.
34. Angle, Jim, *Merle Watson Remembered*, from *All Things Considered*. 1985, National Public Radio: USA.
35. Grosz, Terry, *Interview with Doc Watson*, from *Fresh Air*. 1988, National Public Radio.

Photo by Nic Siler ©
*Merle & Doc Watson on stage.*

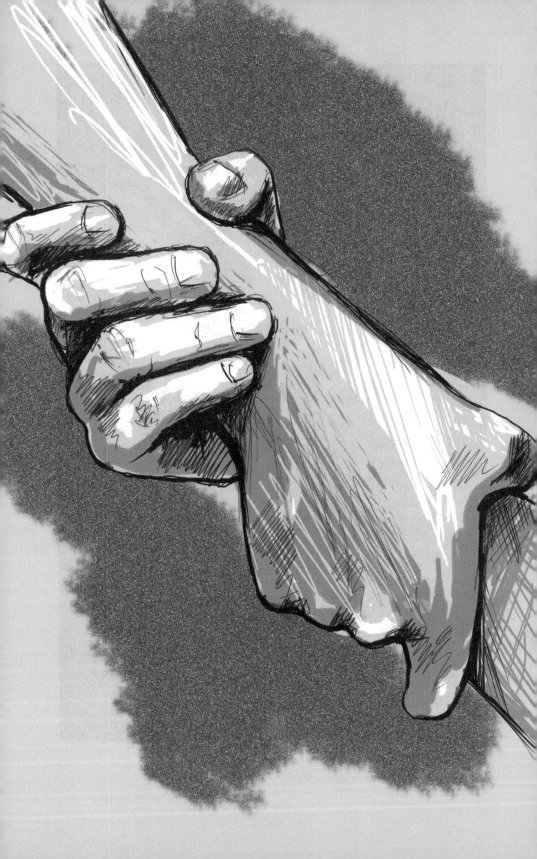

# CHAPTER SEVENTEEN
## After Merle

*"I'll always realize that I need him there. Ain't nobody who could ever sit in his seat – in that other side of the stage over there. I don't know of a soul that I could think of that could sit in that chair."*

- Doc Watson, 1985[1]

*"I still dream of him and hear him speak, and [he] talks to me as clearly as he did the day he died, and it's 12 years ago this fall. And the hurt, it's a deep hurt. I've accepted it, but it's a deep hurt, much deeper than when it first happened."*

- Doc Watson, 1997[2]

At the Laurel Springs Baptist Church on a sunny autumn Saturday afternoon, three days after Merle's death, Merle Watson's body lay in the front of the sanctuary during the memorial ceremony commemorating his life. The church pastor had planned a standard Southern Baptist funeral. Doc and Rosa Lee received friends, family members and well-wishers from all across the region at the small church just down the road from their home in Deep Gap.

Tony Cartledge, a Southern Baptist preacher who served a nearby church for most of his career described the standard service: "You normally have the person's pastor, and maybe another pastor too, who knew the person well. They'll read scripture and say prayers, and, hopefully they'll have someone that will say some words, kind of a memorial eulogy about the person. Baptist funerals traditionally are designed to comfort the family, to assure them that the person is now in a better place, because he's trusted in Christ."[3]

Despite Doc's mourning, he was confident that his boy was in the arms of God. Three weeks before Merle's death, on the way home from Nashville with his son, Doc had said, "Son, I'm not the best candidate I can think of to talk about this with you, but if old Death was to slip up on you, how is it between you and the good Lord?"[4] Merle answered his father with strong assurance: "I've been on my knees in the woods, and I've made my peace with God, and if I have to die I'm not afraid."[5]

That memory was surely great comfort to Doc as the preachers spoke that October day. Cartledge commented that such a statement would be "comforting to a parent, to believe that their child is 'right with God,' and would have eternal life... It would have been extremely meaningful to Doc and Rosa Lee. For most Baptists, that would mean that he had 'accepted Christ.' The great comfort of that is that one would typically believe that, because he has made this decision, that he would have eternal security, and be in heaven."[3]

Another element included in most regional Baptist funerals was a challenge from the pulpit to the survivors present. Cartledge explained: "Sometimes there's an element of challenge directed towards the congregation; to the people who are there, to encourage them to accept Christ as well, so they'll have the same eternal assurance that the pastor bestowed upon the family regarding their loved one."[3]

Jack Lawrence recalled that the preacher at Laurel Springs in Deep Gap, as was customary, preached to Merle's surviving friends and family about "hellfire and damnation."[6] He recalled, "At the funeral, Coleman and I were sitting there, alongside Mitch Greenhill and some of the other pallbearers in the front row. So this preacher was going on. He was a hellfire and brimstone kind of preacher, and it was like, 'Get yourself right with God before something like this happens to you.' So Coleman and I are going, 'Oh, man, this is not right. We should send him out with some music.' Merle was also really not a churchgoer. So we're sitting there, and they bring out this terrible gospel quartet, which consists of people who, I guess, are in the congregation at the church or whatever, and they start singing. Well, there's this door at the back of the pulpit that leads outside. During the first verse that this quartet sings, this door opens up very slowly and then slams shut. I mean it opens up wide, and then slams shut, and there was nobody there, of course. And I turned around to Coleman and said, 'There goes Merle. He's out of here, he can't stand it.' And then the quartet finishes singing and the preacher is going on and on. It was a pretty long service. So that door opens up again, this time just a crack for a second, and closes again. And I was saying, 'Yeah, he's checking to see if it's over yet.'"[6]

After the service, a procession of cars followed the hearse out of the church's driveway, down the highway, then off the main road through a field, across a creek, and up into the trees where Merle had been building his parents' house. His grave was directly outside the kitchen window of their home, so the pallbearers carried the casket to the back yard, and the family and a few close friends gathered around.

Before Merle died, Doc's daughter Nancy had planned on building a house across from the main house. But, as Doc told his old friend Eugene Earle in 1988, "The day between the funeral and [Merle's] death, she came and said, 'Mama, I'm not going to build a house at all. I want you and Dad to put Merle out there. That's his place.'"[7]

The pastor then read another passage from scripture near the grave, most likely from 1 Corinthians 15, verses 51-58 of the King James Bible: "Behold, I shew you a mystery; We shall not all sleep, but we shall all be changed, in a moment, in the twinkling of an eye, at the last trump: for the trumpet shall sound, and the dead shall be raised incorruptible, and we shall be changed..." After the preacher was done, he said a final prayer, after which Doc went to the coffin and wept over his son's enclosed remains. The coffin was lowered into the ground of the new Watson family plot, and people said their last goodbyes and walked away. Merle's friends then sang "Midnight Rider" over the grave, and it was finished. Merle was gone.

Family and close friends gathered together after the funeral at Doc's home, including Jack Williams, Doc's bandmate from the 1950s; Ralph Rinzler, Doc's friend and discoverer from the 1960s; and Merle's friends from the road in the 1970s and '80s. As the talking faded out, and the day rolled on towards night, Doc said about Merle, "I wish to God I had done him right, but I don't think I did. He was, for 19 years, my eyes. He was not just a son but close to one of the best friends I've ever had."[8]

Only two years later, Doc Watson began recording his first all-gospel album, *On Praying Ground*, which was later released in 1991. The songs that Doc recorded on that album are heart-rendingly personal, and loss is tangible with each breath and phrase on that record. On a few of the cuts, Doc even seemed to be at the edge of tears, putting every ounce of sadness and memory into each word he sang. Ketch Secor spoke to the power in Doc's voice that came from the pain and loss he felt each day: "I think that part of the power of Doc is, and over the past 20 years, one of the things that I have loved about listening to Doc, is that I can feel in his voice the despair; the grief of having lost his son. And probably having lost his son years before he was ever killed. Having lost his son during their career. Having their career pretty much be about him holding on to his son."[9]

Among the most beautiful tracks on the album is the song "Christmas Lullaby." The lyrics were written by Isaac Watts in the late 18th century and set to the melody "Restoration" that is most familiarly associated with the hymn "I Will Arise." The melody is haunting, especially with Doc's quivering voice, thick with the memory of his son.

*Hush, my babe, lie still and slumber,*
*Holy angels guard thy bed.*
*Heavenly blessings without number*
*Gently stealing on thy head.*

*How much better art thou attended*
*Than the Son of God could be,*
*When from heaven He descended*
*And became a child like thee?*

*Soft and easy is thy cradle,*
*Coarse and hard the Savior lay,*
*When His birthplace was a stable,*
*And His softest bed was hay.*[10]

Doc clearly remembered the tiny hands and feet of his firstborn son in his emotional rendition of the traditional hymn, as his singing grew softer and softer throughout. And he surely prayed that his little boy Merle was well attended wherever he was, with angels guarding his bed.

When Merle died, it was as if someone reached into Doc's chest and pulled out a large portion of his heart. Maria Muldaur recalled seeing Doc for the first time after the tragedy: "When it first happened, he took my hand...Since Merle died, he's never been quite the same. There was a whole bunch of people who wanted to talk to him, and he said, 'You stay here, I want to talk to you.' We share very deep spiritual conversations when I occasionally run into him now."[11]

Doc took his son's death very hard, partially because he had seen it coming. In a 1985 interview, Doc remembered having said to Merle not long before his death: "Son, if I lose you, I don't mean to lose you as a musician and partner, I mean lose you permanently...I don't know what it might do to me.'"[12] He had been terrified of losing his friend, companion, manager, soul mate, and only son.

Doc had a dream shortly after Merle's death within which his son appeared to him. His dream was just as vivid as the dream he had while morphine-ridden in the hospital 19 years previous. But this time, instead of fighting with a monster, Doc fell into quicksand, and there was no one to rescue him. From a 2002 interview with Daniel Gewertz, Doc recalled the dream: "Before the funeral I had a dream. I was in a desert-like place. It was hot and dark, with quicksand. I was so miserable. I knew I'd never get out. And then a big old strong arm reached up, and a voice said: 'Come on, Dad. You can make it.' He helped me out of that place 'til it was cool and sunshine. And I waked up and told my wife that Merle wanted me to stay on the road. Merle never liked a quitter."[13] Doc went even further to say, "I think God sent him to me to show me that I couldn't quit. My family came first over my hurt. I had to grit my teeth and face the storm of my heartaches."[14] Doc believed that God was speaking to him through his son's familiar, strong, workman's hand, guiding him out of the quicksand. Doc did indeed go back out on the road a few days later, and went on for many years to come. He contemplated retirement, but never got there.

Part of the reason Doc never retired is that he still had to support his wife and grown daughter. According to Doc, his daughter Nancy suffers from allergies that cause her to rarely leave her home, and Rosa Lee has suffered several health problems, including three heart attacks right after Merle's death. In a 1989 inter-view, Doc spoke softly to the interviewer about Rosa Lee's reaction to Merle's death: "His mama says it's the hardest thing she has ever faced... It broke her heart."[15] Doc truly believes that his wife's heart nearly gave out because she had lost Merle, and no scientific evidence could possibly prove him wrong.

After Merle's burial, Doc and Rosa Lee brought in workers to finish their home, and to realize the dream that Merle had started for the beautiful house in the woods. Over time, the earth over Merle's grave settled, and from the kitchen window, Rosa Lee could look out and remember her son. Although they thought to be a way for Rosa Lee to cope with her son's death, many feel that she was never able to let Merle go because his grave was so close to the house. Jack Law-rence said: "They buried him out behind their house. You know, in hindsight I think that was a mistake for Rosa Lee's sake..."[6]

Ketch Secor remembered entering the kitchen at Doc Watson's home: "That family is so marked by the loss of their boy. He was the only one. And if you've been around people who are addicts, or if someone that you love dearly is a drug addict, like a dear friend of mine, you read into people's stories when you don't even know them. And I couldn't help but read into the dynamic of Merle in that family. I couldn't help but see everything as a sign towards the tragic loss of Merle. Being in their kitchen, it was very much a place of somebody missing. The feeling of bereavement was tangible. There was somebody missing, and it wasn't Doc's grandson Richard. Richard came, and there was still somebody missing."[9] Secor still felt the sense of bereavement nearly twenty years after Doc, Rosa Lee, Nancy and Richard had lost their son, brother and father. Deep emotion runs through the Watson family, and it always did; that's why the folk audience in New York and across the country clamored to see them play and sing on stage. There was true heart and honesty in the music, and there was true frailty and suffering in the life of this family.

Jeri Rowe, in a 1997 interview with Doc, wrote of Doc's suffering, more than a decade after his son's passing, after sitting down and playing one of Merle's instrumental songs, "Thoughts of Never." The song was originally released in 1975 on Doc and Merle's album *Memories*, and later also put onto the album *Remembering Merle*. The tune, recorded as a duet between piano and classical guitar, with its melancholy melody and circus-like bridge, represented the two sides of Merle Watson, but especially the dark side that few people knew. Before mentioning that Doc had only played the song once on stage since his son's death, Rowe wrote that Doc began playing the song for her that day, "cradling [the] guitar between his carpenter-solid forearms."[2] Doc spoke to Rowe of the song's lonely beauty: "You don't think [when you play it]. You're buried in the melody...and it suspends your mind. It's [a] very lonely kind of thing. I have no idea what he thought of when he wrote it. I could only guess...Merle had some heartaches, and they're all wrapped up in that melody."[2] Doc often got emotional in interviews when he thought of certain songs or personal stories about his boy. The writer of a *United Press International* article about Doc in 1989 wrote, "He weeps as he talks about the son who for more than 20 years was his eyes, his companion, his musical complement, as they criss-crossed the nation, playing to audiences not yet addicted to 'rock n' roll'...."[15]

The music business changed a great deal after the mid-1980s when Merle died. Many of his friends remember how things mellowed out, in some part because of his death. His death and others were warnings to those who were living on the same edge that Merle had teetered upon. Everyone who knew Merle agreed that he had died far too early, and would have gone on to do great things with his life and his music. Marty Stuart compared Merle's death to many other young musicians who died before they came into their own: "I think Merle's death was kind of like when Clarence White died. You can put Merle and Clarence White kind of as bookends, and stick Keith Whitley in there from that world, too, because those were three masterpieces in progress that we'll all just have to scratch our head and wonder how they would have turned out musically. And they were, as men, cut down way too early. The same thing with Jimi Hendrix and Hank Williams, those kind of figures. I think a lot of people had to take a look at what they were doing. I'll speak for myself; I had to take a look at how I was living. There should have been a million people at the bottom of that mountain under that tractor instead of Merle, and I'm one of them. But for the grace of God."[16]

Warren Haynes of Gov't Mule and The Allman Brothers Band, after talking about his enjoyment of Merle's slide guitar playing, spoke with deliberation to having lost friends in the music business around the same time as Merle's death: "I think anybody that's been in the business for a long time has lost friends, and in a lot of cases extremely talented friends that should be here still with us. It's unfortunately a part of the environment, and the lesson to be learned from other people's mistakes is you want to be here to spread your joy and your music."[17]

The music scene was changing quickly; calming down. But the party kept going for a little while, stumbling along on its last legs. Jerry Douglas remembered: "Festivals were different then. Everybody thought a festival meant Woodstock. It meant babies were born, and people died from drug overdoses. That's what festivals were like in the '70s and early '80s. And then it calmed down. I mean, everybody calmed down, and those things pretty much stopped. It was just too dangerous and we all figured it out. It was a little crazy out there, and we were all part of it to some degree, but we all lost too many people, and Merle was one of them. And it was all totally, totally sad."[18]

Jerry Douglas knew Merle well, and had crossed paths with him many times on the road. He remembered, "It was a huge loss when Merle died. Everybody went into a coma for a while. He was sort of an icon to everybody, and was there to help you. Whenever you needed help, Merle was there. Merle was a really good fellow. Big hearted, like Doc. It was a tragedy, and it was also a wake up call for a lot of people. I think that after that everybody was a little more careful. Everyone needed to go through that slowdown."[18]

Ricky Skaggs, who had risen to popularity in the bluegrass crowd for his work with Ralph Stanley, J.D. Crowe and Emmylou Harris, witnessed first hand as the music scene changed around the time of Merle's death. He recalled, "It seemed as though that rock and roll crowd had started growing up and taking a little more responsibility for having children and really trying to settle down. It's like they were burned up. It was like, 'Okay, we did that, we lived through it, now this is a new decade, let's let the past be the past and try to start over in our lives again.'"[19] Skaggs has always been as well-known for his gospel music and Christian values as he has been for his fast picking and high tenor, and he spoke to the change he saw in the country around the same time towards Christianity. He spoke of a turn away from the sin-soaked 1970s: "There was a revival that kind of swept the land in the '80s as well. There were a lot of people turning to Christ and there was just a real revival going on. I saw a lot of people really moved by that, and I think that was a big part of it."[19]

Tony Trischka noticed the change in the mid-1980s as well, and though he was happy to see a mellower time with more attentive crowds and a calmer backstage life for musicians, he also noticed the music change: "I wish the excitement of the '70s was back in the air, but I don't feel it during the present time. Not to sound overly pessimistic, but I think music right now is saturated. This genre of music is saturated. You didn't think about it in those days. Whoever your musical heroes were, you could hear about four or five notes and that's all it took for you to instantly recognize whomever you were listening to. Let's fast forward to today. When you hear an honest picker out there that you can think of, or somebody comes on the radio or over the satellite that's absolutely red hot or even beautifully melodic for that matter, do you know who it is? No, you probably don't. In those days of the '70s to the early '80s, man, you knew after five notes of fiddle playing that it was Vassar Clements, or you knew it in five notes of hearing a mandolin kick-off that it was Sam Bush. The energy and spirit of those days, to my own ears, has somehow been lost. At some point, maybe later on down the road it can be recaptured again, but until that happens, to me we're in a world of musical saturation."[20]

Within days of Merle's death, Doc was back on the road. Jack Lawrence remembered: "A lot of people think that Doc stopped playing concerts for a while when Merle died. But he didn't. When Merle died, it was only a day or maybe two days before Doc and Michael and I were supposed to go out for a two-week trip."[6] After Merle's funeral, Doc called Lawrence up and said, "We're going to do the second week of the trip."[6] Lawrence remembered that the shows were very emotional, but they "pulled the shows off, and it got easier to do after that."[6] Lawrence said it was the only way for any of the three of them to deal with Merle's death: "It was the only way Doc could come to grips. And it was the only way Michael and I could deal with it, who at that point were probably Doc's two closest friends. It was the only way we could all deal with it."[6]

T. Michael Coleman wrote about going back on the road after Merle's death: "I remember one of the first places we played after the accident was the Great American Music Hall in San Francisco, California. We walked out onstage to a thundering ovation that seemed to go on for ten minutes. Everyone was in tears. This was the audience's way of showing their support and realization of the bravery it took for Doc to get back on that stage and play for them. I will be eternally grateful to everyone in that hall because they gave us all the strength to continue."[21] It was especially difficult for Doc to continue because of the loneliness on the road. He recalled, "There was times on the road when I had to go to my knees at the hotel rooms after we'd do gigs."[4] After a few gigs the pain lessened, but even 25 years after Merle's death, Doc still talks about his boy in every interview, and every night on stage.

David Moultrup saw Doc Watson, Jack Lawrence and T. Michael Coleman in Boston, on their first tour after Merle's death. He remembered that their emotions were written on their faces, but that they got through the concert, and the crowd tried to support the musicians in their grief: "Within weeks of Merle's death, Doc had a gig in Boston. I remember that gig because part of what I do for a living is psychotherapy. While I was watching that concert, I was aware of the fact that I, at least, needed Doc to somehow acknowledge that Merle wasn't there. And Doc didn't and he didn't and he didn't. And I couldn't tell whether I was sort of the only one in the room that needed an acknowledgement or what, but finally, almost at the end of the night, he did say something. And I do not remember what it was, but it sort of punctured the boil. It at least let it out, you know, so that, okay, it was acknowledged. Because you couldn't look at all three of them, Doc and Jack and T. Michael; they all looked terrible."[22]

Though they looked and felt terrible, the three mourning musicians stepped on stage night after night as a memorial to Merle, and what he had built over two decades. It was now up to Jack and T. Michael to pick up where Merle had left off; that much was clear to them. T. Michael only stayed on for just over a year before he left to join another acoustic music group, The Seldom Scene. At that point, Jack Lawrence began his long tenure as Doc's accompanist, partner and caretaker. Doc would never have been able to stay on the road for so many years after Merle's death had it not been for Jack Lawrence. And Lawrence stayed for a reason. His good friend Merle had asked him to care for his father, and Lawrence had accepted the task.

Jack Lawrence not only helped Doc through tours, travel and concerts for 25 years, but he also gave the gift of traditional music to the hundreds of thousands of Doc Watson fans across the world who were able to see Doc Watson in concert because of his service. Lawrence humbly mentioned the people who give him credit for keeping Doc on the road: "I get some people who give me credit for keeping Doc on the road for as long as he has been. And of course I'm touched by that and to a certain degree I believe it to be true. I don't know what would have happened if Doc would have had to break in somebody else when Merle died. We already had a good show down by that point, so we were able to continue."[6]

Because of his loyalty to Merle, and his deep love for Doc and Doc's music, and because he had a family to feed at home, Lawrence at times dealt with situations that weren't necessarily optimal for him. In his interview for this book, he only briefly touched on the fact that there had been some difficult situations in the business side to the organization, saying, "I was deeply saddened by Merle's death. He was my friend, and he made sure I was well taken care of within the organization. Like I said, I could take his word to the bank. It wasn't always like that after his death. There have been some things, which I won't go into now, that have happened through the years that are neither here nor there to this story.

It's more of a personal thing for me, and doesn't need to be aired."[6] Lawrence has remained loyal to Doc and to the franchise for a quarter century, and he continues to be, through both thick and thin. Certainly Merle would never have expected Lawrence to stay on the road for 25 years with his father. He had thought his friend could simply take over from him on the road before his father went into the retirement he had always been speaking of (even before Merle's death). Doc never quite got there, and Lawrence still accompanies him today.

Remembering his last conversation with Merle, Jack Lawrence thought about his old friend: "He would have been 60 in February [2009]. If he were alive today, I think he'd be a contractor, playing music on the side, or for his own enjoyment. I really think that. I could be completely wrong, he could've gotten a second wind on the whole music thing and tried to put together something that showcased his slide playing. And it's possible that he might have done a collaboration at some point with Dickey Betts of the Allman Brothers; I know they were friendly. But, I think if Merle were alive today, like I said, he'd probably be a contractor, going out to do the occasional gig with Doc. But you know, it's something we'll never really know."[6]

Jack Lawrence surely knew the double meaning of his words when he closed his comments about Merle by saying, "My last conversation with him leads me to believe he was ready to be at home and at rest."[6] Merle soon was at rest in the grassy area that he himself had cleared behind his parents' home, forever surrounded by the seasons of the Blue Ridge, never again to wander.

# CHAPTER NOTES

1. Murphy, Joe, *Doc and Merle -The Lives and Music of Doc & Merle Watson (1985)*, VHS, Vestapol, 1996.
2. Rowe, Jeri, *Doc Watson: Remembrance and Regret; Road Has Been Lonely; Sometimes He Wishes He'd Never Left Home*. The News & Record, May 31, 1997. Piedmont Triad, NC.
3. Gustavson, Kent, *Telephone Interview with Tony Cartledge*. Oct. 3, 2009.
4. Terkel, Studs, *Will the Circle Be Unbroken: Reflections on Death, Rebirth, and Hunger for a Faith*. 2002: Ballantine Books.
5. *Doc Watson Biography*. 2005, MerleFest.
6. Gustavson, Kent, *Telephone Interview with Jack Lawrence*. April 13, 2009.
7. Earle, Eugene, *Interview with Doc Watson*, Audio Cassette, Southern Folklife Collection: Eugene Earle Collection, 1988.
8. Emerson, Bo, *The day they buried Merle Watson: Tractor accident a tragic, early end for quiet guitarist*. The Atlanta Journal, October 29, 1985. Atlanta, GA: p. 17.
9. Gustavson, Kent, *Telephone Interview with Ketch Secor*. March 19, 2009.
10. Watts, Isaac, *435. A Cradle Hymn*, in *The Oxford Book of English Verse: 1250-1900*, A. Quiller-Couch, Editor. 1919: Oxford.
11. Gustavson, Kent, *Telephone Interview with Maria Muldaur*. April 1, 2009.
12. Olsher, Dean, *Special Report about Doc Watson from North Carolina's WUNC*, from *Morning Edition*, B. Edwards, Editor. 1985, National Public Radio: USA.
13. Gewertz, Daniel, *Music; Watson brings country blues to Passim's Roots revival*. Boston Herald, March 2002. Boston, MA.
14. Alesia, Tom, *A Good Audience Makes an Old Tune Fresh*. Wisconsin State Journal, March 6, 2003.
15. *Doc Watson*. The Royal Gazette, April 24, 1989. Bermuda.
16. Gustavson, Kent, *Telephone Interview with Marty Stuart*. May 18, 2009.
17. Gustavson, Kent, *Telephone Interview with Warren Haynes*. May 20, 2009.
18. Gustavson, Kent, *Telephone Interview with Jerry Douglas*. April 10, 2009.
19. Gustavson, Kent, *Telephone Interview with Ricky Skaggs*. April 29, 2009.
20. Gustavson, Kent, *Telephone Interview with Tony Trischka*. April 27, 2009.
21. Coleman, T. Michael, *T. Michael Coleman's Biography*. 2002, Doc and Merle Watson Museum at Cove Creek.
22. Gustavson, Kent, *Telephone Interview with David Moultrup*. April 27, 2009.

Photo by John Hudson ©
*Merle & Doc Watson onstage.*

# CHAPTER EIGHTEEN
## Traditional Plus

*"His music is the essence of American music. It's not country, it's not folk, it's not blues, it's American music. And Doc Watson is an American tradition in himself."*

- Ben Harper[1]

*"Doc Watson threw an umbrella over probably five or six genres. We all have to thank him for calling it one thing, whether it was a Jimmy Rodgers tune, a swing tune, a flatpicking instrumental or a Texas fiddle tune. He saw all that as one thing, the Americana songbook."*

- Mike Marshall[2]

C ontemporary singer-songwriter Joe Crookston attempted to explain Doc Watson's importance in one sentence: "Think of what Doc represents; a fierce honesty and a fierce simplicity that is so clear and direct and unpretentious that it just cuts through all the bullshit straight to a place of all the intersections and styles of music and people in the world."[3] Si Kahn echoed him, "Doc is not a purist, and a good thing he isn't. If it's a good song, Doc's going to do it. And his willingness to play with anybody, anywhere, anytime, and his refusal to pigeonhole music will be a large part of his legacy."[4] David Grisman said of his old friend Doc, "He is definitely a major link in the chain of American roots music."[5]

Doc has made a career of breaking through boundaries with his unique brand of acoustic music. Jerry Douglas said: "Doc is an icon. He's one of the reasons that we have the musical vocabulary that we do. He made it easier for us. He broke down a lot of barriers for musicians that came after him. And I don't think that any of us take that for granted. Doc has opened musical avenues for other people and brought them to different audiences that they wouldn't have been able to get to, just by inviting them on stage."[6] And Doc has invited many people on stage with him at MerleFest, the music festival named in honor of his son.

While Doc Watson spent most of his life trying to avoid being put on a pedestal, he worked hard after Merle's death to put his son on one. Each April, in the early days of Appalachian spring, thousands of music fans make a pilgrimage to Wilkes Community College in Wilkesboro, North Carolina for MerleFest. Founded by a horticultural instructor at Wilkes Community College in order to fund a garden, the festival now has great impact on the local non-profit landscape and the worldwide acoustic music scene, with its family atmosphere and traditional plus music.

MerleFest co-founder B. Townes was a young horticultural instructor at Wilkes Community College with a great deal of enthusiasm for his subject, and for his students. He was excited to find that the college would support his idea to plant gardens on campus, though they had no funds for him. He had a master plan to include everything from rose gardens to Japanese gardens, and eventually a garden for the blind. According to Townes, "…a garden for the visually impaired by its very nature has plants that have tactical appeal, or are highly fragrant, or in our case, because visually impaired is not necessarily 100 percent blind, all the walls and all the plants tend to be yellows or whites or contrasting colors."[7] As Townes was trying to raise money for his gardens, a friend suggested that he be in touch with Doc Watson, since the garden was for the blind; perhaps he would agree to perform as a fundraiser. The first idea was to name the garden for Doc Watson, but when Townes first met with Doc, the musician would only agree if the concert could be in Merle's memory instead.

Townes thought honoring Merle with the concert was a great idea, and he was thrilled that Doc had tentatively agreed to perform the benefit concert. He remembered how the memorial concert for Merle began to take shape: "In subsequent meetings with Doc and his family, the idea for a festival in memory of Merle with Doc, a one-man concert in our auditorium, was sort of the impetus for what was to become the first festival. That discussion was happening in the summer and fall of 1987."[7]

Townes was excited about the possibilities, not knowing how difficult it might be to host a concert only a few weeks later. He continued: "I was naïvely approaching our people at the community center about doing a concert literally the next month, and they quickly told me that wasn't going to happen. First of all it was too short of notice, and second, there were a number of things to be considered, the least of which was marketing and having a calendar date and so forth and so on."[7] Townes recalled his next meeting with Doc about the concert: "My second meeting with Doc was to tell him that it didn't look like we'd be able to do it because we couldn't do it on such short notice."[7] At that point, according to Townes, Rosa Lee jumped in and said to Doc, "Well, honey, why don't you just put it off 'til spring, and you'uns can have a festival in memory of Merle. And Doc, you can just invite some of your friends to come."[7] That was the seed of the first annual MerleFest.

Townes admitted to not really knowing what a music festival *was* when Doc's wife and daughter made their suggestion. Still, he worked with the Watsons and with the college to put together a festival-style concert in the college's theater: "We established a date in April when we would have Doc and his friends performing in the 1100-seat Walker Center, and have a situation where Doc would invite some friends. And he threw around names like Chet Atkins, Marty Stuart and Earl Scruggs and a whole list of names, some of which I'd heard of, a lot of which I'd never heard of, including Sam Bush, Bela Fleck, The New Grass Revival, Jerry Douglas, Peter Rowan and a number of others."[7]

The memorial festival sold out, and the pieces began to come together. Townes remembered: "Once the auditorium sold out, I'll never forget talking to Cliff Miller, who had performed music with Doc and Merle. He had started a little sound company, and he told Doc that he'd come do the sound, complimentary. At that time everybody was donating their time, and everybody was buying a ticket, including myself as a fundraiser for what was then to become the Eddy Merle Watson Garden for the Senses, a garden for the visually impaired in memory of Merle. And I was telling Cliff that the phone was ringing off the hook, and people wanting to perform and people wanting to buy tickets, and we basically had sold all the tickets. And we were walking around on the campus, and he said, 'Well, what about this field down here?'"[7] Of course, that moment was the beginning of the outdoor festival that has put northwest North Carolina on the map for music fans across the country.

B. Townes was soon overwhelmed by the responsibilities this burgeoning music festival had brought, and when he approached the local music icon to ask for assistance, Doc referred Townes to his old friend Ralph Rinzler. At first,

Townes received no answer from Rinzler, but he remembered that, only a few days before the festival, he received a call from him: "The week before the festival, I got a call from France, and it was Ralph Rinzler, and he said, 'I've had a lot of calls from you, and I'm headed back to the States. I've been in Europe for several months.' He said, 'I know that I told Doc Watson I'd come and speak a little bit about when he started performing and how we got started, but I'm not exactly sure what I'm supposed to do.' I said, 'Well, he told me that you would help with the schedules.' He said, 'Well, I'm flying in; can somebody come pick me up?' This was Wednesday or Thursday night, whatever it was; it was a couple days before the festival. I picked him up at the Greensboro airport."[7]

As they were riding up the road, Townes excitedly told Rinzler about the more than 100 musicians who would be performing at the festival the coming weekend. Rinzler replied, "Well, who's writing the schedules?" Townes said to him, "Well, I think you are."[7] Without Rinzler's knowledge, Doc had enlisted his old friend Ralph to program these concerts as he had once programmed the sets for the Clarence Ashley Group, and for Doc in advance of his first solo concerts at the Ash Grove in New York. Rinzler replied, "That's news to me!"[7] Rinzler had little time to figure everything out, but knowing what this concert meant to Doc, Townes remembered, "he sat down with one of the gals here in the office, Brenda Shepherd, and basically hammered out who would play when, and who would play with whom."[7] For the sake of ease, Rinzler and Shepherd decided that after the indoor concert, they would just have the musicians repeat the same concert at the outside venue, in front of the 200-year old cabin.

The concert weekend came quickly, and B. Townes remembered: "It really happened on a wing and a prayer, and although we thought we were doing a lot of planning, there wasn't any planning like we have to do today in advance. We set up a festival that maybe shouldn't have happened by anybody else's standards. But as it turned out, when I met these artists and they were arriving, everybody was so gracious. My job was also to meet them and thank them for coming, and say, 'By the way, you're playing here with so-and-so and so-and-so at two o'clock, and then at four, I have some volunteers and they'll drive you down there.' Some of them would frown and say, 'Well I've never played with him,' or 'Who said I'd play with him?' or 'What songs are we doing?' and 'What key?' and all of this stuff. And I said, 'I don't know.'" Townes still knew little about music, but thankfully, Rinzler had organized the musicians' schedules. Otherwise, Townes would not have known whom to schedule when. He just kept smiling, hoping that everything would work out. And the musicians maintained their cool, because they knew this was all in memory of their friend Merle, and a favor to their mentor and friend Doc.

The day of the festival came quickly, and the horticultural instructor found himself running around all over the place trying to get things under control. Miraculously, nothing major went amiss, and the concert was a success. But there were certainly a few difficulties along the way. Townes said, "There were a lot of potential accidents that didn't happen, and a lot of accidents that happened and nobody knew about them."[7] He remembered one such twist: "The New Grass Revival kind of pulled in, and I was in the field at the time. And I'll never forget, the road manager there got out of the van and said, 'What time are we supposed to play?' And I said, 'Well, in an hour you're supposed to be over at the Walker Center,' and he said, 'I don't know about that.' And he rode with me up there and said, 'No way, I can't set this band up to play up here in an hour.' He said, 'Besides, we're not about to move. We'll play one place or the other.' So I talked to George Hamilton IV, the MC, and George just sort of chuckled. He said, 'Well, there's only one thing you can do.' He said, 'You're going to have to go over here to this microphone and tell this thousand people here in the Walker Center that if they want to hear The New Grass Revival, they'll have to go outside.'"[7]

On a scale seldom seen outside of protest marches and marathons, B. Townes would have to march with 1100 people over to the field so that they would all be able to hear The New Grass Revival. Townes remembered stepping up to the microphone: "For the first time I'd ever been at a microphone in front of anybody, I had to tell a thousand people that they weren't going to get to see what was scheduled. And you know, everybody got up and followed me. We walked down the steps and half a mile to the outdoor field. This was Sunday afternoon, and it was all in the spirit of remembering Merle and honoring Doc."[7]

Wilkes Community College made significant profits towards the garden, and the event had been a smashing success. That led to thoughts that they might try it again the next year. Today, MerleFest represents a collection of some of the greatest musicians in acoustic music, with crowds of over 50,000 each year; the local impact of the festival is immense. Townes explained: "Today, we have some 70 non-profits involved. MerleFest is not only a fundraiser for the college; [it] has expanded beyond the gardens to scholarships..."[7] Si Kahn also spoke of the music festival's impact in the local community: "Everything from the cheerleaders to the rescue squad to the school for the developmentally disabled, every county non-profit has a right to set up a stand at the festival, but you can't be a commercial vendor and come in there. And the non-profits make their budgets for the year. That's important in a county where everything is closed or closing: the furniture plant, the chicken plants... It's a pretty rough time out there."[4]

Doc and Rosa Lee were themselves having a rough time financially when Doc Watson showed up at the Clarence Ashley session in 1960 armed with his electric guitar and amplifier. At the time, Doc did what he could to earn a few extra dollars, and they lived mostly on charity and garden vegetables. Doc played the music that would pay the bills, and that was dance music; so he was known around town for his hot licks and rockabilly chops.

After submitting to a decade of tutelage at the feet of Ralph Rinzler, Doc broke free of his discoverer's neo-traditionalist ideology. He started to integrate all of the styles of music he listened to on the radio and had played throughout his career, even before being "discovered" in the folk boom. In order to maintain his existing fan base, Doc simply started calling all of the music he played *traditional plus* music. That meant, *traditional* music, *plus* whatever else he wanted to bring into the mix.

Michelle Shocked spoke to Ralph Rinzler's attempt to keep Doc a traditionalist: "I heard a story that I think is hypocritical, where Ralph Rinzler told him to knock off the *Blue Suede Shoes* kind of numbers because it didn't fit into the stereotype that he was so busy marketing and promoting of Doc. And that's exactly why I love Doc Watson so much, because he would cross those lines. All I can speculate is that it kind of ends up being what his audience would put maybe behind a glass frame or up on a shelf somewhere. It was like, 'Well that's okay for Doc Watson. He's embracing the old time ways, but it's not for us.' That was pure Rinzler marketing."[8]

Edgar Meyer, the brilliant upright bass player who is equally comfortable in classical, popular, and folk music, spoke to the diversity of Doc's music: "Obviously bluegrass and opera are fairly different. But I think the desire to present the true essence of a style is a very misleading thing. I think music is a spectrum, like a color spectrum. I think you can be fortunate to have defining figures like Louis Armstrong and Bill Monroe who define genres, but even that's a little after the fact. It's a tricky business. In general, it's just not as clear and clean as that. Most people have exposure to all kinds of music and it influences them in lots of ways. And they're not just one thing, no matter how they are marketed or how they choose to present themselves."[9] In other words, no matter how hard

Ralph Rinzler tried to constrain Doc within the traditionalist world, the true spectrum of Doc's music would eventually emerge.

Tom Paxton, who was a young singer-songwriter when Doc came to New York, greatly admired Doc, and the feeling was mutual. Doc ended up singing several of Paxton's songs through the years, which was thought by many *traditionalists* as something akin to heresy. Paxton was, after all, a contemporary singer-songwriter, and Doc was supposed to be a traditionalist. Paxton spoke about Doc's perceived authenticity: "We all thought that Doc was the *real thing*. But Doc could appeal to a much broader spectrum than just the purist folk scene. If you were to sit Doc down in front of a Chamber of Commerce meeting – it didn't matter where – and let him play, you'd have them eating out of his hand because he was brilliant, and still is brilliant. Certainly you would have in the Village, among young people, these fierce arguments between *purists* and so-called *sellouts*. I heard someone dismissed once as being 'so pure he had surface noise in his voice,' which I thought was one of the greatest putdowns I ever heard. I was one of those who kind of had a foot and boot in both camps. I mean, I always believed in the value of entertaining people, but I also believed in making the best music you could make."[10]

North Carolina singer-songwriter Jonathan Byrd's idea of what *traditional* music should be is similar to Doc Watson's: "Before recordings, everybody played it however they played it, whether they had a guitar or a piano or a comb and a jug. Verses were made up, melodies evolved, and nobody really gave a damn, as long as it was fun, meaningful, or danceable. Now that everything can be recorded, people take a record and say, 'This is the authentic version of this song.' That's bullshit. Charlie Poole, one of the most influential old-time musicians ever, was told not to bring his pianist to the sessions, because it wasn't *hillbilly* enough. That one decision practically erased the piano from southern string-band music."[11]

When Doc apologized to fans in the liner notes of *Southbound* for going away from *pure* traditional music, he was not *selling out* in order to sell more records. He was actually coming closer to what his own pure traditions were. Sure he heard his granny singing on the front porch, and his father singing hymns in church, but that was only a small part of his musical world. Doc really began to learn about music not from his parents, but from the radio and records, and from friends at the Raleigh School for the Blind. In that way, he was not being authentic when he played only Ralph Rinzler's idea of traditional music. When he was able to open up his playing style a bit after Merle joined him, Doc was grateful and excited about the possibilities. He felt that the broader new style was much truer to how he identified himself as a musician.

Legendary southern rock guitarist Warren Haynes spoke of Doc's diverse influences: "I think Doc must have been very open-minded about what his influences were, because you can hear different musical genres coming through him naturally, in his playing and his singing. In fact, I remember Derek Trucks and I were having a conversation one time. We were listening to an old Doc Watson record on the bus, when all of a sudden, we got this sense during this one song that Doc was singing that there was some Burl Ives influence there. And neither one of us had thought that up until that moment."[12]

Darol Anger, famous for his genre-bending musical experimentations, talked about the new genre that Doc created by including every different kind of music in his repertoire: "He wasn't averse to singing contemporary folk or pop songs, if he thought it was a good song and reflected his standards. It basically comes down to the fact that Doc invented his own genre, which became the touchstone and departure point for thousands of acoustic string musicians."[13] Beppe Gambetta agreed: "Doc always moved freely within the big spectrum of American roots music (from old-time music to early country, to bluegrass, to blues and much more) in order to build a repertoire only his own."[14]

Each year, music fans make a pilgrimage to see Doc Watson play at MerleFest alongside so many of those young musicians who broke through boundaries because of Doc and Merle Watson's lead. And the *traditional plus* genre grows and evolves each year, bringing fresh talent to the surface.

Rebecca Lovell, speaking for Doc Watson's great-grandchildren's generation of acoustic musicians, said: "Doc's music has universal appeal and honesty that effortlessly spans any and all social and musical barriers."[15]

Greg Brown described Doc's contribution to traditional music best: "Doc Watson bridges many styles of American music. That stew is very rich, made up of all the music that came in here from the British Isles, from Africa, from all over. Doc's bowl of that stew is full and runneth over."[16] Indeed it spills to the new generations, hungry to follow in their musical idol's footsteps, to play the music they love and become innovators in their own unique way.

# CHAPTER NOTES

1.     Gustavson, Kent, *Telephone Interview with Ben Harper*. June 4, 2009.
2.     Gustavson, Kent, *Telephone Interview with Mike Marshall*. March 26, 2009.
3.     Gustavson, Kent, *Telephone Interview with Joe Crookston*. March 25, 2009.
4.     Gustavson, Kent, *Telephone Interview with Si Kahn*. May 26, 2009.
5.     Gustavson, Kent, *Email Interview with David Grisman*. March 25, 2009.
6.     Gustavson, Kent, *Telephone Interview with Jerry Douglas*. April 10, 2009.
7.     Gustavson, Kent, *Telephone Interview with B. Townes*. July 10, 2009.
8.     Gustavson, Kent, *Telephone Interview with Michelle Shocked*. March 12, 2009.
9.     Gustavson, Kent, *Telephone Interview with Edgar Meyer*. June 10, 2009.
10.    Gustavson, Kent, *Telephone Interview with Tom Paxton*. April 14, 2009.
11.    Gustavson, Kent, *Email Interview with Jonathan Byrd*. April 2, 2009.
12.    Gustavson, Kent, *Telephone Interview with Warren Haynes*. May 20, 2009.
13.    Gustavson, Kent, *Email Interview with Darol Anger*. April 24, 2009.
14.    Gustavson, Kent, *Email Interview with Beppe Gambetta*. July 23, 2009.
15.    Gustavson, Kent, *Email Interview with Rebecca Lovell*. March 28, 2009.
16.    Gustavson, Kent, *Email Interview with Greg Brown*. April 1, 2009.

# CHAPTER NINETEEN
## Doc's Guitar

*"His guitar playing is off the chart. It's otherworldly."*

- Marty Stuart[1]

*"Doc Watson...can play the guitar with such ability... just like water running."*

- Bob Dylan[2]

I f everything else about Doc Watson faded to the background, his flat-picking tunes will remain in collective memory for the next several hundred years, like the chorales of Bach, and the motets of Palestrina. Doc Watson was, and is, the father of flatpicking guitar.

At the peak of his ability, Doc was like the Usain Bolt of guitar; he did things that no one else could do. After seeing Doc in concert, guitarists would go home and either practice like the devil for weeks on end, or put their guitars away forever. And Doc's skills on the guitar were not simply in speed; they were in timbre. He pulled sounds from the acoustic guitar that are simply unmatchable.

Ricky Skaggs described the lineage of Doc's musical influence: "As a guitar player, Doc is kind of like the father of Clarence White and Tony Rice. You think of the people that Clarence White influenced all over the country. Then you think of the people that Tony Rice has influenced in his generation. Now you think of the people that Bryan Sutton and Cody Kilby and Clay Hess and Kenny Smith and all those guys, how they have influenced the next generation. But it all comes back to Doc's style of playing, because there's only a few guys that were playing any kind of lead guitar solos on any bluegrass type records in any kind of music like that. You had Bill Napier with the Stanley Brothers, and then George

Shuffler, and that was about it. Then Doc was playing lead solos, but he was playing almost like fiddle tunes and banjo tunes. He would sit and pick them out just like a mandolin player or a banjo player would play it and that was really unheard of back then. So it really sparked a whole new sound and a whole new style."[3] Every acoustic guitar player of the 21st century will owe at least part of their technique, tone and timing to Doc Watson's innovations on the instrument.

Doc's virtuosity and tone take root in his passion for the guitar. George McCeney relates what is possibly the finest illustration of Doc's relationship to his instrument and his music: "My friend Gary and I were down at Doc's for two or three weeks in 1962. Doc would get up really early in the morning before anybody else. His and Rosa Lee's bedroom was on the second floor of this little small house, and the stairs came down into the kitchen. Doc would come down with his shoes in his hand so he wouldn't wake anybody up. And then he'd walk into the living room and sit on the sofa and put his shoes on."[4] This was Doc's routine every morning, and for the weeks that McCeney stayed with the Watsons, he grew accustomed to the habit. He witnessed the blind man's simple ritual each morning through his open door: "The bedroom that I was staying in was just off the living room, and it was blazing hot at night. So I'd keep the door open on one side and the window on the other, so it wouldn't get too hot."[4]

McCeney continued his story, "Well, one morning, I remember waking up, just lying on my side and looking out that door in the living room and watching Doc come down with his shoes in his hands, and his socks stuffed in the shoes. And he sat down on the sofa in the living room. And I had a dead 90-degree angle right to it. So he put on one sock and he stops. And he just sat there on the sofa with the other two shoes and one sock on the floor. And he sat there and he sat there. All of a sudden, he reached under the sofa and he pulled out his guitar. He opened the case, took the guitar out and played a short lick. Then he did it again, a little bit tighter. And the next time, he got the run just right. Then he put the guitar back in the case, closed it, put it back under the sofa, and then he put his other sock on, and then his shoes."[4]

McCeney remembers how stunned he was: "I thought to myself, 'You really have a musician there.' I mean, it was the first thing that struck him in the morning. He had that run in his head and he woke up with it, and he just had to confirm it, and then he could begin the day. It just took my breath away."[4]

Tony Trischka spoke to why Doc was so revered among guitarists, and why it was an education just to listen to his records, watch his hands, and play with him onstage: "Doc was certainly an influence on me. If I had to describe how, I would say that, between him and Clarence White, the bar was raised real, real, real damn high. Not that I ended up being able to play like them, but they certainly set a standard to adhere to."[5]

Musicians would listen to Doc and realize that there was no limit to what they could do on the guitar, or on whatever instrument they chose. However, sometimes Doc's incredible ability dissuaded guitarists from picking up their instrument for a few weeks. Trischka, now revered as one of the best banjo players to ever live, remembered that he thought he would never be able to play guitar like Doc: "The first record I heard of Doc's was his first Vanguard album, the one self-titled *Doc Watson*. My perception of Doc Watson at the time when I first heard the early Vanguard albums, was just, you know, for myself to be able to play a guitar like that was unattainable. Of course, I also felt the same way about eventually playing like Clarence White. It took me well into my teens to figure out that I couldn't play like either one of them anyway, which turned out to be good. As a result I sort of followed my own path."[5] Thankfully, Trischka did follow his own path, or the music world would never have experienced his virtuosic banjo stylings.

Other musicians deconstructed Doc's style, learning each note and nuance, trying to see how the man was able to make such music with his own two hands. Beppe Gambetta, the Italian flatpicking guitarist, described how he studied Doc's guitar playing: "I first started to learn and play Doc Watson note for note, but, while doing this, the learning process turned out to be much more complex than I thought. Transcribing and learning every single note of many tunes was actually just a little step in a long journey, and I had to continue to work on the same piece over and over to try to go closer to the real beauty of Doc's style. The big challenges turned out to be the tone, the timing, the sense of syncopation, the use of cross-picking, the dynamics, the intonation, the subtle importance of some ghost notes and strums, the variety of solutions and licks in the accompaniment. From this point of view surely no other guitar player will be able to reproduce Doc Watson's sound in every nuance and detail. Sometimes I think that part of his uniqueness comes from the choice to move his whole right arm instead of just the wrist, and I was fascinated to discover that this same characteristic was the trademark of the style of [19th century violin virtuoso] Niccolò Paganini."[6]

Other musicians were lucky enough to have personal coaching from Doc Watson himself; in Doc's early years, he taught hundreds of workshops around the country at colleges and universities, reaching thousands of young guitarists and budding folk musicians. David Moultrup remembered one of these workshops when he was a college student in Michigan: "Back in the early '70s Doc came to Ann Arbor and was scheduled to do a workshop and a concert. He and Merle came and I was one of only a handful of people at this workshop. It was held at the Ark, which is one of the fine old folk venues in Ann Arbor. We got to spend a couple of hours with Doc working on the guitar, so it was very special. Doc proceeded to sit down and just win everybody over."[7] For Doc, it was not important that only a few students were gathered; he engaged with them and talked with them for those couple of hours as if they were the most important people in the world.

Moultrup remembered how much it meant to the students to meet and learn from Doc in person: "At that point there was simply not the availability of teaching in the way that there is now. There might have been a book or two around, but it was hard to understand anything from a book, and so to have an opportunity with Doc at that point was delightful. No one had guitars. As I recall it was very much, 'Here, this is the way I do it; here's how you hold the pick...' With no one around to teach me anything I just started holding the pick however, and it turned out that I was holding it the wrong way, at least as to the way Doc and almost everyone does it now. So he changed the way that I was holding the flat pick. And I talked to him, I said, 'All right, also about speed?' So he worked with me on the elbow motion. He said, 'Watch my elbow.' There again, these are all minor things to most people, but they were the kind of intricate changes that truly made a difference in my playing."[7]

Doc gave a gift to thousands of young musicians in person at these workshops; a gift he himself had received partially from his father, brothers, and friends at the Raleigh School for the Blind, but had mostly acquired from long hours in front of records and the radio. He shortened his students' learning curve significantly.

When Doc was growing up, the only music he heard before his father brought home their first Victrola was the music in church and the music from the front porch. Mike Marshall spoke about the new generation of musicians who grew up with records and radio: "If you think of the generation before Doc Watson and Bill Monroe, these were mountain people who, before radio, only heard the music that was played around their villages, and it was the radio that changed all of that. Doc is in the first generation of pickers who had radio in the home and so he heard swing, he heard classical and popular songs, all the crooners of the '30s in his home. Doc Watson, Flatt and Scruggs, and Bill Monroe were the generation who fused this stuff into hillbilly music. They were the mountain people who said, 'Wait a second, there is this swing thing, rockabilly thing, there is this popular music, this classical music...'"[8] Doc integrated all kinds of music into his playing, and he loved just about everything he heard. Except for a few years in the early 1960s, he played all kinds of music from the stage, which is how he eventually developed his *traditional plus* style.

Marshall continued to explain the new generation of which Doc was a part: "I see that generation of musicians as people who fused that stuff in their own way. They didn't go to Berklee School of Music in Boston to study it, but they heard it, and whatever we hear as musicians, and think is great, we will do whatever it takes to incorporate it. 'What is that? How does it go? How can I work that into my playing?'"[8]

Marshall then made the point that today's world is not distant from the world in which Doc grew up, with its diversity of music styles, but that tools have improved for accessing that material: "Really the musicians of today are doing the same thing, but of course, now, we have the Internet and YouTube to work with. So if you are a mandolin player in East Tennessee and you say, 'Gee, I want to play the mandolin,' its not just going to lead you to Sam Bush and David Grisman, Mike Marshall and Chris Thile, you know. Pretty soon, you're going to realize there is a whole tradition to mandolin playing in Brazil and Venezuela, and there is a classical thing going on in Germany, and what are these Irish guys up to? Our reach is just greater now, and I think the spirit of what we are doing is the exact same spirit that Doc Watson was doing it from."[8] Doc had taken all of the music he could find around him, and tried it all on his guitar; jazz, hillbilly, blues, popular music, rock and roll. Whatever sounded good, he kept in his repertoire.

In a world where the shuffle feature on iPods has changed the way most people listen to music, it might seem uninteresting that Doc integrated so many forms of music into his own style, but in Doc's day, musicians chose one genre, and stuck with it. Doc broke the mold, and he inspired musicians like Mike Marshall who came after him to cross boundaries in their music as well, whether that meant Appalachian mountain music or Peruvian mountain music. Marshall said, "Doc was our teacher; he was the guy who showed us that you can be both things. You can have your own music, from your own country, from your local area, and you can be a keeper of the flame from the generation before you... But you can also have your ears open, and be exposed to things, and be the person who says, 'This is really nice. I want to learn. I want to play this music and in- corporate some of what this great musician has contributed to my own playing."[8]

Before Doc was "discovered" by Ralph Rinzler, he had been in the proverbial woodshed. Musicians are said to have spent time in the "woodshed," when they have had a chance to develop skills for a long period of time before gaining recognition. Doc remembered first developing his skills: "Sitting in a little porch swing, at 15 or 16 years old, I would sometimes spend three to four hours figuring out guitar licks. At that time my mind was like a blotter. I could listen to the records a few times and then go work them out. I had never seen anyone play with a flat pick before. My style just happened."[9] While it may be a little simplis- tic to say that his style just "happened," Doc clearly said that he acquired techniques from listening to records and the radio, and with a few pointers from friends and relatives.

Doc Watson mastered the guitar as if playing on its steel strings was like conversing in a familiar language. He learned every technique he could. He later demonstrated the many styles within which he was proficient in the workshops he taught at various folk festivals. He would play rock and roll, blues, open tunings, fingerpicking, flatpicking, and whatever else people asked about. He could do anything, and if there were something he had never tried, he would quickly pick it up. And Doc's technique was impeccable. No one could match him, or even dream of playing the things he was able to play.

Peggy Seeger, the legendary folk guitarist and singer, said: "Doc was one of the most precise guitar players I think I've ever heard. He was crisp, he was inventive. He sang totally with his instrument. I know other musicians do this, but there was never even a hint of sloppiness in him. I always had a vision of him seeing it in his head when I heard him play."[10] Seeger remembered trying to play in Doc's style one time: "It was a total failure and I've never heard anybody come close to doing his pieces like he does."[10]

Doc also had the unique ability to make *any* instrument sound beautiful. Blind singer-songwriter Donna Hill remembered thinking that Doc's incredible tone on the guitar came from the quality of his instrument, until one day she met Doc and spent time with him before a concert: Doc took a decrepit old guitar that a stage-hand brought to him, tuned it up, and made it sound, in her opinion, as good as his prized Gallagher.[11]

Ellen Harper-Verdries remembered being completely mesmerized by Doc's instrumental ability. She and her fellow musicians in the 1960s said to one another: "What is he doing? How's he playing that?"[12] When Doc visited her home, she remembered, "He'd just pick up a guitar and start picking, you know, because we had instruments everywhere. He'd sit down and he'd feel this thing, 'Hmm, what is this?' Then he'd pick it up and start playing it."[12] Doc loved any kind of guitar, whether a Martin or an unknown beater. He tried them out as if they were all new flavors of ice cream. He simply loved to touch guitars, see how they were made, and hear how they would sound.

Doc played guitars with great passion, and by the time he emerged on the folk music scene in 1961, he had already refined his touch on the instrument, experimented with every style of guitar he could get his hands on, and learned every lick of all of his favorite guitar players. In addition, he had already created his own unique sound on the instrument, though after years of playing on stages across the country his style only grew in its power and definition. George McCeney said of Doc's guitar playing: "Doc had the ability to understand what a song was about and then just to sharpen it to where it couldn't be sharpened any more. He understood the song so completely that he knew how far he could take it without going too far. And since Doc has been on the scene I don't think anybody has superseded him."[4]

In 1972 reporter Michael Brooks wrote: "Listening to him play is almost wholly an emotional experience. Aside from random mutterings such as, 'No – what I just heard was impossible on a guitar; he couldn't have done that,' few listeners have the energy to both listen to him and mess around with a technical analysis of what's going on. Tone quality is even more important an identifying mark than speed, and the 'hot runs' he uses for ornamentation have the effect of hitting everyone in the audience in the chest at the same time, forcing out an involuntary 'Hoo!' Doc's playing doesn't make people sad, but it often makes them cry…"[13]

From the time he was a boy, sawing wood with his father and brothers, Doc loved the feeling of hard work. He surprised people along the road who shook his hands and realized that this blind guitarist had workman's hands. Beppe Gambetta, the wizard Italian guitarist, remembered being surprised by Doc's hands: "I saw a Doc Watson performance for my first time in 1986 at a bluegrass festival in Dahlonega, Georgia during my first trip to the United States. The atmosphere in the audience and in the campground was fantastic. On that occasion I experienced for the first time Doc's extraordinary charisma on stage. After many years of listening to him only from the few albums I could find in Europe, I enjoyed feeling how the energy of his live playing was even more intense than I had thought, and I also noticed his intelligence in structuring and conducting the set. I tried to absorb every little movement and nuance of his playing, and I was really excited when he agreed to meet me briefly backstage. I didn't speak any English, and a friend translated for me. Doc was gracious and kind, and when we shook hands, I was shocked to feel callouses on his hand, like on the hand of a worker."[6]

Doc *was*, after all, a worker. It was in his blood as much, or more, than the music was. He had been doing different kinds of manual labor since he was a teenager, despite his disability. He learned how to repair things by trial and error. His brother remembered that Doc had disassembled their family record player when they were children, and Doc was known to fix cars, guitars, appliances and everything in between. And he later came up with contraptions to make life around the house a little easier for his wife and kids.

Marty Stuart remembered that his old boss Earl Scruggs was amazed by Doc: "Earl was always fascinated by the fact that Doc wired his own place, he cut his own grass, he chopped his own wood. All those things that were just kind of fascinating to even think of. And I remember Earl saying one time that he was over there picking with Doc at his house, and he went back in the bedroom or something and got a couple guitars. And when it was time to put the guitars up, Earl put the guitars up, and Doc said, 'No, that one goes on the other side of the bed.' And Earl always wondered, 'How did he know? He was sitting in another room.' And Doc told him it was the sound of the latches. So Doc is tuned-in in ways, and sees things that you and I can't."[1]

At the beginning of Doc's experimentation on the guitar, he taught himself to play with the *thumb and strum* style made popular by Maybelle Carter in the late 1920s on the Carter Family records: "The Maybelle Carter thumb-lead strum…came natural. I figured it out by listening to the records and messing around with the guitar."[9]

Next, Doc caught the Jimmie Rodgers bug in his teenage years. His father would bring home new records every once in a while, and Rodgers was a family favorite. It was only a matter of time until Doc tried to emulate Rodgers' yodel and runs on the guitar, as every young aspiring singer did at the time. Doc recalled: "I was just a kid going to school when Jimmie left us, but his music means everything to me: from good ballads, blues, to a sweet song. I loved everything Jimmie did."[14] Like Rodgers, Doc was fearless in his incorporation of all kinds of music, from black or white singers, from the mountain or the city, both modern and old-time. Doc also began, for the first time, to use a flat pick. He recalled, "When I began to listen to Jimmie Rodgers I figured out there was something being done there besides the thumb and finger. So I got me a pick and started working on it."[15]

Around that time, Doc started to sit with old-time musicians around the local area, playing with them for dances, and sitting around with them, learning tunes on their front porches. Gaither Carlton taught Doc many fiddle tunes that Doc later played on the guitar to the amazement of folk audiences. John Cohen recalled speaking with Ralph Rinzler in 1961, just after Doc visited New York for the first time: "We were amazed that he could play these fiddle tunes on the guitar…"[16] It was not just Doc's speed, but also his tone. He played fiddle tunes using a flat pick, and somehow still kept the old-time feel to the tunes. Doc was not simply playing runs on the guitar; he was fiddling. He was playing the tunes he had learned at the feet of Gaither and other masters.

Doc also listened to licks on the radio and on records, and among his favorite guitarists was Riley Puckett, a well-known blind guitarist who recorded on his own and played with The Skillet Lickers and several other groups in the 1930s. His guitar playing had rock-solid rhythm, with occasional bursts of arpeggiation; runs and brief fiddle licks for flavor. Doc's style in even the recordings of the early 1960s still had a large element of Puckett's style, and Doc's solid yet playful flatpicking technique ultimately originated with Puckett. When listening to Riley Puckett's 1927 record of "Red Wing" or some other old tune, with eyes closed, one could almost mistake Riley Puckett's strong bass runs on the guitar for Doc's runs four decades later.

The next great phase in Doc's guitar playing was when he began attempting to play the Delmore Brothers' songs. Their hot guitar licks on songs like "Nashville

Blues," recorded in 1936, around the time when the Delmores were the most popular act on the Grand Ol' Opry, prefaced the virtuosic runs that Doc would record on the same song nearly 30 years later on his first self-title album in 1964. The duo's duet guitars, and the jaunty rhythms of their music also sound uncannily similar to the music that Doc and Merle produced on the road in the 1970s.

The Delmore Brothers also lent Doc their song "Deep River Blues," which he spiced up with Merle Travis-style fingerpicking, amazing folk guitar players everywhere. Texas singer-songwriter Guy Clark spoke about first seeing Doc live, and going home to learn the song: "Doc Watson is one of a kind, just stunning. The first time I saw him play was in a little folk club called the Sand Mountain Coffeehouse around 1965 or 1966 in Houston. And I was just aghast. Have been ever since. I remember watching everything during that first show. And listening. He's a phenomenal player, and I still sit and practice 'Deep River Blues' every day and I still can't play it. I broke my leg last year, and was holed up for about three and a half, four months, and every day I got to play 'Deep River Blues.'"[17]

Merle Travis was a big influence on Doc; so much so that Doc named his only son after him. Ironically, just after Doc got married to Rosa Lee, Travis' single "Divorce Me C.O.D." hit #1 on the country music charts. Doc later had the chance to play with Merle Travis several times: most famously during the recording session for the *Will the Circle Be Unbroken* album. Doc recalled that, after their first appearance on stage together, Travis said to him, "Doc Watson, I used to think of you as a good musician. I still do, but now I think of you as a friend."[18] That blessing from Travis meant the world to Doc; he had followed Travis' career at that point for more than 20 years.

Not unlike his guitar heroes in Nashville, Doc began exploring the electric guitar in 1952 after he traded in his Martin for a Les Paul. He additionally started learning how to play *lead* guitar as opposed to *accompaniment*-style guitar. When Doc was essentially forced to play acoustic guitar by Ralph Rinzler in the early 1960s, he simply applied the techniques he had used on the electric, and played leads on the steel-string acoustic guitar, something that had never been done before in such a way.

Don Rigsby, brilliant mandolinist, high lonesome lead singer and director of Morehead State University's Kentucky Center for Traditional Music, spoke about Doc's lead playing on the acoustic guitar: "Lead guitar was something more or less pioneered by a few folks, and Doc is one of those. His phrasing on guitar is one of a kind. There is nobody else who played with phrasing like he did. It was so spot-on perfect, the things he played. I just love what Doc does with a guitar; it's so much about the melody. I think a lot of people get away from that.

They get to thinking they need to play other things they know. Doc knows way more than he plays."[19]

Alan O'Bryant spoke about Doc's tone while flatpicking the guitar: "I think there's few people that have the command of touch that Doc does. You know, there's people like Norman Blake. There's other wonderful flat pickers, David Greer and Brian Sutton and people like that that have been able to pick up on how it is that these guys, through their command of touch, can pull that kind of tone, and the other aspects of their technique that they use to get that sound on the guitar. But Doc did it; Doc's always done it with such taste. That always came first, the rhythm and the taste of it; it always seemed to come first. You know, this is one thing I always said about Doc, that he had more taste in the end of his little finger than most people had in their whole approach. But I think that's what it is for me; it's just the tasteful approach and the command of being able to convey emotion when he's telling the story with his instrument."[20]

Jerry Douglas first heard Doc Watson on the *Strictly Instrumental* album as a lead guitarist with Flatt and Scruggs: "I was just knocked out by the fact that a guitar player could play fiddle tunes. And he didn't just hint at the melody and play around the melody, but he played the exact melody the way it was supposed to be played. And that was a revelation to me. It was the first guy I ever heard do that. And the melody was crystal clear."[21] The moment when Douglas heard that record, his life changed forever. He remembered: "Doc wasn't messing around. He was playing the melody. I've taken that rule to heart my whole career, too. The first thing I want to know is, what is the real melody? Don't give me the pseudo-melody, or the counter-melody, I want to know what the real melody is, and Doc Watson's always gone straight to the heart of that, and if you play with him onstage, the thing you are most aware of is what the melody, the true melody is. Then you start to scope in on little tiny increments of diverse melody, where you can go to change the melody ever so slightly, but still be true to the original melody. I think that's what Doc does. Doc can play outside as well as anybody else, but he prefers to play the melody because that's where the essence of the song is. And that's what really connects with the audience as well. He's a true master of that."[21]

Don Rigsby also spoke about the importance of melody in Doc's guitar playing: "It's what you leave *out* that makes the song. He'll rip it up, he'll blister it, he'll play the melody as fast as you want it played and he'll vary it a little bit. You can play a song and mess around the melody a bunch and still play the melody and he'll do that. I've got some live recordings from where I saw him for the first time in 1986, I think, in Louisville at the old Kentucky Fried Chicken Bluegrass Festival. He had Mark O'Connor playing with him. T. Michael Coleman, Jack Lawrence too. Those guys were just tearing it up."[19] But of course, he was still playing the melody. Tom Paxton recalled Doc's flatpicking in his early years on the scene: "The thing about Doc was he was fast as lightning but every note was distinct. He's one of the clearest players you'll ever hear, and he knows how to leave space between the notes as well. He is the most melodious of flatpickers."[22]

Doc had first heard melodies on the electric guitar after listening to Fay "Smitty" Smith play the melody on several of Ernest Tubb's hit songs released in 1941. Smith was the staff guitarist at a radio station in Fort Worth, Texas, and played simple melodies incredibly smoothly on his electric guitar. Doc recalled, "[I] purposely tried my best to copy every lick Smitty played on the early Ernest Tubb recordings. That man was some kind of guitar picker, I thought. He was a jazz player turned country. God, I loved his guitar picking! Whew! Did I ever! I swore by it."[23] But the first guitarist Doc ever heard play fiddle tunes on the guitar was Grady Martin, on Red Foley's version of "Alabama Jubilee," which also featured the Nashville Dixielanders, and had a New Orleans feel to it with a horn section. The song was released as a single in 1951, and hit #3 on the country music charts, and #28 in the national charts. Shortly after that, Doc first heard 19-year old Hank Garland play "Sugarfoot Rag" on his electric guitar like a fiddle, on a record that spread around the country like wildfire. Doc remembered the Nashville guitarists' influence on his playing: "I never tried to do too much lead with the flat pick until I began to hear Hank Garland and Grady Martin. Hank was a jazz guitar player, but in the early days he played some country music up in Nashville with Red Foley and different people. I heard them play fiddle tunes and I thought, 'By golly, if they can do that, I can.'"[24]

Si Kahn spoke about the importance of Doc's work on the electric guitar to his eventual acoustic styles: "It's very hard to pigeonhole Doc. Most people don't know that he spent so many years playing rockabilly in honkytonks. And that shows up in Doc's music. Doc's guitar work is really sinewy, it's really animated, it's very forward leaning without being bluegrass. I think those are the rockabilly echoes. Doc can play anything; he's got an amazing repertoire. I think his music's got a level of energy that opens him up to other kind of stuff. And he has covered so many kinds of music. Doc doesn't care what kind of music it is; if it's a good song, he's going to play it."[25]

Doc's sound has always been unmistakable on the flattop guitar. Ben Harper said of Doc's playing, "The second you hear a note, you know it's Doc Watson, and if it ain't Doc, boy, it's someone who's listened to about 10,000 hours of Doc."[26] Jerry Douglas said, "Doc Watson is the king and the father of flatpicking guitar."[21] And Jack Lawrence agreed, "He wasn't the first flatpicker on the scene, but he was the one who really put it out in front of the world and presented it well."[27]

Norman Blake, himself a legendary finger- and flatpicking guitarist, recalled first hearing Doc Watson play the guitar on record, which also first introduced him to the use of a flat pick on the acoustic guitar. He recalled, "I was teaching guitar in the late 1960s in Chattanooga, Tennessee, and one of my students brought in an early Vanguard Doc Watson record. Up till then I played guitar with a thumb pick and one finger, much like Mother Maybelle, Lester Flatt, Riley Puckett, Carter Stanley and others. I used a flat pick for mandolin, but it never occurred to me to use a flat pick on the guitar until hearing Doc's LP that showed me this as an avenue one could go down... Doc was a very self-contained guitar player in that he played in the open chord positions, a very full sound without a band."[28] Blake soon performed on stage many times next to Doc, most famously in 1973 at the second annual Winfield, Kansas Walnut Valley Music Festival, where legendary guitar picker Dan Crary also joined them. Blake recalled the day, "Doc seemed surprised that I played guitar, as he knew me as a Dobro player. Doc, Dan Crary and I did this big jam set. It got very cold and windy during our performance. Doc said he couldn't play below 55 degrees so nobody told him it was 47 degrees. Later, Doc was talking about trying to electrify the neck on his guitar to keep it warm."[28] At this point in the interview, Blake's agent jumped in and added, "The impact of this performance is still being talked about from those who were there or wished they had been..."[28] Of course, any acoustic guitarist would have given nearly anything to be a fly on the wall for the meeting of those three great guitar pickers on one stage.

Besides Doc's open-position melody guitar flatpicking, he also used many difficult techniques to accent the melodies he picked out. Pat Donohue recalled, "In listening to Doc's flatpicking stuff, I learned he really had a nice way of phrasing things. There were only so many notes that he would use, but there were so many different ways to play them; using open strings, pull-offs, and hammer-ons in a way that really makes the tunes sound funky, as opposed to just running up and down with a pick. I think the thing that influenced me the most was just the way he sounds when he plays. It was such an attractive sound he played. And it was not so much the type of music he was playing or any of those things. It was an unnamable thing in music where you hear something and you just want to hear more. That's all I can say; I just love the sound of him picking that thing so much, it really inspired me to want to be a good guitar player."[29]

Mike Seeger echoed Donohue's comment when he also talked about how Doc had inspired many young players to push their limits: "I think Doc's work on behalf of flat-pick guitar playing in the early '60s was very, very important. And I think that that's one of the things that people will really remember about him, and his effect is going to continue, if you think of the history of flatpicking."[30] Coming from Mike Seeger, himself a master of multiple guitar, banjo, and fiddle styles, and a musician known for his deep musical honesty and integrity, such a comment was very high praise.

One of the reasons Doc's flatpicking has always been revered is that it was fast but understated, virtuosic but humble. Doc always stayed near to the melody, and played clearer notes on the guitar than any guitarist before or since. Si Kahn said of Doc's musicianship: "Part of Doc's legacy is in his cleanliness of playing on the guitar, and his restraint. There are what I call the techno pickers, who can pick harder and faster than anybody else. But the interpretation and soul are not there. Doc could techno pick if he so desired. Even in his eighties, he is stunningly fast and clean. But with Doc his playing is almost always understated and beautiful. Even when Doc is doing a brilliant passage, it's clean and clear. You can hear every note. Every note. It's never muddy. It's never jumbled together."[25] Young guitarists across the country had never dreamed that the instrument they thought they knew intimately turned out to have so many more notes and so much more tone than they had ever imagined.

Pat Donohue recalled heading out early so that he could be at the front of the line when the doors for Doc Watson's concerts were opened. He got as close to Doc's hands as he could. He remembered, "I knew what chord shapes looked like at that point when someone was playing, because I could play at least that well when I first saw him. For example, I could tell if he was doing a C chord. But when he started playing all those melodies, I just watched what he was doing with his left hand fingers. With the right hand it was a little harder to zone in for me. But I learned a lot about the left hand stuff and the phrasing. There are a number of different ways to play any three-note phrase, for instance and the way he did it was the way you wanted it to sound. So I watched that really closely. There was not a lot of movement either, with his left hand. There was an awful lot of stuff going on, but his fingers didn't move any more than they had to. That was the same thing with Chet Atkins and really any truly great instrumentalist. They learn how to economize their hands and their movement."[29]

Doc also economized his notes. His old friend George McCeney said, "What made Doc so great is that each note is unique. Somebody told me one time that it only takes a single note to make a song. And that's true in a lot of Doc's songs; there's just that one note in the right place, and then everything else is assumed underneath that particular note, or run, or something."[4] Doc also played notes that no one was expecting. McCeney continued, "I think the thing that drew people to Doc in those early years is that he was so imaginative."[4]

But what made Doc the official king of the flatpicked guitar? Doc would never say that he was the best, but all of the musicians around him always knew that he was; he had a sound like no other, and he inspired thousands of young guitarists to explore their own sounds with the flat pick.

After he began forging out into new territory with his use of a flat pick, Doc changed the flattop acoustic guitar landscape for all who came after him. Paul Chasman, a master fingerpicking guitarist and member of the 1960s group, The Heavy Gauge String Band, said, "Doc Watson is to flatpicking what Bach is to classical music."[31] James Reams echoed that sentiment, and said, "Whenever they talk about flatpicking lead guitar, Doc Watson's name is going to be mentioned for all time."[32] In his prime, Doc Watson's approach to folk music on the guitar was like Horowitz's approach to the piano; no one could match his stylings and subtle intricacy. His ability to touch on the full range of the guitar's intimacy and timbre, as well its clean, bell-clear qualities, will inspire many future generations of musicians and musicologists to mention Doc alongside the greats of American folk music.

Sarah Bryan, a musicologist and the editor of the *Old-Time Herald* magazine, remembered the first time she ever heard Doc play live. She was with her parents at a concert at the Smithsonian Institution, and remembered attempting to watch the master's hands from a distant seat. Bryan distinctly recalled the discussion her parents had about Doc's playing: "I remember my parents having an impassioned argument afterwards about whether Doc was flatpicking or fingerpicking. One knew he was flatpicking, while the other maintained that it was physically impossible to play so many notes so fast with only a flat pick; that he must have been using at least three fingers."[33] Of course, Doc was playing with a flat pick, but it is very illustrative to hear that audience members often strained their eyes to see how Doc could possibly play all of the notes that were emerging from his guitar at any one time. After all, his body barely moved, and from a distance, Doc looked like a man sitting with good posture in a straight-backed chair, not moving a muscle to the left, right, top or bottom. The reason for that was his incredible economy of movement. But at the time, it must have seemed like some kind of magic that allowed Doc to produce so much wonderful sound while barely moving an inch.

Doc is also known as a fantastic fingerpicker, and is able to play styles from Mississippi John Hurt or Merle Travis-style country blues stride picking to open-tuned blues. In his performances in early years, Doc particularly developed his fingerpicking techniques, since he often did not have accompaniment on stage. Once Merle came on the road with him full time, Doc was able to play more leads, resting on his son's solid accompaniment.

Guitarist Paul Asbell, a teacher of electric, acoustic, finger- and flatpicked guitar, as well as an excellent guitarist in his own right, spoke to the huge range of styles that Doc was able to play on his instrument: "I was aware enough that the stuff that he was playing was kind of like the bluegrass that I had heard, Flatt and Scruggs or Bill Monroe, you know, and I was aware that the flatpicking thing he did was very much out of that tradition. But then he did Mississippi John Hurt stuff, he was fingerpicking, and to me these were kind of different worlds in a way. It was puzzling to me, or amazing to me, that he was so adept at that stuff, but also just that he was such an incredible exponent of both flatpicking and fingerpicking. I was aware that there were sort of two Doc Watsons that I really dug, and I knew they were the same guy, but I didn't quite understand how he could do both. It has utterly influenced my choice of what I do when I'm doing solo stuff. Doc's guitar playing paved the way for a lot of people to understand that these different worlds of southern white music and southern black music aren't nearly as different as you might think if you hung out with musicologists or bought a bunch of anthologies of diverse music styles or something like that. And that was something that really changed my life, I think."[34]

Doc merged all of his styles together in performances, and he was, because of that, a walking American music history lesson, and he did a great deal to bring diverse techniques and styles to the forefront of young guitar pickers. In one 1960s workshop recorded by Mike Seeger, Doc covered ten different styles of guitar playing within his brief session. Doc spoke about thumb picks and flat picks as he explained the blues, and how he could use the thumb pick to fingepick a song, then grip it in the middle of the song to use it like a flat pick and have greater ability to play 16th notes. He then played "Dill Pickle Rag" and spoke about ragtime music on the guitar. Next, Doc played "Dream of the Miner's Child," and demonstrated the syncopated 4-beat pattern of cross-picking, a style that had been largely invented by mandolinist Jesse McReynolds (of the group Jim and Jesse) and later used by guitarist George Shuffler in his work with the Stanley Brothers. On "Way Downtown," Doc played his well-known runs in between lines of singing, and when he was asked how to play them, Doc was able to slow down the runs for the young guitarists in front of him. He then demonstrated the open tuning of blues player Blind Lemon Jefferson, playing a guitar arrangement of an old-time song in 6/8 rhythm; a gospel hymn; two rock and roll songs, "Rock Around the Clock" and "Jailhouse Rock;" a rhythm and blues song; and the popular Elvis crooner, "Love Me."[35] Doc was not only able to do just about anything possible on an acoustic guitar, he was always able to slow it down and teach it to young guitarists.

Mike Marshall paid tribute to Doc and his guitar playing with the following: "Doc Watson's legacy is his old world gentlemanliness, the classiness in which he presented himself in public, his warmth and open-heartedness, and of course his unbelievably gorgeous, fierce, guitar playing. He set such a standard in the early '70s that every flatpicker who has come after him has to tip their hat to him and thank him for playing really all the notes of a fiddle tune so cleanly. He was one of the first guys to do that; to play "Black Mountain Rag" and "Billy in the Lowground" and really hit all those notes. I think everyone in the music world felt the same way about Doc. He was legend. When I think back, he was my age in 1972 when I first heard him, and I'm 51 now [in 2009]. He would have been around 49 then, and even at that time he was a legend. He was this iconic ideal of perfect guitar playing."[8]

Like the mahogany, spruce and cedar of his guitars, Doc's sound has improved with age.

# CHAPTER NOTES

1.   Gustavson, Kent, *Telephone Interview with Marty Stuart*. May 18, 2009.
2.   Cohen, John, *Conversations with Bob Dylan*. Sing Out!, 1968. 18(4): p. 6-23,67.
3.   Gustavson, Kent, *Telephone Interview with Ricky Skaggs*. April 29, 2009.
4.   Gustavson, Kent, *Telephone Interview with George McCeney*. May 22, 2009.
5.   Gustavson, Kent, *Telephone Interview with Tony Trischka*. April 27, 2009.
6.   Gustavson, Kent, *Email Interview with Beppe Gambetta*. July 23, 2009.
7.   Gustavson, Kent, *Telephone Interview with David Moultrup*. April 27, 2009.
8.   Gustavson, Kent, *Telephone Interview with Mike Marshall*. March 26, 2009.
9.   Holt, David, *Liner Notes to Doc Watson and David Holt: Legacy*, High Windy, 2002.
10.  Gustavson, Kent, *Telephone Interview with Peggy Seeger*. July 1, 2009.
11.  Gustavson, Kent, *Telephone Interview with Donna Hill*. May 6, 2009.
12.  Gustavson, Kent, *Telephone Interview with Ellen Harper-Verdries*. July 3, 2009.
13.  Brooks, Michael, *Doc Watson on Bluegrass Guitar*. Sing Out!, 196?: p. 5-6,9.
14.  *American Roots Music*, DVD, Palm Pictures, 2001.
15.  Humphrey, Mark, *Liner Notes from Legends of Flatpicking Guitar*, Vestapol, 2001.
16.  Gustavson, Kent, *Personal Interviews with John Cohen*. April 8 & August 6, 2009.
17.  Gustavson, Kent, *Telephone Interview with Guy Clark*. March 18, 2009.
18.  Ohlschmidt, Jim, *The Life and Legacy of Thumbpicking King Merle Travis*. Acoustic Guitar, 1998(72): p. 63.
19.  Gustavson, Kent, *Telephone Interview with Don Rigsby*. April 1, 2009.
20.  Gustavson, Kent, *Telephone Interview with Alan O'Bryant*. May 6, 2009.
21.  Gustavson, Kent, *Telephone Interview with Jerry Douglas*. April 10, 2009.
22.  Gustavson, Kent, *Telephone Interview with Tom Paxton*. April 14, 2009.
23.  Ledgin, Stephanie P., *Father and Son*. Acoustic Guitar, 1993: p. 49-57.
24.  *Doc Watson Quotes*. 2005, MerleFest.org.
25.  Gustavson, Kent, *Telephone Interview with Si Kahn*. May 26, 2009.
26.  Gustavson, Kent, *Telephone Interview with Ben Harper*. June 4, 2009.
27.  Gustavson, Kent, *Telephone Interview with Jack Lawrence*. April 13, 2009.
28.  Gustavson, Kent, *Email Interview with Norman Blake*. Sept. 5, 2009.
29.  Gustavson, Kent, *Telephone Interview with Pat Donohue*. March 11, 2009.
30.  Gustavson, Kent, *Telephone Interview with Mike Seeger*. May 23, 2009.
31.  Gustavson, Kent, *Telephone Interview with Paul Chasman*. April 13, 2009.
32.  Gustavson, Kent, *Telephone Interview with James Reams*. April 9, 2009.
33.  Gustavson, Kent, *Telephone Interview with Sarah Bryan*. March 25, 2009.
34.  Gustavson, Kent, *Telephone Interview with Paul Asbell*. March 16, 2009.
35.  *FT 2752c #1*, from *Southern Folklife Collection at The Wilson Library*. University of North Carolina at Chapel Hill: Raleigh, NC.

Photo by Nic Siler ©
*Doc Watson on stage.*

# CHAPTER TWENTY
## Amazing Grace

*"Doc Watson sings like an arrow straight to a place that is true."*

\- Joe Crookston[1]

From "Amazing Grace" at PS 41 to "Tennessee Stud" on the *Will the Circle Be Unbroken* album, Doc Watson has always been able to sing straight to the heart of a tune. Greg Brown said of Doc's soul, "Like all great musicians, he expresses things that cannot be said any other way than by the sounds coming out of his voice and guitar, a sound full of sorrow and joy, whimsy and trouble, a sound that comes out of the land itself."[2]

As if speaking in the same voice, Ben Harper continued, "And his voice and his guitar are inseparable. They just accent and play off of each other so perfectly. I won't say 'effortless,' as the term sometimes to me sounds like an insult because I know how much effort it probably took him to learn it. But it looks as effortless as, say, a professional gymnast, or an ice skater or something. You know, it took work to get there, boy, but once he arrived, there was just a grace and an effortlessness and a fluidity to his musicianship and singing that is nothing short of miraculous."[3]

While pushing the envelope of technique and virtuosity with his guitar playing, Doc has always had a steady baritone voice that anchors his tunes back to the earth of Deep Gap, and the well of tradition. Tony Trischka recalled coming to Doc through his voice: "The main thing that got me into Doc's music was that he had this wonderful voice. He had a rich, warm voice, and just his whole persona was so inviting and so great. Of course his guitar playing was something that I gravitated towards, being an instrumentalist. But as the years rolled on I started tuning in to his singing more, and his vocal phrasing. These days, that's what blows me away when I listen to him, the way he syncopates; the way he puts his words together and has them falling across the beat. As the years roll on I've started thinking, 'Man, this guy's an amazing singer.'"[4]

David Moultrup echoed Trischka's comment: "When I listen to Doc I almost get into a hypnotic trance. I love it. It's almost like the sound of his voice and the grittiness of the lyrics and the willingness to sort of touch a part of life that people don't like to acknowledge very easy, he does it so gracefully in his songs. He's just so graceful and so charming about it."[5]

Ellen Harper-Verdries said: "Doc's voice is just so rich, and so present, and it's just so Doc Watson. Anytime I hear that voice, I can just picture him. It takes me right back to the first time I saw him. His voice just reaches very deep."[6] Wayne Henderson added, "He don't sound like anybody else. Once he sings one lick, you know who it is."[7]

And Tom Chapin remembered first hearing Doc from a distance: "I first heard Doc in person at one of the summer folk festivals. I remember one time walking across the festival ground with my instruments on my back, having just arrived from the parking lot by bus, and hearing this voice on stage in the distance and thinking, 'Now, that's the voice of American folk music.' And it was the voice of, as I discovered walking closer, Doc Watson."[8]

Most traditional musicians have one volume setting for their voices: *loud*. Doc, on the other hand, uses a wide dynamic range, and sings from within the emotions of his songs, whether joyful or mournful. John Cohen spoke about the difference between Doc Watson's baritone voice and Roscoe Holcomb's *high lonesome* tenor: "I once played Doc Watson and Roscoe Holcomb for a woman who was doing her PhD dissertation following up on music I had recorded in Peru, and doing very great work, going much further than I had ever gone. First I played her Roscoe. Then I played Doc for her, and she said, 'He's got a full range of tonality.'"[9]

Alan O'Bryant explained this tonality further: "I think that Doc has a very highly developed ability of conveying emotions through his music. If you think of music as a language and him just being very fluent in it and very articulate, it's just very refined. Doc's voice tells a story, and I think that's the height of what any musician can do. He can excite you or kind of penetrate you with whatever kind of emotion he's trying to get across."[10]

Sam Bush has always gravitated towards the joy in Doc's music: "It's obvious the man is not faking it. You can feel the joy in his playing and hear it in his voice and the way he talks to the audience. You can just feel the joy, and it still brings him joy. And if anything, it's very inspirational to me. This is going to sound crazy, but I want to be like Doc when I'm that age. I still want to have the ability to play. It still brings him joy, you know. In that way he's an inspiration to all of us people as we age, to keep yourself together and just realize why you're there. You're there because you love playing music."[11]

Doc has been singing since he can remember, and by the time he was "discovered" in 1960, Doc could sing any part from bass to high tenor, in countless styles of music, from rock and roll to a capella hymns. In developing his voice, Doc did not necessarily set out to forge a new style. Like most great artists, Doc imitated other artists until his own voice emerged.

Peter Rowan spoke about Doc's unique voice: "I think that Elvis Presley always said he was trying to sing like Dean Martin. In other words, Elvis wasn't trying to be Elvis, he was trying to be someone else. I think Doc Watson has tried to honor the people he loves, like Tennessee Ernie Ford and Merle Travis, and he just sang their material without trying to sound like them. The great thing about Doc is his very natural style. The thing is that Doc is *Doc*, it's going to come out. You know what I mean? He doesn't have to try. Whatever he does has got that flavor to it."[12]

In speaking about learning to sing like Jimmie Rodgers early on, Doc discussed how he developed his own voice: "In the early days, one of my favorite singers of all the time back then was Jimmie Rodgers... I don't try to copy him, but I know he influenced my style... I like his songs but I think if you don't try to imitate or emulate a singer or singers, you develop your own style, you just do it... And they inspire you to sing – you sing what you are able to sing... I never was too good at vibrato – I can do a little of it, on some songs, a slight vibrato in my voice, but I never could get those, where your Adam's apple goes and bobs up and down in your stomach, and your diaphragm goes in and out about 2-3 inches – I can't do that..."[13]

Doc's vocal style was a true bridge between old-time music and modern music, and between city and country. Doc's ability to connect to both a rural and city, educated and uneducated, highbrow and lowbrow audiences, was highlighted in a 1967 New York Times article: "Watson is located dead-center in the forward thrust of country music toward highbrow as well as lowbrow respectability. The very impurity of his style, coupled with the exhilaration his work generates, goes a long way to accomplish this aim. Like a select few before him (John Jacob Niles, Merle Travis, Clarence Ashley), he forms a bridge between America's primitive folk heritage and the sophisticated listener."[14]

Alice Gerrard noted that Doc had a mountain sound, but he did not have the sound that was in a sense "expected" for a mountain singer. She said, "His voice hasn't got that sort of edgy high lonesome sound that a lot of more traditional mountain musicians like Roscoe Holcomb or Ralph Stanley have."[15]

Instead, Greg Brown spoke about what Doc's voice *did* have: "Doc's music and the stories coming out of his life are part of the fiber of American music. They come out of the country and that whole life; small farms, hard times, people getting together to work, fight, eat and play music. That was a vivid life, strongly influenced by the cold hard facts of life, and with an underlying gumption and spirit it took to make it through. I think that is what you can hear in Doc's music, the vividness of a life rooted in a certain place, and a rural life, all that entails. It hardly exists any more; country music is pop music now."[2] Like Greg Brown's voice, Doc's voice was rooted to the land, vividly expressing the true heart of the country.

Doc's old friend Clint Howard addressed the mountain quality in Doc's voice: as far as I'm concerned, we sound like the mountains. That's what it comes down to. No way you can change it."[16]

Part of the mountain sound that Doc's singing has evoked throughout the years comes from its simplicity. His baritone voice rarely was cloaked in mordents and trills, had little or no vibrato, and no contrived tone. The sound he produced was straight from his vocal cords, with little modification of any sort. He never needed reverb or effects. The sound of his voice was enough to express the emotions and story of a song.

Peter Rowan said of Doc's great ability to sing a song simply: "Doc is a force of nature. In fact, without Doc there would have been no anchor for the last 40 years to keep us remembering the simplicity of the old tunes."[12] Sam Bush echoed Rowan's sentiment: "When he sings, he'll never throw in a fancy lick to show off."[11]

Folk singer Tom Paxton expressed the importance of the simple "straight ahead" quality of Doc's singing: "I always loved Doc's singing because it was straight ahead, where the song is the star, not the singer. If Doc were to be asked to sing the 'Star Spangled Banner' at a football game, he'd sing it straight through the way it ought to be sung instead of seeing how much of a spin he could put on it."[17]

Si Kahn said: "I think Doc lifts up the value of simplicity in music. Simplicity is not simple-mindedness, it's not an over simplification, but an understanding that there is such a thing as modesty in music. I think this is partly Doc's traditional heritage, the simplicity."[18]

Larry Long pointed out how Doc is able to tell stories through his songs: "Doc is a natural storyteller. He brings each of these gifts to every live performance he does. Seamless. Simple. Direct. Honest. Inspirational."[19] He continued to write about Doc's ability to combine words and music into something incredible: "Words and notes written on a page are simply words and notes. But once you start singing and playing, you put breath, or life, or spirit, into those words and notes. It becomes something much larger and more mysterious. When it's done right, you lose yourself in it, and become part of that breath, part of that spirit. Your ego no longer gets in the way. You become part of something far greater than yourself. You become who you truly are. Folk music restores our collective memory. It reminds us that we're all human and that we're all in this together. Folk music is a tie that binds. When people sing along together there's no room for hatred."[19]

Not only did Doc always honor the words and story, he also honored the *song* itself. Alan O'Bryant remembered, "Doc Watson was probably one of the first people that I heard that had a huge impression on me as far as what you could have called at that time a contemporary treatment of folk music. Because he was just so tasteful. And you know, it's just the way he used his voice. He was so expressive and so emotive in his ability to be able to tell the stories in song, and just the way that he wove the guitar around it and all that. It was just killer."[10]

Jonathan Byrd wrote: "Doc explores every piece of music and wrings the best out of it."[20] George McCeney echoed that statement: "I think Doc understood songs more deeply than most of the people that played them. Some people have those nuances with their voice, you know. There are just certain singers that can do things that make a song so very different than when its sung by somebody else."[21] And Paul Chasman said of Doc's ability to present a song: "Doc's real innovation, I think, comes from his way of presenting a song. I always feel that with whatever he's doing, whether he's singing a song or flatpicking a fiddle tune or playing banjo or whatever, the song is always the most important thing, and it comes from this really deep place."[20]

Si Kahn continued, "Doc believes in the song. When Doc does a song, he *does* that song. He's not playing another song. There are artists who, no matter which song they're doing, they're essentially treating it the same way musically and instrumentally. And if you're only listening to the instrumental break and the break is not on the chorus, you don't know which song it is because they're playing it exactly the same. Doc does the heart of the song, and his vocal delivery and his instrumentation are always appropriate to that song. He's paying attention to what is there in the moment."[18]

Michelle Shocked even went one step further into Doc's belief in the song: "I believe when Doc is singing a tune, he's actually actively repenting. And to repent is the one act that people don't want to bring themselves to do; the humbling of one's self-pride to repent and say, 'I was wrong, I've made mistakes, I've erred, I've sinned.' And I believe so firmly that Doc was working out his own salvation."[22]

Despite Doc Watson's brilliance, kindness, and honesty on the surface, and his ability to connect with his audience through music, Doc has retreated into a protective shell since Merle's death. Even old friends often find it next to impossible to contact him, and he is often tight-lipped when it comes to interviews.

Pat Donohue, one of the best acoustic blues guitarists alive today, and the house guitarist for Prairie Home Companion, said: "I remember one time ten or fifteen years ago when I opened for Doc [in Saint Paul, Minnesota] at the Fitzgerald Theater for one of his concerts. I had another concert coming up with him about six months hence, and the producer had asked me if I would talk to Doc about possibly doing something together at the end of that concert. So anyway, I played my set, went down, and was in the dressing room with Doc, and I brought it up to him. I told him about this concert that we had coming up together and said, 'Do you think there's anything we might do together on that show?' And he didn't say anything but, *'No sir...'* That was the end of the conversation."[23] Donohue knew that Doc wasn't joking when he didn't say anything else, continuing to sit in silence. Perhaps Doc thought to himself,

"It would be too much work to figure out a tune that we could play together onstage," but whatever he might have been thinking, he didn't vocalize it for Donohue, who was stunned by the older guitarist's flat refusal.

Despite Doc's open door policy for his New York friends in the early 1960s, fifty years later, Doc takes quite the opposite approach. Since Merle's death, he stays secluded even from his neighbors and friends, preferring most often to be left alone; the one exception being each year at MerleFest, when he spends the entire weekend with other musicians onstage and off. He has directed his agent Mitchell Greenhill in California to run interference on all correspondence with him, and Greenhill obliges him religiously.

John Cohen, who first met Doc as he stepped off the bus at Port Authority in New York for the first time in 1961, and is one of Doc's oldest friends in the music business, now finds it nearly impossible to contact him: "When Doc became managed by Mitch Greenhill, after [his father] Manny Greenhill [got out of the business], he became inaccessible. I tried to persuade Doc to be on the soundtrack of *Cold Mountain*, because I was involved in the music for the movie. And it was so humiliating for me. The only way I could talk to Doc was backstage at an outdoor concert in New York City. After the concert I was given five minutes, and Mitch Greenhill was right there, listening to every word. It was like he was supervising everything I said. And I was forced to resort to saying, 'Hey, Doc, remember the old days when we first put on the first concert?' I was trying to re-establish any credentials, knowing that anything I said was being shaped by Mitch."[9]

At the same time, Doc, who is now 87 years old, likes to be left alone, so that he can spend time with his wife of 65 years, his daughter Nancy, his grandchildren, great-grandchildren, and great-great grandchildren. It is a feat for any great-great-grandparent to even remember all of the names of their progeny, let alone the words to folk songs, but Doc still steps out on stage and pours his heart out for audiences everywhere.

Doc has repeated over and over for most of the duration of his career that he never wants to be "put on a pedestal." The funny thing is, he *literally* was, by the man some think is the greatest country guitar player in history, Chet Atkins, who had a bust of Doc Watson made and put on top of his piano. However, by saying that he did not want to be "put on a pedestal,"

Doc was able to live humbly, and maintain his simple life, keeping his professional and personal identities separate. When he stepped off that Greyhound bus at the end of March in 1961 after returning from New York City, and every time he returned home after that, he was going back to the same simple home and day-to-day lifestyle he had left behind.

Doc has taken every chance he can to speak badly about the pedestal, but he has always loved the stage. The stage allowed him to be near the audience; to hear their sighs and singing. He never thought of the stage as a pedestal, and that is why he was so effective over 50 years on the road. He always told his audience to imagine that they were on the front porch *with* him, even though he was on the stage. And though he disliked being placed on a metaphorical pedestal, filmmaker Joe Murphy, in his 1985 film *Doc and Merle*, captured a scene with 60-year old Doc climbing onto his roof.

While standing on the roof of his own home, the Doc told Murphy that he didn't want to be put onto a pedestal: "Appreciation is a thing I feed on. Not worship or stardom. I don't give a *Katie* about that... Hell, we're all people; you, me...we're just human beings, and if we do what we do well, others should appreciate us for it, but not worship us for it, or make lords out of us or something."[24]

Doc might have been frustrated that people often tried to "make a lord" out of him, but it is hard *not* to be astonished when Murphy then captured images of the elderly blind musician gently feeling his way to the edge of the roof, finding the ladder with the tips of his fingers, then backing down to the ground, seemingly without fear. While hauling the screen up the ladder, Doc had said with a grin on his face, further building the tension, "I like to be careful on this ladder, boys – man could fall and break his neck..."[24] Although Doc might want to be treated like any ordinary man, he is anything but... He is the greatest flatpicker who has ever lived, and he is a blind man who is able to climb onto his own roof, repair an air conditioner, build a fan out of a washing machine, and sing a thousand songs. He is extraordinary.

However, Doc has always been uncomfortable in situations where he is receiving honors for his accomplishments, no matter whether an honorary degree or a Grammy award. During the ceremony in which he was awarded an honorary Doctoral degree from Appalachian State University in Boone, Doc said to his friend Professor Rogers Whitener, "Rogers...I don't know whether to shake your hand for this or hit you. I'm going to feel like a fool wearing a cap and gown, man... I ain't never been to a college or a university, and why in the world would you give a man some kind of honorary degree for getting off his lazy tail and playing music for people who love it and earning a living for his family?"[25]

Doc never desired to be a celebrity or a household name. He would have preferred to be a great entertainer living in complete seclusion from the world. But when he is onstage, his personality transforms him from a recluse to an entertainer. And when he steps onto a stage and gets a standing ovation, or finishes a blistering solo on some instrumental tune to wild shouts and applause afterwards, he always breaks out in a smile. What musician wouldn't? Jack Lawrence said, in 2009: "Doc also likes the audiences, and he likes performing more than he lets on sometimes. Otherwise he would have quit a long time ago."[26]

Often going far beyond simple admiration, Doc's adherers frequently express that Doc is nearly a deity. Well-known fiddler Darol Anger remarked that, among musician friends, "There was a feeling, on the west coast at least, that Doc was sort of like a spectacular natural feature of the landscape; inevitable, fully formed, iconic. He seemed ageless, and his so-called disability and spectacular transcendence of that along with his folksy manner made him a kind of mythic character, sort of a household god."[27]

Doc was in fact held in such high esteem by some musicians that he often intimidated them, even when he would be sitting silently backstage. This man who was a musical giant onstage appeared as a slight, frail old man when backstage, sitting as if thinking, usually all alone. In a story about Doc from his book *Cathedrals of Kudzu*, Hal Crowther wrote about the time that he first saw Doc up close: "I found him sitting alone in a classroom behind the stage area, waiting for an escort. I don't think he heard me come in. It was an unfair advantage to take, but I watched him for five minutes before I spoke. It wasn't much of a conversation – two polite strangers, each caught out of his element in a different way."[28]

Abigail Washburn, with her gorgeous voice and clawhammer banjo playing, has now shared the stage with every major acoustic act in the country. But when she was first getting recognition with her band Uncle Earl, Washburn recalled seeing Doc for the first time backstage: "Doc was on at the same time as we were, and there were two sides to the backstage; there was a little room that was almost like a little shack or something on each side of the stage. Uncle Earl got dressed behind a curtain and he was on the other side, and somebody said, 'You know, Doc's on the other side practicing.' And I was like, 'Oh, my gosh!' And this was the first time other than paying to see him in concert that I was somewhere with him, so I walked over to the other side and sort of peeked in the door, and there he was."[29] Washburn had the reaction that most musicians have when they first run across Doc backstage. She watched without speaking.

Abigail Washburn continued, "He didn't seem to notice that I'd opened the door, or if he had, he didn't say anything. So I just peeked in the door and I watched for about 15 minutes while he just picked his guitar and hummed along, and I cried. I just was so...it was such an intimate moment, even though he didn't...I don't know that he knew I was there."[29] Doc's finest music has been sung off stage, on porches and in back rooms. And Washburn, watching from across the room, felt that to disturb him would break some kind of boundary: "I didn't want to be there, you know what I mean? I was just glad to have this real intimate moment where I got to actually be in his presence and in his spirit. And it's funny that I didn't want to make myself known at all."[29]

Abigail Washburn is well-loved musician, and has a seat in the modern pantheon of acoustic pickers, as does her husband Bela Fleck. Yet to see Doc Watson the first time was such a profound experience for her that she wept at seeing the intimacy with which he played his guitar privately backstage. If even the greatest musicians treat Doc Watson with such respect and reverence, how could fans not also put Doc on the highest pedestal?

Musicians do not just revere Doc because he is a great musician. He is a catalyst in many of their careers, and has helped countless young artists. Scores of musicians find themselves saying, "It all started with Doc." Ketch Secor of Old Crow Medicine Show is one such artist. His band had never recorded for a major record label when they met Doc. They had never even played a large concert, or recorded more than a brief demo recording. But Doc came across them on the streets of Boone, and their lives changed forever. Secor related the entire story about his band being "discovered" by Doc Watson in Boone, who himself had been "discovered" only a few miles down the road in much the same way by Ralph Rinzler four decades before.

The members of Old Crow Medicine Show moved to the mountains near Boone in the late 1990s, learning from the locals. Secor described the result of their moonshine experiment: "We made all this liquor with a steam keg. We had the corn mash going for about 60 days, and everything was ready to roll on this project. And we made the liquor on the night of July 4th, and then we drank almost all of it. And, on the morning of the 5th of July, we woke up really [messed] up and hung over, and it was somebody's idea that we should go busk. I mean, we had played on the street corner in Boone before, but on the 5th of July, all the tourists were out, so we got it together, and about lunchtime we made it down to King Street."[30] The story so far seemed as if it could have taken place 70 years earlier, in the time of the Skillet Lickers and Jimmie Rodgers.

Secor continued to weave his tale: "We were playing in front of the pharmacy real hung over, that kind where you're just still kind of drunk, and your mouth tastes terrible; splitting headache kind of stuff. And we played for a couple of hours, at the end of which a woman came up and asked us a couple questions, and said, 'Are you guys going to be here for a while? My dad really likes this kind of music.' And we said, 'Well, I don't know if we will or not, but we're here now.' And she said, 'I hope you're here in 20 minutes.' So she disappeared and she came back, and we saw her little red Jeep Cherokee pull up across the street from us, and then she walked her dad out. And there was Doc."[30] Little did the young men know that this moment would change the rest of their lives.

Secor remembered, "Doc listened to us play on the corner there before walking in to have his lunch at Boone Drug, which has a great lunch counter. And right there on the street corner after we played a song called 'Oh My Little Darling,' which is an old folk song, he said, 'That's some of the finest old-time music I've heard in a long time. Boys, I've got a festival down in North Wilkesboro, and I'd love to have you on it.' We said, 'Gee, thanks Doc,' and we took a picture with him. It was taken of us right there, and it was taken with infrared film, so Doc's hair is cotton candy pink. I have a Mohawk, and Arthur Grimes is in the background, because he was dancing during the show, and about three of us are there."[30]

Doc had, in a few moments done something that had never happened to him in all of the years he had played on the street corners. He heard something in their music, and he wanted to help them become great. The sound that Old Crow Medicine Show is able to produce live is unlike any other band; the sound of the moonshine and the mountains is in their music, as well as a certain intellectual worldview. Doc knew that they had it in them to become great. And since that moment, Old Crow Medicine Show went straight up the charts, and now sells thousands of records. And it all started with a few words on a street corner.

The interesting thing about Secor's story is that the band's relationship with Doc pretty much started and stopped at that moment. The old sage had given them his blessing, and he did not have any more time to devote to them. He was busy enough taking care of his own family. He had already grown old and tired, and this was but a brief pause in his retirement. Secor remembered, "I feel like Doc's shine to us started and stopped right then and there. It was more like recognition than it was a taking under the wing of."[30] It was a blessing by the chief priest of acoustic music, and it took them far. Secor said, "Doc gave us such a huge break, and that encounter on the street corner is why we moved to Nashville, is why we met the people who we met. I mean, we went from meeting Doc to playing on the Opry in about a year and a half's time. And meeting Doc was this great point of acceleration. Things really lined up after that meeting with Doc. I mean, just *bing, bing, bing*. We did MerleFest. Well, we played just some little set on a lousy stage and nobody was there, but we busked, we got drunk, and we played out, we made our own stage. I'm not real crazy about MerleFest, actually. But we made the most of it, and somebody from Nashville, from the Opry, this lady named Sally Williams heard us, and we moved off the mountain less than four months later, after that gig."[30]

Abigail Washburn is another artist who could say that her career started with Doc. She first came across his music when she was living abroad: "I was living in China, in Schezuan Province... I was so obsessed with this other culture, other way of living, talking, thinking, that I just got pretty removed from my own, on lots of levels. I was starting a new life in China, a different kind of life, and I realized that I was just missing out a lot on where I came from and my own native heritage. One of the things that I would struggle with about being in China and trying to relocate there and build a life there is that I realized I could never truly be Chinese. And that was a strange concept to me, because in America, anyone can come and become American...And I wanted to explore more about why that was possible in America...And when I came back to the States after living in Schezuan I was just hanging out with some friends, and somebody put on an LP of Doc Watson singing and playing 'Shady Grove,' an old LP. And I was just struck by it. I said, 'Wow, that is a truly American sound,' and I just felt like I knew it was, I just had no doubt about it…It was like a call in the night, or like a beacon of light back to my own roots. And I pretty well became obsessed with the sounds of Doc Watson and what he represented to me, and to music in general in America. And I went out and I bought a banjo and started with 'Shady Grove.' And then I went from there."[29]

Marty Stuart, Doc and Merle's old friend, went one step further, speaking quite literally of the light around his mentor: "The last time I went to MerleFest, I was walking through the crowd, and Doc was on with somebody, and there were a lot of people onstage. He was standing up, and the way the light was shining down on him, I just stopped and took it in for a minute. I thought, 'Man, that is an American treasure standing there.' And he is a spiritual treasure. The way the light was shining down on his silver hair, I thought he looked like a mountain angel. He has been an angel to a lot of people."[31]

The word *angel* comes from the Greek root *angelos*, which means "messenger." Doc was indeed a mountain messenger in many ways. He brought the music of the mountains to the rest of the world. And he brought the message of kindness and love to the world with the hymn "Amazing Grace."

Jean Ritchie told an amusing story about walking in Doc's shoes for a few moments in Washington: "I don't think of Doc as blind. I'll tell you a funny story. My husband and I were down in Washington at a festival one time. We weren't on the program; we were just there walking around one time, and we saw Doc sitting in a big circle of people, and we went in to hear him sing. Somebody ran in to tell him that Jean Ritchie was there. He said, 'Jean, Jean, come in, let's sing a song.' So we sang 'Amazing Grace,' and you know, when I sing, I close my eyes. It just makes the song come out better; I don't have to look into other people's faces. So when it was over somebody said, 'Oh, what a beautiful song, and poor thing, she's blind.'"[32]

Most of the musicians who knew Doc closely through the years felt that Doc had a different kind of seeing. He held a guru-like status for these young musicians. He gave them life advice and music advice, and treated them all as if they were his long-lost sons and daughters. And thus Doc's blindness became a lovable afterthought for those who knew him well, and a spiritual center for others.

Ricky Skaggs said, "Doc has a spiritual sense and a spiritual eye that I think is so keen and so right, and that's how he loves people."[33] Maria Muldaur said, "He's an incredibly aware and conscious human being. He just so overdeveloped his other faculties to an unusually remarkable degree to make up for not having sight. I mean most sighted guys couldn't do what he did. He is a really incredible presence on this planet, I have to say."[34]

Peter Rowan recalled having long conversations with Doc about spirituality while they were on the road together in the 1970s. Doc was, of course, a devoutly Christian man, but Rowan remembered their conversation about all kinds of spirituality: "We talked about the American Indians and the vision thing and what it's like to not be able to see a little bit. You know, I didn't want to pry, but I sat with him for hours and we talked about the mystical side of things. He told me that he used to feel the vibration of the American Indian, he said, 'But I don't any more.'"[12] Rowan explained how he saw Doc's *light* and *darkness* in a different way after those conversations: "I don't know what Doc means to other people, because my impression is that, for Doc, the darkness of being blind kind of highlights the brilliance of his emanation as a person and as a musician. In other words...some people are scared of blind people because they seem to have a sixth sense. But Doc was so in tuned to his vibe...He'd call me nicknames, you know, and he made you feel at home, you know."[12] Rowan finished by speaking of Doc's special sensitivity to people and sound: "Somehow the idea of all this darkness made his articulation and his emanation very, very, very present and very bright. You know, Doc's sensitivity became stronger and stronger because of his loss of sight, I believe."[12]

Despite his blindness, Doc has been able to achieve extraordinary things in the world of music, influencing acoustic musicians of all subsequent generations. But he has always been self-effacing, even talking about the fact that blindness had been given to him by God to keep him humble. Donna Hill, also blind, remembered well when Doc told her that: "And he also talked about his religious convictions and how he felt that God had given him the handicap basically to prevent him from becoming over prideful. And he says he's positive that knowing what he was like as a young man, that he would have gotten himself a real big head. And he feels that that's why he has the blindness."[35]

Doc also did his best, despite the constant care he required through the years when traveling to foreign places, to appreciate everyone around him, often using humor to put others at ease about his disability. Sam Bush recalled the great honor of walking Doc onto stage after Merle's death, and one mishap: "When

I was growing up I played with a guitar player named Gib Cassidy. And Gib played electric guitar, and Gib was a blind man. Their hands reminded me of each other, the way they played, Gib and Doc. And I grew up learning the way Gib liked to be led when we walked with each other, which was one step behind you, with his hand around your bicep. That way when you step up they feel you step up, and when you stop they stop. It seemed natural to me whenever I would have a chance to lead Doc, because I had done that with another guitar player when I was a kid. One time we were going on stage at the Strawberry Music Festival out in California in Yosemite Park, and I tripped going up the steps while I was leading Doc. I was so embarrassed, and I said, 'Oh, Doc, excuse me, I'm so sorry.' And Doc is such a gentleman, he said, 'Oh, Sam, you know I pushed you.'"[11] Bush was so struck by the kindness of that event, he has been telling that story for two decades.

On August 23rd, 2009, Doc, in an expression of piety and gratefulness to God, spoke to a local Todd, North Carolina audience about his faith: "I said, 'Lord, I don't want to die and go to hell. I thought I was a Christian for all these years. I was baptized when I was 14... The [preacher] did his best to explain the love of Christ. But it didn't get across to me. I was too young, and he was a beginning preacher. All of those years I made too many willful mistakes. I couldn't have been a Christian.'"[36] As well as enduring Rosa Lee's many recent medical problems, Doc had also just gone through an operation removing a spot from his lung, and at age 86, it made him consider his own mortality.

Doc continued, "Bless His heart and name, He knew the future and I didn't. I was let live to provide for my family."[36] Indeed, Doc had been saved as a young man, supine in the Nashville hospital bed, and now he had been spared again. His greatest purpose in life had always been to support his family, not to become famous or to become rich.

At this point, Doc broke out into sobs, then continued to *witness* to the audience: "One morning I was listening to Randy Travis sing 'Doctor Jesus,' and the third time it come around to where it said, 'Lord I need you to mend my heart and save my soul,' I accepted. And He comes up right here in the Holy Spirit..." At this point, Doc motioned somewhere above his shoulder, beside his face, and continued, "He said, 'I'm here. Open your heart.'" Doc finished his passionate statement, again breaking down into tears, saying: "Tears of joy still flow when I think of that. And I'm glad I've not backslid in spite of my weaknesses.

He knows me. He knows my heart. And I'm glad that I'm here."[36] The lyrics of the song "Doctor Jesus" had inspired Doc to become *born again* within his faith: "Doctor Jesus, will you help me? / Make me better, make me whole / Doctor Jesus, Lord I need you / to mend my heart and save my soul."[37]

In a similarly intense performance from one year previous in Bristol, Tennessee, Doc sang a stunning a capella version of "What a Friend We Have in Jesus" on stage, choking back tears during the hymn's words: "Can we find a friend so faithful? / Who will all our sorrows share? / We should never be discouraged, / Take it all to Him in prayer..." Doc had a personal relationship with God, and this was the embodiment of that relationship. And the words of this hymn brought back memories of his son, of his own father, and of his big brothers, most of whom had already passed on.[38]

Three nights later, Doc sang an a capella version of "Amazing Grace," the song that he had brought to the folk music crowd's attention back in 1961 at PS 41 in New York City. He choked back tears during the hymn, while he was singing the lines he had once sung solo on the stage in New York City: "I once was lost / but now I'm found / was blind but now I see."

Just down the street from PS 41, the Twin Towers of the World Trade Center were built in 1965, only four years after Doc's strong baritone first rang out the words to "Amazing Grace" in the elementary school's auditorium, supported by his father-in-law and friends, humming in four-part harmony. Forty years later, New Yorkers gathered nearby to honor their dead, paying tribute to the fallen with the sounds of bagpipes tolling "Amazing Grace," a song that Doc Watson had never owned, but delivered to the world with his workman's hands and steady voice.

# CHAPTER NOTES

1.  Gustavson, Kent, *Telephone Interview with Joe Crookston*. March 25, 2009.
2.  Gustavson, Kent, *Email Interview with Greg Brown*. April 1, 2009.
3.  Gustavson, Kent, *Telephone Interview with Ben Harper*. June 4, 2009.
4.  Gustavson, Kent, *Telephone Interview with Tony Trischka*. April 27, 2009.
5.  Gustavson, Kent, *Telephone Interview with David Moultrup*. April 27, 2009.
6.  Gustavson, Kent, *Telephone Interview with Ellen Harper-Verdries*. July 3, 2009.
7.  Gustavson, Kent, *Email Interview with Wayne Henderson*. April 2, 2009.
8.  Gustavson, Kent, *Email Interview with Tom Chapin*. Oct. 22, 2009.
9.  Gustavson, Kent, *Personal Interviews with John Cohen*. April 8 & August 6, 2009.
10. Gustavson, Kent, *Telephone Interview with Alan O'Bryant*. May 6, 2009.
11. Gustavson, Kent, *Telephone Interview with Sam Bush*. April 9, 2009.
12. Gustavson, Kent, *Telephone Interview with Peter Rowan*. June 1, 2009.
13. Holt, David, *Liner Notes to Doc Watson and David Holt: Legacy*, High Windy Audio, 2002.
14. *Folk Singers: Champion Country Picker*. Time, 1967. **90**(8).
15. Gustavson, Kent, *Telephone Interview with Alice Gerrard*. June 2, 2009.
16. Bane, Michael, *White Boy Singin' the Blues: The Black Roots of White Rock*. 1982, New York: Da Capo Press.
17. Gustavson, Kent, *Telephone Interview with Tom Paxton*. April 14, 2009.
18. Gustavson, Kent, *Telephone Interview with Si Kahn*. May 26, 2009.
19. Gustavson, Kent, *Email Interview with Larry Long*. June 30, 2009.
20. Gustavson, Kent, *Email Interview with Jonathan Byrd*. April 2, 2009.
21. Gustavson, Kent, *Telephone Interview with George McCeney*. May 22, 2009.
22. Gustavson, Kent, *Telephone Interview with Michelle Shocked*. March 12, 2009.
23. Gustavson, Kent, *Telephone Interview with Pat Donohue*. March 11, 2009.
24. Murphy, Joe, *Doc and Merle -The Lives and Music of Doc & Merle Watson (1985)*, VHS, Vestapol, 1996.
25. Rowe, Jeri, *Doc Watson -- in his own words*. 1997, Greensboro News and Record Online.
26. Gustavson, Kent, *Telephone Interview with Jack Lawrence*. April 13, 2009.
27. Gustavson, Kent, *Email Interview with Darol Anger*. April 24, 2009.
28. Crowther, Hal, *Cathedrals of Kudzu*. 2002: Louisiana State University Press. 192.
29. Gustavson, Kent, *Telephone Interview with Abigail Washburn*. June 8, 2009.
30. Gustavson, Kent, *Telephone Interview with Ketch Secor*. March 19, 2009.
31. Gustavson, Kent, *Telephone Interview with Marty Stuart*. May 18, 2009.
32. Gustavson, Kent, *Telephone Interview with Jean Ritchie*. May 6, 2009.
33. Gustavson, Kent, *Telephone Interview with Ricky Skaggs*. April 29, 2009.
34. Gustavson, Kent, *Telephone Interview with Maria Muldaur*. April 1, 2009.
35. Gustavson, Kent, *Telephone Interview with Donna Hill*. May 6, 2009.
36. srvjbgblues, *August 22nd 2009 - Todd NC Concert*. 2009, YouTube.
37. Bolen, Justin and Tony Stampley, *Doctor Jesus*, 2000.
38. deneicee, *Doc Watson ~ Bristol 9-20-08 What a friend we have in Jesus*. 2008, YouTube.

*"When you hear Doc Watson singing Amazing Grace, there is something that happens. Something else enters the room."*

- Ben Harper[3]

Photo by John Cohen ©

# ACKNOWLEDGMENTS

Although I only distantly remember my first moments at the keyboard, my father recounts vividly the way I would sit at the piano, pound on it, and then, wide-eyed, beg my parents for lessons. My father was the first to give in, and he likes to take credit for my musical beginnings, with due cause. That was certainly the moment when my love of music took root and brought me towards this joyous obsession I now have.

My greatest memories are of sitting down with my mother, father, and sister as a child, singing *Kumbaya* or *Puff the Magic Dragon*, or *Annie's Song*; the songs of Pete Seeger, John Denver and Joan Baez our fare... My first exposure to bluegrass was on Saturday nights, during my family's sacred two-hour family tradition: listening quietly to Prairie Home Companion while eating Chicago-style whole wheat pizza, steaming hot out of the oven. Kate McKenzie, a regular on the program, often played bluegrass at our little country Lutheran church in Marine on St. Croix, Minnesota, a little town on the river... Soon, my mother joined the Bloodwashed Band at the church, strumming her parlor-sized koa wood Harmony and singing gospel hymns in ear-splitting Midwestern harmony.

We never listened to popular music at home when I was young. So, outside of school trips to the roller-skating rink, my first exposure to contemporary pop music was when my sister lent me her old tape collection in 1989 upon leaving for college. I discovered many musical treasures in that dusty stack of hand-labeled cassettes, lovingly assembled in shoeboxes through the years of her angst-driven teens: Suzanne Vega, Sting, Depeche Mode, REM, U2, Peter Gabriel, and every great band of the 1980s. Much to my dismay, my parents soon confiscated them from me, having discovered the album Talking Heads: *Naked*.

I wouldn't have become a musician without your love and support, Mom, Dad and Britta. Thank you.

Thank you to Katharina for falling in love not only with me, but also with this music that I love. She might just be the only German woman who can really *sing* bluegrass tenor.

Thank you to Micah Spicher-Schonberg, who took a folk music-loving kid from the Midwest and countrified him. We would go to the little local Baptist church on Sundays in Vermont, and after church, we'd go to a practice room in the art center at our college, and play gospel songs all afternoon in the shadow of the Green Mountains. And then, in the mountains of Washington, where we later both worked as cooks at Holden Village, we would run, not walk, during break time to the porch of my little house, and let songs ring out into the cold Cascade Mountain air. And I won't forget the times we bushwhacked up into the mountains, and looked down over the valley and sang "Talk About Suffering" for the world to hear. In those moments, this music became real for me.

Thank you to Peter Winkler for supporting me through my PhD, and believing that this American traditional music that we both love is every bit as important as the mathematical music that academics contrives within us. I couldn't have finished without his belief and support of my oddity and passion. Thank you also to all of the teachers who supported me through the years. To John Koziol, who first taught me to love improvisation. To Evan Bennett and Su Lian Tan, who taught me to see outside the box. To John Elder, who first opened the door for me towards creativity as a career. To Greg Vitercik, who encouraged me to pursue a music career; pointing me towards Stony Brook. To Daria Semegen, for helping me to listen each day with new ears. And a special thank you to Michael Chorney, my greatest music teacher, who taught me to be free. Thank you also to my friends at Sabreen in Jerusalem (especially Wissam Murad), who made me realize how much I love my own country's traditional music.

Thank you to Gabe Shuford and Nicholas Walker, my bandmates in Stolen Shack. From the time we began to unite Baroque and bluegrass music, I have been able to reconcile my academic and vernacular talents, and I now feel like a *whole* musician. I continue to be in awe of their talents. Thank you to my musical brother from across the sea, Dejan Ilijic, for his faith in my music, and his unshatterable willingness to experiment with both tradition and innovation. Thank you to Patrick Lo Re, who taught me more about music than any class during the countless hours we have worked together.

Thank you to the incredible musicians and scholars I had the great honor of interviewing during the course of this book project, including Abigail Washburn, Alan O'Bryant, Alice Gerrard, Annie Bird, B. Townes, Bela Fleck, Ben Harper, Beppe Gambetta, Clint Howard, Darol Anger, David Grisman, David Moultrup, Don Rigsby, Donna Hill, Ed Pearl, Edgar Meyer, Ellen Harper-Verdries, George McCeney, Greg Brown, Guy Clark, Guy Davis, Jack Lawrence, James Reams, Jean Ritchie, Jerry Douglas, Joe Crookston, John Cohen, John Pushkin, Jonathan Byrd, Ketch Secor, Larry Long, Maria Muldaur, Mark Moss, Marty Stuart, Michelle Shocked, Mike Marshall, Mike Seeger, Norman Blake, Paddy Moloney, Pat Donohue, Paul Asbell, Paul Chasman, Peggy Seeger, Peter Rowan, Peter Siegel, Rebecca Lovell, Ricky Skaggs, Roland White, Sam Bush, Sarah Bryan,

ACKNOWLEDGMENTS

Si Kahn, Tao Rodriguez-Seeger, Tom Chapin, Tom Moore, Tom Paxton, Tommy Emmanuel, Tommy Sands, Tony Cartledge, Tony Rice, Tony Trischka, Warren Haynes and Wayne Henderson.

This book is dedicated in part to the memory of Mike Seeger, who passed away only a few weeks after our conversation. He was and will always be a giant in the traditional music world. Rest in peace.

Thank you to the photographers whose images are included in this book: Bill Revill, Bill Walsh, Bob Voors, John Cohen, John Hudson, John Rocklin, Mark Reid, Nic Siler, Peter Shenkin, Rob Garland and Tony Cartledge. You make it possible for us to glimpse the past through the window of your photographs. This book wouldn't be the same without your contribution.

Thank you to Kristina Tosic for the incredible illustrations she created for this book. You and your artwork are both an inspiration.

A special thank you to Amber Bean, who was tireless in her pursuit of interviews for this book, and was able to hold together a seeming logistical nightmare. Thank you also to Jamie Gough and Andrew Smith for editing, and to Victoria Judd for assisting me with research funding.

Another special thank you to Jeff Place and Stephanie Smith at the Ralph Rinzler Folklife Archives at the Smithsonian Institution in Washington, for your patient assistance during the several days I spent there researching, and to the staff at the Southern Folklife Collection at the University of North Carolina in Chapel Hill as well.

Last, but not least, a special thank you to everyone who has supported me along the way. To Dave Nogueras, thank you for your friendship & hospitality in Washington while I was researching there. To Duff Lyall, for sharing your tape collection with me, expanding my horizons immensely. To everyone at Holden Village: thank you for being part of my lifelong community. To my friends at Seeds of Peace; I still plan to write the book about Israel and Palestine that I always intended to write; I think about you every day. To the John Hokanson family, the Windgasse family, the Florea family, Lars Clausen, Jennifer Powers, Nadia & Matthew Bolz-Weber, and all of the other families and advisors I have sought advice and shelter from in my wanderings.

To my friends Jim Sparnon, Ryan Case, Jared Baird, Katie Lichtenstein, Eric Carlberg, Matthew Avanzino, Kate Stevens, Rolf Vegdahl, Gary Sontum, Jeshua Erickson, Callista Isabelle, Bethany Spicher-Schonberg, Chrissy Post, Jeremy Blyth, Jonathan Winters, Kaethe Schwehn, and everyone else who has shared music and fellowship with me through the years.

# ABOUT THE AUTHOR

Dr. Kent Gustavson earned his PhD from Stony Brook University in New York, where he now teaches music, leadership, & language. He speaks around the world on both music and publishing, and has interviewed hundreds of award-winning musicians and authors for his radio show Sound Authors. Dr. Gustavson has released more than a dozen audio recordings on his small independent record label Ninety and Nine Records. He lives and works in Sound Beach, New York.

Find out more at *www.kentgustavson.com*

*Part of the proceeds from the sale of this book go to...*

## NATIONAL FEDERATION OF THE BLIND, PERFORMING ARTS DIVISION

The non-profit, volunteer-run Performing Arts Division of the National Federation of the Blind works to provide opportunities for and acceptance of blind performers through scholarships, subsidies and networking. The Performing Arts Division believes that performers are uniquely positioned to spread the good news about the capabilities of blind Americans and shed light on the problems of declining braille literacy and its impact on the massive unemployment rates for working-age blind Americans.

With more than 50,000 members, the National Federation of the Blind is the largest and most influential membership organization of blind people in the United States. The National Federation of the Blind improves blind people's lives through advocacy, education, research, technology, and programs encouraging independence and self-confidence. It is the leading force in the blindness field today and the voice of the nation's blind.

Find out more at: **www.padnfb.org**

*Part of the proceeds from the sale of this book go to...*

## PLAYING FOR CHANGE & PLAYING FOR CHANGE FOUNDATION

The Playing For Change Movement was born several years ago when a small group of filmmakers set out with a dream: to make a documentary film about street musicians from around the world. That dream has grown not only into a reality, but into a global sensation that has touched the lives of millions of people.

While traveling to around the world to film and record these musicians, the crew became intimately involved with the music and people of each community they visited. Many of these people lived very modestly in communities with limited resources; nevertheless, they were full of generosity, warmth, and above all they were connected to each other by a common thread: music.

In an effort to ensure that anyone with a desire to receive a music education would have the opportunity to do so, the Playing For Change Foundation was born. The Playing For Change Foundation is dedicated to connecting the world through music by providing resources to musicians and their communities worldwide. We are committed to creating positive change through music education. To learn more, please visit **www.playingforchange.org**

Photo by John Hudson ©